THE MAVERICK GUIDE TO AUSTRALIA

mav.er.ick (mav'er-ik), *n* 1. an unbranded steer. Hence [colloq.] 2. a person not labeled as belonging to any one faction, group, etc., who acts independently. 3. one who moves in a different direction than the rest of the herd— often a nonconformist. 4. a person using individual judgment, even when it runs against majority opinion.

The MAVERICK Guide to

AUSTRALIA

Robert W. Bone

PELICAN PUBLISHING COMPANY

Gretna 1980

Library of Congress Cataloging in Publication Data

Bone, Robert W.
  The maverick guide to Australia.

  Includes index.
  1. Australia—Description and travel—1951– Guidebooks. I. Title.
DU95.B66   919.4'04'6   79–1384
ISBN: 0-88289-263-0

Excerpts from the poem "Dunciad Minor" courtesy of
A. D. Hope, % Curtis Brown (Aust.) Pty. Ltd.,
Sydney, Australia.

Manufactured in the United States of America
Published by Pelican Publishing Company, Inc.
1101 Monroe Street, Gretna, Louisiana 70053

For Christina and David,
Who had to sit this one out

ACKNOWLEDGMENTS

Sara and I want to thank the scores of friends Down Under and Up Top who gave us dinkum oil and an equal measure of sympathy in this project, especially the following:

Ian Anderson, John Anderson, Ken Boys, Keith Castle, Ian Cotton, Anne De Wolfe, Mike Fisher, Marlene Freedman, Gael Golla, George Golla, Jack Gregory, Anne Harpham, Sandra Holmes, Alison Hudson, John Hudson, Maggi Jones, Paul Kendall, Ed Kaptein, Sally Kaptein, Leonard Lueras, Sheree Lipton, Alison Fan MacLaurin, Duncan MacLaurin, Stan Marks, Jim Matheson, Neil McDonell, Dan Myers, Gale Myers, John Myers, Sylvia Pager, Alexandra Piechowiak, Robin Prestage, Eduard Rodgers, Anne Ross, Tony Salisbury, Jim Sanderson, Joan Sanderson, Cile Sinnex, Wayne Storey, David Tong, Dorothy Van Kuyl, David Ward, Ellen Ward, Maria Williams, Ann Wu, Tong Wu, Sanford Zalburg, George Gibson, and Jennifer Price.

Contents

CONTENTS

List of Maps

THE MAVERICK GUIDE TO AUSTRALIA

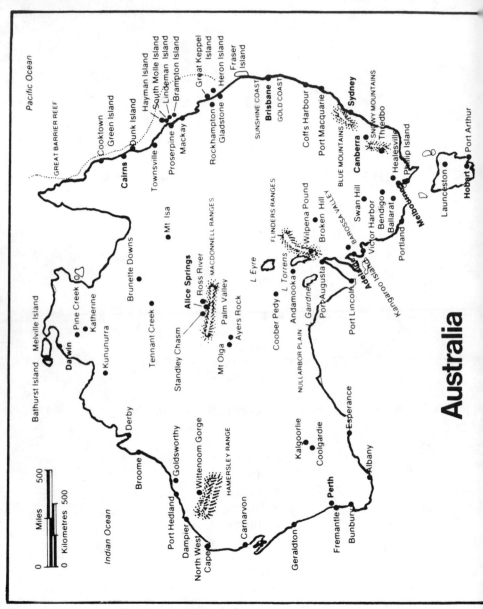

Map courtesy Australian Tourist Commission

1

Why Go Down Under?
An Introduction

Have you been to another planet yet? Or are you even likely to visit one in your lifetime? Most of us probably doubt that we'll live long enough. Or even if we do, surely it will be too expensive for just an average bloke, anyway.

But imagine for a moment what we might find if we did indeed take off from home to land in some obscure, though physically hospitable, corner of the universe: There are surely many strange animals there, some of which we've never seen or heard of before—not even in a zoo. Probably some of these creatures won't divide neatly into the great zoological classifications in the textbooks—a mammal (like us) who lays eggs, for example.

The dark of night, spangled of course with an unfamiliar pattern of constellations, obscures the origins of a cacophony of weird cries. Perhaps we'll catch sight of one bizarre bird with twin tall tails. He seems not to possess a voice of his own, but to burst forth instead with the vocal tricks of hundreds of other creatures—even with the realistic noises of non-living and mechanical objects like lawn mowers and car horns.

Naturally, on this strange planet, there are flowers, plants, and trees that look, act, and smell like nothing else in your previous experience. Grass that cringes when you walk on it, for instance. Trees with elephantine, bottle-shaped trunks that actually do hold water. How about some lovely blossoms which thrive on a protein diet—trapping and consuming insects?

And the insects themselves. Some of them seem to behave differently. Would you believe flies that catch and devour other flies—or even bees—on the wing? What about termites who don't tear down houses but instead construct some complex condominiums of their own—skyscrapers, relative to their own size, with some models of these buildings designed in thin wedges, always pointing north and south, and using the effects of the sun for central heating and cooling?

Some of the land itself on this other world should be very different. Let's color the ground red and occasionally sculpt it into strange, massive, and beautiful shapes that seem . . . well . . . unearthly.

Say there are thousands of square miles in some areas composed of nothing more or less than flat, glaringly white salt. Or put in a mountain which has been on fire, always burning out of control, constantly for thousands of years. And there are other vast acreages where fiery-colored precious stones are scattered willy-nilly just under the surface of the ground—where amateur gem hunters can strike it rich with little more equipment than that provided by patience and determination.

And all this—could it be where you can have snow in July and where Christmas means summertime?

If these conditions *were* on another planet, would you go see them if you could? Understandably, you might be worried about the inhabitants, if any. Would they be dangerous, aggressive, living in heaven knows what way and speaking some unintelligible gibberish?

The strange "planet" we have been describing—as you knew all along—is Australia, the world's largest island and smallest continent. Separated by thousands of miles of ocean from the more familiar paths around the globe, Australia has all the things we've been talking about and a thousand times more. There are strange things, indeed, alien to all other parts of our Mother Earth. And 200 years ago, the place might just as well have been another planet. It was almost that inaccessible to the rest of the world.

The people, of course, are not to be feared. Far from inhospitable, living in caves, and munching only on strange yucky objects, they are by and large just like you and me. Fourteen million strong, they're friendly, have many lovely homes, and run excellent hotels and superb restaurants. They are interested in art, fashion, movies, cars, music, sport, and talking to foreigners.

And most of all, the folks who are surrounded by all this weird and wonderful nature speak English! Er . . . well, it's English *most* of the time, although many a Yank, Pommie, and Kiwi (American, Englishman, and New Zealander) has had to cock his ear carefully to catch the exact meaning of the common language that is sometimes mutilated before his very ears.

But once he does catch it, it's a fascinating game—one where the sound "A" comes out like "I," and words like "our" became "air." It's best learned over a "schooner." That's 15 ounces of beer if you're in Sydney or seven ounces for elbow benders in Adelaide.

They call the language "Strine." That, you'll notice, is the word "Australian," itself spoken in Strine.

You may never completely master this condensed communication, but you'll have a wonderful time trying, once you learn the basics of it—like the fact that Strines like to eat something called "semmiches" (sometimes an "M-semmich," sometimes an "X-semmich").

Note that "shower" comes out "share" in Strine ("Wine chevva cole share?"). In fact, Strine, spiced with a group of colorful slang terms (e.g., "dinkie-die"—the whole truth; "tucker"—something to eat), plus a whole new set of antipodean jokes, could turn out to be your cheapest and best souvenirs of Australia.

Australia has the charm of Great Britain, the excitement of America, and the intelligence to have a character all its own.

There's a refreshing feeling of space in underpopulated Australia. It's still pioneer country, in many ways—one of the very few left. There's a wild Outback "Beyond the Black Stump" that most Australians themselves haven't ventured into. A century ago, explorers died of hunger in this wilderness, often while food lay all around them, free for the taking. These nutrients were strange and different, and hidden from view, although the Aborigines, of course, lived quite well on such "bush tucker."

Today you can get to many of the wild areas—but not all of them—by modern means of transportation. And if you've a penchant for rough living, you can explore even more rugged areas with a kangaroo-proofed Land Rover and other survival equipment.

Whether on safari or on the standard tours, you can pick up some tall tales and take some pictures the neighbors couldn't get in Greece or Japan last year. There's no other place in the world where you can readily hold a koala bear in your arms, go on a mile-long hike accompanied by a high-stepping emu, or climb a thousand feet on one single red rock.

The Confessional

You can, of course, visit Australia without using a guidebook. There are plenty of people to point you toward the things they consider interesting and significant or whose brother-in-law owns the concession stand there. You'll find lots of "free" literature where the freight is actually paid by advertising. They generally don't write about the places that don't pay up.

Unlike many guidebooks, this one contains no advertising, either overt or covert. All opinions expressed, and there are many, pro and con, are those of myself or my wife and co-researcher, Sara. Readers familiar with the first book in the series, *The Maverick Guide to Hawaii*, know that we allow no one to cross our path with friendship or favors to influence our coverage of their commercial interests.

In the full spirit of confession, however, we have to say that unlike the Hawaii book, for which we accepted no economic assistance, we could not afford to remain quite so Simon-pure this time. If we were going to hit just a few high spots, as most visitors to Australia do, we might have been able to swing it all with no help. But the expense needed to visit and revisit the major parts of Australia to prepare the manuscript for this book was just too horrendous.

We did not make the traditional travel guide turn to members of the tourist industry to subsidize our research. We managed to forswear allegiance to any commercial interest, accepting instead an offer by the government-owned Australian Tourist Commission to cover a portion of our expenses.

We accepted the offer only on the firm understanding that no one from the ATC or anywhere else would have the right to see our words before they were published or to approve or disapprove anything we wrote. The ATC, for its part, was more than understanding. All it asked in return was that I write a book about Australia. I could be as critical as I liked, the Aussies said.

This I have done, and I wouldn't have had it any other way.

The Maverick Guide to Australia is the second in the Maverick series which began in 1977 with the publication of the guide to Hawaii. The Hawaii book has been widely accepted and has been published in a new edition every year since. For any travelers who may be stopping in Hawaii on their way Down Under (or back up), we firmly suggest you tuck it in your suitcase first.

Our family has now traveled to virtually every part of the globe. We have been in travel journalism since 1968 after joining the well-honed team assembled by Temple Fielding, author of *Fielding's Travel Guide to*

Europe and many other books. Today, in our own series, we have no connection with the Fielding operation, but if the Maverick guidebooks show an influence by the Fielding techniques, it is a heritage of which we are very proud.

But while Fielding's interest remains in Europe and the Atlantic, ours is now tied to Pacific climes, where we have lived since 1971. As a U.S. citizen, my outlook is naturally American. Sara, however, is a New Zealander, and her antipodean attitudes are reflected throughout the text. Her common cultural background with the Australians has helped at least one poor Yank and the Diggers to come close to understanding each other.

Getting the Most Out of This Book

We have arranged this guide in a specific pattern which we believe will make for super-smooth reading. After a chapter on timely basics and two others on nature and people, we devote the next eight "area chapters" to the capitals and surrounding areas of the six states and two territories in Australia. The order—Sydney, Canberra, Melbourne, Hobart, Adelaide, Perth, Darwin (with Alice Springs), and Brisbane—represents a hypothetical clockwise swing around the continent.

But the chapters need not be read in that sequence, of course. In fact, those areas which you will not be visiting need not be read at all, if you don't want. Nevertheless, we advise you to peruse it all in advance of your trip so that you can determine which areas you will (and will not) be able to visit in the country.

Each of those area chapters is divided into exactly 12 numbered parts, and after you become familiar with them in one chapter, you should know where to look for these same subjects in each of the other chapters.

The categories are as follows:

1. The General Picture
2. Airports and Long-distance Travel
3. Local Travel
4. Hotels and Lodging
5. Restaurants and Dining
6. Sightseeing
7. Guided Tours and Cruises
8. Water Sports
9. Other Sports
10. Shopping
11. Night Life and Entertainment
12. The Address List

We have set up this book to be used two ways. First, you should look it over before you leave home, to help plan for your trip. There are several ways to travel to Australia, for instance. These and their different price scales are thoroughly described in the following chapter. Also, the individual hotels and other facilities for which advance reservations are required or advisable are discussed throughout the area chapters.

Next, the book is also designed to be used on the scene—to help solve those day-to-day concerns that get in the way of smooth, fun traveling. How to get a bus to King's Cross, where to find a hamburger, when to look for kangaroos, and most of all, how to budget money and time everywhere as you travel throughout Australia.

A Few Bits of Miscellaneous Advice

If you're serious about planning a great vacation in Australia, be sure to take advantage of the colorful and free literature available. Write to the Australian Tourist Commission and ask for the latest information. (The independent national consumer travel magazine, *The Travel Advisor*, recently rated the ATC as one of the most helpful foreign government tourist offices in America.) In the U.S.A., you'll find the ATC at 1270 Avenue of the Americas, New York, N.Y. 10020, and at 3550 Wilshire Blvd., Los Angeles, Calif. 90010. They also have offices in London, Auckland, Tokyo, and Frankfurt.

Write to other addresses you'll find throughout this book, both those in the U.S. and in Australia, and tell them of your interest. Many will respond with a considerable amount of up-to-date illustrated literature.

If you have a well-stocked public library in town, you'll find many large picture books on Australia. The beauty of the land and the strong characteristics of its inhabitants have been attracting professional artists and photographers for years. These will help you decide what areas you want to explore yourself on the great southern continent.

And most of all, after you've made your trip, would you please write us (in care of the publisher) and tell us about it? The traveling experiences of persons such as you will help us tremendously in preparing the next edition of this guidebook.

Use either the enclosed letter/envelope form or, if that's not enough space, copy the address onto your own envelope and include as many pages as you like. Your reactions to both the book and the country are earnestly solicited and will be warmly appreciated.

"Good-on ya!"
Bob and Sara Bone

2

Smooth Sailings
and Happy Landings

The major cities of Australia, virtually all perched on the rim of the continent, are served by dozens of the world's airlines, plus about 14 large shipping companies.

One important exception is Canberra, the federal capital, which has neither seaport nor international airport. (It does have frequent flights to and from other Australian cities, however.) Visitors to Australia generally land first in Sydney, Brisbane, Melbourne, Perth, or sometimes Darwin, and most often they come by air.

Nevertheless, for diehard surface travelers, there are still a few ocean liners and passenger-carrying freighters on the high seas bound for Australia. In the following paragraphs, we have considered mostly those who list convenient ports also in North America and presumably may be boarded there.

Sailing to Australia. Most international travelers today agree that ships are either (a) too expensive, (b) too time-consuming, or (c) both. But old salts who want to plow full speed ahead may still consider some alternatives.

Two of the most elegant tours are the winter cruises launched by the Norwegian-owned **Royal Viking Line,** both leaving from—and returning to—San Francisco and Los Angeles. Usually the 22,000-ton *Royal*

Viking Star leaves in January to make a 45-day swing through the Pacific, calling at about 10 ports, including Sydney. The *Royal Viking Sea,* a twin of the *Star,* casts off in February to ride the ocean for 70 days, stopping at Sydney and Cairns in Australia and several more ports in the Pacific and the Far East. A minimum fare will break down to about $130 a day.

Details on the Viking operation are available from the Royal Viking Line, One Embarcadero Center, San Francisco, Calif. 94111.

California's well-known **Princess Cruises,** now owned by P & O Lines, sends its British-registered, 600-passenger *Island Princess* on voyages from Los Angeles to Sydney and back about once a year. The 28-day trip down—via Lahaina, Honolulu, Raiatea, Papeete, Nuku'alofa, Auckland, Christchurch, Melbourne, and Sydney—will cost a minimum of about $4,844. The return trip, taking around 27 days and stopping at fewer ports, is cheaper, but you should still figure on paying at least $175 for each day on board. Perhaps you would shave a little off the fare if you chose to leave the ship at Honolulu on the return voyage and fly back to the U.S. Mainland.

For full information, write P & O/Princess Cruises, 2029 Century Park East, Los Angeles, Calif. 90067, or contact their offices in New York, Chicago, Dallas, San Francisco, or Seattle.

Princess' adoptive parent, the century-old **P & O Lines,** generally assigns its 42,000-ton, 20-year-old *Oriana* to the Southampton-Sydney run, which calls at Port Everglades (Florida), then slices through Panama and briefly nuzzles other American ports, including Los Angeles, San Francisco, and Honolulu before it heads for Auckland and Sydney.

The 45,000-ton, 1,800-passenger *Canberra*, flagship of the P & O fleet, may make another 90-day world cruise this year, calling at all the above on its 21-port itinerary.

For details, write P & O at the same address given for Princess Cruises, above.

Other passenger lines who sail to Australia from England (but do not normally call at U.S. ports) include **Chandris Lines** (on the *Ellinis*) and **Sitmar Cruises** (on the *Fairstar* and the *Fairsky*).

However, one outfit we know of, Airsea Holidays, Inc. (1900 Avenue of the Stars, Los Angeles, Calif. 90067), has set up a special air/sea cruise with Sitmar Lines and Air New Zealand. Under the plan, you fly from Los Angeles to Fiji, cruise on the *Fairstar* through several exotic ports to New Zealand and Australia, and then sail back to Fiji, where you reboard a plane for Los Angeles. Fares begin at about $1,400 for a 17-day vacation.

We have had no personal experience with any of these trips, and can offer no firm opinion on their quality. But in general, we feel strongly that any cruise that does not allow you to break your trip significantly in Australia will not allow you the time to enjoy the things Australia is famous for.

If you like passenger-carrying freighters, we know of two interesting possibilities. One good New York-to-Australia run is on **Farrell Lines,** which has two sailings a month on its brand-new *Austral Pioneer* and other container ships. They each carry 12 passengers in commodious accommodations on a 21-day trip through the Panama Canal to Sydney, Brisbane, or (usually) Melbourne. One-way fares for that voyage average about $1,400. Mile for mile and meal for meal, this sounds like a very good deal.

If interested, get all the information from J. Robert Bielskas, Passenger Traffic Manager, Farrell Lines, One Whitehall St., New York, N.Y. 10004.

And a really unusual cruise to Australia is possible on the Norwegian freighters of the **Knutsen Line.** You can sail from San Francisco and spend about 45 days and $2,000 to travel by way of Hong Kong, Manila, Singapore, and thence to Fremantle—the Indian Ocean port for Perth, the capital of the state of Western Australia.

Then, if you make your way overland through the Outback to the east coast (and perhaps take a Farrell Lines freighter back home via New Zealand and Mexico to New Orleans), you'll have some very different experiences and a few unique stories to tell your friends. (Write Knutsen's American representatives, Bakke Steamship Corporation, Agents, 650 California St., San Francisco, Calif. 94108.)

Well, for most of us, this has been merely drifting and dreaming. Let's now step ashore and return to the solid realities of the jet age:

The Air Ways to Australia. Want to fly First Class to Australia? You can, of course. You can get the champagne, red carpet, Captain Kangaroo treatment for from $2,700 to $3,000 round trip from San Francisco, Los Angeles, or Vancouver to and from Sydney or Brisbane.

But is it really worth it? With the advent of jumbo jets (DC–10's, 747's, 767's, etc.), the much-cheaper Economy Class (sometimes called "Tourist" or "Coach") is virtually as comfortable for most of us at present. So what if you have to cough up a little extra for the liquor or the movies? Will that extra charge add up to more than $1,000—we said One Thousand Dollars—additional for a few shots of scotch, the rubber earphones, a pair of cheap slipper sox, and a fancier meal? No way!

That whopping amount is what you'll save if you choose to go Economy instead of First Class. We've tried both categories on flights to and from Down Under, and we've decided we'd rather sit in the back of the plane, taking comfort in the knowledge that we could use the savings to spend another two weeks or more in Australia.

The Economy Class round-trip tickets (from the West Coast gateways mentioned above) normally run around $1,600. For that, you can stop off when and where you want on the way, travel any day of the week, and return any day of the week. You can tool around Australia for up to a year, or until the money runs out (whichever comes first).

(Some airlines offer a cheaper Economy Class. You might save $200 if you do *not* take a stopover. Worth looking into.)

As an Economist, if you want to watch the movie, that'll be $2.50 extra for the earphones the First Class passengers are getting "free" in exchange for their weight in gold.

But is that the best you can do? No. Not by a long shot.

Last year the airline fare revolution finally invaded the South Pacific, and more and more types of bargain flights are taking off at jet speeds. The pattern is changing rapidly as the various airlines jockey for competitive position and also count in the rising cost of fuel. You should get all the up-to-date details from a travel agent or the airlines, of course, but meanwhile here's approximately what it looks like:

Qantas Airways has put into effect a 45-day advance purchase deal—a "Super APEX" fare—between San Francisco and Sydney. (In honor of its Koala symbol, it calls it the "Bear Minimum" fare.) It varies in price at several levels from a high of $1,084 to a low of $573 round trip, depending on a formula determined by the month you choose to fly Down Under and the month you're coming back up in. (Qantas has low seasons to Sydney March through June, but low seasons back to San Francisco are February, March, October, and November. There are also "Shoulder" and "Peak" seasons determined for each direction.)

Incidentally, the lowest round-trip—the barest Bear Minimum— is $564, from Honolulu.

Pan American also has inaugurated a competitive Super APEX fare, and it runs from $1,269 down to $671. But Pan Am also has a "Budget" fare, which also varies between Peak, Shoulder, and Low seasons, similar to the APEX fare. Pan Am's Budget fare reaches at this writing a low of $648 round trip during the off-peak season to Sydney from either Los Angeles or San Francisco.

And the airline's round-trip budget fare is as low as $949 from New York and $567 from Honolulu.

Budget fares are less convenient for many passengers than the APEX system, for which you reserve a specific date. Under Budget provisions, however, you may choose only the *week* you want to fly, and you must buy your tickets at least 21 days before that week begins. Then, at least seven days before the departure week, the airline notifies you of the exact date and flight you have been assigned. (We took the Budget Fare once, on Air New Zealand. The system worked very smoothly, and for our kids, the Budget tickets were even less than the regular children's half-price Economy fare.)

Be aware, however, that there is usually a 50 percent cancellation fee if you decide to pull out after you've paid for a Budget flight!

Air New Zealand still has in effect some attractive budget fares to Auckland, but has apparently dropped its Los Angeles to Sydney deal.

CP Air and *UTA French Airlines*, the only other lines that fly from North America to Australia, have finally jumped into the discount fray. CP Air now matches Qantas' APEX of $722 from Vancouver. UTA has a 14 to 45-day excursion from L.A. at $1,129.

Continental Airlines, the new kid on the South Pacific block, has some of the best prices from its Los Angeles base to Sydney. First Class passengers are charged only $2,240 at this writing, and Economy Class tickets total just $1,400. Both are considerably off the usual fares and allow free stopovers.

The airline also chalks up some super Super APEX fares on three levels, from $1,010 Peak Season down to $610 Low. (March–June are Low Season southbound, and February, March, October, and November are Low for returning passengers northbound.)

And unlike APEX fares on other lines, a free stopover is allowed in Honolulu—a big plus from our point of view.

Before we leave the air fare situation, take note also that some airlines will probably still offer "tour basing" fares this year—ITX or group GITs, for instance. These are sold at similar bargain prices, but they require you to purchase a ground package, too—hotels and/or rental cars, usually. These can be very good deals if you are going to have to buy some ground arrangements anyway—not so good if you're going to keep a strong spirit of independence.

There are several advantages to these IT fares. One is that unlike most APEX fares, you can usually arrange free or nominal-charge stopovers along the way. A point to remember about all the bargain fares—IT, APEX, Budget, etc.—is that these allow your travel agent to set up some lower *internal* airfares in Australia called "See Australia" fares, if you log more than 1,000 kilometers (621 miles) flying around the country.

A way to keep up with the latest on cheap flights is to join clubs composed mainly of antipodean expatriates. Examples are the Australian Kangaroo Club, P.O. Box 4230, Irvine, Calif. 92716; the Australian-New Zealand Society, 41 E. 42nd St., New York, N.Y. 10017; the Southern Cross Club, P.O. Box 19243, Washington, D.C. 20036; the Down Under Club, P.O. Box 3143, St. Paul, Minn. 55165; and the Friends of the Koala and Kiwi Association, 56 Aberfoyle Cres., Toronto, Ont. M8X 2W4, or Suite 618, 470 Granville St., Vancouver, B.C. V6C 1V5. Many of these are composed of Australians and New Zealanders who want to head home for the Christmas (summer) holidays.

And from elsewhere around the country? There are several domestic air fares in the U.S. that can be used in conjunction with the rates across the South Pacific.

As an example, if a New Yorker pays about $250 for a mid-week Super Saver round trip to Los Angeles to connect with a West-Coast-to-Australia APEX tour, his trip to and from Sydney could cost him less than $1,000. At rates like these, today it costs only a little more for an easterner to vacation in Australia than a westerner—an almost negligible amount compared to the awesome differences of only a few years ago.

Tours. Many travel agents and travel wholesalers (tour operators) make up their own tailored tours, either escorted or for FIT's ("free and independent travelers").

Tour companies have several fly/drive deals, but we are only interested in the ones which allow you to roam over several cities. One good deal is a Qantas 14-day tour, which offers a car with 250 free miles and vouchers for several hotels all over the country, currently running about $450 per person, two sharing. An unlimited mileage plan is also available for around $500. (Be sure to add your airfare to these prices.)

Another intriguing Qantas tour is the fly/campervan, a darn good way to cut restaurant and hotel costs virtually to zero. It also gives you the flexibility to be in exactly the right place at the right time to see Australia's bird and animal life. Two in a fully equipped Volkswagen camper, *including* GIT airfare, now may run about $1,000 each for 14 days (or if the flights are up later in the year, figure $440 plus the air fare).

Pricewise, it's a bargain, unless you don't relish wheeling a right-hand drive camper around left-hand sides of highways. And of course your grocery shopping will be in unfamiliar markets selling strange brands. Think carefully about this one; what's fun and challenging for one couple could be a drag for another pair of travelers.

If you're seriously interested in joining a tour, you might start by trying to get hold of a Qantas Airways tour catalogue from the Qantas address below. This attractive, free publication lists several tours run by Qantas and other U.S. based tour operators. No doubt it is not the *only* group of tours to be offered this year, and we can extend no particular recommendation except to say that most of them seem very well designed.

If you don't have a Qantas sales office near you, write to the Qantas Holidays address below. And (as always) mention this book in your letter.

Tour Operators. Here are a few travel wholesalers who offer Australian itineraries. Your travel agent may know of more, but we believe these at least will be reliable:

Australian Travel Service
7175 Sunset Boulevard
Los Angeles, Calif. 90046

Euroworld
3175 Waialae Ave.
Honolulu, Hi. 96816

Brendan Tours
510 West Sixth St.
Los Angeles, Calif. 90014

Islands in the Sun Tours
2814 Lafayette St.
Newport Beach, Calif.

Intercontinental Tours
609 So. Grand Ave., Suite 612
Los Angeles, Calif. 90017

Overland Tours
P.O. Box 100
Agincourt, Ont. M1S 3C6

International Travel Planners
21 East 40th St.
New York, N.Y. 10016

Qantas Holidays
360 Post St.
San Francisco, Calif. 94108

International Tours
12401 Wilshire Blvd.
Los Angeles, Calif. 90025

Westcan International Treks
8906 –112th St.
Edmonton, Alberta, CANADA

Kuoni Travel Inc.
11 East 44th St.
New York, N.Y. 10017

World of Oz, Ltd.
3 East 54th St.
New York, N.Y. 10022

Which airline to fly? Choosing an airline is like choosing a spouse: It's a very personal thing, but it has important practical elements, too.

Briefly, you pick an airline based on how well the things it offers seem to suit your needs for the price to be paid. (Please see our discussion a few pages previous on air fares.) But also, you should seek the advice of friends and objective fellow travelers whose opinions you respect.

There are six carriers—two American and four foreign—who fly from North America to Australia. In our own general order of preference for this trip they are Qantas, Pan American, Air New Zealand, Continental, UTA, and CP Air. Here's why:

Qantas Airways Limited. Flight QF-4 leaves San Francisco every evening at 9:00, arrives in Honolulu around midnight, picks up more passengers and then continues non-stop to Sydney. (On Sundays, the flight leaves Vancouver about 5:30, then picks up the San Francisco passengers at 9:00.) Frequent travelers to Down Under have this schedule memorized. But in late 1979, Qantas added three daytime departures from San Francisco, leaving at 10 a.m. Sunday, Wednesday, and Friday, and arriving in Sydney at 9:35 p.m. Monday, Thursday, and Saturday.

All flights are in our favorite plane, the Boeing 747, so that's a big plus in our book. Seats in the Economy section, however, have just been increased from a former 9 across to 10 across, with two aisles in a 3–4–3 configuration. There's a new Business Class section this year, however, with 8-across seating (2–4–2) and equipped with wide, executive lounge chairs. (It costs about $200 more than Economy.) First Class has taken a cue from Pan Am but moved even a step beyond, installing full-length sleeper chairs that recline into long, contoured beds.

You'll get dinner and a movie between San Francisco and Honolulu, and usually another movie, plus supper and breakfast, between Honolulu and Sydney. There are no longer any on-board charges in any class for drinks, headsets, etc. The overnight flights arrive around 7:00 in the morning, depending on the winds, some 16 hours after leaving San Francisco. Most days, QF-4 continues to Melbourne—on the same or a different aircraft—landing there at 9:00 or 10:00 a.m.)

On the return trip there are two movies—one after dinner and the other in the late morning on the Honolulu-San Francisco leg of the trip.

Generally speaking, some people prefer to fly the airline of the country to which they are traveling, and this alone may be a good reason for choosing Qantas. On these runs, all the flight and cabin crew members are stationed in Sydney, so you have a group of experts on the city to advise you on where to go and what to see after you get there.

The flights also feature Aussie beer and wines (both are justly famous). Often there are other Down Under specialties like lamb dishes and beef pies, Sydney rock oysters, and perhaps even a Pavlova for dessert. And if you can shut your eyes during the early morning flights between Honolulu and Sydney—10 hours flying time—you might pick up a full night's sleep before breakfast.

Pan American World Airways. Pan Am is proud as a puffed-up kookaburra of its speedy 747-SP service from Los Angeles (three days a week) *non-stop* to Auckland, New Zealand. SP, which stand for "special performance," indicates a model of the Boeing jumbo which allows a far greater range. (It flies at a much higher altitude, increasing speed and saving on fuel.)

Pan Am's SP reaches Auckland, now, in 12 to 13 hours over a distance of about 7,400 miles. Passengers going on to Sydney arrive about 8:30 a.m. That's a convenient time, but with the pause in Auckland, the trip for Australia-bound passengers totals about 17 hours. That's still an hour or so longer than Qantas' elapsed time on the San Francisco-Honolulu-Sydney run. But for passengers from Los Angeles, who would otherwise have to make a two-hour head start to catch that Qantas flight in San Francisco, Pan Am via Auckland *is* more convenient and, in effect, about an hour faster. And flying non-stop from L.A. to Auckland, Air New Zealand's home base, Pan Am beats that carrier at its own route by at least 2½ hours.

But even more dramatic for our purposes, Pan Am turns around its SP in Sydney two days a week and flies it from the Australian continent on a bee line to Los Angeles for a scheduled elapsed time of only 13 hours and 20 minutes. A distance of more than 7,500 miles, the flight may be the longest non-stop passenger service in airline history. For a fast trip home from Australia, it can't be beat.

If you stop over in Auckland or someplace else on the way to Australia, you may be better off for baggage allowance with Pan American. Once you break your trip on your way to Australia from the United States, some airlines, including Air New Zealand, switch from the two-bag system to the old-fashioned weight allowance—66 pounds in First Class and only 44 pounds in Economy—for the balance of your trip. Pan Am tells us it won't do that to you if you're flying Pan Am for all legs of the journey to Australia.

We've never flown First Class on Pan Am, but some who have tell us its most attractive feature is "sky dining"—reserved seats in the upstairs lounge converted to a special dining salon at meal times. Also, Pan Am has also put its popular Sleeperettes on board for high rollers on the Sydney service now.

Air New Zealand. Most ANZ flights leave Los Angeles about 8:00 in the evening and make at least two stops before landing at Australian destinations 21 or 22 hours later—late morning, Australian time. The stops are at Honolulu and Auckland, or Papeete and Auckland, and some stop at Honolulu, Nadi and Auckland (where most passengers to Australia change planes and flight numbers).

The airline's three-engine DC-10s have seats in the coach section with aisles separating them into a 2-5-2 pattern. All together, they carry about 270 passengers.

Air New Zealand might be our first choice for flying to Auckland for a visit to New Zealand—certainly it would be if we wanted to see something of Tahiti, or perhaps Hawaii or Fiji on the way. It has more flights to Auckland than its competitors, and it arrives there some 15 to 17½ hours after leaving Los Angeles, depending on the stops along the way.

Inflight service is usually excellent on ANZ, and we've enjoyed our trips several times over this route. It serves good New Zealand wines, and First Class passengers relax on comfortable New Zealand sheepskin seats. If you want the stopovers, it could be the ideal airline to fly.

Continental Airlines has seven weekly round trips from Los Angeles, three serving Auckland, New Zealand and four to Sydney, Australia. As previously indicated, Continental has set up strong financial competiton with the other carriers, although the differences are not as dramatic this year as they were last year. Still, if you make the right deal, Continental could turn out to be the sleeper in the value-per-mile sweepstakes.

The airline rolls out its McDonnell Douglas DC-10 jumbos for the Sydney and Auckland runs, and regardless of what other facilities it may adopt, that still gives it a firm edge over CP Air, at least.

Continental has dedicated its galleys exclusively to First Class. Economy Class meals are pre-prepared. They also have a new tape-TV movie projection system for in-flight entertainment. (We prefer the conventional type, although the cabin doesn't have to be so dark for the new system.) The airline also has provided 14 seats in a "quiet zone" for those who decide to forego the film.

Continental has been leaving Los Angeles at 8 or 9 a.m. daily (depending on daylight savings time), stopping in Honolulu 4½ elapsed hours later. From Honolulu, three days a week it flies via Pago Pago to Auckland, and four days a week (via Nadi Monday and Wednesday, via Pago Pago Thursday and Saturday) to Sydney. At this writing, those Sydney flights via Nadi land in Sydney at about 8:45 p.m. local time, a little under 17 hours from L.A. But those via Pago Pago are running about 17½ hours from L.A. due to a longer stopover in Samoa than in Fiji.

The return trip also begins as a daylight flight, but because of the dateline and time difference, the flight that leaves Sydney at 11 or 11:30 a.m. arrives at Los Angeles at 10 or 11 a.m. on the same day! (Elapsed time is more than 18 hours, however, and remember that these departure and arrival times will vary depending which of the two cities, if any, are on their respective opposite-season daylight savings times.)

U.T.A. French Airlines flies from Los Angeles Friday night to Sydney via Papeete and Auckland, or Thursday night to Sydney by way of Papeete, Nadi, and Noumea, perhaps providing some interesting stopovers on the way. (Sydney itself can be a stopover on UTA, since the flight continues through the Far and Near East and ends in Paris.)

All flights Down Under are on wide body DC-10s, but they don't arrive in Sydney until the early afternoon, about 19 hours after leaving L.A.

We know little more about UTA, having never flown them ourselves. As we mentioned previously, the airline is slower to get any discount fares into operation, although these are expected to come.

CP Air, the Canadian airline, until just now has always held one trump card in its twice weekly flights from Honolulu to Nadi and Sydney. It was the only one offering the convenience of daytime departures.

It still has that distinction from Vancouver, where it leaves at 8:00 a.m. Thursday and Saturday. It touches down at 12:35 p.m. in Honolulu (where it competes with Continental and Qantas), and lands in Sydney at around 9:00 p.m., after a total trip of more than 18 hours.

But the daytime trip would not make up for one big disadvantage: It does not yet make the run in a jumbo jet.

Temporarily hampered by some international agreements, CP Air does plan to put DC-10s on the route, and then the whole picture could change. In the meantime, they gamely carry on with stretched DC-8s, which despite their reputation for good service just cramps our traveling style too much.

One word about day flights to Sydney, whether on CP Air, Qantas, or Continental. The bad news is that most folks will immediately have to shell out for a night's hotel room after arrival. The good news is that in the Australian summer time, at least, there's still light in the sky in Sydney after 9:00 p.m., so the evening seems young. And a good night's sleep soon after you get in will go a long way toward fighting off a case of jet lag.

Transportation Within Australia

Getting around the country is a lot of fun, but it could be strenuous and expensive, too. We'll talk about it some more in the "Transporta-

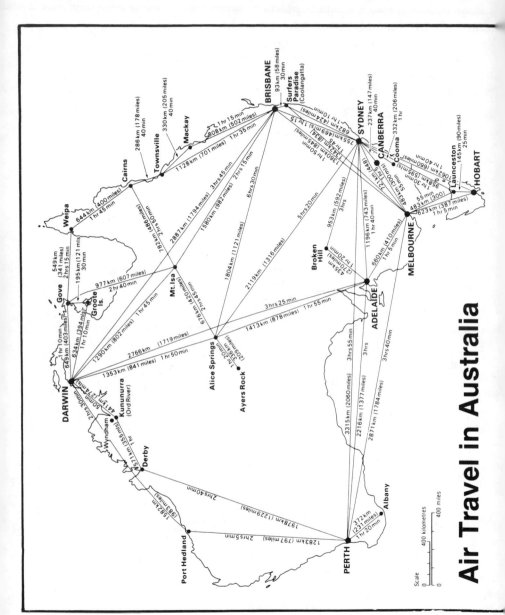

Map courtesy Australian Tourist Commission

tion" sections in the following area chapters, but some of your plans on how to go from one place to another should be considered before you leave home. For instance, any kind of transportation can be difficult on national holidays or at the beginning or end of school vacations ("school holidays").

Domestic Air Travel. Australia boasts a long and honored aviation history. That befits a country which early embraced the airplane in its attempts to bridge vast, lonely distances in a sparsely settled land. The past is alive with Aussie air heroes, and passenger flights have developed to the point where Australia's airlines have just been ranked safest in the world by *Flight International,* the respected British aviation magazine.

Now pushing 60, Qantas may be the world's oldest airline. (It's also famous for giving the world its only Q word without a U following it. It was an acronym for Queensland And Northern Territory Aerial Services.) But today Qantas is devoted to international routes, leaving two big internal airlines (and a few others) serving within the nation's borders.

The 43-year-old **Ansett Airlines of Australia** is an enterprise of that dynamic mogul of the transport business, Sir Reginald Ansett, whose name you may hear frequently. Ansett Airlines competes (sort of) with the government-owned **Trans-Australia Airlines**, more often called TAA (and sometimes sounding like "T-I-I" to American ears).

These two airlines rely principally on three-jet Boeing 727's or twin-jet Douglas DC–9's, two comfortable, well-built planes. In addition, TAA has just ordered a jumbo jet—the A300 Airbus. Ansett is expected to follow suit. (Economy class meals on either airline are non-existent, but they have good coffee and delicious cookies!)

All seats are assigned ("allocated") in advance, incidentally, and you can request such options as smoking or non-smoking, aisle or window, and even (photographers, take note) forward or rearward of the wing. Be aware that you may have more choice of seat position if you arrive early and check in at the airport itself. Checking in at the various city air terminals is convenient, but since seat allocations are made only at the airport, you could find that your choice is already taken by the time the bus from town lets you out at the aerodrome.

The only criticism we have of Ansett or TAA is that they are so competitive—or noncompetitive, depending on your point of view—that they fly to the same destinations at virtually the same time. "In tandem," some grumbling Australians put it. Sometimes both planes are only half full, and it seems a wasteful practice in this energy-conscious age. If either one of these lines is closed down by a strike for a few days, somehow the other seems to manage to pick up the slack with relatively little trouble.

Another important company is **MacRobertson Miller Airline Services**, which is now a subsidiary of Ansett. Headquartered in Perth, MMA flies several important routes in Western Australia, generally connecting towns and villages between Perth and Darwin, up in the "Top End" of the Northern Territory.

The workhorse of the MMA fleet is the Fokker F–28, a fine twin-jet aircraft especially designed for quick takeoffs and landings on the short runways often existing in these far west outposts. But avoid the Fokker's Row 12. This back bank of seats is noisy, has no windows, and they don't recline. Unfortunately for those in Row 12, the seats in Row 11 do! We felt like a pair of marsupials trapped in the same pouch for 1,116 miles and two hours and 40 minutes between Perth and Derby recently, all because we were last to show up for seat allocations on a busy holiday.

Some other domestic air companies include **East-West Airlines,** which flies principally in New South Wales and southern Queensland between Sydney and Brisbane; **Ansett Airlines of New South Wales** (also an Ansett subsidiary), covering some smaller ports in the same general area; **Connair,** which buzzes hither and thither almost entirely within the Northern Territory still flying DC–3's; and **Bush Pilots Airways,** which flies light planes between communities along the Queensland coast as well as to islands in the Great Barrier Reef area.

Air Bargains in Australia. Get the latest dope directly from a travel agent, but North American visitors who hold some types of round-trip tickets to Australia (generally promotional point-to-point fares, without stopover privileges) qualify for 30 percent discounts on air trips totaling more than 1,000 kilometers—621 miles—within the country. No longer must they be purchased outside Australia, but they are only available to passengers from the U.S.A. and Canada, and most still find it more convenient to arrange them in advance.

If you're going to see anything of Australia at all, you'll have little trouble using up that 621-mile minimum. Round trip Sydney to Melbourne, for example, equals nearly 900 miles, a trip that will cost about $91 (at this writing) instead of the usual fare of around $131. An intensive trip around the continent—about 10,000 miles—might tote up approximately $800 instead of $1100 (Sydney, Canberra, Melbourne, Hobart, Adelaide, Perth, Darwin, Alice Springs, Cairns, Brisbane, Sydney).

Other passengers can choose from among a series of around-

Australia air routes calculated in advance by Ansett and TAA, which cut about 15 percent off Economy fares. Since the savings are much less dramatic, and since only a few readers would not qualify for the better deals on the previously mentioned "See Australia" fares, we won't go into more detail. For either of these, see any Ansett or TAA office in Australia. The two airlines also have addresses in the U.S.A. In Los Angeles, you can write or see either at 510 West Sixth St., Los Angeles, Calif. 90014. (They're on different floors there.) Ansett is also in the New York phone book, and you'll find TAA in both New York and Chicago.

All of Australia's domestic airlines seem to have some sort of special deal, many of them with complicated ifs, ands, and buts. Check them out at the offices or representatives of MacRobertson Miller, East-West Airlines, and Bush Pilots Airways, all of whom will happily launch you into dozens of airports out in the wopwops.

A couple more cheery notes: If you don't want to go flying for at least 1,000 Ansett or TAA kilometers, you might still save 30 percent on some selected short hops now that those two airlines have introduced *standby fares* between certain routes—probably at least from Sydney to Melbourne, Hobart or Launceston, and from Melbourne either to Hobart or Launceston, and perhaps to some other cities by now. Other than that, TAA and Ansett also have another 15 percent savings plan called "BudJet Fares," applicable during off-peak periods between certain east coast cities.

Taking the train. For more than 100 years, railroad travel in Australia has been plagued by the short-sightedness and stubbornness of the original six different colonies, all of which—incredibly—adopted different track gauges. In the past decade this has been partly—but not totally—overcome. So today there are no sleepy 2:00 a.m. changes of carriage at Albury. Rail travel has become sometimes convenient, occasionally comfortable, and often fun.

Australia's newest and only prestigious train, the trans-continental Indian Pacific, travels 2,500 miles between Sydney (the Pacific Ocean) and Perth (the Indian Ocean), and may be only one of two in the world which carries a functioning piano on board in the lounge car. After traversing the rolling country of the east, it shoots across the great Nullarbor Desert in the west, at one point barreling along for 300 miles straight as an arrow, with not a single curve—the longest stretch of straight track in the world.

Other passenger trains link Brisbane, Sydney, Canberra, Melbourne,

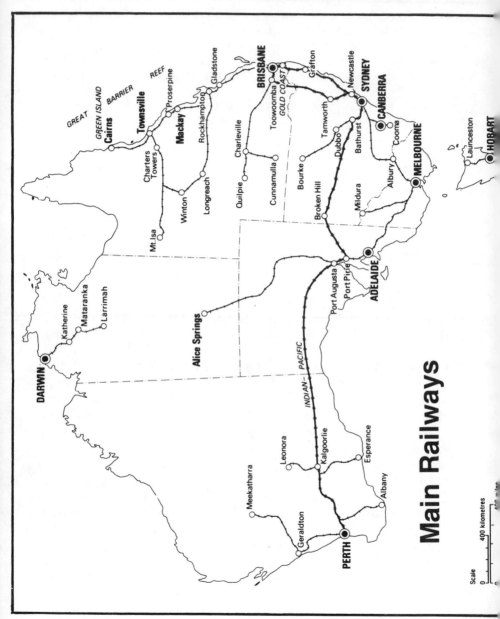

Main Railways

Scale
0 — 400 kilometres

GREAT BARRIER REEF
GREEN ISLAND

Cairns
Townsville
Charters Towers
Mackay
Proserpine
Rockhampton
Gladstone
Mt. Isa
Winton
Longreach
Quilpie
Charleville
Cunnamulla
BRISBANE
GOLD COAST
Toowoomba
Grafton
Newcastle
SYDNEY
CANBERRA
Tamworth
Bourke
Dubbo
Bathurst
Cooma
Broken Hill
Mildura
Albury
MELBOURNE
Launceston
HOBART

DARWIN
Katherine
Mataranka
Larrimah
Alice Springs

Port Augusta
Port Pirie
ADELAIDE

INDIAN – PACIFIC

Meekatharra
Leonora
Kalgoorlie
Esperance
Geraldton
Albany
PERTH

Map courtesy Australian Tourist Commission

Adelaide, etc. The famous—or notorious—Ghan runs (when it can) between Adelaide and Alice Springs, and it carries the other piano. Both these trains are discussed again in the chapters that follow.

If you're going to travel around Australia by train, you'll save a tank car full of dollars if you buy the **Australpass.** Now stop, look, and listen, because this bargain card *must be purchased outside of Australia.* There are five types varying between a 14-day pass for about $A150 (about $US170) and a three-month version for about $A420 (about $US480). Either gives you unlimited first-class travel on the rail systems of Australia, including city and suburban lines.

When you consider that the price of a round-trip first-class ticket on the Indian Pacific, for instance, is now $A560 *alone*, it's a good deal. (You will have to pay modest amounts extra for berths and meals in the IP and other long runs, however.) With the Australpass, you can generally hop off and on other trains whenever you want, making reservations where and when necessary. You can buy the pass through your travel agent or through Thomas Cook Australia, 9363 Wilshire Blvd., Suite 206, Beverly Hills, Calif. 90210. We like this plan a lot.

Bargains by Bus. Besides booking on the scene, there are at least six types of passes you can use for bus ("coach") travel in Australia, but be careful to make the exact arrangements you want. There's a potential source of confusion in the two companies you can deal with. One is **Ansett Pioneer,** which is represented in the U.S. by Greyhound International, 625 8th Ave., New York, N.Y. 10018. The other is **Greyhound Australia,** which is *not* connected with the North American Greyhound and has *no* U.S. representative.

Ansett Pioneer, the large operation controlled by the same people as Ansett Airways, etc., offers five bus plans, four of which, like the Australpass, must be purchased outside Australia.

First and most famous is the **Aussiepass**, currently selling in four versions: 60 days for $A295, 35 days for $A245, 21 days for $A190 and 14 days for $A140. There are also two plans which may be purchased in Australia at somewhat higher rates—60 days for $A330 and 30 days (not 35) for $A265. Aussiepasses allow unlimited travel in Pioneer coaches throughout the country.

Some long distance buses have toilets and air conditioning on board, but neither the Aussiepass nor Sir Reggie himself can guarantee that these modern devices won't "go crook" somewhere in the wild country Beyond the Black Stump.

Prior to the advent of mobile dunnies, the traditional Outback answer by the driver to the passenger who feels a call of nature hundreds of miles from any plumbing is to stop the coach and hand over a shovel with the instructions that the user can go dig in the desert as far away as is necessary to become inconspicuous.

According to the veteran bus driver who explained it to us, the passenger, who he said was more often a woman, soon learns that it's more practical to walk 100 yards or so *in front* of the bus—not to the rear. Under that procedure, she needs only to walk one way and then wave the shovel in the air as a signal to the driver that the job has been done, and it's time to be picked up. (Trudging off *behind* the coach may seem more modest, but it's exactly twice as far to walk, of course.)

Nevertheless, traveling by bus is quite respectable in Australia, and the meal stops are usually at fairly nice cafes. Many Americans say these long-distance trips are an ideal way to make good friends among the Diggers.

Ansett Pioneer, which calls itself the country's only national coachline, also has four passes which must be bought before leaving for Australia. The **Unlimited Sightseeing Pass** will allow you to take any number of their bus sightseeing tours (half-day or all-day narrated trips) in capital cities and major tourist areas. They vary in price from 14 days for $A85, 21 days for $A120, and 30 days for $A145.

If you're in doubt on this one, let us suggest that you could live without it. We found that Pioneer sightseeing tours vary widely in quality, and we would rather make up our minds on tours only after arriving at each individual general destination. If you already have the Aussiepass, you can get 10 percent discounts on the sightseeing tours anyway; but even without that advantage, we doubt you would take enough tours to make up the initial outlay. (Of course some may disagree.)

Ansett Pioneer has three types of "Gold Passes," at least one of which may be a good deal. That one is the tried and true **21-day Australian Gold Pass.** It allows 20 nights' accommodations at certain hotels, and 21 days of unlimited travel for $A598 (at this writing, and on a share-twin basis), plus a couple of extras such as working out a personal itinerary for you, meeting you on arrival in Australia, etc. It does not include meals or other expenses.

Then there is the **21-day Australian Super Gold Pass "A,"** a mouthful which is like the above except that it also includes air travel back to Sydney from either Cairns or Alice Springs. This one costs $A735, or $137 more for a trip that currently totals less than that if you were to buy the plane ticket separately. The last is the **21-day Super Australian Gold Pass "B,"** which is similar, but at $A778 (again a share-twin), it includes the airfare back to Sydney from either Perth or Darwin. (Again the airfare can be less than the additional amount by using the "See Australia" plan.)

Last on this busman's holiday, the other company, Greyhound Australia, offers a 30-day and 60-day **Eaglepass** plan which is competitive with Pioneer's Aussiepass. At the moment, the price is the same for both. (Remember Greyhound has nothing to do with North American Greyhounds, a different breed.) Its headquarters are at Greyhound Travel Centre, 79 Melbourne St., South Brisbane 4101, Queensland, Australia.

Note: Nearly all bus lines allow you to take two suitcases along. Children generally travel for half fare on all buses. Overnight express buses, equipped with washrooms and toilets, do not stop en route. At least, they're not *scheduled* to do so.

Rental Cars. There are five big outfits throughout Australia. **Avis Rent-a-Car System,** the good ole Number Two in America, is Number One Down Under. And **Hertz Rent-A-Car,** until recently known as Kay/Hertz in Australia, is coming along right behind. The third biggie is **Budget Rent-A-Car System.** Rates on all three are similar, running from a minimum of about $A10 per day, plus 14 cents a kilometre (about 23 cents a mile) for standard-shift minis up to about $A20, plus 20 cents per km. for big cars. Unlimited mileage (er, kilometrage) rates may run from about $A150 per week in these outfits.

Avis, incidentally, increases its rates during the "peak seasons"—winter on the Gold Coast and summer in Tasmania.

The other two nation wide firms are **Thrifty Rent-A-Car** (Sydney address: 83 William St., Tel. 33–5058) and **Letz Rent-A-Car** (Sydney address: 110 Darlinghurst Rd., Tel. 31–3178). Both appear to offer significant savings on weekly rates.

The way to get the best deal, of course, is to shop for car rentals on the scene. All the above publish rate sheets. It may not make much difference renting a car for a day, but if you take an hour to compare the different deals available, it could save you a hundred Aussie dollars or more over a long vacation.

By the way, don't go to the trouble of getting an international driver's license. If you're a genuine tourist, your regular U.S. license is good for a year in Australia. British, Canadian, and New Zealand licenses are also accepted.

Gasoline (called "petrol" Down Under) is extra and costs about 30 Australian cents per litre—$1.37 American per U.S. gallon. (If you rent a Leyland Mini, with manual transmission, you'll get about 30 miles per

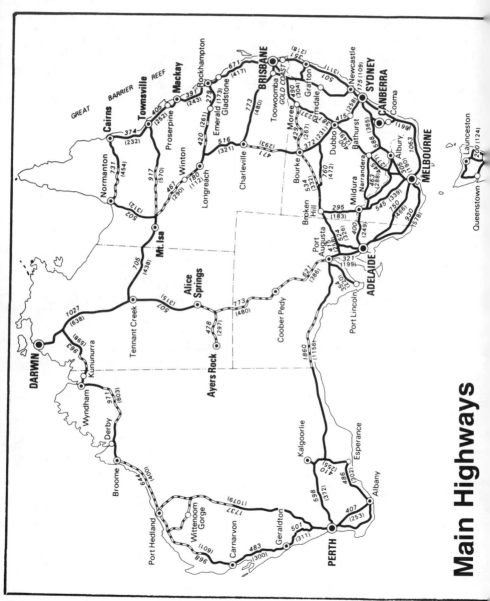

Map courtesy Australian Tourist Commission

Main Highways

gallon.) Popular petrols include Shell, BP, Caltex, Mobil, Amoco, Golden Fleece, and AMPOL.

A few driving tips: Traffic signs are similar to the international signs we have at home today, and are generally clear and easily understood. As in Britain and New Zealand, you drive on the left, of course. You pass ("overtake") on the right. Until you get used to it, use caution making right-hand turns across the traffic lane, and don't forget to go *clockwise* around traffic circles ("roundabouts"). Generally speaking, we prefer to rent an automatic drive car for it gives us just one less thing to think about for the first 100 miles while we are grimly chanting, "Keep left! Keep left! Keep left!" and learning not to look for the rear view mirror somewhere in outer space.

Don't forget that the vehicle on the right at intersections has the right of way unless otherwise indicated. And look out on main highways for the *ocker* (hillbilly) who comes off a little dirt country road insisting on his rights! And above all, remember that wearing a safety belt is the law in Australia. If you don't buckle up, you could be fined $20!

If you're going to be traveling extensively in the Outback, there are many, many precautions to be taken. It's exciting country, but genuinely wild. Motorists are still found dead when they ignore the lessons of the past—forgetting to take extra water, getting bogged in "bulldust," etc.

Before you leave home, try to pick up a little Pan Am pamphlet on driving through Australia, although it may be out of print now. Otherwise and furthermore, after you arrive in the country, look for some of the several publications with good advice and hints for effective motoring through specific rough areas of Australia.

Also, the Automobile Association in Australia offers a lot—road service, general driving assistance, travel information, maps, etc., *but only if you are already a member of an affiliated organization* like the American Automobile Association (AAA) or the Canadian Automobile Association. (And you'll be asked to prove it, too.)

Campers. You can rent campers (called campervans) from several places in Australia. Some of the best bargains are those equipped to sleep five persons. You can get lots of good information on the subject from the Australian Tourist Commission (see page 8). Avis is affiliated with John Terry Pty. Ltd., corner Hillcrest St. and Parramatta Rd., Homebush, NSW 2140. Some family rates have been running about $A250 a week, including linens, dishes, and a free 625 miles (per week)—a good deal for combining sleeping and wheeling expenses. (But don't hold us to that. That rate is a sample one only.)

Camping grounds ("caravan parks") are located near cities and towns all over the country. With electric outlet you'll pay $3 to $5 a day, and $10 for "unpowered sites." And, of course, you can also rent or buy caravans (house trailers) in most parts of Australia.

We've never had the opportunity to seriously evaluate caravan parks, but if you're serious about this kind of travel, try to get hold of the annual **Caravan Camping Directory,** published by the NRMA (National Road & Motorists Association), 151 Clarence St., Sydney 2000, N.S.W. (If worse comes to worse, join the outfit for about 10 bucks.)

Hitchhiking. If you hitchhike elsewhere, you'll probably get away with it in Australia, too. Aussie drivers are gregarious, and hitching men and hitching couples usually seem to get along okay. As at home, it is dangerous for women to hitchhike, however, either alone or in pairs.

Members of the Society of the Upturned Thumb report good luck carrying (1) an American or Canadian flag, and (2) a signboard which can be marked with the immediate destination. Cops, like cops nearly everywhere, might interfere. Savants of the Australian open road say that when you see the "white hats," you should step back off the right of way. Then you're not standing on an illegal portion of the road.

Choosing a Travel Agent

Don't pick a travel agent blindly from the Yellow Pages. If you don't already have a trusted travel expert, your best bet is to ask your friends and associates who they've used—especially if they recently took a trip to Australia or the South Pacific.

After you have a few names of agencies in your area, call them up. Some just won't talk to you over the phone at all about your proposed trip. Throw those rascals out immediately. A good agency may understandably not feel like going into great detail over the phone, but you can get a pretty good feel for their operation if they seem pleasant and willing to jaw with you for a few minutes.

Ask them some questions about Australia. If they seem vague or confused, they just might not be able to do the job for you. If they seem to have facts and figures at their fingertips, then make a date to drop in and speak to someone about your ideas for a vacation.

We heartily recommend you choose an aggressive, enthusiastic travel agency. Avoid "assembly-line" operations (and these can be the tiny, one-man office or the giant, international outfits)—those who seem anxious only to ship you out in one of their own pre-wrapped packages or just to jet you off into space on any old flight. Australia is not a single, simple destination; there are many kinds of tours and other options, and a travel agency should be ready to spell them all out for you and then follow through and make your reservations.

Your travel agent should be a member of ASTA (the American Society of Travel Agents) or the ARTA (the Association of Retail Travel Agents). The most respected agents today also have the initials "CTC" (Certified Travel Counselor) after their names. And of course the agency should be licensed by the ATC (the Air Traffic Conference), so it can legally issue your tickets.

If your agent has been to Australia, that may be a help, but it's not an absolute requirement. Agents who have received only one or two "familiarization" trips hosted by commercial outfits in the travel industry may be inclined to book their clients with those few firms to whom they feel grateful for the freebies. (Incidentally, in case you missed it before, we have made no arrangements of any kind with any companies in connection with this book.)

It's quite possible for a good agent who has never been to Australia to be thoroughly familiar with many of its facilities and book you into a terrific vacation, and it's also possible for a dumb or gullible agent who has been to Australia a dozen times to completely foul up your trip.

A good travel agent will try to give you what you want, so we suggest that you rely on this book for the important basics and then let your travel agent try to put your requests into a final practical itinerary.

Your travel agent's service should be free, remember. They generally make their money from commissions (7 to 11 percent from airlines, 10 percent from hotels, tours, etc.). It costs them money in postage, cables, phone calls, and the like to set things up, of course, and if their client suddenly decides to cancel everything at the last minute, it's not unreasonable that the agency would then send the would-be customer a bill. We've heard that some travel agents charge their clients outright, anyway. Maybe they've got a good reason, but personally, we'd stay away from those people.

If you prefer to make all your arrangements yourself, that can be a very self-satisfying experience. Just be sure to write letters that are specific about your requirements. (See our remarks on hotels, rental cars, bus tours, etc., before you do this.) And be sure to save all your confirmation letters and deposit receipts. You'll need those for proof at every turn.

Travel Facts and Figures

Here's a set of considerations that may be boring after you've learned them all, but they are essential for first-time visitors to Australia:

Weather and Climate. Antipodeans think it gets cold in their country. Don't believe it. Without the opportunity to experience the "temperate" zone in North America, bless their hearts, they don't know what cold really is. Even the island state of Tasmania—which Aussies sometimes describe in terms reserved in most places for deepest Siberia—grows an occasional palm tree. And how cold can any city be where practically the only snow is the white stuff that sometimes appears in the hills and mountains?

It does, however, get hot—damned hot—in Australia, and more on that in a moment.

The most important thing to remember about weather and climate Down Under is that the seasons are exactly opposite to ours. When we're hot, the Australians are cold (or think they are). When we're cold, the Aussies are hot—or warm, depending on the part of the country.

Because of the upside-down weather pattern, remember that the hottest parts of the country are those in the north, while the temperature gets generally lower the further south you progress. This puts cities like Brisbane and Darwin *up* in the tropics (closer to the equator), while Sydney, Canberra and Melbourne are *down* in the cooler southland. (Perth, like Los Angeles, is in a separate category. It's west and warm nearly the year around.)

The seasons are considered to run like this:

Spring . . . September to November.
Summer . . . December to February.
Autumn . . . March to May.
Winter . . . June to August.

In practical terms, this means that the ideal time to visit Australia would seem to be during our northern winter—the southern warm months—September to April, when most Aussies are enjoying swimming, sailing, and other outdoor sports in temperatures in the 70's and 80's. (We've felt comfortable in a suit or sport jacket in sunny Sydney even in late May.)

An important exception is Darwin and the "Top End" districts of the Northern Territory, which will be suffering through the hot and humid summer monsoon season December to March, and also in the desert Outback where temperatures reach over 100 degrees F. around Christmas time.

Darwin is ideal during its dry season—about April to November. The skies are clear and the weather is usually ideal in Alice Springs and at Ayers Rock then, too. You'll find warm weather in Perth and in Brisbane also at that time of year. In Sydney, Canberra, and Melbourne, they think it's cold in the winter seasons because their daytime temperatures run between the mid 40's and the mid 60's on the Fahrenheit scale June to August. Hobart does get down as low as 40 F. in deepest July.

And snow? You'll find it in abundance, appropriately enough in the Snowy Mountains. Within easy traveling distance from Sydney and Canberra, they host a flourishing ski season there at winter resorts from June through September.

To sum it up optimistically, a country as large as Australia always can point to some area blessed with ideal vacation weather at any time of the year. By the same token, there is always some place in Australia which is not dependably comfortable at any particular time of the year.

However our own recent two-month trip took place under near ideal conditions. We found ourselves generally in the southern part of the country in April (early autumn) and in the warmer northern areas in May (late autumn). We enjoyed perfect traveling conditions nearly all the time.

Be aware, though, that spanning the temperate and tropical zones means a wider selection of wearing apparel. We packed sweaters as well as shorts, for instance.

Packing and Wearing. We've alluded to it before, but the most important thing to remember is that the international baggage allowance for persons (including children) traveling directly between the U.S.A. and a foreign destination is two checked pieces of luggage and a small amount of hand luggage.

Technically, each of the two checked bags may not exceed 62 inches; that's adding up its length, width, and breadth. And unless you're traveling first class, the two together may not exceed 106 inches, all told. Virtually no commercial suitcase made in America comes close to exceeding 62 inches, so the chances are you'll be okay if you take your two largest bags. (But if in doubt, measure it out.)

You're allowed one or more pieces of carry-on luggage small enough to fit under the seat (camera bag, airline bag, etc.), and the maximum outside dimensions of all those pieces combined may not exceed 45 inches per person.

If you have an extra suitcase, well, it'll cost you about another $100 or so to bring it to Australia, so don't do it. And another good reason for keeping your luggage requirements modest is that while traveling around Australia by plane, the official requirements are more strict. Here you're allowed one checked bag plus a piece of carry-on luggage.

If you have extra checked bags, and if the airline decides to charge you for them, it may do so on a sliding scale of between $2 and $10 per bag, depending on how far you're traveling.

So if you're planning on doing any heavy buying Down Under, you may want to do it after your last Australian domestic flight so that you can carry it back home in your two cases.

Now, what to take? If you're an experienced traveler, you'll believe us when we plead that you should travel as light as you possibly can. You may also know that it never seems to be possible to travel as light as you plan to.

The male traveler. Even if he's only in Australia on vacation, the American man will feel out of place on occasion if he doesn't have something to wear a tie with. Take at least a sport jacket or a blazer. A dark-color suit, either summer or winter weight, would also be a good idea, and if you're worried about airline overweight, you can wear it on plane trips.

Australians don't like to think of themselves as class conscious, to be sure. But in my experience, I nearly always receive a little better attention when wearing a coat and tie than wandering around bare necked. Also, many of Australia's nicer restaurants have dress codes; like it or not, you just won't be allowed in without that noose around your neck.

A couple pair of easy-care slacks will do for most day-to-day needs. A pair of jeans is a must if you're going to do any exploring in the bush at all.

Take maybe one or two long-sleeve shirts, two or three knit pullover shirts, and perhaps two two-way shirts with short sleeves, which can be worn with a tie or open necked. (If you're going to be traveling entirely in winter, substitute another long-sleeve shirt or two for these.)

I'd have a sweater along any time of the year, either a pullover or button-up cardigan. Some men might like a zipper jacket for cold weather.

There's considerable debate about top coats among antipodean traveling men. My personal choice is a knee-length all-weather coat (with or without lining), unless I were going to spend all the time in dependably warm weather. In that case, you could consider a folding raincoat. I also like to have a collapsible black men's umbrella in the suitcase, just for insurance.

For your feet, try to find something that's comfortable but also looks good with your suit or jacket. Hush Puppies or similar suedes might do it. I felt equally at ease in good dining salons, tramping around animal reserves, and exploring old gold mines in shoes like that last year. Businessmen on the job, of course, may prefer to have a pair of black-leather shoes along, as well.

Take an old, well-broken-in pair of sneakers, too, if you'll be trudging over sand and gibbers in the Red Centre—certainly for clambering up Ayers Rock or for picking your way carefully over the coral at the Great Barrier Reef.

We saw no great need for a hat, except possibly for days of excessive rain or sun. A roll-up or crushable model to keep in a coat pocket most of the time is not a bad idea. And if you want to buy an Aussie bush hat, well, there are many to choose from.

Throw in underwear, pajamas, lightweight robe, ties, etc., to suit your fancy, and several pair of socks. As a general guide, automatic laundries do exist in Australia, but they are hard to find as compared with the U.S.A. (You'll find automatic washing machines available for guest use more often in the less expensive "family" hotels and motels.)

In the good ole summer time, or in the northern, tropical parts of the country, you'll find Australian men *dressed up* in shorts. They are considered acceptable for many occasions and locations where they would not be at home. Generally shorter than our Bermudas, shorts are usually called "stubbies." They are more or less the length of American walk shorts, but virtually always worn with long socks. (You can take your walk shorts along for this uniform, but you'll probably have to buy the socks on the scene.) With a short-sleeve shirt, tie, long socks, and stubbies, you're dressed to kill in many areas of Australia, particularly in the warmer climes of Queensland or the Northern Territory.

Of course if you're going to take part in athletic activities—swimming, skiing, hiking, etc.—then your Down Under wardrobe requirements will be pretty much as it would be at home for those things.

The woman visitor. Decide whether or not you want to wear a pants suit. They're comfortable, flexible, and convenient for traveling in, to be sure. However, if you're fashion conscious, it's our duty to tell you that Australian women seem almost to have deserted trousers, now, except for the fancier jeans. (Women's fashion in Australian cities seem to follow what they were wearing in London or New York the previous six months, if you want to remember that.)

We'd suggest taking shorts, trousers, and skirts with tops that mix and match, but keep in mind that you may not wear shorts as often as you do at home. You'll want a couple of dresses for evening wear, of course, and take a sweater—pullover or cardigan—as evenings can be cool any time of year.

In the winter, a medium weight, all-weather coat would be nice, and certainly take some kind of casual jacket. Sara was also glad she carried her folding umbrella to Australia.

On your feet, we might mention that ladies' longstemmed boots have been very popular in Australia lately. Of course you must have comfortable walking shoes for everyday sightseeing, and a pair of evening shoes. And like the men, you, too, will need sneakers (and a pair of jeans) for the rougher style of Aussie outback experiences.

Men and women. Take your favorite toiletries, of course, but with the full knowledge that you can replace nearly anything you run out of. They will often be unfamiliar brands, though, and you can buy things only during Australia's rather restrictive shopping hours.

Strangely, we find plain old bottles of regular aspirin hard to get hold of. (Plenty of dissolvables, aspirin in chewing gum, and other pain killers available.) And we were glad we tucked in some rub-on fly and mosquito repellent.

We imagine you will take your camera. If you have a telephoto lens, don't think of leaving it at home. (Too many animals way up in the trees.) We also enjoyed using our miniature tape recorder to capture the cockney of the tour guides and the laughter of the kookaburra. (Film and cassette tapes are readily available.)

If you have a pair of binoculars, toss them in. A portable transistor radio is also good to help you keep in tune with Australia and Australians all along the way. (Their AM stations use the same general broadcast band frequencies we do.) And we always carry our pocket calculator, now, to check hotel and restaurant bills, exchange rates, conversion from centigrade to Fahrenheit, and a zillion other little logistical tasks which might otherwise get in the way of a dinkum holiday.

Avoiding the Crush. As in any other country, foreign visitors who find themselves casually on the go during peak periods for local traffic are due for sudden disappointment and sad inconvenience.

Look out especially for vacation times—they call them "school holidays" Down Under—when every kid in the continent seems to be traveling between boarding school and home at opposite ends of the country. Trains and planes are particularly jam packed at the beginnings and ends of these periods.

Christmas Holidays (the big summer vacation) begin in mid-December and continue until early February. Although the worst strain on public transportation appears to be at either end of that period, there will be considerable traffic by oldsters and youngsters alike throughout all of January. If you travel then, have your reservations firmly locked in in advance, and avoid any changes in plans.

Planes and trains are also overflowing with small fry for two other difficult periods—for about two weeks in mid-May and another two weeks at the end of August/beginning of September.

Public Holidays. Australia has about 30 public holidays, counting all the ones that are celebrated in different states on different dates. There are about 11 holidays agreed upon nearly nationwide, however. They are as follows:

January—New Years Day; last Monday in January—Australia Day; in April—Good Friday and Easter Saturday, Sunday, and Monday (four days); April 25—Anzac Day (the national memorial day); a Monday in early June—the Queen's Birthday; first Tuesday in November—Melbourne Cup Day (official only in Victoria, but observed everywhere); December 25—Christmas Day; and December 26—Boxing Day.

Time Zones. Queensland, New South Wales, the Australian Capital Territory, Victoria, and Tasmania—states that make up the eastern third of the continent—set their clocks at Greenwich Mean Time plus 10. Since Pacific Standard Time in the U.S. is GMT minus eight, that places Brisbane, Sydney, Canberra, Melbourne, Hobart, etc., at 18 hours later than American west coast cities. Or, since the International Date Line is between the U.S. and Australia, you can say these places are six hours earlier, but on the following day. Thus, when it is 12:00 noon Saturday in San Francisco, it's 6:00 a.m. Sunday in Sydney—provided both are on standard time.

(Since you "lose" a day traveling to Australia across the date line, conversely you "gain" a day coming back home. Leaving Sydney Saturday evening, for instance, you'll find yourself arriving in San Francisco on Saturday afternoon. In effect, it will be two or three hours before you left!)

Australia is one of the few countries in the world to use a half-hour split time zone. But to add to the confusion, it's only in the center of the country. Therefore, it is a half-hour earlier in Darwin and Alice Springs in the Northern Territory and in Adelaide in South Australia than it is in Sydney.

The vast state of Western Australia is back in step with the rest of the world, eight hours ahead of Greenwich Mean Time. This places Perth, of course, 1½ hours earlier than Adelaide and two hours ahead of the east coast cities.

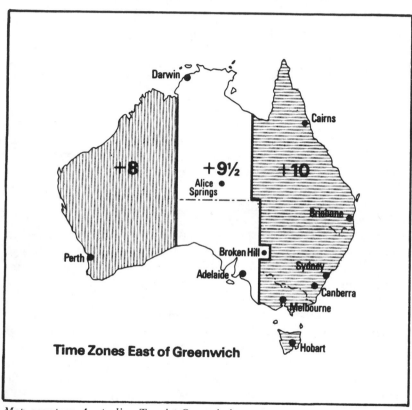

Darwin

Cairns

+8

+9½

+10

Alice
Springs

Perth

Broken Hill

Brisbane

Adelaide

Sydney

Canberra

Melbourne

Hobart

Time Zones East of Greenwich

Map courtesy Australian Tourist Commission

The three time zones are called Eastern Standard, Central Australian, and Western.

During the summer months (from the last Sunday in October to the first Sunday in March), some states shift into Daylight Saving Time, making those times one hour later. (Western Australia, the Northern Territory, and Queensland do not.) And because much of the U.S. also goes on Daylight Saving—but in the approximate opposite months— there are periods each year when Australia and the U.S. are separated by one hour more than normal or by one hour less than normal. Thus, when it is noon in San Francisco, it would be 5:00 a.m. in Sydney if California is on PDST, or 7:00 a.m. in Sydney, if N.S.W. is observing Daylight Saving, or 6:00 a.m. if neither city is on it.

But unless you're calculating airline schedules yourself, perhaps you won't have to get involved with this perplexing refinement of the clock game. American businessmen in Australia pondering when to phone the home office do find themselves performing these mental gymnastics and usually at about two o'bloody clock in the morning!

Jet Lag. Daylight Savings, Greenwich Mean, and all the king's men can hardly put you together again if you suffer from jet lag—the familiar disorientation for those who fly long distances in short amounts of time.

One of the best reasons for flying to Australia overnight, however, is that it somewhat minimizes the adverse effects of jet lag. You leave California after dinner, see a movie, go to sleep (if you can sleep on a plane). Then, when you awake in the morning, you eat what might seem like a rather late breakfast, then arrive in Sydney at 6:00 a.m.

Nevertheless, your first effect thereafter might be finding yourself famished an hour or so later and then compulsively eating again in the mid-afternoon. First thing you know, you're dead on your feet at 6:00 in the evening. That's midnight back in California—much later than that in Cleveland and New York.

Some claim they are never affected by jet lag. Personally, it takes us a day or two before we stop propping open our eyes, quit yawning in everyone's faces, and are able to again walk a reasonably straight line.

We suggest six steps to alleviate—somewhat—the effects of jet lag: (1) Sleep as much as you can on the plane. (2) Set your watch to Australian time as soon as you take off. (3) Take no sleeping pill and little alcohol during the flight, but eat when food is offered. (4) After you arrive at your hotel, pull the shades against the daylight and try for a good nap. (5) Schedule no business appointments or any demanding sightseeing your first day in Australia. (6) Eat lightly with familiar foods your first day.

Metrics and Electrics

According to one story, it was the U.S.A. who convinced Australia about 10 years ago to convert to the metric (decimal) system of weights and measures. Americans said they were about to do it themselves and, in the interests of improved international trade and communication, the island continent should quickly do the same.

Australia then set out on a well-organized program that now has the whole country easily dividing and multiplying by tens while the U.S.A. is still stumbling around with 12 inches, 16 ounces, four pints, and countless short and long tons.

The money came first and easiest. Pounds, shillings, and pence were smoothly changed to dollars and cents. But steadily, the adaptable Aussies also came to accept the kilometer, the centimeter, the litre, the gram, and degrees centigrade.

To try to learn the decimal system while on vacation is, of course, absurd and a contradiction in terms. But here are a few thoughts on how to keep from mixing your millimeters throughout Australia.

Temperature. Anybody who gets up in the morning without listening to the weather forecasts on the radio deserves to freeze or burn on the day's sightseeing. But the temperatures will be given on the Celsius (centigrade) scale.

We were a bit pedantic last trip and often took out our midget calculator, marked it with the figure the radio gave us, and then punched out "$\times 9, \div 5, + 32 =$" and came up with the familiar Fahrenheit. If you're not carrying your own trusty LED, however, remember that the most comfortable temperatures are generally in the 20s. (20° Celsius equals 68° Fahrenheit; 29° C. = 84° F.) Of course the freezing point of water is zero degrees and the boiling point is 100 degrees, which is the principle behind the whole scale.

Distance. How far is it to the next town? Strangely enough, middle-aged and older Australians will still give you longer distances estimated in miles. Closer to home, where they often see signs printed in kilometers—like 32 km from Sydney to Parramatta—they may use the modern figure.

A kilometer is .621 of a mile, but for quick conversion while zipping along the highway, we move over the decimal point or maybe even lop off the last digit, multiply by six, and then round off the result. In the example above, 32 becomes either 3.2 × 6 or 3 × 6, depending on how lazy we're feeling. One equation gives us 18 and the other 19. Either one we would round off to 20 miles. And if the speed limit on the road is 100 kmh, we calculate that at 60. (Of course it's really 62.1 mph, but few traffic cops are going to care much about 2.1 mph anyway.)

For small distances, well, one centimeter is about the width of your little finger nail, and there are about 2½ finger nails per inch. 100 centimeters, of course, equal a meter, and that's about as far as a man's outstretched arm can reach from his nose—39 inches, or a little more than a yard. And since "kilo" means thousand, there are a thousand meters in the kilometer.)

Volume. Gasoline and milk are sold in litres, and a litre is close enough to an American quart to our way of thinking. Therefore, four of them are darn near an American gallon. (Not the British imperial gallon; that's larger.)

Now if some Digger tells you his car gets 11 km per litre of petrol, you can quickly multiply 1.1 by six (6.6) and then by 4 litres to get 26.4 miles per U.S. gallon.

Weight. Here's an anachronism. You might find Aussies giving their body weight still in stone (that's singular and plural), an old British system which amounts to 14 pounds per stone. However a kilogram, which you'll meet while grocery shopping, is 2.2 pounds, so you can double that weight quoted at the butcher shop to get the approximate weight of the meat in the system we're familiar with. You'll also hear the weight of coal or wheat given in tonnes. That's 1000 kilograms, which works out to be 1.1 tons. Not being in the coal or wheat business, we've mentally equated the two for all practical purposes.

Area. If you think about buying land, you'll get into hectares. A hectare, which is 10,000 square meters, works out to 2.47 acres—two and a half acres is a pretty close estimate. And a square meter, if anyone wants to know, is 10.8 square feet.

Electricity. Luckily, electric current, like units of time, is *measured* Down Under the same as at home. The important thing to remember about Aussie house current is first, that it's powered at 240 volts, or more than twice the zap we get in the U.S.A. or Canada. This means you'll instantly cremate your razor or hair dryer if you manage to plug them in without a transformer. And as transformers are generally too bulky and expensive to travel with, perhaps you'd better forget these devices.

The more expensive hotels do have 110-volt outlets fed by small transformers installed in the bathrooms. You can run light-duty appliances like razors from those—no hair dryers, irons or the like. We do find it handy for the AC adaptor for our tape recorder, pocket calculator, transistor radio, etc., when we are out of or want to save on batteries. (Take an extension cord, too, so you're not always listening to your tapes in the bathroom!) Incidentally, you can buy standard battery sizes in Australia, but it often seems you have to hunt around, the stores are closed, etc. We take some spares.

Australian alternating current (AC) also alternates at 50 cycles per second (versus 60 c.p.s. in the U.S.). This means that U.S. motors will run a little slower, even if the voltage is transformed from 240 to 110 volts. Such items as American electric clocks and phonographs, where exact speed is important, will not perform satisfactorily unless they are electrically or mechanically converted—a complicated process. It doesn't matter much if your razor motor revolves a little less rapidly than usual.

If you've been to Europe or England, don't think that your two-pronged adaptor is going to work in an Aussie three-pronged socket. If you have a 240-volt appliance like a traveling iron, and you can't find an adapter at an electrical store, go to Woolworth's or some place similar and have a look at an iron cord or an electric teakettle cord. Sometimes the American plug—or at least the European adapter—will fit into the appliance end of that cord and the other end will fit into the three-pronged "point" in the wall. One American firm sells adapters for American plugs to Australian sockets for two or three bucks. That's Traveler's Checklist, Cornwall Bridge Road, Sharon, Conn. 06069. (They've got a lot of other stuff for sale too, of course.)

Notice that it's probably a "switched point," too. Unlike in the U.S., most electrical outlets in Australia are controlled by a switch—a darned good idea.

Changing a light bulb? Be aware that Australian light bulbs—like British ones—don't unscrew. They're held in place with two little pins, like some of our automobile and flashlight bulbs. You push in and turn to the left to take them out. And if the socket is dangling from the ceiling, for heaven's sake, use two hands—one to hold the socket and the other to twist the bulb.

Money, Currency, and Prices

In November, 1976, Australia officially devalued its dollar by 17½ percent on international exchanges. Bargains became good for American travelers in the wake of this action, but the bickie has gradually been revalued upwards in the world currency markets over the past four years.

Today, there is again more than just a dime's worth of difference between the Yankee and the Aussie dollar. At this writing, the Australian dollar is worth about $1.14 American. Expressed another way, every time you spend 88 Australian cents, you've spent an American dollar. But remember that with the vagaries of international economics, there can be no guarantee that the exchange rate won't take a kangaroo jump forward or backward at any time.

When writing specifically about prices, the traditional way to make things perfectly clear is to use something like "$US114," or "$A100," the "US" or the "A" indicating which country's dollars you're talking about.

In this volume, we sometimes do that, too, or make some other specific indication when it seems appropriate. But generally speaking throughout the balance of this book, we quote and estimate prices in *Australian dollars*. This makes things easier for everyone, including travelers from other countries, to make their own conversions when calculating prices at hotels, restaurants, and other tourist facilities in this guidebook. (An exception is in the earlier part of this chapter. The prices quoted there for air and sea trips to Australia from America are in U.S. currency.)

One thing seems clear at the present time. Your money will go much further in Australia than it will in many of the expensive European countries which have served as traditional vacation destinations. We'll bet the price of a good Aussie steak dinner will be less than half the tab you'd pay for a comparable meal in London or Paris, for instance. And you'll do almost as well on the cost of good hotel rooms. Internal transportation, by plane, train, or bus, might be a third off what you'd pay mile per mile around Europe.

Be sure to pick up at least a small amount of Australian currency before you leave on your trip, so you can begin to become familiar with it. Also, it's always a good idea to land in a country with some of its currency immediately in your pocket. (Your bank will sell you some or will tell you where to buy it.)

Sensibly, the bills (Aussies call them "notes") are printed in different sizes and colors for different denominations, so you're not likely to find out too late that you gave the taxi a ten by mistake. They come in $50, $20, $10, $5, $2, and $1 versions. The $2 note *is* green, by the way. The $1 note, a tan color like a certain Australian cookie ("biscuit") is sometimes called a "bickie." The Aussies also use the term "bucks," an American influence on the lingo. But they have lost the colorful slang they had for coins before the country adopted decimal currency. A 10-cent coin is dully called a "10-cent piece." ("Tanners" and "two-bob bits" have gone the way of spats and corset stays.)

Coins come in 50 cents (a 12-sided coin about the size of the American half-dollar), 20 cents (slightly smaller, with a platypus swimming on the back), 10 cents (the size and value of the old shilling but with the sheep replaced by a lyrebird), 5 cents (dime-size, bearing a spiny anteater), 2 cents (a copper coin about the size of a nickel and featuring the frill-necked lizard), and one cent (a small copper stamped with a feather-tailed glider).

As with most British commonwealth countries, the profile of Queen Elizabeth (looking very young) is featured on the obverse with the value and regional designs on the reverse sides.

If you're curious as to who all those people are on the folding money, we've researched it all out for you.

The only person on the "bickie" is the Queen again, with a stern expression and a very long neck. Two dollars gives you John Macarthur, the irascible settler who established Australia's wool industry. On the back is William J. Farrer, who developed the excellent hybrid wheat now grown in the country.

The five-dollar note features Sir Joseph Banks, the scientist on Cook's voyage who catalogued and described much of Australia's strange natural life. On the reverse is a woman, Caroline Chisholm, who worked to improve immigrant conditions in Australia during the mid-nineteenth century.

On the $10 note is Francis Greenway, convicted of forgery in England, but who became a great architect in colonial Australia. Opposite him on the same bill is Henry Lawson, Australia's best-known writer. Sir Charles Kingsford Smith, the most notable of the nation's aviation pioneers, appears on a $20. Lawrence Hargrave, who experimented with the theory of flight by using kites, is engraved on the back. And John Curtin, the wartime prime minister who defied Churchill, is honored on a $50.

There are no strict currency regulations that you're likely to run afoul of in Australia. You can bring whatever money you want into the country, but you're only allowed to take out $250 in Australian notes and $5 in coins.

Credit cards. Visa and Master Charge are scheduled to come to Australia this year for some retail outlets. Meanwhile the only American cards generally accepted are Diners Club (often), American Express (sometimes), and Carte Blanche (seldom).

We used our Diners Club infrequently on our latest trip, fearing that the exchange rate would be horrendous. Back home, we were pleasantly surprised to see that the rate used was very fair.

Exchange rates. Remember that you will get your best rate *within* the country, and that only at genuine banks. ("Trading" banks, by the way—not at reserve or savings banks.) You'll virtually never get good exchange rates at hotel desks, although it is handy to be able to exchange small amounts—$10 or $20 travelers checks—at the desk when the banks are closed.

Travelers checks. No problem, except for the fact that you'll have to cash them at banks (or hotel desks). Don't expect a restaurant or a shop to make the current conversion to Aussie currency. (Or if they do, the chances are the exchange rate will be weighted heavily in the firm's favor.)

Unlike in Europe, incidentally, Aussie banks virtually never have asked us for a passport or other identification, although we certainly are not well-known in that country. It seemed to be enough for most banks that our signatures matched the samples. Most banks are open from 10:00 to 3:00, Mondays through Thursdays, and until 5:00 p.m. on Fridays.

A minor annoyance, however, is that it takes a little longer to cash checks at some banks in the hinterlands. These are ones where the tellers have no money at the windows, and all the paperwork has to be sent to a cash cage somewhere in the rear. There it waits in line with others requesting spending money.

This did not occur in Sydney or Melbourne, but in other cities you may as well wait it out. Sit down, and they'll call you by name when your money arrives.

Governmental Fiddle Faddle

Your travel agent should guide you firmly through all this. But just in case, here are a few basic requirements set up by Australian authorities.

Passport. Unless you're an Australian or a New Zealand citizen, you'll need a passport and visa to enter Australia. Americans can apply directly at a passport office in major cities or any U.S. Post Office. It now takes only a few days once you deliver or send in the filled-out form with the required photographs and fee.

Visa. You get an Australian visa—free—from any Australian consulate. Take in your passport and fill out an application, and you can probably pick it up the next day. By mail, send your passport to the consulate and include a stamped, self-addressed envelope. (Be sure there are enough stamps on it and that it's large enough for the thing to fit in when they send it back.)

Tourist visas are issued for a six months' stay—unless special arrangements are made with the consulate prior to your trip. Your travel agent should know which is the nearest Aussie consulate. If not, you can find out by writing to any one of them, say the Australian Consulate General, 636 Fifth Ave., New York, N.Y. 10020, or in Canada, the Australian Consulate General, Suite 2324, Commerce Court West, King & Bay Streets, Postal Box 69, Toronto, Ont. M5L 1B9. (There are also Australian consulates in Chicago, San Francisco, Los Angeles, Washington, Honolulu, Ottawa, and Vancouver.)

Health. Unless your situation is unusual, you won't need a health card or a vaccination certificate. But you'll have to get one if you'll be traveling in some infected countries on the way.

Immigration officials. These fellows at the airport will want to see a few things before they allow you in the country. Your passport and visa are required, of course, and you'll probably have to show your return (or onward-going) ticket. If the inspector thinks you look like someone who could become a drain on the economy, he might also ask to see evidence that you can support yourself—cash, travelers' checks, credit cards, etc. If you're genuinely on vacation, and are not trying to put something over on these chaps, don't worry. It'll all go smoothly.

Customs. Australian customs officials will allow you to take into Australia most normal things for your own personal use. If you're going to strain things by toting along firearms, gallons of liquor, and the like, then special arrangements will have to be sought. But you can even come in with a bicycle or motorcycle nowadays. We didn't have any vehicles, but we have so far managed to speed through Australian customs without incident.

Animals, fruits, and veggies are strictly controlled, however. Ask especially if you want to get into this kind of thing. One thing we might mention right off the bat: It's practically impossible to get into Australia with a live dog or cat unless your furry friends have lived all their lives in neighboring New Zealand.

Departure tax. Australia currently levies the largest national departure tax of any country in the world, but it may not seem so much of a bummer if you're prepared for the idea ahead of time. It's $A10 for all outward bound passengers 18 years of age or older, and no charge for the youngsters. So you might save one last picture of Francis Greenway in the bottom of your shoe to fork over before you get on the plane.

3

The Land and Life of Australia

To many travelers, Australia's dominant characteristic is also the one most difficult to grasp—its almost incredible size of just a little under 3 million square miles.

There are five countries with a greater total acreage. China, Russia, and Canada are all much bigger. Even the United States and Brazil have a slight edge. But those countries are each part of continents, contiguous with other nations, and culturally and economically influenced by the flow of people and communication across and along their common borders.

Australia is an island unto itself and by far the largest island on earth. It is so massive and so distant from almost anywhere else that geographers have universally agreed that it should be labeled a continent in its own right. Today it is the only continent which belongs entirely to one single nation.

After its size, another ponderable for travelers from the Northern Hemisphere is that Australia is, in effect, "upside-down." The north, near the equator, is warm. In fact, 39 percent of Australia is officially in the northern tropics. The south, which looks toward Antarctica, is cool by comparison. And the seasons are also reversed in time. The Southern Hemisphere is tilted further toward the sun at the same time Europe and North America are having their deepest, darkest days of winter.

Australia

PLACES OF INTEREST

1. Cairns — Atherton Tableland
2. Great Barrier Reef
3. Brisbane — Gold Coast
4. Hunter Valley
5. Sydney — Blue Mountains
6. Canberra — Australian National Capital
7. The Australian Alps
8. Melbourne — Murray Valley
9. Tasmania
10. Adelaide — Barossa Valley
11. Flinders Ranges
12. Perth — The South West
13. Australia's Great Outback
14. Lightning Ridge — Gem Fields

TIMOR SEA

JO
BON
O
Wyndham
YAMPI SOUND Kunu
O
Derby
Broome
GREAT SANDY DESERT
BARROW ISLAND Port Hedland
Dampier
Onslow HAMERSLEY
RANGE GIBSONS DESERT
**WESTERN
AUSTRALIA**
Carnavon

INDIAN

GREAT VICTOR

Mt. Magnet O

OCEAN Kalgoorlie NUI
O
Geraldton

Perth 12
Fremantle G
Kwinana
Bunbury
Pemberton
Albany

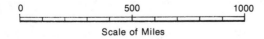

0   500   1000

Scale of Miles

TORRES STRAIT

o Thursday Is

ARNHEM LAND

Weipa

o Katherine

GROOTE
EYLANDT

GULF OF
CARPENTARIA

CORAL   SEA

CAPE YORK
PENINSULA

o Cooktown

o Daly Waters

Great

1

ATHERTON
TABLELAND

Karumba o

TABLELAND

Cairns

GREEN ISLAND

BARKLEY TABLELAND

DUNK ISLAND

o Tennant Creek

2

Barrier

Townsville

ORTHERN

o Mary Kathleen

HAYMAN ISLAND

ERRITORY

Mt.Isa

QUEENSLAND

SOUTH MOLLE ISLAND
LINDEMAN ISLAND

ACDONNELL RANGES

Proserpine

Mackay

Springs O o Ross River

o Longreach

HERON ISLAND

Reef

13

o Emerald

yers Rock

THE CHANNEL
COUNTRY

Rockhampton

Gladstone

Maryborough

FRASER ISLAND

STURTS STONY
DESERT

Charleville o

o Roma

Kingaroy

SOUTH

Cunnamulla o

Coober Pedy

LAKE EYRE

Toowoomba
Moonie o

o

Brisbane

Southport

TH

14 o Lightning

Warwick

3

Surfers Paradise

TRALIA

Andamooka o

LAKE
TORRENS

Bourke Ridge

Coolangatta

PACIFIC

11

Woomera o

o Grafton

FLINDERS RANGES

NEW

o Ceduna

Wilpena
Pound

Broken o
Hill

Wilcannia

SOUTH

Armidale o

Tamworth o

Kempsey

OCEAN

BIGHT

Port
Augusta

Port Barossa
Pirie Valley

WALES

Dubbo

4

Port Macquarie

10

Adelaide

Renmark

o Parkes

Newcastle

Port Lincoln

Mildura o

Hay

o Griffith

Bathurst

5

Sydney

Murray
Bridge

Wagga Wagga

6

Wollongong

KANGAROO ISLAND

Albury

7

Canberra

VICTORIA

Cooma

Mt. Gambier

Bendigo o

8

Ballarat O

Melbourne

Geelong

BASS STRAIT

TASMAN   SEA

Devonport

Queenstown o

o Launceston

TASMANIA

9

Hobart o   o Port Arthur

July and August, therefore, are Australia's coolest months (and in southern Australia, the wettest). Christmas Day can be boiling hot, although January and February are the warmest months usually.

In this jet age, it is possible for a person of means to spend the summer in the U.S. and then spend the summer again in Australia, year after year never experiencing winter at all—just jumping directly from fall to spring as he crosses the equator every six months. (And avid ski enthusiasts have been known to operate just in reverse of this. They'll spend an American winter on the slopes of Stowe, Vermont, perhaps, and then an Australian winter in the aptly named Snowy Mountains of New South Wales.

Once you begin travel to the South Pacific, strange things begin to happen—events you might win bets on in future years. Sara once had 30 days in February, for instance: On a ship from New Zealand to Honolulu, she crossed the International Dateline during that month in a leap year. And both of us lay claim to experiencing the longest day of the year and the shortest day of the year on the same day: We flew from Perth to Singapore across the equator on June 21, the Summer Solstice. (The fewest hours of daylight occur in the Southern Hemisphere that date and the most in the Northern Hemisphere—exactly the opposite of December 22.)

Australia, then, became known also as "Down Under." And since it was supposed to be directly on the opposite point on the earth from the mother country—the "antipode" (accent on the first syllable) to Great Britain—it also became known as the "antipodes" (accent on the second syllable), with "antipodean" (accent on the penultimate syllable) for the adjective or else meaning "one who lives Down Under." (The terms are also applied to New Zealand and New Zealanders. Interestingly, New Zealand is technically closer to Britain's genuine geographic antipode.)

All this upside-down-ness and inside-out-ness, massive size, and yet distance from the sophisticated influence of the rest of the world have been addressed in sociological terms by Professor Geoffrey Blainey in his book, *The Tyranny of Distance*.

But an itinerant sheep-shearer downing a cold beer in the western town of Marble Bar, the hottest, dryest spot in Australia, has been credited for summing up the geographic/cultural situation in Australian terms:

"If this earth were shaped like a cow," he said, leaning back on the bar, "This country here would be its arse-end!"

Australia is often described as a very, very old land. It's true. Some of its rock was formed 2 and 3 *billion* years ago. It was already pretty much its present size and shape about 230 million years ago. And somewhere along about 170 million years later—relatively recently—it became totally separated from the Asian mainland.

The continent is also the world's flattest and dryest. The average elevation is about 900 feet, less than half the world's average. It does have a few respectable mountains, though. Most are in the 2,000 to 4,000 foot range, although Mt. Kosciusko, stretching up to 7,315 feet, and a dozen others in the Snowy Mountains are over a mile high.

A considerable portion of the continent is a hot and waterless plain. About 43 percent of Australia is officially "arid" and another 20 percent is "semi-arid." To statistically emphasize the point, evaporation exceeds rainfall over 70 percent of the territory.

Some of this no-man's land in the middle of the continent has been given a prosaic name—"The Centre." Sometimes it's called the "Red Centre," the "Dead Centre," the "Red Heart," or the "Dead Heart." Any of those terms refer to about a million square miles of outback whose hub is marked by the giant monoliths of Ayers Rock (a single, gargantuan hunk of granite, 1,100 feet high and six miles around) and Mt. Olga, a set of elephantine mounds 20 miles to the east. Those mammoth red stones, and the sandy ground around them, are indeed red—and apparently dead, too.

The main use of land in The Centre is for cattle raising—though it's chancy at best, for mining, and for Aboriginal reserves. Winter is warm and dry, and the Red Centre has become a popular tourist attraction for Australians and increasingly more foreign tourists to Australia—especially since it has become apparent that The Centre is teeming with interesting plants and animals and other spectacular sights to see.

On the map you'll find three main deserts: The Great Sandy, the Gibson, and the Great Victoria, and several smaller ones in between. These and The Centre are, in the language of legend, the "Outback," the "back-of-beyond," the "beyond-the-black-stump," or the "back-o'-Burke." The Outback's rugged characteristics have often kindled and then killed the spirits of antipodean explorers—to this very day. (One dusty desert known for its lack of vegetation is called the Nullarbor Plain. The very name of that vast southern flat land means "No trees.")

This physical inhospitality of much of the land toward agriculture and seemingly to life at all has severely limited the settlement of the interior of Australia. The size comparisons of Australia with the U.S.A. are, therefore, superficial. In the Outback, there are no Clevelands, Chicagos, or St. Louises because—despite the almost limitless space for building—there is simply nothing to economically support such development.

Even in areas which receive enough rain to raise some cattle and sheep, the amount is highly unpredictable and very unreliable. There is no guarantee that the station (ranch) that managed to make it through last year won't fail because of floods or drought over the next 12 months. This is another reason for the large property holdings. Animals may have to range over thousands of square miles to find enough food to remain alive, and then compete with the wild dingo and the kangaroo for the available forage.

It's often said that Australia also suffers for the lack of lakes and rivers. For such a vast land, surface water is indeed scarce.

To look at the country on a map, which uses a share of blue ink, you might think there is a respectable interior water supply. In reality, most of the "lakes" and "rivers" shown are cartographic jokes. Lake Eyre, for instance, is seldom anything more than a 3,000-square-mile salt sump. Most years it holds no water at all. There are just vast plains of glaring, white salt—magnificent to see, but useless to any plans for human habitation.

Many of the rivers are that in name only, or at best operate only part-time. The Todd River, one of the more dependable routes, courses through the Outback community of Alice Springs. The Todd is dependably dry, that is. Every August, the Henley-on-Todd "regatta" is held at Alice Springs. The "yachts" are boat-shaped effigies carried by a half-dozen pairs of legs running along the dry river bed.

But even in Alice Springs, no one can count on the weather. The race had to be canceled one year because there really was water in the Todd River—for the first time on race day in memory.

But the Outback is not all dry. Up in the "Top End" of the Northern Territory, in Darwin, for instance, they speak of two seasons. One, to be sure, is called "the Dry," and it lasts more than the winter—from about May to November. The other season, "the Wet," is a monsoon period which continues from December to February and sometimes to April. One of the wettest towns on earth might be Tully (Pop. 3,500) which manages to survive the heavy rainfalls on the North Queensland Coast. Tully often registers more than 200 inches of rain a year, and sometimes it's counted well over 300 inches.

Much of the Outback has, in the past, and even into the 1970's proven to be rich in the minerals and other raw materials sought by man. There have been some famous gold rushes, and mining is still carried on today.

But now it is mostly for other metals like iron, lead, zinc, nickel, copper, bauxite (aluminum), and uranium. Australia also has a large coal reserve and has been pumping about 70 percent of its own oil needs.

Precious stones are still mined from the dusty earth of Australia. A major new diamond strike was made in 1978 in the Kimberly region of Western Australia and rubies were discovered at a remote station northeast of Alice Springs. Other gems are unearthed regularly by amateur weekend "fossickers," particularly the opals of Lightning Ridge and Coober Pedy. Or you can scratch around for sapphire, topaz, and amethyst near Emerald, 625 miles north of Brisbane.

The greater part of Australia may be Outback, but it is certainly not *all* Outback. Most of its visitors, like most of its citizens, probably get no further inland than its green and fertile coastline, site of all the great cities.

Australia on the Map

It may be confusing, but basically Australia has six states and two territories, most of them accounting for large amounts of land, and eight major cities. Beginning in the northeast and progressing clockwise, Brisbane is the capital of tropical **Queensland,** home of acres of sugar cane, pineapple, and banana plantations.

Just south of Queensland is **New South Wales.** (You'll almost never see that spelled out. It's abbreviated N.S.W., but you still *say* "New South Wales.") Capital of N.S.W., of course, is Sydney, the largest city and perhaps the cultural leader of the country. N.S.W. boasts a population of some 5 million, well over a third the number of persons in the entire nation.

Entirely surrounded by N.S.W. is the A.C.T.—the **Australian Capital Territory**—about 750 square miles artificially carved out for Canberra, the fully planned Federal capital of Australia. It was designed 70 years ago by an American.

The southeast coast is commanded by the state of **Victoria,** whose capital, Melbourne, is Sydney's rival for size and influence in the country.

Across Bass Strait, 200 miles south of Melbourne, is the island state of **Tasmania.** Appearing deceptively small beside the Mainland on maps of the world, Tasmania nevertheless consists of 18,605 square miles— about the combined size of New Hampshire and Vermont (much larger than Denmark or Holland). Its capital is the attractive little seaport of Hobart.

West of Victoria is **South Australia,** home of most of the length of the

Murray River ("Old Man Murray") and capitaled by the well-planned city of Adelaide. South Australia is also the home of the Barossa Valley wine country.

The huge state of **Western Australia** is next. At 975,920 square miles, it is nearly one-third the area of the entire country. (That's bigger than Alaska, Texas, and New Mexico combined.) It's not only abbreviated W.A., but actually *called* W.A. by most of its citizens. (Incidentally, no one has ever been able to tell us why one state is South Australia and the other is West*ern* Australia, and not "South*ern*" or "West" respectively.) Perth, on the Swan River, perhaps Australia's most attractive city, is the capital.

The last political unit is the **Northern Territory,** sometimes called the "Top End," and whose capital is Darwin. The N.T. last year was given many self-governing powers and many expect it to become a full-fledged state of the Commonwealth.

Living Things In Australia

Australia's land bridge to Asia disappeared millions upon millions of years ago, and so its flora and fauna began to develop and evolve in different ways to plants and animals in the rest of the world.

Trees and Bushes. Of Australia's trees, the most famous is the **eucalyptus.** Actually there are about 600 different kinds of eucalypts, what the Aussies commonly call "gum trees." Crush the leaves and smell them; the pungent, oily odor may help to clear out your sinuses.

Koala bears live on the leaves of certain kinds of eucalyptus, the reason you can hardly keep a koala supplied with food anywhere else in the world. (Many eucalypts are grown in other places on the earth. All originated in Australia, however.)

One type of box gum is the **coolabah tree,** sung about in "Waltzing Matilda." And another eucalypt, sometimes called the **mountain ash,** could be the tallest tree in the world. They often reach heights of more than 300 feet, rivaling the California redwoods for that honor. And among the most startling of the eucalypt family are the **ghost gums** where bleached branches beautify the Outback. You'll probably see them near Alice Springs.

Thirsty Aborigines have always known they could quench themselves from gallons of water stored naturally in the trunks of **bottle trees**, of which the most famous is the "baobab," renamed the "boab" by the Australians. If you find your way to the western down of Derby, you'll see one so grotesquely swollen that it was hollowed out and used as a jail cell. The "Prison Tree" is still alive, and you can walk inside. The Aborigines say the boab tree is immortal. None have been known to die from old age.

You may hear a lot about the **wattle trees** or acacias, of which there are hundreds of types. The yellow spikes of wattle flowers have become the official blossoms of Australia and they appear on its coat of arms. An Aboriginal word for one type of wattle is **mulga**. Early settlers called it wattle because the stems were used in "wattling," a type of thatching and packing used in making houses.

A weird-looking thing is the **grass tree**. The leaves are grass-like, but above them grow long, black sometimes snake-like spikes, on occasion covered with white flowers. A 10-foot tall grass tree may be 1,000 years old. After a bush fire, the blackened stalk and spike look something like an Aboriginal warrior standing with his spear. In some states they are called "black boys."

The **casuarina**, a graceful tree the Aussies have dubbed the "she-oak," has tiny, needle-like branches and virtually no leaves. The **pandanus**, in the tropical north, has aerial roots and is the same as the Hawaiian *hala* tree. Its orange fruit is good "bush tucker" in an emergency. The **banksia**, often only a tall shrub, is named after Joseph Banks, who collected specimens on Cook's voyage in 1770. Its cylindrical flower is more familiar than the tree.

Look out: The **black bean** tree has seeds that are harmful eaten raw. Aborigines sometimes know how to safely prepare them. It's more dependable for furniture making, though. Don't eat the **cheese tree** either. Its fruit is a hollow disc and *looks* rather like a Dutch cheese. The red flowers on the **coral tree** are dramatic, but watch out for sharp prickles on the leaves and branches. The wood is very light weight. **Cycads** are rather like palms or tree ferns. They are descendants of Mesozoic plants which grew 100 million years ago. The **bottle brush tree** bears a fuzzy flower that looks like a crimson version of one of Fuller's products.

Davidson's Plum trees, in Queensland rain forests, grow purple plums eaten by fruit bats and used by humans for jams and jellies. You may know **pawpaw** trees better as papaya trees. The delicious tropical fruit grows in Queensland. The **flame tree** blooms bright red overhead but is different than the flame trees (poincianas) known in other parts of the world. The **lillypilly** tree has bunches of tiny white fruit. One Australian encyclopedia says they are eaten "by Aborigines, small boys, and birds." **Paperbark** trees are well named. The bark readily peels off in thin flakes. Some produce oil used in insecticides. **Queensland nut** is the tree which produces macadamia nuts commercially in Hawaii but not much in Australia, its native habitat. And **woollybutt** is one of those no-nonsense Australian names for a eucalypt with a fluffy, loose bark on the trunk.

Australian Flowers. There are thousands upon thousands of distinctive Australian flowers, and many will just have to be seen to be believed. Some, in addition to those mentioned under trees, above, are the following:

The **kangaroo paw**, official flower of Western Australia, actually looks and feels like one—but in red, white, and green. **Sturt's desert pea** is a large crimson flower which grows wild in dry country. **Christmas bells**, a waxy, flower-like bloom, are gathered from swamps in December. **Chocolate lily**—it's colored purple, but *smells* rather like a Hershey bar. A **lamb's tail** looks just about like one, too. **Bindi-eye** is a daisy-like flower, yellow-and-white or yellow-and-blue. **Bird-flowers** are shaped like birds; sometimes they're called parrot flowers.

The **bladderwort** has purple blossoms but is more interesting for its ability to catch and devour insects. Some other insect eaters include the **Albany pitcher** and the **pigmy sundew**. **Blindgrass** is a type of lily which can cause blindness to cattle and sheep. **Blue devil** is a blue, thistle-like flower. **Desert roses** are found in the form of blue flowers on cotton plants. **Early Nancy** is an attractive pink flower seen all over the country. An amber flower called **fairy lantern** is rather like an iris. **Finger flower**—each purple bloom bears five petals and five stamens. **Hairy-tails** are a little like hairy clover. **Ladies tresses** are a type of orchid. **Milkmaid**—a purple and white star-like lily. **Orchids**: there are dozens of types, some of which grow underground, another which reaches lengths of more than 40 feet, and another (the bearded orchid) looks like an old man with a lavender beard. **Pigface** is a bright red fruit with two "ear-like" leaves. **Trigger plant**: If you bother it, it shoots pollen at you, no doubt figuring you'll spread some of it around. The **waratah** grows into a fantastic, 10-foot tall plant seemingly supporting dozens of crimson cabbages.

The Mammals from Down Under. Nearly all Australian mammals are "marsupials"—meaning their young are born immature and then develop in the pouch or pocket outside the body. Few are "placentals," like the rest of us. But when the first animals of Australia were described to the European scientific community they were called hoaxes. The learned world was not ready to accept "animals the size of greyhounds who leap like grasshoppers."

The most famous Australian marsupial is the **kangaroo** and his smaller cousin, the **wallaby**. They seem to come in all colors and sizes, ranging from big red or great gray kangaroos—seven foot tall "boomers," weighing as much as 200 pounds and able to hop over the plains at 30 m.p.h.—down to the tiny quokkas, rat kangaroos, and narbaleks.

Among other types are tree kangaroos, pretty face wallabies, agile wallabies, short-tailed pademelons, red-bellied pademelons, ringed-tail rock wallabies, banded hare wallabies, and one whose name seems to come from both the kangaroo and wallaby, the wallaroo. There are supposed to be 45 kinds of "roos," all together, all native to Australia.

A marsupial now almost as famous as the kangaroo is the **koala**, Australia's "Teddy Bear." Once an endangered species, koalas have been preserved in sanctuaries, and chances are, you'll be able to pick one up and give him a hug somewhere in Australia. (The Lone Pine Sanctuary in Brisbane is a good place.) According to one theory, the slow-moving koala is constantly drunk due to the intoxicating powers of the eucalyptus leaves he eats. They spend most of their time in trees, and because of their slow movements, many have perished in the frequent Australian bushfires.

Other interesting marsupials include the **wombat**, a chunky, fuzzy fellow of perhaps 50 pounds who burrows underground and sleeps during the day, the **Tasmanian devil**, a small, black beastie who can tear through a henhouse in nothing flat, but can still be tamed, the **bandicoot**, a small marsupial who lives in trees and likes both meat and veggies, the **numbat**, a slow-moving creature incredibly possessing 52 teeth for a diet of termites, and the **native cat** and the **tiger cat**, neither of which, of course, are cats. Actually they're tough fighters and related to the aforementioned Tasmanian devil.

Other marsupials include several kinds of possums or "phalangers" which live in trees. Some, like the **feather-tail glider** stretch out flat like a four-pawed magic carpet to swoop from one branch to another. The **sugar glider** and the **greater glider** are also arborial acrobats. The **brush-tailed possum** loves to chomp on mistletoe, an undesirable wood parasite in Australia. The **honey possum** has a long, sharp tongue for picking up nectar and pollen directly from flowers. Our favorite phalanger, though, is the **cuscus**, a white fuzzy tree-dweller, drowsy by day but adventurous and fun-loving after dark.

Although most mammals in Australia are marsupials, there are just a few notable ones that are not. Australia's most famous zoological enigma, of course, is the **platypus**. European scientists refused to believe this animal, with a bill like a duck, a tail like a beaver, furry and amphibious, who lays eggs but still suckles its young, was anything but a fake. As late as 1884, it was still debated as to whether the platypus—of a group called monotremes—really laid eggs. Then a young English zoologist named W. H. Caldwell came to Australia at just the right time to find some eggs in a pregnant platypus. In a famous laconic telegram to the British Association for the Advancement of Science, then meeting in Montreal, he managed to report that the animals were indeed egglayers and to say just exactly what kind of egg it was: "MONOTREMES OVIPAROUS, OVUM MEROBLASTIC," Caldwell cabled.

Platipi are almost impossible to keep in captivity because of their appetite for more than a thousand earthworms, 50 crayfish and oodles of other edibles per day. In the wild, it's in danger of extinction due to pollution in the rivers along the east coast. You can see a platypus either at Taronga Park, a ferry ride from Sydney, or at the Mackenzie Wildlife Sanctuary at Healesville, near Melbourne.

The platypus' fellow monotreme is the **spiny anteater**, although they seem different at first glance. Note that it also has a bill, although much thinner. He was first described in a ship's log by Captain William Bligh. Both monotremes are considered previously missing links between reptiles and mammals.

You may hear of the **flying foxes**—or hear from them directly, because there's practically a whole island of them setting up quite a ruckus a few miles upstream in the Brisbane River. Actually, they are not much different than large fruit bats. Australia has a few smaller bats around, too.

Two animals have been the scourges of the nation. The **rabbit**, carelessly introduced to the country in 1859, practically devoured all vegetation on sheep and cattle stations before they were brought (relatively) under control by the introduction of myxomatosis—rabbit fever. A rabbit-proof fence running more than 1,100 miles blocks off a considerable piece of Western Australia.

The other is the much-maligned **dingo**, a distinctive type of wild yellow dog domesticated and used for hunting by the Aborigines, but hunted down by sheep graziers. The dingos are officially classified as "noxious vermin" in Australia, but recently a few have been trained for drug detection. (The dingo is not supposed to bark—only howl—but we've heard a couple barking during a disagreement and have taped the sound in case anyone is interested.)

Two other familiar wild animals are hunted in Australia. **Brumbies**, or wild horses, are sometimes shot for pet food but sometimes brought in alive to be broken as riding animals. **Buffalo** (actually water buffalo) are considered wild in the tropical Outbacks up north. **Camels**, first brought to Australia in 1841 to help open up the interior, were later allowed to go wild. Some are now considered pests. Some others are raised for export—even to Arabia!

Australia also has a goodly share of **seals** and **sea lions**. Although these are not unusual to North Americans, it is unusual to be able to mingle with them. You can do just that on Phillip Island, near Melbourne, and on the beaches at Kangaroo Island, near Adelaide.

The country's two most economically important animals, of course, are **sheep** and **cattle**. There are about 150 million sheep in the country, producing nearly a third of the world's wool. Australian sheep have been developed from the Spanish merino type, to suit different climate and grazing conditions found over the continent.

In the past decade, cattle have become a major industry. The nation is now the world's leading beef exporter, not to mention the producer of some of the best and most affordable veal, chops, and steaks for consumption right at home.

Reptiles of the Outback. Australia boasts a number of **snakes**, easily as many deadly ones as in North America, although none will attack a human unless provoked. The most poisonous is the **taipan**, although an antitoxin has recently been developed. The **tiger snake** and the **death adder** are also widely known. Perhaps the most dramatic snake is the **amethystine python**, which can reach about 25 feet in length and has been known to gulp down whole wallabies. The **black whip snake**, slightly poisonous, is known for its speed. It can outdistance a running man in the desert. (Luckily for the man, it is usually speeding in the opposite direction.) Of the harmless snakes, farmers encourage the **carpet snake** and the **children's python**, keeping them around the station even after they become seven feet long. They prey on rats and rabbits.

Not really snakes, of course, but none the less dramatic are the **giant earthworms**. About ¾ inch in diameter, they can be heard munching, gurgling, groaning, and sucking their way along under the swamps in the Bass River area of Gippsland, on the route between Melbourne and Phillip Island.

There are several different kinds of **lizards**, including the **monitors**, which can grow as long as six or eight feet. The monitors and their smaller cousins, the **goannas**, are the only creatures known to stagger away victorious in a fight to the finish with Australia's most poisonous snakes. They use their tails like lethal whips. Goannas have also been known to mistake horses—and humans—for trees. In the face of danger, they might just scramble up the nearest leg!

The **mountain devil**, which out-horns our horned toad, is fierce looking but harmless. The **skink**, often called the blue-tongued lizard in Australia, does indeed have a bright, cobalt-colored tongue. All types are harmless. **Crocodiles** (with the exception of one supposedly gentle fellow) can be counted on to be as dangerous in Australia as in anywhere else in the world. There are salt- and fresh-water species.

The World of Insects. Australia has all the common insects—and more. Flies, particularly **bush flies**, are more bothersome. In the warm Outback, frequent brushing is the only way to keep them away from eyes, noses, and mouths:

"I see you've learned the Barcoo salute, your highness," said the bush-roughed Australian.

"Oh? What's that?" asked Prince Phillip, wiping away yet another squadron of flies which had settled on his face.

"That's it!" the man replied.

Not all Aussie flies are as languid, however. The assassin fly or robber fly, for instance, grows up to 3½ inches long and is able to catch and devour other insects on the wing—even bees and dragonflies. (Recently, some beetles have been imported from China in an attempt to cut down the breeding of Australian flies.)

As with every other living thing, there is also a strange selection of insects alive and well in Australia. One innocuous fellow, the **giant stick**, grows to be a foot long. Other outsize insects include the Australian **dragonfly**, with a wingspan of 5½ inches and the ability to fly a mile a minute; an **earwig** which can grow to be two inches; **ants** and **termites** that grow up to an inch long. (Some kinds of termites are called "white ants" in Australia.) Some termites build nests up to 24 feet high. Some flat ones are called "magnetic ant hills" because they point directly north and south. They were built so the termites could take advantage of the heat from the sun as it proceeds from east to west.

There are quite a few **spiders** in Australia. Some huntsman spiders are encouraged to settle in Outback homes to catch flies and mosquitoes. Black widows exist, but are called the red-back. Another deadly poisonous variety is called the funnel-web. The country's largest is the barking spider, with a *body* up to two inches in length. It has been known to kill chickens and drag them into its nest. **Scorpions** live in the Australian desert. Although they sting, they are not considered deadly to humans.

The only insect honored by a memorial is, no doubt, the **cactoblastis**. This moth was introduced to Australia, where it successfully began to blast the cactus called the prickly pear from the face of the nation. The prickly pear is no longer the pest it was, and the Cactoblastic Memorial Hall was erected at Boonarga in Queensland.

The **fungus gnat** acts as a kind of glowworm in its larval state, lighting up the caves of Bundanoon in N.S.W. and the Mole Creek caves in Tasmania. Of the many **grasshoppers**, the interesting ones are more often heard than seen. One sounds like someone winding up a cheap pocket watch. Australia has more than 20,000 separate species of **beetles**, several of them, like the jewel beetle, with such startlingly beautiful colors that they are sometimes actually set in jewelry.

Of course there are also hundreds of brightly colored **butterflies** throughout the country, many of which are found only there. Some Aussie butterflies, incidently, wear a perfume as strong as the flowers they visit. You probably won't see this one, but one of the many **moths** is the giant atlas-moth of northern Queensland. Its wingspan has been reported up to 10½ inches. Another type of moth, the cossid moth, is more famous in its larval state. Found at the base of the witchety bush, they are the "witchety grubs" enjoyed by Aborigines as delicacies. Raw, they taste like heavy cream. Cooked, they're compared with sweet pork rind!

Australian Birds. There are 736 species of birds in Australia, about twice the number in North America. Two of the country's most famous birds are flightless. First is the **emu**, a five-to-six-foot tall creature, weighing about 120 pounds, inquisitive but generally as dumb as they come. Its feathered body looks like a Phyllis Diller wig. They've been clocked running at speeds of up to 40 m.p.h., though, and have a habit of crashing into fences at those velocities. Fully emancipated, the female emu does the courting. She changes partners each season, and leaves the male to sit on and hatch the eggs. The emu also shares with the kangaroo an honored place on the Australian Coat of Arms.

The **cassowary**, almost as large, also never gets off the ground, spending most of his time in Queensland rainforests. He runs with his head lowered, and he wears a permanent bony "crash helmet" to assure him a clear channel through the jungle.

Australia's most famous bird is the appealing fuzzy creature with the flattened head called the **kookaburra**. Also known as the "laughing jackass," he is the largest in the kingfisher family (although they don't fish). Some call him the bush alarm clock because he wakes up farmers with a long call much like mocking laughter. As a predator of reptiles and rodents, he is a welcome resident in the agricultural lands of Australia.

Until the Dutch captured some **black swans** near the present site of Perth in 1697, it was axiomatic in Europe that all swans are white. They helped to further establish Australia as a land of paradox.

The most interesting bird for our money is the **lyrebird** (pronounced "liarbird"). In addition to creating some beautiful songs of his own, he imitates other sounds—other birds, barking dogs, or even objects like a squeaky wheel, a buzz saw, a violin, a baby, or an old truck. Virtually nothing is beyond this feathered Rich Little. One story is told about a lyrebird who used to let everybody off work an hour early when he "blew" the factory whistle. He also has some fascinating courtship habits, and that's when he shapes his two tails into a classic lyre shape. Listen to the lyrebird at the Taronga Park Zoo in Sydney or in the Sherbrooke National Forest in the Dandenong Hills near Melbourne.

There are about 50 families of **parrots** native to Australia, many of them so garishly colored they almost hurt your eyes with their orange, green, blue, and yellow feathers. The pink and light gray **galah**, often seen in flocks of 20 or more, is also the slang word for a loud, ignorant person. That's an anomoly because galahs can be kept as pets and will even learn to talk. A magnificent pink and white bird, the **Major Mitchell** is named after the early inland explorer who discovered it. **Cockatoos** are also parrots. You might find the sulfur-crested cockatoo wild even in a city park. (We watched them frolic from tree to tree right in the center of Canberra.) In farmlands, look for the startling red, yellow, blue, and green **rosellas**. Also the **budgerigah**, now known throughout the world as "parakeets," "budgies," or "love birds," are native to Australia.

The activity of the male **bower-bird** makes him a curiosity. He builds a fancy bachelor flat, equips it with as many flashy objects as possible—beads, coins, etc.—and if the female likes the place, she moves in with him. The most ubiquitous Australian bird surely must be those big, black-and-white **magpies**. You'll see these crow-like monsters and hear them everywhere. Often called "butcherbirds," they have a habit of hanging uneaten prey from thorns (like butchers hanging meat on hooks). They are not related to European or American magpies.

Another favorite bird of ours is the **willy wagtail**. In a world of uncertainties, he can be counted on to bob his head and wag his tail every time he lands—always. Last, but certainly not least, are the wonderful **fairy penguins**. They put on a penguin "parade" nightly at Phillip Island in Victoria, returning to their nesting burrows come people or high water. No visitor to Melbourne should miss them.

Life in the Water. There are no fewer than 180 kinds of fresh-water fishes in Australia, of which the most well-known is the **Queensland lungfish**, an air-breather found in the Burnett and Mary Rivers, growing to a length of five feet. The lungfish is protected as a scientific curiosity, but the **barramundi** is a delicious freshwater fish popular on the plates of Australian homes and restaurants.

Much of the world's salt-water life is attracted to Australian shores, some of the most interesting specimens to the 1,250-mile strip of coral called the Great Barrier Reef, off the coast of Queensland.

Everyone asks about **sharks**, and it's true that Australian beaches have a sharky reputation, although all public ones are now protected by shark nets during warm weather. According to Sidney J. Baker, an Australian with a penchant for statistics (in the *Ampol Book of Australiana*), shark attacks are most common in January, between 3:00 and 6:00 p.m., in about 4 to 6 feet of water, between 10 and 50 yards offshore.

When an Australian talks about **crayfish**, he means big fellows—what we would call lobster. In fact, tails exported to the U.S.A. are marketed as Australian lobster tails. There are, however, delicious fresh-water crayfish called **yabbies**. Australia's most famous shellfish, however, are the Sydney **rock oysters**—some of the most succulent in the world. Other Australian fish considered delicacies and often found on restaurant bills-of-fare include snapper, whiting, John Dory, gemfish, jewfish, silver bream, pearl perch, and flounder.

Big game fishing for marlin, tuna, etc. is popular along the east coast, particularly along the Great Barrier Reef in Queensland.

The barrier reef itself, of course, qualifies as sea life since it is built from the skeletons of millions of tiny coral polyps over thousands of years. When an Australian oil company wanted to drill along the reef one year, public indignation drove them away with red faces. Unfortunately the reef, which harbors many beautiful and intricate forms of marine life, has been under attack by the crown of thorns **starfish**, an animal which feeds on the coral. Recently, however, the threat to the reef seems to be receding.

4

Who Are the Australians?

Australia's convict beginnings were once said to be the source of a continuing national inferiority complex, and among a few Aussies that may still be true. But in the latter half of the twentieth century, this has largely given way to a new sense of pride in a national character stimulated by early adversity. It is this temperament that developed a talent for building both a modern nation and "the good life" for most of its citizens.

Among Americans who know nothing about Australia, it's often criticized for "lack of tradition" and "paucity of culture." If these snobs paused from peering down their noses, they could look around and see Britain and Europe laughing over their shoulder. To those whose history runs to a thousand years or more, what is the difference between countries like the U.S. and Canada, whose formative steps were taken in the 1600's and 1700's, and Australia and New Zealand, who got a later start—by fewer than one hundred years?

What is not true in America, then, is equally false Down Under. Australia's character was shaped by experiences very much like the background of the United States. In fact, Americans and American history often played key roles in the formation of Australia, and they are still doing so.

A RAMBUNCTIOUS MARCH THROUGH THE PAST

"Australian history," said Mark Twain, "does not read like history, but like the most beautiful lies. And all of a fresh new sort, no moldy old stale ones. It is full of surprises, and adventures, and incongruities, and contradictions, and incredibilities; but they are all true; they all happened."

This description, in his book *Following the Equator*, is always quoted in writings about Australia for the rest of the world. Allowing for typical Twain hyperbole on the one hand, and the fact that Twain's visit to the country might be considered only halfway through Australia's history on the other hand, we are certainly left at least with something worth finding out about. Here is a brief synopsis of the country to date.

Voyages of Discovery—to 1770

Australia was named, and it appeared on the maps of the world, long before it was even found by modern man. Terra Australis Incognita, they called it: "Unknown Land of the South." It was daubed in a misshapen blob on the charts just because someone had theorized that it just had to be there—something to do with balancing the weight on the rest of the earth.

Fifteenth and sixteenth century Portuguese and Spanish navigated much of the Pacific, and it seems almost incredible that such a large hunk of *terra firma* could have been overlooked. Indeed, on a series of surviving French maps, produced between 1536 and 1567, and based on Portuguese travels, a land called "Jave le Grand" bears a remarkable resemblance to a portion of the Australian coastline.

China is reported to have explored part of Australia as early as the sixth century B.C. and there is some strong evidence that a Chinese landing was made near Darwin in 1432.

All this notwithstanding, the first written record of a landing on Australia was provided by the Dutch ship *Duyfken* ("Little Dove") commanded by Willem Jansz in 1606. The point of discovery was the red bauxite cliffs along the western shore of the Cape York Peninsula. The ship's log described the area as "for the greater part desert, with wild, cruel, black savages." Bauxite and its product, aluminum, were unknown, and Jansz dismissed the land saying they found "no good to be done there."

The blacks mentioned by the captain had been the human inhabitants of Australia for some time. Discoveries just made in 1978 indicate the first ancestors of the Aborigines migrated over a now-submerged land bridge from Asia not later than 100,000 years ago.

The Aborigines had no weapons, except for sticks and the boomerang—not an Aborigine invention, by the way, but a holdover from the stone age on other parts of the earth. They became a short, lean, and tough people, with excellent teeth from their habit of chewing sand and ashes along with their food.

They remained nomads, and although they developed a rich culture, they did not learn to read and write, keeping no history of their background. Even today, confronted with the beautiful and artistic evidence of their past, the Aborigine is apt to say the images were drawn in the "Dreamtime." Dreamtime has religious significance, as well. That's when the world itself was created in Aboriginal song and story.

Throughout the 1600's, the Dutch made several landings on the island continent, without realizing it was such, virtually always followed by a negative report of the area's potential worth. One such explorer was Abel Tasman, who discovered what is now Tasmania in 1642. He caled it "Van Diemen's Land," a name that lasted for 214 years, and he didn't know it was an island.

Most of the Dutch encounters with Australia were made by accident when unfavorable winds carried their ships off their established trade routes between the mother country and the rich colonies in Indonesia, and perhaps their perception was colored by these misfortunes. Some vessels were wrecked off the western shores of Australia, and even today, archeologists and treasure hunters are exploring the remains of Dutch ships.

The contemporary view of the poverty and uselessness of the land was echoed by at least one Englishman, the buccaneer William Dampier, who spent three months on the northwest coast of Australia in 1688. He wrote a best-seller about his travels and then returned in 1699. Dampier, too, had little good to say of the land which by now was called New Holland. He also wrote of the native inhabitants, calling them "the miserablest people in the world."

Due to this kind of bad press, Australia was virtually ignored for nearly a century. No European seemed to admit making any more landings until its east coast was explored for the first time by Lieutenant (later Captain) James Cook of the British Royal Navy, in command of the HMS *Endeavor* in 1770. Cook made his historic landing at Botany Bay, near the present Sydney Airport, on April 28 that year.

The British commander found a green, more pleasant landscape on this eastern shore, and apparently more friendly, self-sufficient natives than were seen 100 years previously in the west. After making his way up the entire east coast, and almost coming to grief on the Great Barrier Reef, Cook named the entire area after South Wales, a countryside he was familiar with back home. "New South Wales," then, had as undefined a boundary in the east as New Holland did from the western aspect.

Cook didn't know it, of course, but Possession Island, on which he stood while declaring New South Wales to be British evermore, bore riches under his feet. A century later it was found to contain considerable amounts of gold, an irony at least equal to the disparaged bauxite cliffs of Jansz and his "Little Dove" a century and a half before.

The First Penal Colonies—1788 to 1810

American history sparked the development of modern Australia. The 1775 revolution of the 13 colonies not only robbed Britain of tobacco and other products but it also took away the traditional New World dumping ground for England's convicted criminals. For the next decade, convicts who were formerly banished to Maryland and Virginia at the rate of 1,000 a year were instead sent to overcrowded British prisons to await the end of the American uprising.

Decommissioned ships became "prison hulks" where the only deliverance from cruelty and disease occurred when the worm-ridden old vessels began to sink at their moorings. Clearly some more humane treatment was called for.

A decade and a half after Cook's discoveries, someone got the idea that the countryside around Botany Bay was the answer, and King George III approved. Under the command of Captain Arthur Phillip, what is now called the "First Fleet" of 11 ships, carrying 1,486 persons, about half of whom were convicts, arrived in New South Wales on January 18, 1788, to begin the settlement of Australia.

The town was built at Sydney Cove, on what was accurately described as "the finest harbor in the world," and Phillip was declared to be the first governor of the colony.

Australia served its original purpose well. In the 80 years it accepted convicts, about 157,000 were sent there—three times as many as had ever been sent to America.

The first year in Sydney was equally unpleasant for convicts, guards, and settlers. There was little food, crops failed, sheep died, the weather was cold, the first buildings were crude, and supply ships from England were wrecked. Also relations with the Aborigines were difficult, and most of all, the land looked so different and was so far away from England, that some people literally died of homesickness.

One of the interesting early residents of Sydney Cove was an intelligent and friendly Aborigine named Bennelong, befriended by Phillip so that the colony could learn something of Aboriginal culture and language. Bennelong turned out to be something of a tragic/comic character, especially when dressed in English formal wear. He was even given his own brick hut on what is now known as Bennelong Point—site of the Sydney Opera House. After Phillip, however, he became an outcast from both British and Aboriginal society. He drank heavily and was finally killed in a fight.

Conditions began to improve after two or three years, but back home in England, "Botany Bay," as it was called there, held a worsening reputation. Convicts would almost choose death over "transportation," as the sentence was termed. (In Australia and Britain, the word "transportation" seems still to carry the same meaning. For public transportation, they use the word "transport.")

Once in Australia, however, some of the first convicts seem almost to have taken on a philosophical resignation—to make the best of a bad job. A line of verse said to have been written for the opening of Sydney's first theater in 1796 is now famous:

True patriots all, for be it understood,
We left our country for our country's good!

Although rough by today's standards, life for the convicts became at least on a par with and often better than that of honest common laborers in eighteenth-century England. Few of the first convicts spent any time behind bars in Australia. They were just too busy building houses, barracks, and the like, and learning to raise food. And it wasn't long until a few of the best behaved ones were pardoned—emancipated—and, like the marines who guarded them and other free men, were given plots of land on which they might begin to scratch out a living in the colony.

Meanwhile, two explorers, George Bass and Mathew Flinders, used Sydney as a base to begin detailed examinations of the coast. They proved that Van Diemen's Land (Tasmania) was an island. The channel is now called Bass Strait.

Van Diemen's Land became a penal colony in 1803, initially for incorrigibles from Sydney. Macquarie Harbour and Port Arthur were perhaps the most hated prisons in the colonies. (You can visit the peaceful ruins of Port Arthur today.)

Things became a little difficult with the appointment of the hot-tempered Captain William Bligh—of HMS *Bounty* fame—as governor in 1806. A complicated series of stormy events took place, culminating in something called the Rum Rebellion. While guns were trained on Government House, Bligh was arrested and deposed by army officers in 1808. The Army was in the alcohol importing business on the side, something opposed by Bligh. The governor was later exonerated in London, but the rebels received only light sentences.

Sadly, no structure remains in Sydney today from the first two decades of the colony. But an honest approximation can be seen at Old Sydney Town, a theme park 44 miles north of the city at Somersby. Many of the events of day-to-day life in pre-Macquarie Sydney are acted out daily.

Exploration, Expansion, and Emancipation —1810 to 1850

Both the new governor, Lachlan Macquarie, and his arch-enemy, rancher John Macarthur, were in their own ways fathers of Australia. Macquarie encouraged the emancipation of convicts, exploration of the unknown territory to the west, and the creation of small farms. Macarthur opposed him on much of this, undermining Macquarie considerably by writing letters to sympathetic and influential friends in London.

But Macarthur, the first to import the hardy Merino sheep, is credited with establishing the wool industry in Australia. Until very recently, it was the country's most important export.

Macquarie tried to resist the growing class system in which the soldiers and free settlers attempted to hold themselves above the emancipists. Macquarie once opined that the colony then consisted of "those who had been transported and those who ought to have been!"

Several public buildings were constructed under Macquarie, including the "Rum Hospital," put up entirely without funds. It was built by a trio of emancipists in exchange for a three-year rum import monopoly. Many of the finest buildings, some of which have managed to survive, were designed by the convict Francis Greenway, still thought of as Australia's greatest architect. Today his picture is on a ten-dollar bill, quite an honor for a man transported for forgery.

The Blue Mountains, the barrier along the Great Dividing Range, were finally crossed in 1813 in an expedition led by journalist William C. Wentworth, and lands began to be developed on the other side. Free immigrants and the offspring of prisoners were becoming important settlers of the country. John Bigge, sent out from London to inspect the running of the colony, was amazed at the second generation: "The class of inhabitants who have been born in the colony affords a remarkable exception to the moral and physical character of their parents," he wrote. The population passed 30,000 in 1819, and only about half were convicts.

In the north, settlers around Sydney were attempting, without much success, to establish some churches and schools for Aborigines. In Van Diemen's Land, however, the colonialists and the natives continued at loggerheads with clashes destined eventually to wipe out the entire race of Tasmanian Aborigines.

Elsewhere, similar attempts at genocide were unsuccessful, but for a significant period of the colony's history, English settlers and the Aborigines were engaged in constant guerilla warfare. This had all the brutality seen in fights with the Indians in America and elsewhere where the haves and have-nots, usually speaking different languages and following different cultural drums, have come into conflict.

Through it all, however, the Aborigine seems to have been reacting more than he was on the offensive. He did not understand, for instance, why white men could kill his kangaroos but he was not allowed to kill their sheep. And if he was a little slow at math, it was understandable. On one typical occasion, in reprisal for a raid on his tribe, he massacred 19 settlers at an outback station. Then he saw 70 Aborigines—any Aborigines—killed in counter-reprisal by righteous "police" forces.

When the Aborigines developed a taste for bread, some colonials left poisoned flour where they knew it would be stolen. The white man's guilt toward the natives is no less a burden in Australia than it is anywhere else in the world.

In the 1830's and 40's, several excursions were made into the immediate interior, often by following rivers that flowed westward from the formerly formidable Dividing Range, including the 1,609-mile Murray and the 1,702-mile Darling Rivers. They were charted in 1827–29 mainly by Charles Sturt, a journey then difficult enough to make him temporarily blind. In 1844, Sturt also became the first man to explore central Australia in a vain search for the long-rumored "great inland sea." (He thought he would find it where two great bird migrations crossed.) There was no sea, and the desert nearly killed him.

In 1841, Edward Eyre *walked* the entire south coast of Australia, finding to everyone's amazement that there could be 1,500 miles of coastline with not a single river or stream to break it. And Paul Strzelecki, a Pole, explored the Blue Mountains, naming the tallest peak after Tadeusz Kosciusko, the Polish nobleman who served under George Washington at Yorktown.

In a series of explorations on foot, Freidrich Leichardt, a Prussian, mapped out the land between Sydney and Moreton Bay and then explored from Brisbane across to the Gulf of Carpentaria and Arnhem Land, which is still as wild today. In 1848, Leichardt set out upon a transcontinental crossing but was never seen again, one of the many Australian disappearances which have never been solved to this day.

The city of Melbourne was founded in 1835 by John Batman after he "bought" 600,000 acres of land from the Aborigines for a collection of tomahawks, knives, scissors, mirrors, and blankets. Adelaide was laid out with military precision—and considerable vision—by Colonel John Light in 1838. Perth was founded entirely by free settlers in 1829. It remained generally poverty-stricken until convicts were shipped in to provide badly needed labor 20 years later. Brisbane grew out of the repressive 1824 penal colony at Moreton Bay. Like Tasmania, it was for particularly intractable convicts. It had a justifiably fearsome reputation until the cruel regime was finally ended after the military commander was killed by Aborigines in 1830.

As hopeless a situation as existed in many of these penal institutions—where the mere possession of a fishhook was worth 100 lashes—the convicts began to try to escape at all costs. Confronted by impenetrable jungle and hopeless odds, they seemed to have developed a stubbornly optimistic "give-it-a-go-mate!" philosophy which has continued in the Australian character up to today.

Some of the same attitudes may have caused a certain resignation, or an acceptance of the outcome even if things just don't work out very well in the end: "It'll do, mate." Or, "She'll be right!" (Even when it won't "do" or "be right.") Today these feelings are cited by some as evidence of a sort of national intellectual laziness—almost a Latin-style tendency toward inefficiency in general.

By 1850, Australia had become four colonies. Besides New South Wales, the massive area of Western Australia was already delineated. Van Diemen's Land also governed itself and was thinking about changing its name to Tasmania, and South Australia was carved out of New South Wales. Three groups dominated political life—first, the government party, second the landowners ("squatters," a respectable term in Australia, and other wealthy settlers); and last, the merchants and workers in the cities. From these three groups evolved the Liberal, Country, and Labor parties of today's Australia.

Bushrangers, Booms, and Busts—1851 to 1900

The 1849 discovery of gold in California attracted many from the people-poor colonies of Australia. (In California, they were called the

Sydney Ducks, and achieved an unsavory reputation there.) This in turn led alarmed colonial officials to reverse a government policy which formerly suppressed gold information in Australia.

But no one thought there was much gold anyway until the big strike was made by Edward H. Hargraves. He was an Australian who became a forty-niner in California but returned after he noticed the California gold country geologically resembled his own home in the Bathurst area of New South Wales. He panned gold in Summerhill Creek on his very first try, February 12, 1851. And the rush was on.

Convict transportation to eastern Australia was immediately halted. As the governor of Van Diemen's Land noted, "There are few English criminals who would not regard a free passage to the gold fields . . . as a great boon." Transportation did begin to the west, though, where the poor settlements on the Swan River badly needed the labor. (Western Australians hadn't discovered *their* gold yet!)

Labor was short everywhere else as servants and masters alike caught gold fever and became "diggers" (a word that came to mean Australians to much of the world). Miners from California and other areas began pouring into Australia, along with thousands of Chinese. Some of the gold lumps found were gigantic, and more diggings were soon opened up further south, in Victoria.

The Chinese, who did not bring their women to Australia, and largely kept to themselves, were soon the target of racial enmity among the diggers—the unwitting formation of a national philosophy which continued almost up to today.

As in America, some diggers got rich, but most remained poor. Like the explorers, they put up with incredibly difficult physical hazards far from civilization. But many were turned against their government by the imposition of gold digging license fees to be paid monthly whether or not the digger ever found any gold. Police stopped nearly every man they saw—sometimes several times a day—and asked to see his license, marching him off to jail if he couldn't produce it immediately.

Australia's most notorious clash between police and diggers, now known as the Battle of the Eureka Stockade, took place December 3, 1854 at Ballarat, Victoria, 70 miles west of Melbourne. Under a flag depicting the Southern Cross, 500 miners lined up against 100 police. Forty people, mostly miners, were killed in the resulting melee. Only then were the licensing laws finally relaxed, but the average Australian's distrust of authority today, particularly the police, may be caused in some part by the memory of this event.

A battle almost as well remembered as Ballarat is the incident in which the fiery dancer Lola Montez publicly horsewhipped the editor of the Ballarat *Times* after he panned her famous Spider Dance. (Today there is a nearby re-creation of the Ballarat of that day called Sovereign Hill. Tourists pan for gold in the stream that runs through the park and see performances on a stage like the one used by Ms. Montez.)

Travel during the period was still considered only comfortable and practical by ship, even though there were dramatic disasters among both coastal steamers and trans-oceanic ships. One of the best-remembered tragedies was the wreck of the *Dunbar*, which took the lives of 121 persons, mostly wives and daughters returning from England. The event is well worth reading in Mark Twain's book *Following the Equator*: " . . . Not one of all that fair and gracious company was ever seen alive again . . . " To look at the dramatic, sheer cliffs of Sydney Heads today is to imagine easily enough a cruel sea pounding the *Dunbar* to pieces against the unyielding rocks.

Some inland travel was accomplished via river boats, although not to the extent they were used in America. Many rivers were just not dependable enough, drying out one year and flooding another. One which was consistently navigable, however, was the Murray River, which still keeps a few riverboats sentimentally in service. (You can even book passage on one.) A famous riverboat captain of the day was George Bain Johnston, who pulled so many nearly drowned colonials from the water that he was dubbed the River Murray Spaniel. At the height of the river trade in the 1870's, more than 200 paddle-wheelers operated over 4,000 miles in the Murray and Darling Rivers.

Railroads were slow to become established in Australia, partly because of the bickering between the separate colonies. (This resulted in trains being run on no less than six different track gauges, a legacy that plagues Australian rail travelers to this day.)

The country first turned to America for a practical means of traveling long distances between the far-flung cities and towns of the colonies. Freeman Cobb and a group of fellow Yanks imported the plains-proven Concord coach to Australia and started a highly successful service called Cobb & Co. It became every bit as famous as Wells-Fargo in the U.S.A.

The drivers became characters almost as famous as the leading political, entertainment, and commercial figures whom they carried jolting and bouncing over the rough landscape. One, named Mike Dougherty, was known from Brisbane to Ballarat as possibly the most prolific bush liar in Australia, and one *grande dame* of the day is said to have booked a seat atop his coach especially to test the veracity of that appellation.

For 50 miles, though, Mike would hardly speak to her. But late in the afternoon, when the coach was traveling deep in the country, he dropped a few casual remarks about a kangaroo he had trained to meet the coach. The roo would catch the mail bag, sort through the letters, and then deliver them to settlers who lived on some widely scattered stations in the area.

Mike fell silent again, and the woman wasn't sure she took much stock in the story—not even as a respectable lie. She had almost forgotten it, in fact, when the coach rounded a curve. There in the middle of the road stood a large, "old-man" kangaroo, pausing intently in that special way of kangaroos and staring inquisitively at the approaching vehicle.

Mike didn't hesitate a second: "Nothin' today, Red!" he shouted, and then cracked his whip. Whereupon the kangaroo turned and bounced easily off into the spinifex, apparently on his way to take care of some other important business.

The coaches carried gold and other cargo, of course, as well as passengers. And these and other means of travel were occasionally stopped by another prototype of the American West who had his counterpart in the wilds of Australia. Outlaws Down Under were known as "bushrangers," and all through the nineteenth century, they were an inescapable fact of colonial life.

The most famous—not to say notorious—bushranger was Ned Kelly, a murderous blackguard who nevertheless is still worshipped today by schoolchildren and elders alike as a genuine folk hero. His story has been told countless times in prose, poetry, drama, canvas, and song. More revered by Aussies than Jesse James ever was by Yanks, Kelly led police a merry chase for two years, from 1878 to 1880.

Like many misfits in the latter half of the century, he was the son of an English-hating Irish ex-convict. He made friends among and was abetted by some poor settlers in what is now called Kelly Country, northeast of Melbourne. At the final shootout, Kelly and some members of his gang donned some crude home-made armor, which was saved and may still be found in the museums. His jail cell, death mask, the armor, and other appurtenances are still popular tourist attractions.

The explorers, too, were still active throughout the late nineteenth century, building up genuine tales of dedication and sacrifice which should—but often didn't—far outweigh the somewhat trumped-up importance of the bushrangers.

One of the most successful, but certainly the most tragic of the later explorations was the expedition led by Robert Burke and William Wills in a south-to-north continental crossing from Melbourne to the Gulf of Carpentaria in 1861. Nearly everyone died, including Burke and Wills, many of them because of a bizarre series of events which left help and food close at hand but hidden to the principals involved. To touch on the story briefly is a literary injustice. It is early Australia at its most heroic and most tragic, and the entire account should be sought out by anyone who wants to know something of how this adventure was stamped into the character of the country.

The Australian's love of horse racing and other sports also developed during this period. The Melbourne Cup, the derby for which all Australia still comes to a halt, was first run in 1861. An early style of football came in with the first settlers. But after rugby was invented, a unique Australian form of mayhem called Australian Rules football was developed during the 1850's. (It requires an oval-shaped field and no less than four goal posts!) Soccer matches were first held in Sydney during the 1880's. And two types of rugby are still played in the country.

Golf and tennis were introduced during the last years of the century. Cricket, of course, was played by the earliest settlers, but not seriously until after 1856. The first Australian team to visit England in 1868 was composed entirely of Aborigines, perhaps insuring a good attendance by its shock value alone. But English/Australian cricket rivalry became intense with a famous Australian victory in England in 1822. Prompted by a sports pundit's claim that English cricket had just died, the two countries have played for the "ashes" of that sport ever since. (The trophy is in the shape of a funeral urn.)

Although sport (as well as gambling, which is intimately related) became supreme in the occupation of Aussie leisure time, the finer arts were not completely ignored. Landscape painters who could capture the unique (and to the Englishman, strange) panoramas of Australia achieved some deserved fame. Abram Louis Buvelot is considered the father of that field, after beginning works in Victoria in 1865. John Glover also proved adept at capturing the charm of the elusive eucalyptus. The first native-born landscape artist was W. C. Piquenit.

Some artists were also peculiar Australian characters, of course. Frederick Garling developed an expertise in marine painting reportedly while painting every single vessel that tied up in Sydney Cove between 1830 and 1870!

While the French were developing impressionism in Europe, a group of Melbourne artists called the Heidelberg School was exhibiting similar works with Australian subject matter between 1888 and 1890.

Victorian sentimentality did not escape Australian art and literature, but in still-wild Australia such emotionalism was more real, less contrived. Frederick McCubbin's painting of *The Lost Child*, relating to a common tragic occurrence in Australian frontier life, is as stark as Marcus Clarke's realistic story on a similar horrible theme, *Pretty Dick*: "They looked for him for five days; on the sixth, his father and another came upon something, lying, hidden, in the long grass at the bottom of a gully in the ranges. A little army of crows flew heavily away. . . . Pretty Dick is lying on his face, with his head on his arm. . . ."

Clarke, more famous for his convict-era novel, *For the Term of His Natural Life* (1874), was one of Australia's important nineteenth century writers. He was a member of a Melbourne literary group which included the poets George McCrae and the melancholy Adam Lindsay Gordon. Gordon wrote a wide variety of pieces, from masterful poems to simple homespun proverbs popular with—and often embroidered by—even the most unpoetically minded outback Australian:

> "Life is mostly froth and bubble,
> Two things stand like stone
> Kindness in another's trouble,
> Courage in your own."

It was a fine thought, but one perhaps lost on the author himself. Faced with loneliness and financial problems, he killed himself in 1870.

"Bush ballads" became the folk songs of Australia, and many of them are still sung today, long after the authors have been forgotten. "Waltzing Matilda," written by "Banjo" Patterson in 1895, has been voted in and out several times as Australia's national anthem in recent years.

At that date, a new gold rush was on in Western Australia, and back east, the colonies were on their way to setting up a new nation—not by revolution, as it might have been formed by the flag-bearing diggers at the Eureka Stockade, but by a Federation of the seven formerly separate colonies. One final impediment to the union was the continued rivalry between Sydney and Melbourne, the capitals of New South Wales and Victoria respectively and the two most populous cities. This thorn was only plucked for good when it was agreed that a new capital would be formed. It would be in New South Wales (to satisfy that state), but it could not be less than 100 miles from Sydney (as demanded by Victoria).

Canberra and the Commonwealth—1901 to 1979

The Commonwealth of Australia came into being on the first day of the new century, January 1, 1901, with the approval of Great Britain, and still very much under its protective wing. Australia was not then a fully independent nation. That status was developed gradually, but is in some doubt even today.

The flag adopted in 1901—what the Sydney *Bulletin* called a "bastard flag"—bears the Southern Cross, inspired by the Eureka diggers' banner, but a quarter of the field is the British Union Jack, a prominent symbol of crown power.

Parliament met temporarily in Melbourne, and one of the first new items of governmental business was the building of the permanent capital. Two Americans figured prominently in the project. One was the colorful King O'Malley, who was elected to parliament and there led the land acquisition program for the new city. He also helped conduct the international design competition for it, a contest won in 1911 by a young Chicago architect, Walter Burley Griffin. (Virtually unknown in his own country then and now, his name is probably a household word in Australia—certainly known in every schoolroom.)

Griffin eventually resigned in the face of bureaucratic meddling with his designs. And with World War I, the Great Depression, and World War II, the growth of Canberra went very slowly. ("A good sheep paddock, ruined," one early cynic called it.) But today it stands as one of the loveliest and most successful of the planned capital cities of the world.

The form of government adopted has both British and American elements. The federal parliament consists of a House of Representatives and an upper house called the Senate. Each of the six states elects 10 senators for six-year terms, and the house membership (about 124) is based on population. Representatives are elected for three years at the most. But there the system turns British, for the prime minister, if defeated on a vote of confidence, must call for new election in the house.

In Australia, it still seems like there's an election every time you turn around—perhaps appropriate enough in the country that actually invented the ballot box (in 1856). And if you are Australian, you must vote or pay a fine. It's the law.

As in Britain, the prime minister is not elected by the voters at large. The leader of a political party, like all other nominees, runs for representative (or M.P.—Member of Parliament) in his own district. If he and his party are elected, he will then become prime minister. He will pick his cabinet from the members of the House of Representatives, and perhaps a few from the Senate. The cabinet then meets in secrecy, but their proposals are enacted publicly by the parliament.

Parliament is stronger than the individual prime minister, and the federal government is also much stronger than the U.S. federal government in relation to the states. (Australian federal government has the only power to borrow money, it controls all social services, and it is the

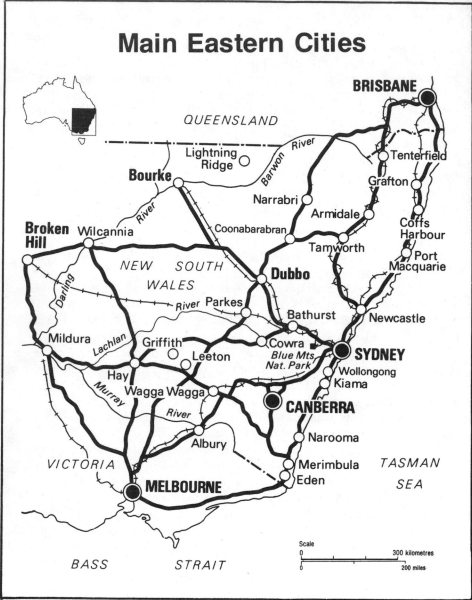

Main Eastern Cities

QUEENSLAND

BRISBANE

Tenterfield

Lightning Ridge

Barwon River

Bourke

Grafton

Narrabri

Armidale

Coffs Harbour

Broken Hill

Wilcannia

Coonabarabran

River

Tamworth

Port Macquarie

NEW SOUTH WALES

Dubbo

Darling

River Parkes

Bathurst

Newcastle

Mildura

Lachlan

Griffith

Cowra

SYDNEY

Leeton

Blue Mts Nat. Park

Wollongong

Hay

Kiama

Murray

Wagga Wagga

River

CANBERRA

Narooma

VICTORIA

Albury

Merimbula
Eden

TASMAN

SEA

MELBOURNE

BASS STRAIT

Scale
0   300 kilometres
0   200 miles

Map courtesy Australian Tourist Commission

only government which can set income taxes. It does have a revenue-sharing program with the states.)

But standing in the wings of the Australian government is the Queen (or King) of England. The head of state still rests with the crown. These are the true "executive powers," and when push comes to shove, Great Britain still has the strength. This was evidenced in 1975 when the governor-general, an appointee of Queen Elizabeth, was so opposed to the Labor government policies that he dismissed the prime minister and his party from office.

From the start of her commonwealth status, Australia was still loyal to Great Britain. Beginning with the Boxer Rebellion and the Boer war, she began a policy of sending off her sons to fight and die in British campaigns.

Commonwealth status also formalized the White Australia Policy, designed at first to keep Queensland plantations from capturing Chinese, Kanakas, and Pacific Islanders as cheap labor. But beyond this humanitarian motive, it remained in effect as a political and philosophical policy against non-white—mainly Oriental—immigration. It began to fade from the scene after World War II, but only disappeared entirely less than a decade ago.

Contrary to some world opinion, it was never a repressive practice like the racial laws in the American South or the separation by color system of South Africa. Some Chinese families, for instance, have been citizens of Australia since the 1850's.

With some regional exceptions in attitudes toward the Aborigines (the "bloody abos" or the "boongs"), the Australians seem to be generally free of racial prejudices, although some of the exceptions have been highly visible. The conservative prime minister, the late Sir Robert Menzies, once became the only delegate at the United Nations to defend South Africa's attitude toward its blacks. He was soundly condemned for this attitude in his own country, but the damage on the world stage was done.

During World War I, Australia's troops, together with New Zealand soldiers, formed the Australian New Zealand Army Corps, known from its initials as the ANZAC's, and they sailed off to Europe to help England fight the Hun. They distinguished themselves in several fights, but their most famous campaign was their first—the disastrous attempt to land on the impregnable Turkish coast at Gallipoli, April 25, 1915, along with British, French, and Indian troops. Beachheads were held and a few temporary small, costly gains were made from April to December when the soldiers, decimated by the battles, were successfully withdrawn.

The famous British war correspondent Ellis Ashmead-Bartlett then wrote of the Anzacs scaling their first, nearly perpendicular cliff on April 25: "Here was a tough proposition to tackle in the darkness, but those colonials, practical above all else, went about it in a practical way . . . this race of athletes proceeded to scale the cliffs without responding to the enemy's fire . . . I have never seen anything like these wounded Australians in war before. Though many were shot to bits, without the hope of recovery, their cheers resounded throughout the night. . . . They were happy because they knew that they had been tried for the first time and had not been found wanting. . . ."

The number of Anzacs killed in the campaign was 8,587. Some 25,000 were wounded. April 25, "Anzac Day," is now the solemn memorial day national holiday in both Australia and New Zealand.

The attack, incidentally, was ordered by Winston Churchill, then First Lord of the Admiralty, despite considerable advance doubts on the practicality of the tactic. This resulted in Churchill's general lack of popularity in Australia throughout World War II and for the rest of his life.

Between the wars, Australia, like the rest of the world, embraced automobiles, airplanes, radios, and moving pictures, and many modernists fought the increasing "wowserism," or prudery that burgeoned incongruously along with drinking and gambling. (The latter was abetted by racing news which now came by "wireless.") Despite the censorship, art and literature was very much alive, largely centered around novelist Norman Lindsay (*Saturdee*, 1933). The motion picture industry developed to the point where Australia could boast the largest number of cinemas per capita in the world.

The nation's two great aviation pioneers were Charles Kingsford Smith and Charles Ulm, who mapped the routes that eventually became the nation's aviation network—a formidable task in a continent so large and sparsely settled. In 1928, Smith and Ulm made the first flight to Australia across the Pacific, flying from Oakland, California, via Honolulu to Fiji and thence to Brisbane in a Fokker tri-motor named the Southern Cross.

The Southern Cross may still be seen in a special museum hangar built for it just outside the passenger terminal in Brisbane. Both Ulm and Smith gave their lives for flying, however, disappearing at sea in different incidents in 1934 and 1935.

On a very different level, Australia became well known during the 1920's and 30's for developing a strain of confidence men who played on the world's rich and gullible—often English or American—bilking them out of millions. One of the most flamboyant was James Coates, who traveled the world first class, pretending to be whomever he needed to be to conduct his elaborate swindles. But whether it was the advent of the depression or of war, the flashiest Australian con men had nearly faded from the scene by 1950.

Less harmful, surely, was the literary prank played on Max Harris, the editor of a poetry magazine. He received in the mail a set of modern poems said to have been written by a deceased telephone lineman named Ern Malley. Harris devoted an entire issue to the writings. Two real poets then revealed that they had deliberately written nonsense lines taken from miscellaneous newspapers and technical manuals to expose the "pretentiousness" of contemporary poetry. Harris insisted they had literary merit, but ironically he was later prosecuted and fined for printing some of the "obscenity" in the works. Today the term "Ern Malley" is sometimes applied to any unorthodox literary effort in Australia.

Severely underpopulated, Australia suffered greatly during the Great Depression, although it maintained its world reputation as a nation of athletes with gold medals won at the Olympics and with the tennis titles awarded at Wimbledon and elsewhere.

In the 1930's, Australians worried about a Japanese invasion, but when war came in 1939, they dutifully sailed off to help the British fight the Germans again. They distinguished themselves from 1940 to 1942 in the North African campaigns against Rommel, becoming the famous "Rats of Tobruk" who defended that post from March to December 1941. Churchill, now British prime minister, would not withdraw them from the seige.

After the Japanese attack at Pearl Harbor and the Philippines in December 1941, Australian troops began to return home to the Pacific. More than 15,000 Aussies were captured at Singapore in February 1942. During the same month, Japanese air raids were carried out on Australian soil at Darwin. Later, Broome, Derby, and Wyndham were also hit.

The same year, Australia took another step toward independence from Britain. When Churchill wanted to move the 7th Division, on its way back home from the Middle East, to Burma, Australian Prime Minister John Curtin refused. A plan by the Japanese to capture Port

Moresby, the capital of the then Australian territory of New Guinea, was thwarted when Australians joined with Americans to fight the naval Battle of the Coral Sea off Australia's northeast coast. It became a major turning point in the war.

American and Australian friendships were firmly sealed during World War II. General Douglas MacArthur moved his headquarters from the Philippines to Melbourne, and later to Brisbane for most of the balance of the war. Yanks and Aussies fought together in New Guinea and in the island-hopping campaigns toward Japan. Thousands of American troops were stationed in Australia, and although the battles at the pubs for booze and girls were highly publicized, by and large the Diggers and the Yanks became mates in the common effort to "beat the Japs."

By the end of the war, 29,400 Australians had been killed in action. An amazing total of 31,000 became prisoners of war, of whom nearly 8,000 died while held by the Japanese.

In appreciation, the electorate kept Labor in power for a few years after the war, and Prime Minister Ben Chifley was credited with seeing that the veterans all received jobs, getting automobile manufacturing in gear (with the Holden car), opening new universities, and beginning an immigration policy to bring thousands of "New Australians" to the country, most of them British, Italian, Greek, Dutch, German and Polish. (Due to this post-war policy, a quarter of the Australian population today are immigrants and their children.)

But an attempt to nationalize the banks, the rising influence of labor unions, and the fear of communism brought Chifley's government down. In came the forceful, conservative, and arrogant Robert Menzies, destined to guide Australia from 1949 to 1965. (In Australia, remember that the liberal party is called Labor—or the A.L.P. The principal conservative party is the Liberal party, and there's also a rural party called the Country party, which usually rules in conservative coalition with the Liberals.)

Australian troops took part in the Korean War, under American command, from 1950 to 1953. During the 50's, Australia's wool profits reached all-time highs, and mineral prospecting and mining were increased throughout the country. Oil was discovered in 1953 and commercially pumped beginning in 1964. Iron ore and other natural resources have continued to be found ever since. A major diamond strike occurred in Western Australia as late as 1978. Some new oil wells were also brought in.

In 1952, Australia, New Zealand, and the United States joined in a mutual defense treaty called the ANZUS pact. Each country would come to the aid of the others in case they were attacked in the Pacific.

More than two dozen U.S. bases were established in Australia. Two of the most well known, still in use today, are the U.S. Naval communications stations at North West Cape, W. A., and at Pine Gap, N. T. (near Alice Springs). They are super-secret installations, but are probably related mainly to communicating with nuclear submarines world wide. Missile bases were also built, and in cooperation with the National Aeronautics and Space Administration in the U.S., Australia set up several satellite tracking stations and played an important role in the American space program.

The authoritarian Menzies continued as prime minister through 1966 before retiring. The founder of the Liberal party, he had served nearly 21 years as P.M., the final 18 consecutively. To much of the world, he had become almost Mister Australia himself. He was extremely loyal to the monarchy, yet he worked hard for increased trade and friendship with the U.S. An imposing figure until his death in 1978, he is remembered for his oratory and his wit. (A reporter who once began his interview with, "I'm from the Daily *Mirror*, Mr. Menzies" received an immediate response: "You have my deepest sympathy!")

He was succeeded by Harold Holt, the Menzies protege, who did not return from an ocean swim in 1967.

Somehow it seems that Australia has always suffered more than her fair share of natural disasters from floods, droughts, cyclones (hurricanes), locusts, and especially bushfires. Bushfires have been endemic to Australia for thousands of years; some kinds of seeds have evolved to the point where they will not germinate until after a fire has passed over the area. Most bushfires that occur far from human habitation are just allowed to burn themselves out.

One of the worst bushfires in recent years took place in February 1967, when a fire with a 90-mile front destroyed part of Hobart, Tasmania, killing 62 persons. (See the gripping account by one of the survivors, writer Patsy Adam-Smith in her book, *Footloose in Australia*.) And in February 1977, five persons, a million sheep, and 800,000 head of cattle were killed in a 300,000-acre bushfire not far from Melbourne.

In 1974, Australia was the victim of two weather extremes. The first, a massive January flood in Brisbane, killed a million sheep, 11 people, and left 8,000 persons homeless. But this was eclipsed by the horror of the Christmas Day strike of Cyclone Tracy in Darwin. It destroyed 90 percent of the town and killed 50. At the time of this writing, Darwin still hasn't entirely recovered from that tragedy.

On December 30, 1976, it was Adelaide's turn. A giant swarm of locusts descended on Adelaide that day, destroying local vegetation. Wheat, millet, alfalfa, and rice crops were ravaged.

The Liberal/Country party coalition held the country into the 70's, during which time America's influence and the fear of Asian communism was so strong that Australia took part in the Vietnam War (474 died), despite growing civilian protests. As in America, much of this dissent was centered in the universities and contributed to the students' disillusion about the country and its values. They began to refer to the nation as "Oz," and to heavily criticize the materialistic, militaristic, and narrow-minded tendencies they saw in much of Australian society.

By this time, it had already long been fashionable to heap abuse on Australia. One of the first to do it with bitter effect was Donald Horne, editor of the newsmagazine, *The Bulletin*. In 1964, he published a book criticizing Australia's attitudes toward almost everything. He called the book *The Lucky Country*. Strangely the irony of that title has been generally lost, and now many Australians have come to accept the idea that they are really the Lucky Country. If so, it is certainly more true today than it was in 1964.

In 1970, Pope Paul VI visited Sydney and demonstrated that philosophical criticisms of Australia could also come from outside the country. He warned Aussies against "self-centeredness, hedonism, eroticism."

The Australian Labor Party adopted a promise to bring home the troops from Vietnam. The withdrawal had already begun, however, before Labor was returned to power in 1972—for the first time in 23 years. Party leader Gough Whitlam became the P.M.

Under Whitlam, Australia immediately declared itself to be anti-apartheid in South Africa and said it would no longer play segregated athletic teams. It also adopted sanctions against Rhodesia, due to its racial policies, and announced plans to reform the Aborigine education system at home. For the first time the emphasis was on saving what was left of Aboriginal culture.

The government also upheld measures to give equal pay for women on the job. It recognized mainland China, and it granted full independence to Papua New Guinea after it had been ruled by Australia for more than 90 years.

In one of the first acts of 1973, "skin color" was officially barred as a factor in admitting immigrants, thereby dissolving the last shades of the

White Australia policy. Many more Asians began to immigrate. The government also further reduced ties to Great Britain.

All this took place over a short period of time, and Liberals began to criticize Labor for trying to do "too much too soon." In retrospect, it seems rather that if they hadn't done these things when they did, they would not have come about for some time in the future.

The world economic situation in the early 1970's, an unusual condition combining high unemployment and high prices, took its political toll in Australia. The Liberals heaped the blame for this "stagflation" on the governing A.L.P., and this led to the political confrontation late in 1975.

Australia's most dramatic political event since the formation of the Commonwealth was on November 11, 1975. The governor general, Sir John Kerr, used his previously untested royal powers to dismiss Prime Minister Whitlam and the Labor party from office. (Since he dissolved both the House and the Senate, it was called a "double dissolution" of Parliament.)

Kerr said he did it because Whitlam had refused to bow to long-standing tradition and call for new elections himself, even though a budget bill passed by the House had become stalled by the Liberal majority in the Senate. It was later suggested that Liberal leader Malcolm Fraser had led blockage of the bill in an attempt to force just such a new election.

No matter how roundly some Australians condemned Kerr's autocratic action, the Australian electorate has traditionally voted the dictates of their pocketbooks more than their consciences. When the elections were held the following month, the Liberals, helped by the National-Country party, routed the A.L.P. The London Economist labeled the whole affair a "political earthquake."

They're still talking about the event that no one thought could happen in Australia. It was brought startlingly back to life last year when Fraser attempted to appoint Kerr as Australia's ambassador to UNESCO in Paris. But Kerr quit the job the day he was to accept it because of all the hullabaloo over the "reward" for his wielding the ax against the Labor government three years previously.

Entire books have been written about November 11, 1975, and no doubt arguments still burn in pubs from one end of the country to the other. When Queen Elizabeth visited Australia in 1977, she was booed and jeered by anti-royalists. (Bless her heart, she probably didn't know anything more about the fuss than any of the rest of us. Even though

Kerr was a "royal appointee," his name had been put forth by Whitlam, the man he later sacked.)

During the worst years of the economic slump, Australia cut back on her immigration quota but has raised it again, now accepting about 70,000 "New Australians" annually. About 30,000 refugees from the former South Vietnam have arrived in Australia, many of them in crowded, derelict fishing junks after a hazardous 2,500-mile trip to Darwin Harbor. The humanitarianism toward the "boat people," who are admitted outside usual immigration channels, has not been universal, however. Some politicians and headline writers have referred to these destitute newcomers merely as "queue jumpers."

Throughout the 1970's, Australia has moved into more active trade with its Asian neighbors, largely through an organization called the Association of Southeast Asian Nations (ASEAN). The country's former market in Britain was largely erased when the U.K. entered the European Common Market in 1973.

Uranium mining has become highly controversial in Australia. At first it seemed to some that the nation was selling off an important future resource, but then when many more heavy deposits were found, objections centered around the lack of tight nuclear safeguards and the ineffective or unsafe radioactive waste disposal systems available throughout the world. Occasional demonstrations are held against nuclear power in Australia, some of them led through the auspices of established trade unions.

Another aspect of the controversy is that much of the uranium has been found on Aboriginal reserves, but historically the tribes have not owned mineral rights on the land. The government, for its part, virtually gave the land to the mining corporations. But now in response to Aboriginal protests and public opinion in general, it is finally beginning to make royalty payments to the Aborigines, too.

In the face of rising unemployment, taxation and interest rates, plus difficulties in the public health field, the Fraser government has been losing considerable credibility and popularity over the past two years. A regular three-year election is due this December, and some Liberal supporters of Andrew S. Peacock, now the foreign minister, see him as a more attractive standard bearer than the current party leader and prime minister. Others strongly disagree.

Under the Liberals, Australia doesn't seem to have rejected many of the important philosophies it put into action during the short life of the Labor government. Recently, the government took a firm anti-racial stand, for instance. When a cabinet minister suggested that a South African type of apartheid system might work in Australia, he was immediately fired by Prime Minister Fraser:

"Any policy based on the belief that one race is superior to another is an affront to human dignity and must be condemned," Fraser said.

A List of Notable Aussies

The best way to enjoy any new country, especially an English-speaking nation, is to keep up with who's doing what via its newspapers, magazines, television, and radio.

This may be a little easier, however, if you have a ready reference to some of the well-known people of the day who are active in several different fields.

An exhaustive list would be prohibitively long. But here is an alphabetical roster of 75 "names" in Australia today, whether they are famous in politics, sports, the arts, science, or are just current darlings of the press. All were chosen somewhat capriciously from a list twice as long.

You'll be surprised at how many Aussies you already know and how many you'll learn about even in a short visit to the country. We believe all these folks are living, but some of them—particularly the few politicians and sports figures we've included—may have had a change of professional fortune by the time these words appear in print.

ANDERSON, Dame Judith. One of Australia's greatest dramatic actresses. Now lives in the U.S.A.

ANSETT, Sir Reginald. Self-made transportation magnate. Owner of bus services, airlines, and related industry.

ANTHONY, Julie. Popular singer and actress.

BADEN-POWELL, Frank. Highly successful restaurateur and former actor. Ended up buying the theatre-restaurants he played in.

BAKER, Tom. Trumpet player and singer. Leader of Tom Baker's San Francisco Jazz Band.

BARRASSI, Ron. A top Australian Rules Football star.

BJELKE-PETERSEN, Joh. Authoritarian and strong-willed premier of Queensland.

BONNER, Neville. A former carpenter, he is the first Aborigine to be elected to parliament.

BUZO, Alexander. Young, Sydney-born playwright. His plays "Tom" and "Makasar Reef" also opened in the U.S. in 1978.

CAWLEY, Evonne (Goolagong). Tennis star with several wins at Wimbledon to her credit.

CLARK, Charles Manning. Eminent but currently controversial historian. In 1979, a visiting professor at Harvard.

CLEARY, Jon. One of the country's most successful novelists. Several have been made into films and TV serials.

COURT, Sir Charles. Aggressive premier of Western Australia.

COURT, Margaret. Outstanding tennis player. Won her first tournament at 13. Now holds many world titles.

DARGIE, Sir William Alexander. Portrait painter of many famous persons.

DART, Raymond. Doctor and anthropologist. Found and named the Australopithecus in Africa.

DAVIDSON, Robyn. Sydney fashion model known as "The Camel Lady" after her trek across the Gibson Desert in 1977.

DRYSDALE, Sir George Russell. Internationally known artist, famous for his harsh Outback themes.

DUNSTAN, Don. Intellectual former premier of South Australia. Published a popular book in 1978. Resigned for health reasons, February 1979.

DUNSTAN, Keith. Melbourne-based writer and columnist. Has written several excellent books on the Australian character.

ECCLES, Sir John. A neurologist and a winner of the Nobel Prize for medicine. Now lives in the U.S.

EVANS, Len. Sydney restaurateur and leading wine writer in Australia.

FOWLES, Glenys. Operatic soprano. Formerly with New York Met, now with the Australian Opera.

FRASER, Dawn. One of the best swimmers in Australia with several Olympic medals.

FRASER, Malcolm. Leader of the Liberal party and prime minister of Australia since 1975.

FRETWELL, Elizabeth. Resident soloist with the Australian Opera. (Formerly principal soprano with Sadler's Wells in London.)

GREER, Germaine. Writer and outstanding Women's Liberation activist. Now lives in the U.S.

HANCOCK, Lang. Millionaire industrialist and the man most responsible for the development of iron ore deposits in W.A.

HARDY, Frank. Novelist, playwright, and TV personality.

HARRIS, Rolf. Well-loved songwriter and entertainer. Famous for his "Tie Me Kangaroo Down, Sport" of the 1950's.

HAWKE, Robert. President of the Australian Council of Trade Unions. One of the most influential political figures.

HAYDEN, Bill. Leader of the Australian Labor Party (A.L.P.), and leader of the opposition (shadow prime minister).

HELPMAN, Sir Robert. Internationally acclaimed ballet dancer, choreographer, actor, and producer.

HIBBERD, Jack. Contemporary and prolific playwright. A recent musical was "A Toast to Melba."

HOGAN, Paul. A rigger on the Sydney Harbour Bridge who shot to fame as a comedian.

HORNE, Donald. Author and social critic. Editor of *The Bulletin,* a news magazine. Wrote *The Lucky Country* and other books.

HUGHES, Robert. Art critic for *Time* magazine in U.S. who returns to Australia for TV appearances, etc., occasionally.

HUMPHRIES, Barry. Actor, comedian, artist. Played in several British and Australian films. Also appeared on Broadway in 1978.

KENEALLY, Tom. Award-winning novelist. His ninth, *Whispers in the Forest* was published recently.

KENNEDY, Graham. Nationally known television personality.

KINNELL, Galway. An American who is now poet-in-residence at Macquarie University in Sydney.

LANE, Don. An American singer who's become a TV star in Australia. His show seems much like the "Tonight" show in the U.S.

LAWS, John. Controversial and independent radio and TV personality. Also writes music and poetry.

McKERN, Leo. Australian Shakespearian actor who has performed often in England, on stage and film.

MATTIOLI, Rocky. Boxer and currently world light-middleweight champion.

MICHELL, Keith. Lead actor in countless Shakespeare plays in London. Returns occasionally for Australian appearances.

MOOREHEAD, Alan. Beginning as a journalist for Australian and British papers, he became the author of many books.

MURDOCH, Rupert. The head of an international publishing empire, he now lives in New York where he owns the *Post.*

NEWTON-JOHN, Olivia. Now a top singer in the U.S., she returns to her home in Australia from time to time.

NOLAN, Sydney. Painter, now living in the U.K., who became famous for illustrating Australian historical events.

PATE, Michael. Australian actor who has appeared in many American movies.

PEACH, Bill. TV host, remembered for "This Day Tonight," public affairs program, and "Peach's Australia," a travel show.

PINDER, Beverley. 1978 Miss Australia and a karate expert.

PUGH, Clifton. Painter who has done the royal family in London. Also known as a conservationist.

REDDY, Helen. Pop singer who now lives in the U.S.A. She's writing a history of Australia.

RIGBY, Paul. Internationally known cartoonist who has returned to his native Perth from London.

ROWE, Greg. 14-year-old actor who appeared in films "The Storm Boy" and "Blue Fin."

SANG, Samantha. Another Aussie singer who has made it big in the U.S.A. Often returns home to Australia.

SCHEPISI, Fred. Movie producer, director, and screenwriter. Known for 1978's prizewinner "The Chant of Jimmie Blacksmith."

SELBY, Kathryn. 17-year-old concert pianist. Played in 1978 with the Philadelphia Orchestra.

SINGLETON, John. Advertising executive who became a millionaire at 36. Married to a top Australian model.

STRETTON, Major General Alan. "The Hero of Darwin," he led the rescue and reconstruction efforts there in 1975–76.

SUTHERLAND, Joan. "La Stupenda," as the Italians called her, is Australia's most widely acclaimed opera singer.

TAYLOR, Rod. Hollywood actor who comes home to Australia sometimes.

THIEL, Colin. Author of several books, including *Storm Boy* and *Blue Fin,* which have been made into films.

WARBY, Ken. The fastest man on water. Holds the water speed record now at more than 300 m.p.h.

WEIR, Peter. A film director called "an antipodean Antonioni" by the London *Standard* last year. Directed "The Last Wave."

WEST, Morris. Prolific author. Wrote *The Shoes of the Fisherman* and others made into films. Now lives in Europe.

WHITE, Patrick. In 1973, became the first Australian writer to receive the Nobel Prize for literature.

WHITELEY, Brett. Enjoys worldwide fame as one of Australia's most talented contemporary painters.

WHITLAM, Gough. Prime Minister of Australia from 72–75 before being dismissed by the governor-general.

WICKHAM, Tracey. Schoolgirl swimmer with many gold medals. At 16, is expected to do well at the 1980 Moscow Olympics.

WILLESEE, Mike. TV investigative reporter with a style and flair. Almost a one-man "60 Minutes."

WILLIAMSON, David. Award-winning playwright whose works ("The Removalists" and others) are performed in London and New York.
WILLIAMSON, Malcolm. Musician and composer, known for operas and orchestral works in Australia, Europe, and the U.S.

Picturesque Patterns of Speech

Entire books have been written on the Australian language, a tongue that is supposed to be called English. But even as there are differences in British and American speech patterns, Australia occupies its own separate, very large, and quite special niche in a corner of the English-speaking world.

Besides mere differences in vocabulary, there are several other peculiar aspects to Australian speech. One, of course, is that it is somewhat affected by the Aboriginal languages—perhaps more so than the Indians ever influenced the American idiom. The boomerang and the kookaburra are Aboriginal words for things that have no English equivalent. Mulga is a popular Aboriginal word for a type of plant called wattle or acacia in English.

But the most interesting characteristic of Aussie speech is that many of its speakers take the language as a game to be played. There is a large, expressive group of regular slang words, of course, most of which occupy a more or less permanent place in an informal lexicon. These include flip abbreviations like "mozzie" for "mosquito" and "Paddo" for the Sydney suburb of "Paddington."

But beyond that is the rhyming slang and variations on that theme which create a much more fluid form of speech that seems to be invented and changed almost daily.

Rhyming slang is supposed to have begun with the Cockneys of London, and many travelers in England are familiar with some of the old chestnuts—"me trouble and strife" is "my wife." And "a bag of fruit" is a "suit."

But the versatile Aussies have added many more examples of this. And in recent years they have taken it a giant step further with *abbreviated* rhyming slang, which almost becomes a secret code among the linguistically initiated. Thus "trouble" becomes wife and "bag" becomes suit, using the previous examples. "My shoes" can be expressed as "me kangaroos" or even just "me kangas."

Another aspect of the language Down Under is the peculiar pronunciation and enunciation of many words. Also similar to the street talk of London, the sound "A" becomes the sound "I," or at least so close to it that perhaps only another Australian could tell the difference—when "mate" becomes "mite," for instance, or "daisy" becomes "dicey."

The degree of this degradation of the "A" varies so completely in the country as to be completely nonexistent among some who carefully cultivate their speech in the mold of the Queen's English to the other extreme of being virtually indistinguishable between "A" and "I." This inconsistency even confuses the Australians themselves. The town of Mackay, for instance: Is it pronounced Mac-*kay* or Mac-*eye*? (We couldn't find anyone who could tell us for sure.)

Another part of the same problem is the fact that Aussies, in common with many other British commonwealth countries, have troubles traceable to the use of a softer "R" than is used by most Americans. (Not all, though; when Bostonians and some others say "Cuba" it may come out "Cuber.") The Australians sometimes seem to leave R's out where they ought to be. (My wife Sara, a New Zealander who is afflicted with a slight touch of the same Down Under disease, occasionally talks about an "S.L." blanket. She means "air cell.") Or else they seem to insert R's where they ought *not* to be. (There are numerous examples, like maybe "Jack" who often becomes "Chairk.")

Combine this with other idiosyncracies such as the sound "ou" as in "hound," which begins sounding like nothin' but a "hand-dog." And condense things to the point where a two-syllable word like "power" sometimes becomes "par," "pair," or "pah." Now you have what one Australian writer labeled "Strine," a compressed form of shattered Australian spoken by many in the country today.

Some of the examples in the book *Let Stalk Strine* by Alistair Morrison are hilarious. Thus an "egg nisher" is a machine to cool down a room with, a popular nursery rhyme begins "Chair congeal went up the heel," and "Furry Tiles" always begin "One spawner time. . . ."

One of my favorite Strine sentences is quoted in John Gunther's *Inside Australia*: "Hazzy gairt non wither mare thorgan?" Try it first before peeking. Give up? It's translated, "How is he getting on with the mouth organ?"

If you get a chance to pick up a book on Strine, do so. (Some of the examples won't work as well with an American accent, remember, partly because of those harsh R's we Yanks have. Strine speakers and non-Strine speakers alike in Australia are not cursed with those.)

For technical reasons, we've had to leave Strine out of the following list. There are also only a few examples of rhyming slang or abbreviated rhyme. We have confined ourselves generally to popular semipermanent Australian slang and other terms familiar to Australians and

British and not considered slang by them at all, but just plain good English.

Many Aussies are surprised to hear that we don't call a black-top road "bitumen," or that "ringer" means something different in America than in Australia. British readers, I hope, will pardon us. For the benefit of other confused Yanks, we have included some of the essential Pom terms like "petrol" in this line-up.

You won't run into all these on a short stay. However, we have taken the liberty of asterisking the most usual words and phrases. It would be a good idea to learn them before arriving in Australia.

Some of these words and terms are not universally used throughout Australia. Instead of "bowser," for example, you may hear something simple like "petrol pump."

Incidentally, we have attempted to use a certain amount of Strine, slang, rhyme, and other Aussie lingo from time to time throughout the rest of this book. They include some of the terms from this list as well as others that came up in the course of writing the text of the volume. The idea is that if you finish the book, you'll be much better acquainted with the language of Australia than 99 percent of the other foreign visitors to the country.

Australian—A to Zed

A

ABC. Abbreviation of Australian Broadcasting Commission.
ACT. Abbreviation of Australian Capital Territory (Canberra).
ACTU. Australian Council of Trade Unions.
ALP. Australian Labor Party.
AWU. Australian Workers Union.
Accommodated tour. Fully guided tour (with hotels, etc.).
Accommodation. Hotel room.
Airy-Jane. Airplane.
Alf. Stupid person.
Antivenine. Antitoxin.
Amber. Beer.
*Anzac. Member of the Australian and New Zealand Army Corps in World War I.
Arvo. Afternoon.
Auntie. The Australian Broadcasting Commission.
*Aussie. Australian.

B

BHP. Abbreviation for Broken Hill Proprietary, a mining corporation.
Back of beyond. Far away in the Outback.

Back of Bourke. Same meaning, used more in N.S.W.

Back chat. Impudence.

Bail up. To rob, hold up.

Banana bender. Queenslander.

Banana land. Queensland.

Barrack. To cheer at a sporting event.

Battler. Person who struggles hard for a living.

Beaut. Short for "beautiful." (Very good.)

Belt up! Shut up!

Bible basher. Minister.

Bickie. Dollar (originally short for "biscuit").

Bike. Promiscuous woman.

Bike: To "get off your bike" is to become angry.

Bikey. One who rides bikes or motorcycles.

Billabong. Water hole in a semi-dry river.

*Billy. Tin container used for boiling water to make tea.

Biscuit. A cookie (sweet biscuit) or a cracker.

Bitser. Mongrel dog ("Bits a this and bits a that").

Bitumen. Asphalt or black-top road.

Black stump, other side of. Same as "back of beyond," etc.

*Bloke. Man, used like "guy" in the U.S.

*Bloody. All-purpose adjective, once thought to be profane.

Bludge. Live off someone else, "sponge."

Blue. A fight, usually (has many other meanings).

Bone, point the. To hex or jinx (Aboriginal ceremony).

*Bonnet. Hood of a car.

*Boomer. Anything large—a lie, a kangaroo, etc.

Boong. Derogatory term for an Aboriginal. (Don't use it.)

*Boot. Trunk of a car.

Bo peep. Quick look, peek.

Bowser. Gasoline pump.

Brissie. Brisbane.

Brumby. Wild horse.

Buckley's Chance. One chance in a million.

Budgie. Parakeet.

Bullock. Heavy manual labor.

Bundy. Time clock.

Bunyip. Mythical animal (Australia's yeti).

Burl, give it a. Give it a try.

*Bush. Countryside outside cities and towns.

Bushranger. Bandit, outlaw.

Butcher. Five-ounce beer glass in S.A.

C

*Chemist. Pharmacist.

Chips. French fried potatoes.
Chook. Chicken.
Chuck. Throw.
Cleanskin. Unbranded cattle.
Clue. (Used like "idea," as in "I haven't a clue.")
Coach. Long-distance bus.
Cobber. Friend.
Cockie. Small farmer.
Come a gutser. Make a bad mistake.
Commercial traveler. Traveling salesman.
Concession (or concessional). Discount, special rate.
Coee. An attention-getting cry in the bush.
Coolabah. A type of box eucalyptus tree.
Cop it sweet. To take the blame or the loss agreeably.
Corroboree. Aboriginal dancing.
Crook. Broken, sick, or no good.
Cuppa. Cup of tea.

D

Daks. Trousers.
Didjeridoo. Aboriginal droning instrument.
Digger. Australian soldier, but used by foreigners meaning any Australian. (Australians prefer "Aussie.")
Dill. Fool.
Dillybag. Small bag for carrying things.
Dinkie die. The whole truth.
Dinkum. Genuine or honest.
Drongo. A born loser.
Duffer. Cattle thief, rustler.
Dunny. Toilet.

E

Enzedder. New Zealander.
Evo. Evening.

F

Fair dinkum. Same as "Dinkie die" above.
Fair go. A good, reasonable chance.
Facilities. Toilets, lavatories, etc.
Fannywhacker. A marble.
Fill-up station. Gasoline service station.
Flaming. Like bloody, another all-purpose adjective.
Flash. Fancy or ostentatious.
Flat out. As fast as one can go.
Flog. Sell or hock.
Fluff. Attractive woman.

Flyswisher stew. Oxtail stew.

Footpath. What the British call the pavement and the Americans call the side-walk.

*Fossick. To prospect or rummage. Search for gold, shells, or other goodies on or under the ground.

G

Galah. Fool or idiot (after the parrot by that name).

Gaol. Australian/British spelling of jail.

Gear. Clothing or equipment.

Getting on. Moving up in the world.

Gibber. Stone or boulder.

Gin. Aboriginal woman.

*Good on ya! Term of approval (sometimes ironic).

Goods. Freight (as in "goods train").

Grizzle. To complain.

*Grazier. Sheep or cattle rancher.

*Grog. Popular term for any alcoholic drink.

H

Hard case. Amusing person.

Have on. To take a challenge.

*Hire. To rent (you "hire" a car).

Hire purchase plan. Time payment plan.

*Hotel. Sometimes means only a pub.

Hottie. Hot water bottle.

Humpy. Small hut or shack.

I

Identity. A well-known person.

In yer boot. Expression of disagreement.

J

Jackeroo. An apprentice cowboy, station hand.

Jilleroo. Female of the above.

*Joey. Baby kangaroo (in the pouch).

Jumbuck. Sheep.

K

Kanga. Abbreviated rhyming slang for "shoe" (see below).

Kangaroo. Rhyming slang for "shoe."

Kerb. British spelling of "curb" (side of the street).

Kick. Pocket or wallet.

Kip. Bed.

*Kiwi. New Zealander.

*Knock. Criticize.

L

Lady's waist. Five-ounce beer glass.
Lair or *larrikin.* Ruffian, hoodlum.
Licensed. Legally permitted to sell beer, wine, and liquor.
Lob. Arrive.
Lolly. Lollipop, money (several meanings).
Loo. Brit./Aus. slang for toilet.
Lot. The whole thing, bunch, mob, group.
Lubra. Aboriginal word for woman.
Lucerne. Alfalfa (in the U.S.).

M

MP. Abbreviation for Member of Parliament.
Mad. Crazy (seldom means angry).
Marjie. Marijuana.
Mate. Your best buddy or comrade (does not mean spouse).
Matilda. Belongings carried by swagmen, wrapped in a blanket.
Medibank. Aus. public health plan.
Middy. Ten-ounce beer glass (in NSW).
Mob. A group of persons or things (not necessarily unruly, etc.).
Mozzie. Mosquito.
Mum. Mom (almost a school of philosophy in Australia).

N

N.S.W. Abbreviation for New South Wales.
Nark. Spoilsport, unpleasant person.
Naughty. Euphemism for sexual activity.
Never never. Desert land far away in the outback.
Never-never. Time payment ("hire purchase") plan.
Nick. Steal.
Nipper. Small child.
Nit. Fool, idiot.
No hoper. Same as above, but worse.
No worries! "She'll be right!" (everything will come out fine).

O

Ocker. Australian hillbilly or country bumpkin.
Offsider. Follower, helper, sidekick.
Oil. Accurate information.
Old boy. Alumnus.
Old man. Adult male kangaroo.
On the beach. An unemployed sailor.
Outback. The bush, uncivilized, uninhabited country.
Oz. Australia or Australian (ironic term coined by university students).

P

PTC. Abbreviation for Public Transport Commission.

**PM.* Abbreviation for prime minister.

Paddo. Paddington.

**Paddock.* Field or meadow.

**Parcel.* Package.

Packet. Envelope (as in pay packet).

Pastoralist. Similar to grazier.

Perve. To watch a woman with admiration (does not mean "perverted").

Peter. Cash register.

**Petrol.* British term for gasoline.

Pig's ear. Rhyming slang for beer.

Pimple squeezers. Singers of popular songs.

Pinch. Arrest.

Plonk. Cheap wine.

Plug hat. What they call a "bowler" in Britain and a "derby" in the U.S.A.

Poddy dodger. One who steals unbranded calves.

Poker machine. Slot machine.

**Pom* or *Pommy.* Englishman.

Poofter. Homosexual.

Pot. 10 ounces of beer in Victoria, 20 in N.S.W.

**Prang.* Accident, crash.

**Proprietary (usually abbreviated "Pty").* Company (Co.).

**Pub.* "Public house," bar, drinking establishment.

Pud. Pudding, dessert.

Q

Quack. Slang for any kind of doctor.

Quaky Isles. New Zealand.

Qld. Abbreviation for Queensland.

R

RSL. Abbreviation for Returned Servicemen's League.

Ratbag. Eccentric character.

Raw Prawn. "To come the raw prawn" means to try to deceive someone. (Honest!)

Razoo. Fictitious coin ("I haven't a brass razoo.").

Repositioning fee. Rental car drop-off charge.

Ringer. Fast sheep shearer.

Ripper. Something particularly good.

Road train. Tractor with two or more trailers.

**Roo.* Kangaroo.

Rouseabout. Handyman on the farm.

Rum. No good, "crook."

S

SA. Abbreviation for South Australia.

STD. Abbreviation for subscriber trunk dialing (same as direct distance dialing in the U.S.).

*Sack. To fire, dismiss from employment (also as in "get the sack"—be fired).

*Scheme. System or method (no nefarious connotation as in U.S.).

School. A group of drinkers, each of whom is expected to buy a round.

Schooner. 15-ounce beer glass in N.S.W., seven ounces in S.A.

Score. To inscribe.

Screamer. Noisy drunk.

Scrub. Bushland.

Sealed. Surfaced road, tar-sealed, paved.

*Sheila. Young woman.

She'll be right! Don't worry.

Shoot through. Leave unexpectedly.

Shop assistant. Sales clerk in a store.

*Shout. Buy someone a drink.

Shove off! Go Away!

Silk shirt on a pig. Something wasted.

Silvertail. Member of high society.

*Smoke-oh. Short break in work time.

Snoot. Disagreeable person.

Sort. Type or kind.

Square off. Apologize, make amends.

*Squatter. Large landholder.

*Station. Large farm or ranch.

*Stockman. Cowboy, Station hand.

Strewth! An all-purpose exclamation ("It's the truth!").

Strides. Trousers.

Sundowner. Rural tramp.

Surfies. Young men who like to surf.

Swag. Bedroll and all worldly goods of the swagman.

*Swagman. Vagabond, rural tramp.

T

TAB. Abbreviation for Totalisator Agency Board, legal offtrack betting shop.

Take away food. Take-out.

Tariffs. Rates (hotel).

Tattersall's. A type of lottery in some states.

Tazzie. Tasmania.

Technicolor yawn. Vomit.

Telecom. The phone company.

Telly. The TV, also the Sydney Daily Telegraph.

Terrible turk. Rhyming slang for work.

Thimble and pea game. Same as U.S. shell and pea game.

*Togs. Swimming suit (sometimes called a "bathing costume," too).

Toney. Modern, up to date, slick.

Too right! Absolutely!

Track. Country road.

*Trendy. Avant-garde, similar to "toney."

Trunk. Long-distance telephone call.

*Tucker. Food.

Twit. Fool, simpleton.

Two-pot screamer. Somebody who can't take his liquor.

Two up. Popular gambling game involving two pennies thrown in the air.

Tyke. Dog.

Tyre. Brit./Aus. spelling of tire (automobile).

U

U.K. Abbreviation for United Kingdom (Great Britain).

Uni. University.

Up a gumtree. In a quandary.

Up the Cross. At Kings Cross, a section of Sydney.

*Ute. Short for utility truck—a pickup truck.

V

Van Dyke. Country backhouse.

Vic. Abbreviation for Victoria.

W

W.A. Abbreviation for Western Australia.

Waddy. Billy club.

Warder. Jailer or guard.

Walkabout. Traveling on foot for long distances, an Aboriginal tradition.

Waltz Matilda. Carry a swag.

Westralia. Western Australia.

Whack. Fair share.

Wharfies. Longshoremen, stevedores.

Whilst. Brit./Aus. version of "while."

*Whinge. Complain.

Willy-nilly. Small dust twister.

Wog. Minor disease, also an Arab.

Wowser. Bluenose, prude, killjoy.

Wurley. Aboriginal shelter, "humpy."

Y

Yabber. Chatter.

Yabbie. Small crayfish.

*Yank. American.

Yankee shout. Drinking school where everyone pays for himself.

Z

Zed. Australian and British pronunciation of "Z."
*Indicates most commonly used.

The National Bush Ballad

A few final notes before we launch our area chapters. Here are a set of verses from "Waltzing Matilda," *the* song of Australia (voted in and out from time to time as the nation's national anthem, in competition to a more formal composition called "Advance Australia Fair"). By the way, we have seen several slightly different printed versions of "Waltzing Matilda" in Australia, and you may, too.

(1)
Once a jolly swagman camped by a billabong,
Under the shade of a coolabah tree;
And he sang as he watched and waited 'til his billy boiled,
Who'll come a-waltzing Matilda with me?

Chorus:

Waltzing Matilda, waltzing Matilda,
You'll come a-waltzing Matilda with me;
And he sang as he watched and waited 'til his billy boiled,
You'll come a-waltzing Matilda with me!

(2)
Down came a jumbuck to drink at the billabong,
Up jumped the swagman and grabbed him with glee;
And he sang as he stowed that jumbuck in his tucker bag,
You'll come a-waltzing Matilda with me!

(Chorus)

(3)
Up rode the squatter, mounted on his thoroughbred,
Down came policemen, one, two, and three;
Whose is the jumbuck you've got there in the tucker bag?
You'll come a-waltzing Matilda with me!

(Chorus)

(4)
But the swagman he up and he jumped in the water hole,
Drowning himself by the coolabah tree;
And his ghost may be heard as it sings in the billabong,
You'll come a-waltzing Matilda with me!

(Chorus)

5

Sydney
and New South Wales

1. The General Picture

Sydney is where it all began. Downtown, in an area called "The Rocks" just west of Sydney Cove, the first colonials and convicts built houses and barracks. The neighborhood still emits a musty, old-world charm.

But today central Sydney is also a bright city of tall towers, as busy as any of the world's major metropolitan areas, its population of 3 million apparently all on the go at once. Big blue buses—both single and double-decker models—wind through the crowded streets. A fleet of ferry boats is constantly nosing into the piers of Circular Quay and then springing back out again into the bay, en route to the many waterside suburbs. They seem to pass in constant review before the concrete sails, frozen in mid-billow, of the grand Opera House, symbol of Sydney, and now one of the world's most recognized public buildings.

"Sydney-siders" say theirs is Australia's liveliest city, and perhaps it is. Something always seems to be happening in its skyscrapers, its leafy green parks, or along the sparkling, watery shores.

Today's Sydney flows over an area of 1,500 square miles, much of it in a suburban sea of red roofs along both sides of Port Jackson, an almost incredibly lovely crenulated estuary that cuts deeply inland from the shores of the Tasman Sea.

To fully experience Sydney Harbour for the first time, and perhaps to try and fail to take in all its splendor at once, is to empathize with the English writer Anthony Trollope, who saw this 21 square miles of sheltered water as a pictorial dilemma:

"I know the task would be hopeless were I to attempt to make others understand the nature of the beauty of Sydney Harbor. I can say that it is lovely, but I cannot paint its loveliness."

The next major inlet south from Port Jackson is the storied Botany Bay, an infamous name by which the early colony was feared in England for more than a hundred years. But the body of water discovered by Cook was not, until recently, part of Sydney at all. Now the metropolis has indeed sprawled out to encompass Botany Bay. Along the shoreline where the crew of the *Endeavour* picked up specimens of strange plants and trees in 1770 is Sydney's international airport.

Sydney has always been the capital of New South Wales, even when N.S.W. included all the known and unknown parts of Australia. Although much abbreviated, the state still spreads over 300,000 square miles, adding 2 million more souls to Sydney's 3 million. Shaped like a four-sided wedge, N.S.W., like all Australian states, includes both urban areas and bushland. You'll find opera houses and shopping centers as well as billabongs and jumbucks.

The green strip along the shore is neatly lined with the viewful Highway 1. Going west, there are the tablelands, the peaks of the Blue Mountains, then the plains country and finally the farming and mining areas of the west.

Inland, too, are the mighty Murray and the Darling river systems, important highways through the bush a century ago. In the northwest, you can take a train as far as Bourke. "Back o' Bourke" begins the traditional Outback. Lightning Ridge, where amateurs still scratch up an occasional black opal, is out there, too.

New South Wales is not all of Australia, to be sure, but to the visitor who explores it well, it offers a surprising percentage of the items the entire country is famous for. From the wines of Hunter Valley and the Kangaroos of Dubbo, to the silver city of Broken Hill, and back again to the 34 golden beaches of Sydney.

2. The Airport and Long-Distance Transporation

Note: Since much of this should be considered before you leave home, be sure to see our discussion on planes, ships, trains, buses, and cars in Chapter 2, "Smooth Sailing and Happy Landings."

If you're lucky, you'll fly into Sydney from the north, beginning your

Sydney, Great Western Highway

To Newcastle

Gosford

Broken Bay

Palm Beach

Avalon Beach

BRISBANE WATER NAT. PK

DHARUG NAT. PARK

HWY

KU-RING-GAI CHASE NAT. PK

Bobbin Head

Berowra Waters

PACIFIC

Hornsby

Manly

Port Jackson

SYDNEY

Bondi

Coogee

SOUTH PACIFIC OCEAN

Botany Bay

Cronulla

ROYAL NATIONAL PARK

PRINCES

HWY

Campbelltown

Parramatta

Liverpool

HUME

To Melbourne 984km (611 mls)

Windsor

Richmond

Penrith

HWY

Springwood

BLUE MOUNTAINS NATIONAL PARK

WESTERN

Leura

Katoomba

Medlow Bath

Blackheath

GREAT

Camden

Picton

To Melbourne

Lake Burragorang

Lithgow

To Mudgee

To Bathurst

Scale

0

30 kilometres

20 miles

descent over the city itself. On the left side of the airplane, you'll recognize the famous "coat hanger"—Sydney Harbour Bridge—and just beyond it the Opera House.

Landing at Botany Bay, you'll enter the **Kingsford Smith Airport**, known better as "Mascot," by locals, after the suburb in which it sits, about six miles from the city center. There are two main terminal areas at the airport—one for international arrivals and departures, and a mile or so away, a separate pair of buildings for domestic flights. You can take an occasional bus between them for 50 cents, or hire a taxi, of course.

The **international terminal**, built in 1970, is arranged so arrivals are handled on the ground level and departures are made from one escalator flight up. Near the departure gates are several gift shops, a newspaper stand, pharmacy, etc. Prices in these shops are relatively high compared to the tabs in the city, and the exchange rates given for foreign currency are not as good. (Even the duty free shops, for outgoing passengers, we thought not as good a bargain as others—say the shop in Auckland, N.Z., for example.)

There's also a **cocktail bar and buffet** in the departures concourse. For a five-cent piece in the turnstile, you can take in the Airport Observation Deck. Nearby is that wonderful institution, the "Mothers Room," a place where women and their offspring can be alone with others of the same persuasion. (Seriously, it's a good place for feeding, changing "nappies," etc., to be sure.)

There are two large **check-in areas** on that upper level. Pan Am, CP Air, and several others are located on the left side. Qantas and Air New Zealand are at the opposite end near the Au Revoir Bar, snack bar, and coffee shop.

Down the escalator is the bank and currency exchange, the post office, rental cars, taxis, buses, etc. Waiting for a loved one to come out of customs? You have to keep your two eyes on about five doors, all of which are marked "A." Coming through yourself? Be sure to look for a luggage cart to pile your bags on. Or you can use a porter.

There are no Sydney PTC buses to or from the international terminal (you'll have to shuttle to the domestic one to find those). But there is a commercial outfit usually operating mini-buses between town and the international terminal. It's called the **Kingsford Smith Airport Bus Service** (Tel. 667–3221). If you can find one, hop on it. In several trips back and forth between Sydney and the airport, we've found the service terribly unreliable as to departure times, pickups, etc. The fare is about $1.50 for the 25-minute ride. (Its Sydney terminus is in front of Qantas House and the Wentworth Hotel, where they are *supposed* to leave hourly from 6 a.m. to 5 p.m. Don't count on it.) By taxi, the airport-Sydney trip will run about $5.

The **domestic terminal** at Mascot is divided into an Ansett Wing and a Trans-Australia Airlines (TAA) wing, representing the two big interior airlines. (Ansett's wing is newer, just completed in 1978 at a cost of $8.5 million.) You'll find covered accesses, moving sidewalks, escalators, TV screen arrival and departure information (*plus* live loudspeaker announcements, a luxury which is fading from U.S. airports), and a selection of the usual restaurants, bars, coffee shops, etc.

Tip: Some of the gates are a l-o-n-g way from the central services. Get your coffee and newspaper and allow yourself plenty of time. You can use it up if necessary in the departure lounge right at the gate. (And that's where you get your seat allocation, too—another reason for showing up in plenty of time, if you want smoking or non-smoking areas.)

The domestic terminal complex is served from Sydney via public buses No. 302 and 303, although it may seem to take forever to get back and forth. **Ansett Airlines** (Tel. 2–0631) has an airline bus terminal in town at Oxford Square, which is convenient to the hotels in the Kings Cross and Darlinghurst neighborhoods. **TAA** (Tel. 669–0022) has one in the high-rise district at 16 Elizabeth St., which is more convenient to the downtown hotels.

By the way, be sure to take an Ansett bus for an Ansett flight, a TAA bus for a TAA flight, etc. Otherwise the walk with your luggage at the air terminal just might be terminal! Some people reasonably choose their airline on the basis of their hotel location vis-à-vis the bus terminal, or vice versa.

Some other important airline addresses in Sydney include the following. (To our knowledge, none provide bus service to the airport, however.) Air New Zealand (Tel. 233–6888), 10 Martin Place; British Airways (Tel. 233–5566), 64 Castlereagh St.; Continental Airlines (Tel. 232–4108), 60 Martin Place; CP Air (Tel. 233–5711), 62 Pitt St.; Pan American (Tel. 233–1111), 14 Martin Place; and Qantas (Tel. 436–6111), 70 Hunter St.

Arriving in Sydney by sea? If you're lucky, your cruise ship will nuzzle up to the **Sydney Cove Terminal** and tie up just across the cove from the opera house. It's where all the action is, and we can't imagine a more beautiful way to enter a beautiful city.

For travel by train, the main Sydney terminus is the large **Central Railway Station** (Tel. 2–0942), just across the street from Belmore Park, on the opposite side of the city center from Sydney Cove. Railway bookings can be terribly complicated in Australia. We'd let the **N.S.W. Gov-**

ernment Travel Centre (Tel. 231–4444), at the corner of Pitt and Spring Streets, or the **PTC Travel & Tours Centre** (Tel. 211–4255), 11–31 York St., take that off our hands. (Don't even *think* of making a major train trip without booking in advance, and watch out for busy holidays!)

Short-distance trains, particularly in Economy Class, are not very comfortable and sometimes not very clean. Scenery is usually delightful, however, and we enjoyed our recent rail trip up to Gosford to see Old Sydney Town.

There are five railway systems in Australia—four state government and one federal government services. Some still operate on different-size track gauges, which means a change of carriage at places you've never heard of. What with shunting and waiting for single tracks, etc., it often takes a very long time to make a medium-length trip.

One of the most dramatic exceptions to the rule is the famous *Indian Pacific*, the proud coast-to-coast service between Sydney and Perth. Currently that costs about $280 First Class or $214 Economy fare, although you can save a lot if you purchased the Austrailpass outside of Australia (see Chapter 2). You'll have to pay $48 extra for a berth and $50 extra for meals on that trip, if you're traveling by pass.

Other important Sydney train services include the *Southern Aurora*, the *Spirit of Progress* and the *Intercapital Daylight* runs between Sydney and Melbourne. All three are daily. The first two are overnight trips and offer sleeping accommodations for about $8 extra in First Class. Travel time is scheduled at about 14 hours.

Monday to Friday, the *Canberra Monaro Express* runs from Sydney to Canberra in five hours. And daily, the *Brisbane Limited Express* has an overnight run between Sydney and Brisbane. (Again, it's about $8 extra for a berth in First Class.) That trip runs about 16 hours.

Rates will be going up, but we'll make a guess on the fare from Sydney to the following places: Brisbane—$55 First Class, $30 Economy. Canberra—$15 First Class, $10 Economy. And Melbourne—$55 First Class, $30 Economy. (To repeat, please don't hold us to it.)

If you're traveling by **interstate bus**, you'll find the Ansett Pioneer station (Tel. 2–0651) at the corner of Oxford and Riley Streets, and Greyhound Coaches (Tel. 33–4203) at 49 McLachlan Ave., Rushcutters Bay.

Rental cars. The three big outfits in Australia have the following headquarters in Sydney, all almost within honking distance of each other: **Avis Rent-A-Car** (Tel. 669–6226), 214 William St.; **Hertz Rent-A-Car** (Tel. 357–6621), nearby at the corner of William and Riley Streets; and **Budget Rent A Car** (Tel. 33–4231), 93 William St.

Sydney

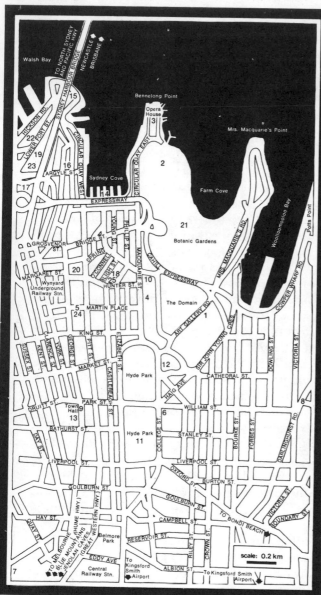

Map courtesy Qantas Airways Ltd.

1. Art Gallery
2. Government House
3. Opera House
4. Parliament House
5. Cenotaph
6. Australian Museum
7. Museum of Applied Arts
8. Kings Cross
9. Town Hall
10. Mitchell Library
11. Anzac War Memorial
12. St. Mary's Cathedral
13. St. Andrew's Cathedral
14. Circular Quay
15. Sydney Harbour Bridge
16. Argyle Art Centre
17. Observatory
18. Wentworth Hotel
19. The Rocks
20. Australia Square
21. Botanical Gardens
22. Garrison Church
23. Cadmans Cottage
24. General Post Office
25. QANTAS

Actually, you'll find Avis almost everywhere, especially at the airports. You may do better financially from **Letz Rent A Car** (Tel. 31–3178), 110 Darlinghurst Rd., near Kings Cross, or **Thrifty Rent A Car** (Tel. 357–5399), at 83 William St. Both of these have offices in other cities. Two local places are **Ajax Rent A Car** (Tel. 357–6791), 85 William St., or **Kings Cross Rent-A-Car** (Tel. 31–4610), 169 William St., corner of Forbes. (Be sure to see our remarks in Chapter 2.)

3. Local Transportation in Sydney

We covered rental cars in the previous section (and in Chapter 2), because we think of them as a mode of long-distance travel. In the city and around the immediate suburbs, "public transport" is usually safer and more convenient. (Note that sightseeing excursions are not covered here. You'll find those in Section 7.)

Get **taxicabs** either by hailing, telephoning in advance, or hopping into one at a cab rank. They look like normal cars except for the light on top.

At last report, rates were still 45 cents to drop the flag plus 32½ cents per kilometer (52 Australian cents a mile), which is comparable to familiar fares at home. There are a few extra charges—perhaps a telephone charge of about 40 cents, if you called them, 10 cents a bag if you're carrying suitcases, and maybe a small Sunday supplement charge for traveling on the Sabbath.

There's some debate about this, but we seldom tip a taxi anywhere in Australia. It's usually not expected, except in special situations. You may, in fact, sometimes find a driver in effect tipping *you*—rounding off the fare with a jolly, "That's all right, mate!" just to make the change even. (That kind of tipping, we do too.)

Taximen usually typify the Australian's determinedly egalitarian nature. A man taking a cab alone ought to be a "regular bloke" and get in up front beside the driver. If you're a woman, or there are two or more of any sex, it's all right to sit in the back.

With all the "New Australians" and students working their way through the University, etc., there may be no such animal as the typical Australian cabbie anymore. But if you get the kind we remember most fondly, you'll probably have an enjoyable trip as well as pick up a little home-spun philosophy with the latest slang and Strine along the way.

Even when such a driver isn't particularly cooperative, he may mitigate his obstinancy with a sardonic sense of humor. John O'Grady, who wrote Australia's all-time best seller about an Italian immigrant and his new Aussie mates—called *They're a Weird Mob*—once told another writer that when he returned from Europe, he was so pleased to be home that he hopped in the first taxi he saw and asked to be taken to his home in the suburb of Oatley, about 15 miles outside of Sydney.

"Oatley!" the driver exclaimed. "Gawd, I wouldn't go that far on me holidays!"

Some radio call cab companies we've called successfully include **TCS**—Taxis Combined Services (Tel. 33–3271), **Cumberland** (Tel. 637–0155), and **Legion** (Tel. 2–0918).

There's nothing wrong with the taxis, but you'll save more, of course, if you take advantage of the excellent **bus services** run by the Public Transport Commission of New South Wales (the PTC). Be sure to pick up an official map, which shows bus as well as train and ferry routes. (It's available at the PTC offices, corner of York and Margaret Streets, or at any newsstand or bookstore.) If you stay up the Cross (in the Kings Cross neighborhood), you'll probably find yourself catching No. 306 and 324 via William Street and George Street to Circular Quay, and returning on those numbers via Pitt and William. You can also take No. 387 and 388 to and from the Quay via William and Elizabeth Streets.

You pay by how far you go, at 10 cents an increment, and it seems to work out that most trips are between 20 and 40 cents. If there's a sign saying "pay as you enter," you hand your money to the driver. Otherwise you wait for a conductor to come around, and you tell him your destination. Yes, the driver or conductor will make change; things haven't come to the stage where they won't do that in Australia.

There's also a free bus (No. 777) which meanders through the central city area. The newer public buses are big, blue Mercedes diesels, by the way, and sometimes they are double-deckers, too. Older models may still have the green paint jobs. If you want to know how to get somewhere, phone the PTC's special bus information number (Tel. 2–0543).

You'll make better time under and above the ground on the electric **Sydney Rail Transport System**, also run by the PTC, and covered by the same map as above. There are seven lines: the North Shore Line, the Main North Line, the Western Richmond Line, the Southern Line, the Bankstown Line, the East Hills Line, and the Illawarra-Cronulla Line. All terminate at Central Station.

There's also a small and handy loop which runs mostly underground from Central Station through the city center with stations at Town Hall, Wynyard Park, Circular Quay, St. James Road, the Australian Museum, and back to Central Station. Called the City Circle Line, it allows you to travel between any two stations for 10 cents.

You may hear something about another suburban line called the Eastern Suburbs Railway, something in the works since the 1870's. (They finally introduced a bill to build it in 1915, passed the bill in 1946, began construction in 1948, ceased work in 1952, and began work again in 1968. Things came to a halt again for awhile. (A Sydney bus driver who keeps up with N.S.W. politics explained it all to us: "When the Liberals are in, they stop work on it; when Labor is in, they start work on it.")

Last year—surprise! The Eastern Suburbs Line finally opened, and it runs from Central Station, with stops at Martin Place, King's Cross, Edgecliff, and Bondi Junction. Eventually it will be extended to Kingsford and Mascot. But the railroad has been a sort of political football, being badly kicked around now for about a century.

If you just want to get on a train and wander, we'd recommend the North Shore Line. Take it as far as Hornsby, and you can come back via a different route. For information on how to get someplace by train, call the PTC's special railway number (Tel. 2–0942).

Probably the most fun division of the PTC is made up of the **ferry boats**, which seem to leap into the water every few minutes from Jetties 2 through 6 at Circular Quay. There are some special cruises we'll cover in Section 7, but here are some of the main ferry services used by Sydney's commuters and shoppers, and which may be enjoyed as a cheap cruise for visitors, too. Fares generally run between 25 and 75 cents. All leave from Circular Quay.

• *Manly Ferries.* Depart Jetty No. 3 for a 30-minute, 45-cent ride to Manly. Check the map; it's a long voyage for your money. Some of these vessels date back to before the war—World War I, that is!

• *Manly Hydrofoils.* Depart Jetty No. 5 for a 15-minute 70-cent ride to Manly. Avoid this one during rush hours. You may queue up for a longer time than you would use if you took the old ferry. The spray may keep you from seeing the harbor as well as you might like from the windows. There's an open deck topside, if you can take the wind. One possibility might be to take the ferry over to Manly and the hydrofoil back.

• *Mosman Ferry.* Departs Jetty No. 5, stopping at Cremorne Point, Musgrave Street, Old Cremorne Wharf, and Mosman.

• *Taronga Park Zoo Ferry.* Departs Jetty No. 5. Note that there is a combination ferry-bus-zoo admission ticket available, for perhaps $3.10.

• *Rose Bay Ferry.* Departs Jetty No. 6 Mondays through Fridays, afternoons only. (Not a PTC vessel.) Call Stannard Brothers Launch Services (Tel. 27–4155) for information.

There are several more. For most, information is available from the PTC (Tel. 27–9251). All newcomers to the capital of New South Wales

who've been out on the water—including us—agree: To leave Sydney
without making some kind of trip on the harbor is to have gone to Sydney without seeing it at all.

One last word for bargain hunters. For compulsive PTC travelers,
there are several special discounts available for heavy local travel. Most
of these are of interest mainly to commuters, but one or two others
stand out. One is the **Day Rover** ticket, which allows you to travel all day
on anything the PTC runs (except hydrofoils) for $2.

There's also something called the **Awayday** ticket, for $4, allowing
you a much wider radius into the countryside of N.S.W. on Sundays (50
cents for children). Stop by the PTC or call its Customer Service Bureau,
7 to 7, Mondays through Fridays, Tel. 290–2988.

4. The Sydney Hotel Scene

If you get into correspondence or conversation with Australian hotels,
make your needs quite specific and look out for problems in terminol-
ogy. A tub is a "bath" to most Australians. If you want a bathtub *and*
shower, be sure to say so. Otherwise you'll more likely get one or the
other.

Remember that if you want a baby's crib, you have to ask for a "cot."
A "double" to Australians will mean a double bed. If you want twin
beds, ask specifically for them. (But in this book, we generally use the
terms "double" or "twin" interchangeably to mean a room for two, regardless of the number of beds in the room.) "Facilities" in Australian is
a rather sappy euphemism for bathroom. "Tariffs" is a synonym for
room rates.

Note also that the word "hotel" in Australia is often taken to mean
merely the local pub, and many buildings you see labeled with the word
"hotel" are nothing more than drinking establishments. Under old laws,
they were required to rent out some rooms in order to have a liquor
license. Although that has been repealed, in some states, a hotel is still
not allowed to call itself a hotel unless it does have such a license. When
it is unlicensed, it will use the term "private hotel," "guest house,"
"lodge," "inn," or something similar. The term "motel," of course, means
that automobile travelers are catered to, although in recent years the
word has been going out of style in favor of terms like "motor hotel" or
"motor inn."

Some hotel miscellany:

• All opinions in this book are based on our own inspections and in-
vestigations of the establishments, of course. We could be wrong, and
probably are in some places.

• For some reason, Australian interior decorators seem to have a penchant for purple. (Not only in hotels, as a matter of fact, but in many other things. We once saw a man in a purple suit!)

• On checking out, leave enough time to look over your bill carefully. Australians seem to be scrupulously honest but often very sloppy in accounting. (Many hotel workers, too, are recent immigrants. The weakness in English may account for some confusion.) A frequent source of difficulty are those "pre-stocked" fridges from which you pay for the beers and mixes used, and the room maids have been given the job of counting the bottles. We try to avoid succumbing to this expensive temptation, although it *is* a convenience.

• As at home, phone calls from hotel rooms are expensive—35 to 50 cents. We have to make so many calls in every city that we stock up on 10-cent pieces and move our office into phone booths in the lobby whenever required.

• If you're *driving* throughout Australia, be sure to pick up the Accommodation Directory published by the National Roads & Motorists Association, even if you have to join the NRMA to do it. In Sydney, they're at 151 Clarence St. (Tel. 290 – 0123). In Melbourne, you can pick up a similar directory from the Royal Automobile Club for about $2, without joining. (See Melbourne Chapter.) Both publish separate directories for budget travel and for trailer parts ("caravan camping").

• Throughout this book, we estimate the price for two in a room. To convert these double prices into single rates, you might deduct about 10 percent.

• There is currently a severe hotel room shortage in Australia, particularly in Sydney. Better have your reservation nailed down tightly before you arrive.

EXPENSIVE HOTELS

These are Sydney's top accommodations, and most prices *begin* at about $55 for two at the present time. Unless otherwise noted, all these "international standard" establishments will have luxury amenities including central air conditioning and heating, color televisions, refrigerator, 110-volt razor outlets (besides 220-volt), electric coffee and tea makers, a free newspaper in the morning, room service, etc.

For a near-perfect combination of luxury, amenities, service and convenience, our top-ranking Sydney hotel is the **Wentworth** (Tel. 230 – 0700), which sits next to Qantas House just off Chifley Square and occupies the block from Phillip to Bligh Streets. Established in the government and financial district, the 448-room, 13-year-old structure with the semi-circular façade is also within walking distance of Circular Quay, the Opera House, and several historic sites. Large, red-carpeted lobby with comfortable leather furniture; several nice shops tucked away in the ground-floor arcades; many decorous and unusual restaurants, including the lunchtime-popular Garden Court, the Last Tram, the Impression Grill (with its changing slides), the Welcome Stranger, and the Ayers Rock Grill; good drinking locations called the Harbour Bar, the Flight Bar, and the Old Sydney Bar; tastefully appointed bedrooms and suites, mainly in solid colors; a few with tiny balconies; some rooms with shower; some with tub and shower; all with deluxe accouterments like color TV's, refrigerators, air conditioning; but windows openable, however, a welcome plus when the "southerly buster" blows through the city; several excellent suites at over $100 on the 17th floor. (You can reserve this Qantas-owned palace through that airline or by writing Box 2686, Sydney 2001.) We call the Wentworth "Number One" in Sydney's Big Six.

Many travelers will logically prefer the 43-story, five-year-old **Sydney Hilton** (Tel. 2–0610), and it is truly a superb hotel. Running between George and Pitt Streets, it is smack dab in the middle of the shopping and theater district: Massive, marble-floored upstairs lobby reachable by escalators from the streets or from the serpentine underground shopping complexes; heated outdoor rooftop swimming pool; gymnasium, including open-air jogging track; particularly lavish convention facilities; large number of dining, drinking, and entertainment locations including the gourmet, black-white-and-gold San Francisco Grill (8 kinds of oysters), the Terrace Cafe, the Market Place steak house, the 24-hour Hilton Coffee Shop, Juliana's supperclub and discotheque, and an incredible collection of pubs, among them the 1893 Marble Bar, the George Adams Bar, the wood-paneled Cedar Bar, the Palace Theatre Bar, and the brassy Americas Cup Bar. A total of 619 accommodations, with all sleeping rooms above the 20th floor, effectively reducing traffic noise; very comfortable bedrooms with thick carpets, double draperies, and all the top amenities; refrigerator pre-stocked with drinks and computerized charges automatically made when bottles are removed; good, high-pressure showers over tubs; lowest rates at $50 to more than five times that for the sumptuous suites. (Reservations through the Hilton reservation system or from the hotel at 259 Pitt St., Sydney 2000.) The Royal Automobile Club and similar organizations give the smooth-running Hilton five stars, an opinion in which we heartily concur.

Just as professionally polished as the previous two choices is the prestigious **Boulevard Hotel** (Tel. 357–2277). We might have ranked it even higher if we liked the immediate neighborhood better, but we think 90 William St. is a relative no-man's land in the auto sales district between the city and Kings Cross. (There was once a plan to turn the thoroughfare into an Antipodean Champs Elysee, a hope the hotel may have counted on.) Large chandeliered lobby in reds and purples; marble-lined reception desk; front doors often bolted against the gusts; garage entrance then open for guests; expensive Cafe Terrazzo at lobby level; well-regarded Palmer Grill one flight up; The Loft, a viewful cocktail and dancing club on the 25th floor; several other bars; indoor heated pool also way upstairs; impressive convention facilities. Total of 280 colorful, well-designed bedchambers; some wonderful overlooks to all of Sydney, the Botanic Gardens, the Opera House, Bridge, Harbor—the whole lot. Bob Hope and John Denver were among last year's celebrity guests, although they may never have strolled the street. (Reservations through the TraveLodge system in several countries, including the U.S.A., or by writing the hotel at Sydney 2011.) The boulevard outside may not be the handsomest, but the Boulevard inside is unsurpassed in Sydney.

Back in the center of the city, right next to Wynyard Gardens (and the Wynyard Station) is the traditional businessman's favorite, the 14-story **Menzies** (Tel. 2–0232). Its roots go back to the 1850's, although it was rebuilt top to bottom in 1964 and a new wing just opened in April 1979. It's the kind of a place where your shoes will be shined if left in the hallway overnight, and you'll find some fresh fruit in the room after checking in: Lots of heavy leather, timber, and warm colorings; large reception area with orange-patterned carpet and comfortable sitting room; 17 bars and six restaurants on the premises, including the Keisan Japanese Restaurant and the Fjord Room smorgasbord; pleasant rooms, some appearing small when the drapes are drawn; 8th through 14th floors slightly higher in price than 3rd to 7th; excellent tub/shower combinations. (Booking through the MFA Homestead organization, Utell International, or from the hotel at 14 Carrington St., Sydney 2000.) A convenient, comfortable choice.

The last two in the category are "up the Cross," and despite its huffy-puffy, hilly location, we think we far prefer the **Sebel Town House** (Tel. 358–3244) where General Manager Henry Rose keeps his staff hoppin' like kangaroos to make things happen for his guests. All together, the hotel probably has more of a distinct personality than any others in this group: Past the little Japanese garden and waterfall to a small lobby; inviting Town House restaurant to one side (crêpes a specialty); cocktail bar with 8 × 10 glossies of local celebs who've come to call; sunny rooftop swimming pool with excellent panoramas of the skyline; poolside food and drink service; large guest rooms, also with good views (usually); excellent furnishings; patterned wallpaper; some king-size beds; children under 12 free in the parents' rooms; draperies and black-out curtains (handy for jet-lag recovery); well-arranged bathrooms (with lots of shelf space, unusual in Australia). (Reservations from Mr. Rose—tell him we sent you—at the hotel, 23 Elizabeth Bay Road, Sydney 2011.) The Town House may seem just a bit out of town, but she's just as sophisticated as her big city cousins.

The **Hyatt Kingsgate** (Tel. 357–2233) has two strong points. One, its location at the very gate to King's Cross is a plus to those who want to dip their toes daily into the spicy sauce of the neighborhood. Number two is the availability of some of the best and most dramatic views over the city that can be imagined. We spent an hour gazing and photographing the wide-angle north-western exposure from our room. The room itself, however, was no more than just okay. The bathroom seemed cramped and we had to coax the water out of the shower head, the light bulbs were dim, the radio didn't work very well. Also, we had trouble locking our door and some of the furniture was broken. To be fair, however, there are many refurbished rooms in the hotel which are better (next time we'd ask specifically for one of those) and prices may begin at slightly lower rates than the others in this group. The layout of the lobby was inconvenient, but the staff was friendly. Altogether we call it not a bad hotel, but far from our favorite in the category.

MEDIUM PRICE HOTELS

These establishments, which will run about $35 to $50 for two, are generally comfortable for everyone. The TV may or may not be in color; some have fridges, some don't; views can be relatively limited, etc. Australians might class most of the following as "motels" or "motor hotels." For most practical purposes, there is little difference, at least in Sydney.

The only place we went through top to bottom at the price level, and which is still in downtown Sydney, is the nicely maintained, well-equipped **Wynyard TraveLodge** (Tel. 2–0254), at York and Margaret Streets, convenient to just about everything in the commercial area: A small lobby in black, white, and orange, sometimes a little crowded; pleasant coffee-shop-style Number 9 restaurant and Howzat Bar also downstairs; viewsome Outrigger Restaurant way up beside the rooftop swimming pool. Some of the 210 units with excellent views; some blocked by new construction next door; refurbishment should be completed this year, leaving nearly all rooms with color TV's and many extras. (Reservations through the TraveLodge network or at the hotel, 9 York St., Sydney 2000.) The Wynyard is a wynner in the group.

In the King's Cross environs, a cylindrical hotel called the **Gazebo** (Tel. 358–1999) has been a favorite for the past decade: Pleasant, open location next to Fitzroy Gardens and its fuzzy fountain at the opposite end of Darlinghurst Road from Kingsgate; bustling reception area in bright orange and reds; attractive Pavilion Room restaurant with some outdoor tables (Beef Stroganoff $7?); heated, roof-top pool with liquor and food service; all air-conditioned rooms with TV, radio, fridge, coffee and tea-making equipment, etc.; each room with a walk-out balcony and many with excellent views (north and northwest the best); specify bath or shower. Gen. Mgr. Silvio Gmur feels his house is large enough to offer all the modern conveniences while still small enough to be friendly. (Reservations from the hotel at 2 Elizabeth Bay Road, King Cross, N.S.W. 2011.) For this area, the Gazebo is a charming garden retreat.

There are three nice choices up Macleay Street from Kings Cross in the Potts Point area, all relatively comfortable. The baronial, 7-story **Chateau Commodore** (Tel. 35 2500) attempts to bring the flavor of Europe to Potts Point in the middle of a tree-lined residential block at a bus stop. Small, dark-wood lobby guarded by suits of armor and crowned by heavy chandeliers; two restaurants spanning culinary gulfs—from the Caves de Montparnasse to Marty's Steak House (cuts for $3?); Grecian swimming pool on the roof; bedrooms in solid colors, heavy on the reds and yellows; nicely designed showers (apparently few tubs); short on vast vistas, but pleasant aspects from the semi-circular balconies. Some rooms are priced higher than the category. (Reservations from the hotel at 14 Macleay St., Sydney 2011). A chateau it's not, but it's still *tres joli* for the price.

Down the street, the pool-less **Marquee Sheraton Hotel** (Tel. 358–1955) boasts a tiny, uncomfortable and too-purple lobby, but nicer rooms upstairs than you might have suspected: A few good views from the upper floors; showers but no bathtubs; all rooms with color television; some with small balconies. (Reservations through the Sheraton or Flag chains or at the hotel, 40 Macleay St., P.O. Box 149, Sydney 2011.) Respectable, but not much like a Sheraton.

Many would prefer the nearby **Macleay Street TraveLodge** (Tel. 358–2777), a nine-story entry with a rooftop pool, and many rooms have an excellent panorama north to the Opera House, etc. Rooms are generally well equipped, although some may seem a little more sterile than the previous Sheraton hotel. Try for units on the ninth floor, but be sure they're not yet priced out of the category. (Reservations through other TraveLodges or from this one at 26–34 Macleay St., Potts Point, N.S.W. 2011.) Not bad at all.

The brand-new **Cambridge Inn** (Tel. 211–5499) opened in mid-1979 at 212 Riley St., an unusual but not inconvenient site near the Ansett Airlines bus terminal. The 15-story hotel includes Cyrano's, a licensed restaurant, and rents rooms for $38 to $50 double.

BUDGET ACCOMMODATIONS

We hope there will still be several hotel rooms in Sydney selling for under $35 for two. Now that the old Welcome Inn has been razed, the best in this category might be the **Canberra Oriental** (Tel. 358–3155), up the Cross, *if* they can hold the line on their rates. (The best rooms are $40 or so, now, but we include it here for the lower-price models, down to less than $25: Convenient Kings Cross location at 223 Victoria St.; generally older clientele; smallish, light-wood lobby with breakfast room off to the side (serving until 9); fresh flowers here and there; a cantilevered stairway to the upper regions; total of about 300 rooms hither and yon, some still without private bathrooms (although they at least have washbasins and hot & cold water); the rooms *with* private "facilities" also have televisions, telephones, coffee and tea makers, etc. (Other rooms can rent TV's for an extra charge.) There's a roof garden for sunbathing and a nice panorama toward the harbor (a view shared by a few rooms). This hotel may still offer single rooms, at prices perhaps ranging between $10 and $16, including breakfast. (Rates may change, so ask for up-to-date price sheets from the hotel. Reservations from the above address at Sydney 2011.) Manager A. C. Allen runs a smooth operation for the tariffs asked.

Another Kings Cross address (or actually, Potts Point) is that old GI R&R favorite, the **Texas Tavern** (Tel. 358–1211), now under new ownership at 44 Macleay St.: An amazing collection of restaurants, bars, and discos on the premises, catering to drop-in and night-time trade; friendly folks at the reception area; 130 bedrooms scattered higgledy-piggledy through the building; many of them renovated with TV's, fridges, air conditioners, etc., but perhaps a few shilling-in-the-slot heaters remaining; doubles around $32; singles around $27, both with breakfast. The Texas Tavern is in transition, to be sure, but Harry Calleia told us he has Texas-size plans for the spread. Good luck, pardner!

If you must have a low-budget address near the city center, the logical choice may be the **Gresham** (Tel. 29–3266) at the corner of Druitt & York Streets, across from Town Hall. More than 107 years old, its façade is protected by the National Trust. The rooms are simple but clean, no TV's (there's a separate lounge with a telly), but perhaps a Flit gun at the ready atop the wardrobes. Some chambers with private baths, some without; short on heaters, but electric blankets provided when needed. We liked No. 26, a large, sunny corner room, but we suspect that light sleepers might find the traffic disturbing when the windows are open. If you're lucky, you'll snag a double for $25, with breakfast, or a single at around $15. You'll carry your own luggage, of course, but the tiny elevator will help. (For reservations, write the hotel at 147 York St.) Though no longer young, Grandma Gresham holds her own at the price level.

The nearby **Coronation** (Tel. 61–8362) might be all right, but we wonder about their public relations. There was absolutely no one available to show us the rooms. It's at Seven Park St., but we can't recommend what we can't see.

Three other possibilities in this price range, but which we didn't get to personally are the **Great Southern** (Tel. 211–4311) at 717 George St., near the Central Station; the **Hyde Park** (Tel. 61–6323) at 231 Elizabeth St., across from the park and the Anzac War Memorial; and the **Grand** (Tel. 232–3755), at 30 Hunter St., near Australia Square.

The **York** (Tel. 29–2613), at 46 King St., was our mistake. We had one depressing inside room there once, and only once. It has a nice pub downstairs, but that's as far as we'll go next time. Virtually last and least there is the Salvation Army chain hotel called in Sydney, as it is over most of Australia, the **People's Palace** (Tel. 211–5777) at 404 Pitt St., near Central Station. You may still get twins for under $20 and singles for $10 there. But it's basic!

Youth Hostels? You must be a member, of course, and if you haven't taken care of that detail, apply to the Australian Youth Hostels Association (Tel. 29–6728), 383 George St., Sydney, N.S.W. 2000. The Sydney hostel itself (Tel. 692–0747), which will set you back about $4 a bed, is a century-old mansion at 28 Ross St. (corner of St. Johns Road) in the western suburb of Forest Lodge, near the university.

Rooms in New South Wales? Since we have not been able to inspect these personally, we'll mention some based on recommendations made to us and other sources in our sightseeing section. (Also, see our note on the NRMA Accommodation Directory at the beginning of this section.) Ski lodges in the Snowy Mountains, however, will be found in our Canberra Chapter, since they're much closer to that city than they are to Sydney.

5. Dining and Restaurants in Sydney

Once was a time that the cuisine of Australia was the cuisine of Liverpool and Houndsditch. There were certain local variations like carpetbagger steak (beef with those wonderful Sydney Rock oysters), meat pies (with a dash of ketchup squirted under the crust), and Pavlova (a rich meringue dessert). These still exist, but today the kitchens of Australia are the kitchens of the world, brought to the country by the tremendous wave of "New Australians" who have immigrated to the country over the past 30 years. Today, Australian cosmopolites can dine on authentic cuisine from all parts of the world, at least in the large cities.

Australian wine. A few words about the fermented grape, which now belongs to Australia as much as it does to France and California. Wines are very good and very reasonable, and no serious meal can be enjoyed without it. The whites are particularly excellent, world-class wines. The reds, though some are a little earthy as compared to their U.S. and French counterparts, are nevertheless inexpensive and absolutely enjoyable—certainly much better than the average *vin ordinaire* served in restaurants in France.

Wineries are in three main areas in Australia:

• The Hunter River Valley, near Pokolbin and Rothbury, 60 miles north of Sydney in New South Wales.

• Throughout much of the state of Victoria, particularly at Rutherglen on the N.S.W. border.

• And the best grape growing area of all, South Australia, mainly in the Barossa Valley (Clare, Coonawarra, etc.), not far from Adelaide. About three-fourths of Australia's total wine output is produced here.

(Some wines are produced along the Swan River in Western Australia. There are also small operations in Queensland and Tasmania.)

White wines. Look for these varieties: Rhine Riesling (and other Rieslings), Moselle, Mosel, White Burgundy, Semillon, Chablis, Traminer, and Great Western Champagne.

Red wines. The best types are Claret, Cabernet Sauvignon, Shiraz (Hermitage), and Pinot Noir. (Red Burgundies may seem a little harsh.)

There are also a few nice sherries, and acceptable ports, and, of course, some brandies, which are wine byproducts.

Some of the more outstanding wineries are represented by the following well-known brands: Elliott, Hardy's, Hungerford Hill, Huntington, Leo Buring, Lindeman's, McWilliam's, Mildara, Orlando, Penfolds, Rosemount, Rothbury, Seppelt, Stanley, Tulloch, Tyrrell's, Wyndham,

Wynns, and Yalumba. (Nevertheless, there are many more good small operations tucked here and there throughout the country.)

Prior to World War II, Australia was almost strictly a beer-drinking country. Many oenophobic Aussies looked down on any wine, which they lumped together as "plonk." (Probably after learning of *vin blanc* during the two wars in France.)

The beers are also excellent (we discuss those further on in our own "pub crawl"). But now that Australian wines have come into their own in the past few years, you'll even find them stocked in limited quantities in Canada, England, and the U.S.

Many Australian restaurants are not "licensed"—i.e., they cannot serve alcohol. These are known as BYO restaurants, allowing you to "Bring Your Own." Even when a Sydney restaurant does receive its license, it may still invite you to cart in your favorite wine, if they might not have it in their own cellar. In some BYO's, you place your order and then run next door to the pub or wine shop to choose your bottle while your meal is being prepared. (Most Australian wine in the shop will cost you from $2 to $4 a bottle. The markup will be about 80 to 90 percent in licensed restaurants.)

AUSTRALIAN AND COSMOPOLITAN RESTAURANTS

One of the most fun of the old-style Australian restaurants is the **Argyle Tavern** (Tel. 27–7782), at 22 Argyle St. in the historic Rocks district. In the rough-brick and candle-lit atmosphere, you might try Convict Broth and then roast beef while joining in the Australian bush ballad singalongs. Dinner will run around $10 and a one-price lunch may be available for $2.50 or so. (Closed Sunday evenings.) Fun for the right crowd.

For breakfast at any hour (they never close) in the same general neighborhood, look into **Pancakes on the Rocks** (Tel. 27–6371), at 10 Hickson Rd. There are a lot more than pancakes on the menu, of course, many with a bizarre touch—would you believe buckwheat mignon, with Hollandaise Sauce? (We haven't tried that.)

Another pancake breakfast we enjoyed was at the **Bourbon & Beefsteak Bar** (Tel. 357–1215) at 24 Darlinghurst Rd. in King's Cross. The service was excellent, but with Australian-style bacon, of course (just cut off the rine). We haven't tried the beef steak and bourbon at the Bourbon & Beefsteak, but we understand they make a pretty fair imitation of an American steakhouse in the evenings.

A high-quality luncheon choice, for those in the know, is not far from Circular Quay down a tiny alley called Bulletin Place. There at No. 16 –18 is Len Evans Wines Pty. Ltd., and almost in a secret upstairs hiding place is the **Beef Room** (Tel. 27–4413, and *do* reserve. We didn't, but were uncommonly lucky.). Apparently furnished and equipped with the castoffs from a fleet of old sailing ships (the sandstone brick walls were carried as ballast), the Beef Room offers a one-price lunch—perhaps $8 by now—including two glasses of Evans' own wine. There's a serve-yourself fruit and cheese bar as well as sailor-size helpings of succulent roast beef, Yorkshire pudding, and lots of other trimmings. The "business lunch" is only served Monday to Friday. (Men, wear a tie in here.) Evans himself is a wine writer of considerable note. We never met him, but we'll be back to his Beef Room again.

One of Australia's highest—in altitude as in charges—is the 47th story location of the **Summit** (Tel. 27–9777). It revolves, of course, once around in one hour and 45 minutes. A la carte, you'll be lucky to leave with a bill of around $25 each. The one-price smorgasbord may be a better deal. Book a table—windowside or nothing—for a half hour before sunset for the most scenic go-around.

A nice little casual place for lunch only downtown is the below-street-level **South Australia Wine Bar** (also known as the Adelaide Wine Celler, Tel. 31–6908). Designed as public relations for that southern state, the tiny niche has several nice quiches, sandwiches, etc., on the blackboard menu in the $1.50 to $3.50 range. We had our quiche with the house white, then a half-litre of Hardy's Riesling for about $2. Go in at 12 to avoid the crush (which begins at about 12:30 in Sydney).

Coffee shops? The **Hilton Coffee Shop** is pleasant, American-like, and certainly pricey. We had a large roast beef sandwich called the Marble Bar for $4.50. (One sour memory was that this place tried to up our Diners Club bill by one Australian dollar after we left the premises. DC later discounted it, of course, when we pointed out the action.) We prefer the orange-and-white striped little **Number 9** restaurant in the TraveLodge for the type. There are light lunches in the $3 to $4.50 range. One we definitely don't like is **Penny's Place**, a 24-hour-bore in the Hyatt. Our table was never clean, and the service was so offhand as to be barely believed.

The **Cahill's** chain of cafeterias are reasonable and reasonably good. Last, if you're looking for American food, well, you'll find McDonald's and Colonel Sanders all over the place. Even Pizza Huts have mushroomed and pepperonied all of Australia.

CHINESE FARE

On Campbell Street, almost next door to the Capitol Theatre is the **Yick On Yuen** (Tel. 212–5958). This family operation is consistently cheap and good. Try the fresh fish in ginger or the roast pork with pickles. No credit cards. Open daily for lunch and dinner.

A more prestigious oriental establishment is the **Mandarin** (Tel. 211–0859), opposite the Barclay Theatre at 754 George St. We haven't tried it yet. Otherwise, just wander the three blocks of Dixon Street and pick one of the dozens of Chinese establishments there. **The Hingara** (Tel. 212–2169) at No. 82 is cheap and good for the hungries. Most of these are open daily.

CONTINENTAL AND FRENCH CUISINE

The little **Le Cafe Nouveau** (Tel. 33–3377), which you'll find in Paddo, but you won't find in the yellow pages, was sought out and praised by James Beard in his syndicated column last year. This Gallic entry at 495 Oxford St., near Moore Park Road, doesn't have to advertise. It's super elegant, super expensive, and has a very changeable menu with many seasonal specialties. Beard had kind words for the steamed fresh tuna with poached oysters and champagne sauce, the cold lamb with pistachio dressing, and the fillets of beef and veal in a watercress-flecked marrow sauce. He didn't say how it all added up, but we'll guess you won't see the door again without leaving $25—plus the wine. (Which did Beard have? A Rosemont Traminer Riesling—those are two grapes blended—and for the red, a Penfold's Grange Hermitage, perhaps Australia's best Shiraz last year.)

Almost as top drawer is the **Pavilion on the Park** (Tel. 232–1322), opposite the Art Gallery in The Domain. Again, the specialties change. The outdoorsy feeling here is just as exciting—and a little less expensive—at lunch. Still, uninhibited diners find themselves toting $20, even for a noonday meal!

Some prefer **Au Chabrol** (Tel. 31–2551), 368 Victoria St. in Paddington. This informal, blackboard menu nook is also BYO, but there's a liquor store around the corner on Oxford St. Try the veal in white wine sauce. (No credit cards.)

In the same general neighborhood, at Taylor Square, we had a happy meal at **The French Restaurant** (Tel. 31–3605). Candles reflect off the stucco walls, and there may be a live accordionist in another niche someplace. The house paté is fine, they trot out excellent French-style steaks with Bearnaise sauce and le works, or an excellent half chicken is the

Spatchcoq au vin Bourguignon. We experienced friendly and efficient service and emerged for not much more than $10 per person (plus wine). Fondly remembered.

An even less-expensive *succes fou* for us was **Le Greedy Pig** (Tel. 31–5675), which specializes in French country-style cooking. The combo BYO/licensed place gives you the choice of taking your own grog or theirs. There's a Provençal atmosphere with exposed wood beams, cafe curtains, etc., and our dinner for two—fillet of sole in herb sauce and beef with *fines herbes* came to less than $13 total. This little restaurant, long known as Le Marseille, may be a little hard to find at the corner of Stanley and Riley Streets, a block off William. But for the combination of price/cuisine, we think it's well worth searching out.

On Albion Street, just around the corner from all those movie palaces on George Street, is another tiny bargain, **La Guillotine** (Tel. 26–1487). Specializing in dozens of kinds of omelettes, there is nonetheless one daily *plat du jour* that we've never heard anything but praise for. You'll dine from $5 to $10 per person here and still have enough time and money left to catch the show.

ITALIAN RISTORANTES

We've had good luck in the nether regions of the **Arriverderci** (Tel. 357–6809) at 77 William St., hidden under the chassis of one of those automobile shops there. Walk past the dramatically presented antipasto table to about two dozen red-and-white, cloth-topped tables. Lots of fishnets and bottles hanging around, and the stucco and stone walls bearing that inevitable mural of the harbor at Naples (or was it Sorrento?). This is an inexpensive trattoria where you can keep the bill even lower by choosing only the entrees, if you want. We enjoyed our Scallopine al burro e limone, which came garnished with peas and mushrooms. (Closed Sundays.) *Molte bene!*

Three other budget Italian entries were recommended by Leo Schofield, the knowledgeable Sydney food writer in a recent article in the *Bulletin*: **Bill and Toni** (no telephone) at 74 Stanley St., offering basic Italian *piattos* for low *prezzos*, the **No Names** (also no phones), 2 Chapel Lane, which is often crowded (Bill & Toni's takes the overflow), and **La Rustica** (Tel. 569–5824), somewhat far out in the western suburb of Leichardt. (Go early.)

More expensive, but on our list for a try, is the **Buona Sera Restaurant** (Tel. 358–1778) at 89 Macleay St., near Kings Cross. (Closed Sundays.) Let us know if you get here first.

Finally, we're not sure if you can call it Italian, really, but the pasta is cheap, hot, and some say good at the **Old Spaghetti Factory** at 80 George St. on the Rocks. There's a fascinating collection of Victorian antiquerie, including a genuine old Bondi tram.

GREEK CUISINE

Newly opened is the **Ethnic** (Tel. 26–5393), at 349 Pitt St., not far from the YMCA. Chef Tassos specializes in Lamb and souvlaki and other Hellenic delights, but you can also get some good honest seafood, perhaps with lemon sauce, for lunches beginning at around $4. And an old reliable on the Greek scene is the **Iliad** (Tel. 61–7644), not far away at 126 Liverpool St., off Pitt. (Try the Ducklings in sour cherries.)

INDIAN RESTAURANTS

We keep hoping that Sydney, like London, will be eventually blessed with an abundance of Indian restaurants. There are few, however, although one we tried, **The Bombay**, (Tel. 358–3946), was quite tasty. Just 9 tables in a tiny spot at 33 Elizabeth Bay Road, near the Sebal Town House Hotel, and when every chair is occupied, service can be frenzied. But the selection of curries may make it worth it. A complimentary glass of sherry comes with every meal. There were several kinds of Indian breads, and a good selection of wines. We might go again.

LEBANESE FARE

There are several of these around, but one of the newest and best is out at Bondi, at 86 Gould St. **Ya Habibi** (Tel. 30–4605) features spit-roasted lamb and things like that, along with an occasional belly dancer on Saturday nights. An old favorite is a little closer in, **Emad's** (Tel. 698–2631), at 298 Cleveland St. in Surry Hills. The decor is undistinguished, but the skewered meat offerings are delicious. If it's closed, look around; Cleveland Street is becoming the Beirut of Sydney, at least as far as restaurants and cafes are concerned.

SEAFOOD RESTAURANTS

Sydney's two top ocean restaurants are both named Doyle's, and they're not really in Sydney. Our last trip, we stopped at the one closer to the city, **Doyle's at Rose Bay** (Tel. 36–4187, but there are no reservations.) Basically it's a box-shaped dining room that extends over the water with no distinguished decor to detract from the views—or the viands. Unfortunately the whiting was off the menu our night. Our $7 snapper fried in batter was great, but this is the place to try the fine Australian fish, John Dory (known as Peterfisch, in Germany). Dining companions David and Ellen Ward let us have a bite of theirs, and it was perfect! One in our group ordered the flounder, which was a little less successful. We chose this site to try some Australian champagne—Seppelts Great Western Imperial Reserve—and fell in love with it. There's often a queue at popular hours, here, but we call the Rose Bay Doyle's worth waiting for. (No credit cards.)

Doyle's on the Beach (Tel. 337–2007), at Watson's Bay, is more scenic, perhaps, but we haven't sat down. Meanwhile, we might mention that columnist James Beard dined there recently and reported to his readers about a "great feast of heaps of steamed mussels, a cold platter of the famous mud crab, blue swimmers, and prawns, and finally white-fleshed, delicate jewfish, batter-dipped and fried, all consumed with plenty of white wine." Mmm. We're trying out Watson's Bay ourselves next time!

• A last note for serious Sydney diners. A valuable listing of nearly 200 restaurants is the annual volume entitled *Eating Out in Sydney*, by Leo Schofield and Rupert Rosenblum, published locally. It's about $4, well spent.

6. Sightseeing in Sydney (and in N.S.W.)

Sydney is a city where it's relatively easy to organize sightseeing excursions, at least to most of the musts. Two important areas—The Rocks and Downtown Sydney—can be efficiently encompassed in walking tours, and ones where you can mercifully cut out those "points of interest" which are not very interesting to you.

THE ROCKS

Sydney's oldest commercial/residential neighborhood, west of Sydney Cove, has been given a laconic name which belies the rich historical and cultural significance of the area. It was here in this winding, hilly area, and against its stone cliffs that soldiers and convicts splashed together the first wattle-and-daub structures of the new colony in the late eighteenth century.

Later it became the squalid slum that eventually fostered the disastrous plague on Sydney in 1900. Scoured and whitewashed from top to bottom, The Rocks then went through a series of other adventures. It was both the haunt of rollicking sailors and the home of wealthy families, but the area fell on hard times again until a few years ago.

Now the Sydney Cove Redevelopment Authority is restoring the Rocks to a position of elegant rusticity and a fascinating place to twist and turn through tiny streets and up and down stairways, peeking into the windows and doorways of the past.

There's only one place to start, at the museum and the **Rocks Visitors Centre** (Tel. 27–4972), at 104 George St., an old court building near the Overseas Passenger Terminal. They'll have suggested walking tours, maps, and all sorts of information available. Don't miss the excellent sound and slide show in the back-room theater, which will give you some dramatic feeling for the area's significance.

Other spots in The Rocks include the nearby little **Cadman's Cottage**, an 1816 stone house that is now the oldest existing structure in Sydney. There's a small maritime museum inside.

At **Argyle Terrace** is the largest restored area of The Rocks. Wander through the arcade of shops that wind around and about the **Argyle Arts Center** (Tel. 241–1853). It's a hefty climb, but some say well worth it, under the expressway and up Observatory Hill to Fort Philip and the **Observatory** (Tel. 241–2478; tours by appointment only). It was built originally to observe incoming ships, but now it's pointed toward the stars.

From here, as well as from many locations in The Rocks below, you can see Sydney's favorite old "coat hanger," the **Sydney Harbour Bridge**. Opened in 1932, it was to have had the longest single span in the world at 1,670 feet, but some more obscure bridge in the U.S.A. bettered it by about five feet just before the Australian project was completed. More than 140,000 vehicles a day now cross the bridge, most of them inch by bloody-inch during rush hours.

A monument to deficit spending, the bridge's price tag once read $9.5 million, but what with interest, inflation, etc., $11 million is still owed on it! They say it may be paid off about 1983. Built during the Depression, the bridge was also known as the iron lung because it kept thousands of construction workers and their families breathing through those hard times.

CENTRAL SYDNEY

What Americans would call "Down Town," Sydney-siders generally refer to as "The City," the compact core area which is officially Sydney. Beginning at a terminus for train, bus, and ferry transportation, right at the end of Sydney Cove, we are at **Circular Quay.** Ruth Park calls it "Sydney's doorstep" in her delightful and exhaustive *Companion Guide to Sydney.*

The quay is no longer circular, however, having long ago been squared off and then fitted out with five ferry boat wharves. It is here where you go to board the boats to the zoo or to take the hydrofoil to Manly.

Very much a part of the background, and easily approachable after a 10-minute stroll, is the famous **Sydney Opera House** (Tel. 2–0588). Designed by the Danish architect Joern Utzon, the opera house took 14 years to build and was finally completed in 1973 at a cost of $102 million. (The original estimate was $12 million.) Incredibly, it's all paid for, due to a unique and very Australian system of financing via public lottery. Still a controversial structure (some say it's more a piece of sculpture than a building), it made architectural history by overcoming seemingly insurmountable construction problems. Some like to speak of the opera house as sails billowing in tile. Unkind critics are apt to call it an orgy of turtles. In any case, it's not a single theater but a huge complex for the performing arts. There are four main rooms—the Concert Hall, the Opera Theatre, the Drama Theatre, and the Music Room. Besides that, add several exhibition areas, two restaurants and six theater bars.

You may not wander the 4½-acre opera house unaccompanied. At this writing, guided tours are given every half hour between 9:00 a.m. and 4:00 p.m., seven days a week, for $1.50 (adults) and 50 cents (children). Be ready to register several kilometers of stair climbing and to carry away baskets of facts and figures.

The Opera House squats on **Bennelong Point**, named for an Aborigine befriended by Governor Philip. Bennelong had just a little hut here when he lived on the site.

Walk from Circular Quay up Loftus Street to **Macquarie Place**, a cool triangle-shaped patch of green which features the 1818 obelisk from which all roads were once measured. There, too, is the anchor from the *Sirius*, the flagship of the First Fleet.

If you move up Bridge Street to the end, you'll have partly penetrated the **Royal Botanic Gardens**. You might save the vast gardens and the wonderful collections of statues, flowers, palms, ponds, and swans for another day, but have a look at least at the castle-like **Conservatorium of Music**. Designed by Francis Greenway, the convict father of Australian architecture, the 1817 alabaster structure was to be a magnificent stable for the governor's horses. Lunchtime and twilight concerts are often given at the school today. **Government House**, the official mansion of the Queen's representative to New South Wales, may not be visited, but you'll glimpse its ghostly towers and garrets from several locations in the area.

Strolling south along **Macquarie Street**, an old thoroughfare laid out and named by Governor Macquarie himself, you'll pass many of the historic buildings of Sydney. One of the few elegant century-old town houses left is now the headquarters of the Royal Australian Historical Society. On the eastern side of the street, first is the **Mitchell Library**, or the Library of N.S.W. (Tel. 221–1388), the center for Australiana research, then **Parliament House**. One wing of this building, as well as part of the next door **Old Mint** were sections of the famous "Rum Hospital," built from 1811 to 1816 at no charge by three emancipists in exchange for a lucrative license to sell rum. And next door to that is the present **Sydney Hospital**, a late Victorian Building. Past the law courts and Hyde Park Barracks, Macquarie Street ends at **Queens Square**.

Two full blocks of **Hyde Park** are filled with fountains and shady trees. To the east rise the Gothic revival spires of **St. Mary's Cathedral**. Also bordering the park, just past William Street, is the free **Australian Museum** (Tel. 339–8111), open daily until 5:00 p.m. Most of the exhibits seemed rather hum-drum to us, with the strong exception of the Aboriginal and South Pacific rooms.

Walk west on Bathurst Street or Park Street to George. The **Town Hall**, flanked by St. Andrew's Cathedral, is one of Sydney's great civic buildings, constructed like many from local sandstone in true Victorian style. In the next block north on George, across from the Hilton, is the façade of the 1893 **Queen Victoria Building** which creates an entire Byzantine block between Druitt and Market Streets.

Near here (at Market and Pitt Streets) is the brand-new **Centrepoint Tower** with its steel basket of four floors that has been jacked up to 902 feet at the rate of about 28 feet per week. It's now the country's tallest structure. The restaurant at the top was not yet open at this writing.

Continuing north, past stores and shopping arcades, you eventually arrive at **Martin Place**, a wide street recently converted to a majestic mall right in the center of the city. The ornate and gargantuan **General Post Office** is there, an Italianesque creation Sydney-siders seem strangely proud of. Mainly, Martin Place seems to be the headquarters of the banking district.

Another couple of blocks along George Street brings us to the round building called **Australia Square**, 50 stories above the street. You can zip to the observation deck called the Sky Walk via a special elevator for $1.20 or so. It's a great spot for photographs of the harbor and environs.

ELSEWHERE IN SYDNEY

The following are listed in alphabetical order, since it would be impractical to design a tour to encompass them all on a logical circuit.

Southeast of the city, the **Bondi Beaches** are the most famous and one of several sites for that strange display of shoreline masculinity called the surf carnival, held in the summer time (December, January, and February, generally). The precision march by lifeguards while wearing full bathing attire—including color-coded caps—may seem ridiculous, but the launching of the surf-boat contests is difficult and thrilling. (The lifeguards are also excellent at their job.) If you're not going into the water, have a seat and a drink at the Bondi Hotel. (Bondi—now pronounced "bond-eye," was originally an Aboriginal onomatopoetic word— "*Boon*-dee"—the sound of a heavy surf breaking on the shore.) It's 25 minutes from Sydney by buses No. 379, 380, 387, and 389.

Botany Bay, as we mentioned before, is the site of the international airport. It was also the port of call of James Cook in 1770, and you can visit the Captain Cook's Landing Place Museum (Tel. 668–9548). It's in the park at Kurnell on the southern peninsula, if you want to "have a Captain Cook" yourself. (That's "take a look" in rhyming slang.) Also, there's a fort on Bare Island built during a Russian invasion scare in 1885. You can reach that via the suburbs of Chifley and La Perouse (Bus No. 394.)

Back near the city—actually between it and Woolloomooloo—lies the **Domain and the Art Gallery**. The grassy common is open to all ("public domain" to be sure), and the favorite spot for weekend soap box orators. Within its green surroundings is the Art Gallery of New South Wales (Tel. 221–2100), which has an excellent collection of late nineteenth and early twentieth century Australian paintings, plus examples of Aboriginal and Melanesian art. It's open daily for a small admission charge.

And while we're thinking about nearby Woolloomooloo for a moment, be prepared for "double-talk" in Australia. The Aussies sometimes seem to bubble with doubles, when reciting numbers or letters. Would you believe it's spelled "Double-U, double-O, double-L, double-O, M, double-O, L, double-O?" The same goes for phone numbers; thus, 299–2211 becomes "two-double-nine, double-two, double-one." Try to say it any other way, and a telephone operator may correct you!

At the very end of the Domain is Mrs. Macquarie's Chair, an enormous piece of sandstone where the early governor's wife supposedly liked to sit at the end of the three-mile road she is also credited with.

About a quarter mile north of this point, out in the harbor, is **Fort Dennison** (Tel. 2–0545, Ext. 292), more popularly known as Pinchgut Island, supposedly nicknamed in honor of ill-fed convicts who once were confined there. You can visit the island and its little museum, but you must book in advance at the phone number above.

Far across the bay, and accessible by ferry from Jetty No. 5, is **Hunter's Hill**, a mid-nineteenth-century settlement of cottages along a narrow peninsula. The streets are a popular stroll on a sunny Sunday.

At the head of William Street begins the neighborhood of **King's Cross**, which for years has had the reputation of being Sydney's "Greenwich Village" (or Sydney's Soho, if London is the comparison). Much of it is, indeed, Sydney on the seamy side. Here are the strippers, the female impersonators, and the like. Ruth Park's poetic description of The Cross is unsurpassed:

"It is a weird, electric place by night, exorbitant, often as bent as a bicycle wheel, offering venal and dubious pleasures as well as four-cornered ones. It swims out of the dusk like a blob of spilled oil, all rainbows and reflections, and gamesome groups of middle-aged tourists, noosed with cameras and excitedly speculating whether the epicene youth in an exoskeleton of painted leather is a drug pusher.

"Upon these aliens, the austerely clad old voluptuary spidering in the coffee bar smiles his abstracted scholar's smile; the adolescent prostitute heaves up her Luxaflex eyelashes and looks right through them. The boy sitting on his kidneys beside the El Alamein Fountain, soaked with the spray, does not even glance their way as they boldly shoot off their flashes and take his picture for a souvenir."

The Cross also has many good restaurants, an often interesting night life, and it is a pleasant walk by day, too. (At night, keep to the main, well-lighted drag.) (There are several buses from the Quay to the Cross, including Numbers 312, 316, 306, 324, 387, and 388.)

The former working-class suburb of **Paddington** ("Paddo," in local parlance), south of King's Cross, has become the height of fashionability in the 1970's with the revival of the "terrace houses" with the wonderfully intricate and lacy wrought-iron balconies. The streets now host little art galleries, coffee bars, and specialty shops, and the atmosphere is somewhat similar to Washington's Georgetown. Also in Paddington is 1841 Victoria Barracks (Tel. 31–0455, Ext. 517), on Oxford Street, where the public watches the changing of the guard at 11:00 a.m. on Tuesdays. (Buses 379 and 380.)

Southwest of the city, where Broadway becomes the Parramatta Road is **Sydney University**. Busily sculpted in Gothic revival style, the university buildings were begun in 1854. The ornate sandstone does provide a welcome relief from the miles and miles of monotonous bungalows which otherwise pave the precinct.

You'll take a delightful 15-minute ferry ride from Circular Quay to get to the **Taronga Park Zoo** (Tel. 969–2777), but be prepared for lots of walking on hilly pathways. In fact, after your boat docks, be sure to climb on the waiting bus (No. 237 or 238) to the *uphill* zoo entrance to allow you to accept the aid, not the hinderance, of gravity while wending your way down to the lower entrance/exit near the dock. Nearly 100 years old, the zoo is about the only dependable location for seeing so many of Australia's animals. Even if your itinerary will take you deep into the bush, there are birds and beasties at the zoo that you probably won't see in the wild.

There's a special koala enclosure, a Platypus House (open daily only 11:00–12:00 and 2:00–3:00, and this could be your lifetime chance to catch the creature in action), the Animals of the Night exhibit (where day and night are switched for Australian nocturnals, and that's only open from 10:00 to 4:00). Also don't miss the Rainforest Aviary, where you walk in the cage with the birds. The main part of the zoo is open from 9:30 a.m. to 5:00 p.m. and costs $2.80 for adults, and $1.40 for children. There's an all-inclusive excursion rate ($3.30 at our last notice) which throws in the ferry and the bus. In our book, the Taronga Zoo and its delightful inhabitants are personal prerequisites for Australian Animal Appreciation 101.

Far out toward the ocean, past Rose Bay to Vaucluse, is **Vaucluse House** (Tel. 337–1957), the home of William C. Wentworth (1790–1872), the first Australian-born citizen to achieve high political office. The colony's first constitution also was drawn up in the house of this patriot and explorer. It's an ideal example of colonial architecture and a pleasant site maintained by the N.S.W. National Parks and Wildlife Service. (Hint: There's a 30-cent booklet sold at the door; buy it *before* you go in to be able to know the significance of the rooms and furnishings.) (Open daily until 4:45 p.m.; take Bus No. 327.)

A little past Vaucluse is **Watson's Bay**, an attractive body of water which boasts the Macquarie Lighthouse, designed by the prolific Francis Greenway in 1816. (It was destroyed and then rebuilt in 1883.) Also nearby is the anchor from the *Dunbar* which was wrecked spectacularly here. Have a look at the sheer cliffs of The Gap, which the ship's captain mistook for Sydney Heads on that fateful night in 1857.

NEW SOUTH WALES

Again in alphabetical order, here are a half dozen sites of historic or scenic interest around the state. (The Snowy Mountains, though part of N.S.W., we'll cover in our Canberra chapter.)

The Blue Mountains. They really are blue, too, due to a thick distance haze caused by oil evaporating from the milliards of eucalyptus leaves and the refraction of light through it. The popular recreation area, about 60 miles from Sydney, includes the resort towns of Katoomba (where you can see the Three Sisters rock formation from an aerial cablecar, Tel. 047 + 82–2577), Leura, Blackheath, and Wentworth Falls. (The Wentworth Falls Motel, about $25 for two, is comfortable.) By train the once impenetrable Blue Mountains can be reached in a little over two hours for about $3.

Dubbo is a busy city of 21,000 on the Macquarie River, 200 miles northwest of Sydney, and a popular air excursion from the state capital. There visitors see sheepshearing demonstrations and visit the Western Plains Zoo. The town is also proud of the local jail, now restored as a tourist attraction. (50 cents to get in.)

Hunter Valley. This is the wine-making district near the town of Pokolbin about 120 miles north of Sydney. You can tour the wineries, including Tyrrell's, Lindemans, Penfold's, Hergerford Hill, Rothbury Estate, etc. Tastings are included, of course. A recommended lunchtime restaurant in Pokolbin is The Cellar. An interesting hotel, recently opened in nearby Cessnock, is the Bellbird Hotel, furnished with Australian antiques.

Incidentally, the wine country is also the beginning of Australian coal country. And if you drive up the road to Mount Wingen, you can see the smoke from "Burning Mountain," an underground coal fire which has been burning steadily out of control for thousands of years.

Lightning Ridge, of course, is the home of the world-famous black opal, 475 miles northwest of Sydney. You can inspect a "walk-in" mine, watch the opal polishers, or even arrange to "fossick" for gems yourself in some of the old mullock heaps. Better not buy an opal from someone on the street, however. In theory, you can get a good bargain from some down-on-his-luck miner. But last year, thin slices of black opal were being mounted behind a convex crystal—striplets—and being returned to Lightning Ridge where unscrupulous types would sell them as solid opals, a difference between a product worth $5 and one worth $50. Buy opals, and any other gems, only from established dealers, and you'll still get a good price. (The Mine and Spectrum are good bets.) We've always wanted to try the Tramway Hotel in Lightning Ridge, made by a man named Harold Hodges from a series of old Sydney trolleys. And a set of Hodges' teeth, a bite of solid opal, are on display at the Diggers Rest Hotel in Lightning Ridge. The Wallangulla Hotel also has a good reputation as a place to stay for about $30 for twins. All in all, Lightning Ridge is only about $100 round trip from Sydney and is a good way to see something of the closer-in Outback.

Old Sydney Town (Tel. 043 + 40 –1104), near Gosford, is one of the most intriguing theme parks we've seen anywhere. In a natural setting very much like that of Sydney in the early nineteenth century, a period which predates any building existing in the real Sydney today, the founder of the town, Frank R. Fox, has recreated the colony as it was about 1810—the "pre-Macquarie" period.

Authentic construction methods and materials were used, and are still being used, for the park is not quite complete. The townspeople—convicts and free settlers—are all in costume, and various pageants are presented throughout the day, usually involving melodramatic conflicts between the two groups. There's an all-inclusive train-bus-admission ticket, or you can drive to the location about 54 miles up the Newcastle Expressway (take the Gosford exit). Admission at the gate is about $3.50 for adults, $1.25 for kids. We had lunch right in Old Sydney Town at Rosetta Stabler's Eating House. Both the food and the strolling minstrels were authentic and good.

Parramatta was founded in 1788, 15 miles inland, less than a year after Sydney. It was once slated to be the state capital. The most interesting building is the Elizabeth Farm House, built by John Macarthur, whose face is on the $2 bill. Old Government House (Tel. 635–8149), Lancer Barracks, and St. Johns church are also traditional sights in Parramatta.

7. Guided Tours and Cruises

If we look on bus tours with a jaundiced eye in other areas of the world, we view them much more kindly in Australia. Reason: This is simply a delightful way to meet the Aussies themselves.

Your fellow passengers will usually not be merely a group of fellow foreigners. Australians are heavy travelers around their own country, and the friendly folk you meet on a bus tour in Sydney might be from Melbourne, Adelaide, Perth or some other city, large or small. And if their home town is on your later itinerary, well, you just might make some new friends to look up when you get there. (No promises, of course!)

Short bus tours, naturally enough, are not nearly as merry as longer ones. Neither the driver nor the passengers can get to know each other very well in two or three hours. But an all-day excursion, or one which includes a meal, is generally the best deal—and the most fun.

Here are some tours of and from Sydney, which we think will continue to be offered, and our guess as to approximately how much they will cost (in Australian dollars).

Some of these trips will be operated daily, others only from Monday to Friday, so you'd better check on the scene to be sure. We've included the names of the tour operators, but if your travel agent hasn't already booked them, you can reserve any seats at the New South Wales Government Travel Center (Tel. 231–4444), 16 Spring St., Sydney, N.S.W. 2000, or at any of their other locations. They'll also have the most up-to-date information on everything available.

Note: Throughout Australia, be aware that many tours do not pick you up at hotels, or might do so only during certain busy periods or for large groups. Generally you'll all have to meet at the point the bus departs. Better be sure to find out from the operator just exactly where to be and when to be picked up for your tour.

Bus (Coach) Tours

Opera House, Historic Rocks, and Inner City. 3½ hours, usually in the morning. $10. Operated by Ansett-Pioneer (Tel. 2–0651), Oxford Square.

Sydney and the Southern Beaches. 3 hours, usually in the afternoon. $8. Operated by AAT Tours (Tel. 669–5444), 16 Elizabeth St., Sydney.

Sydney in a Day. (AAT version includes the Captain Cook luncheon cruise, but lunch itself is extra on both.) 8 hours. $17. Operated by AAT Tours and by Ansett-Pioneer.

North Shore Suburbs, Manly, and the Beaches. (AAT version includes The Rocks.) 3 hours, usually in the morning. $8. AAT Tours and Ansett-Pioneer.

Sydney by Night. 5½ hours. (Includes dinner and floor shows, but recheck.) About $25. Operated by Breakaway Travel (Tel. 232–2911), Challis House, Martin Place, Sydney.

Parramatta, Katoomba, and the Blue Mountains. 7½ hours. $14. AAT Tours and Ansett-Pioneer. Also, the Public Transport Commission of N.S.W. (Tel. 211–4255) has a combination train/coach tour around the same price.

Hawkesbury River, Koala Park, and Pittwater. 7½ hours. $16. AAT Tours and Ansett-Pioneer. (And again, the PTC has a train/coach tour to the same area.)

Hunter Valley Wine Tasting Tour. (Saturdays only.) 11 hours. $19. AAT Tours.

Bush Barbecue. (Sheepshearing demonstrations, etc., and visits to Woolongong, Berrima, Bowral, and Moss Vale, including lunch). 9 hours. $25. Ansett-Pioneer.

Air Tours

A new helicopter operation called **Heliflite** (Tel. 680 –1511) has just been launched in the Sydney area, and we know little about it, but it looks like fun. It offers tours ranging from an overview of the harbor to champagne lunches in the Blue Mountains. Telephone for details or write Lindsay Edmonds, 52 Old Castle Hill Road, Castle Hill, N.S.W. 2154.

Jolly Swagman Tours. There are two, both operated by Ansett Airlines of N.S.W. (Tel. 2– 0631), and for either one you'll have to get up before dawn. One is the *Jolly Swagman to Dubbo*, a 14½-hour tour for about $150, which includes rural activities like sheep shearing, a sheepdog demonstration, boomerang throwing, barbecue lunch, a visit to the zoo and the historic old jail. We rather enjoyed the trip, recently, but suggest it could be more fun with a large gregarious group rather than the few along on our wintertime visit. There is also a lesser-known *Jolly Swagman to Lightning Ridge*, either a one-day tour or a three-day version. The 11-hour, single-day trip costs about $135, but may be available to groups only. The three-day trip, about $280, has the same Lightning Ridge objectives plus some agricultural and wildlife experiences—presumably with jumbucks and coolabah trees. We haven't yet taken the Lightning Ridge Swagmen, but we hope to catch one this year. Either is an ideal way to get a sudden dusty taste of the Australian Outback on a short visit from Sydney.

Cruises on Sydney Harbour

It sounds clichéd, but it's true: No visit to Sydney is complete without getting out on Port Jackson, at least once, even if it's only taking the ferry to the zoo or the hydrofoil to Manly. But in addition to these, we also enjoyed the **Captain Cook Cruises** (Tel. 27–9408). We sailed on the 2½-hour Coffee Cruise (adults $7 and children $4, at the moment), and were amazed at how well our attractive, red-uniformed leader (her name was Tigi Ferris, but there are lots more where she came from) knew her harbor lore. There is also a 1½-hour Luncheon River Cruise (perhaps $5, plus the lunch), which explores narrower areas further up the estuary, that we're going to take sometime this year. All depart from

Pier 6, Circular Quay. (Call the above number to reserve or use the aforementioned N.S.W. Government Travel Center, Tel. 231–4444.)

We haven't tried the **N.D. Hegarty & Son Cruises** (Tel. 27–1879), 1½ hours, about $4, also departing from Pier 6.

And the **Public Transport Commission** (Tel. 211–4255), which runs so many other tours, has set up some attractive 1½-hour harbor and river cruises, still for under $2 at this writing. Bookings are not necessary, but you'd better call to see from which slip and exactly what time they leave.

Last, but at $30 a pop, certainly not least, you can be an all-day guest on an 85-year-old luxury yacht **Tahi Waitangi** (Tel. 919–5555). Denis and Jann Pilkington take you out of Palm Beach, 20 miles north of Sydney, for a cruise on the waters of Pittwater and the Hawkesbury River, serving a chicken and champagne lunch. We've met Denis, but haven't had time to try the trip yet. It sounds like salty fun!

8. Water Sports

Sydney is for swimming and for surfing, and that's a fact which has spread to the outdoor brotherhood in Hawaii, California, and South Africa. The beaches are divided into "Northern," from Manly to Palm Beach, and "Southern," from Bondi to Cronulla. The opening at Sydney Heads provides the dividing line between the two areas.

Unless you're driving, the **Northern Beaches** are best reached by ferry from Sydney to Manly and thence by bus to other beaches. The beaches (going north) include Manly's Ocean Beach, one of the world's best for surfing; Harbord, favored by body surfers; Curl Curl, good for the youngsters; Dee Why, also a good surfing beach; and Collaroy, now being spoiled by sea erosion. One small nude swimming area near Manly is called Reef Beach.

The **Southern Beaches**, between Bondi and Malabar, anyway, are better established than any north of the Heads except Manly itself. In fact, Bondi, Bronte, and Coogee on the southern coast have been famous for 100 years. You can travel by bus to these magnificent strips of sand. When the big name strands are overcrowded, look for smaller beaches like Tamarama, Clovelly, and Malabar. There is a beach in the buff on the southern shore, too. That's Lady Jane Beach, near Watkins Bay.

Sharks? There certainly are some, especially between December and February. And in the same way that visitors to San Francisco are afraid of earthquakes, it may not help much to know that your chance of being struck by a shark in Sydney are one in a million.

Where sharks are most likely to appear, such as in the calm waters of

Port Jackson, there are metal nets to protect the swimming areas. Along the ocean beaches, there are shark patrols by helicopter and by land observers. When a shark is spotted, everyone is quickly shooed out of the water. Then boats close in on the "nasty brute," relentlessly pursuing it until it is killed or driven far away. On no account, never-ever, enter the water anyplace other than a designated, guarded official swimming area!

More likely dangers at the beach would be the occasional rip tides, but then the highly trained lifeguards are ready for those. Perhaps no beaches in the world are guarded better than those of Australia. And last, watch out for the sun. Somehow it seems to burn more quickly and more severely Down Under than it does many other places in the world.

For most of us, **yachting** is more a spectator sport than one in which we can readily join. The sailboat season in New South Wales starts in September and ends in May, with races and regattas held on the harbor nearly every weekend. Some like to watch the 18-footer races while taking the ferry boat to Manly and back.

One boat-rental operation, however, seems to hire out everything, including rowboats, canoes, catamarans, gaffers, corsairs, windsurfers, a 16-foot cabin boat, and a 20-foot cruiser, the latter of which may go for about $10 an hour or $35 a day. That's **Waltons Hire Boats** (Tel. 969–6006) on the Esplanade in Balmoral Beach, near Hunter Bay. We've never had the opportunity to check out either the company or one of its boats personally.

The best **deep sea fishing** is not in New South Wales but in northern Queensland (see last chapter). One popular site in the state, however, is at Coffs Harbour, about 360 miles north of Sydney, where Spanish mackerel and occasionally marlin are taken. Other fishing sites include Port Stephens (marlin from January to March) and Lord Howe Island, if you want to call that dot 325 miles out in the ocean part of N.S.W. Supposedly some of the country's best fishing is there, with dozens of denizens practically yours for the asking.

9. Other Sports

Perhaps no people in the world are more sports crazy than the Australians. Indeed, they are often criticized for this love, usually by visiting English writers who express scant appreciation for the influence of a beautiful outdoor climate that fosters more athletic activities than it does cold cultural pursuits like reading and the enjoyment of classical music.

SPECTATOR SPORTS

Australians have two big seasons, cricket in the summer and football in the winter. There are four types of football, all of which are more fast-moving than the American version. Play is continuous and there are no substitutions.

Football. The two kinds far preferred in New South Wales (and Queensland) are Rugby League and Rugby Union. Union (sometimes called "rugger") is the older, dating from 1864. It is played with 15 men on a side and is strictly an amateur sport.

League dates from 1907 and is a professional spin-off from Union, with only 13 men per team and a few more rule changes. Rugby League is the big sport in this part of the country from about March to September. Although invented in Australia, League is also played in England, France, New Zealand, and South Africa, so teams from these countries often come to give an international flavor to the sport. (However the famed New Zealand All-Blacks are a Union team, so they play the amateur Wallabies in Australia rather than the professional Kangaroos.)

In Sydney, Rugby League can be seen at the Sydney Sports Ground at Moore Park (south of Paddington) or at Redfern Oval in South Sydney.

Soccer. The game has been widely promoted by Australia's recent British and European immigrants and is gaining ground all over the country. It is sometimes called "Association Football." There are 11 on a side, and each team tries to kick or "head" a ball through the opposing goal. Unlike other forms of football, no hands are used. You might catch a soccer match at Marks Field.

Australian Rules football is a big Victoria/South Australia game. Although it is sometimes played in Sydney, too, Sydney-siders will likely put it down in some way—"aerial ping-pong," someone once snorted. Anyway, we cover it in Section 9 of our Melbourne chapter.

The summer activity is **cricket**, played from October through February all over the country. If the crowds seem smaller, it's only because it must compete with the siren calls of the beaches on the weekends. Australian state teams compete for the Sheffield Shield (one home game, one away game for each team). Each of those matches is four days long, usually starting on a Friday or Saturday. Later, England and Australia compete for the coveted trophy called The Ashes in a series of five matches. International games in either cricket or rugby are generally called "test matches."

Cricket in Australia dates back to the earliest days of the colony. It involves bowlers and batsmen, and attempts by the bowler to propel a ball at and to knock down one of two wickets and attempts by a batsman to keep that from happening. There are many refinements to the game, all of which are mysterious to non-players. In Australia, as in England, the importance of cricket is thought to be much beyond that of a game. It is considered an important factor in the development of good character and is an integral part of a child's schooling. (School children also have national and international contests in cricket, incidentally.)

You may catch this gentlemen's game in Sydney at the Sydney Cricket Ground in Moore Park. If you want to make sure you get a seat at a test match, contact the N.S.W. Cricket Association, 254 George St., Sydney 2000.

Some would say that although every Australian male is a football and cricket fan, his absolute passion is **horse-racing**. In truth, it may be much more the gambling instinct that attracts the Aussies to the nags. (Australians are said to love betting on anything, even two flies climbing up a wall.) During the running of the Melbourne Cup, the first Tuesday of November, practically the entire country comes to a halt while the race is run, the citizens glued to radios or televisions.

The Australian satirical poet Alec Derwent Hope once addressed this equestrian obsession in some witty lines which recall a popular assertion that Gulliver's mythical travels took him to a modern Australia:

Far in the South, beyond the burning line,
Where Gulliver, that much-wrecked mariner,
Described their customs, such as they then were,
And found them, like their manners, somewhat coarse,
The yahoos live in slavery to the horse. . .
A sort of costive English, too, they speak,
And sweat and drink and quarrel round the week;
And what they earn in their own time, they spend
On their four-footed masters each week-end.

All over Australia, you can bet on the ponies without going out to the track, quite legally, at the special shops labeled T.A.B. In Sydney, if you want to experience the roar of the horseflesh and the smell of the mob, you can go out during the week to Randwick Racecourse on Alison Road in Randwick or the Rosehill Racecourse on Aston Street in Rosehill. (Take the Carlingford or Sandown train.) Others holding races on Saturdays and holidays include the Canterbury Park Racecourse on King Street in Canterbury, and the Warwick Farm Racecourse on Hume Highway at Warwick Farm. (Several trains run on race days.)

Greyhound racing is also becoming popular. You go to the dogs in Sydney at Glebe—either at Harold Park on Minogue Crescent (Bus 433) or Wentworth Park on the Wentworth Park Road nearby.

PARTICIPATION SPORTS

Some may think the Australians invented **tennis** because of the championship players that have come up from Down Under to win the big tournaments all over the world. But spectator tennis has sparked interest in playing tennis among all Australians, both on paved courts and on grass. You'll find "hard courts" at Moore Park, Prince Alfred Park, Rushcutters Bay, and White City. If you want to find some courts in your neighborhood, call or visit the N.S.W. Lawn Tennis Association (Tel. 31–7144), 30 Alma St., Paddington 2021. Also, have a look in the Yellow Pages under the category "Tennis Courts for Hiere." You'll find lots in every city.

A commercial tennis club, with which we have had no personal experience, is **Fleets Tennis** (Tel. 663–7005) at the corner of Lang Road and Anzac Parade near Moore Park. Our last information indicated private lessons were available for about $12 an hour and court rentals for around $2.

Golf courses in Australia are often on private clubs and not generally open to the public. However, if you are introduced by a member, or perhaps even can prove you are a member of a similar golf club in another country, you may be admitted. Greens fees are around $5, and club rental is about the same.

One good 18-hole public course in Sydney is the **Lakes Golf Club** (Tel. 669–1311), King Street, East Mascot 2020. The top course, however, is the **Royal Sydney** (Tel. 371–4333) which overlooks the harbor at Rose Bay. Unfortunately it's terribly exclusive. You might have better luck at the **Australian Golf Club** (Tel. 663–2272) in Kensington or the beautiful **N.S.W. Golf Club** (Tel. 661–4455), a magnificent site on Botany Bay at Matraville. If you want to let a special agency take over your golf problems, you might try the **Professional Golf Services** (Tel. 212–1325), 220 Elizabeth St., Sydney. You go golfing with a pro on supposedly the best courses at prices ranging from about $25 to $80, depending on the number in your party.

Australia's biggest participant sport is **lawn bowling**, which doesn't come as naturally to much of the rest of the world. If you're into this sport, however, you'll get a friendly reception at the Royal N.S.W. Bowling Association (Tel. 29–6825), 35 Clarence St., Sydney 2000.

Running is Australia's newest sport, in common with many other countries. The big event is the August "City-to-Surf" fun run over nine miles from Sydney to Bondi.

Snow skiing is big during the winter. Although the best resorts are officially in New South Wales, they're closer to Canberra and the A.C.T., so we report on the *schuss*ing scene in the next chapter.

10. Shopping in Sydney

Sydney has the smart shops and clever emporia of all types that you would expect in any of the world's major cities, plus the added accents provided by things specifically antipodean like Aboriginal "X-Ray" artworks, Australian gemstones, wool products, and so forth.

Here are some of the things you might look for in Sydney:

Aboriginal arts and crafts. You can buy boomerangs at any price from one dollar on up, depending on wood, decoration, etc. Didjeridoos, those one-note droners, are from $10 or so for small ones up to about $500 for the deep throat monsters. Spears run from a short $9 up to a long $30. Woomeras, a type of Aboriginal throwing stick, begin at about $7, and woven baskets and mats cost $15 to $50. The best water colors in the Namatjira style run from around $80 to $200. Other Aboriginal creations range from simple bark paintings at around $10 on up to large works sold for $100.

Australian paintings. You can get mass-produced oils of Ayers Rock, the Opera House, etc., starting from around $20 (try the store at 163 King St.), but no really good works for less than $75, and they're more likely to average around $150 to $200.

Here is a list of commercial galleries, some offering works by contemporary Australian artists, others specializing in Aboriginal art, and several displaying both. Many of these grace the fashionable Paddington neighborhood: The **Australian Board of Missions**, 109 Cambridge St., in Stanmore, offers primitive artifacts from all over the country. **Hogarth Galleries** (Tel. 31–6839, and also known as the Gallery of Dreams), 9 Walker Lane, Paddington, is also largely Aboriginal work from all over the nation. The **Collectors Gallery of Aboriginal Art**, 40 Harrington St., near the Rocks, and **Barry Stern**, 19 Glenmore Rd., Paddington, both have extensive collections of Australian works. **Back O'Bourke Art Gallery**, 207 Darlinghurst Rd., specializes in Australiana paintings featuring the Outback. **Artarmon Galleries**, 479 Pacific Highway, Artarmon, has realistic Australian works. The **Macquarie Gallery**, 40 King St., is one of the best-known galleries of Australian artwork, and the **Holdsworth Galleries** (Tel. 32–1364) has new exhibitions every three weeks by well-known Australian artists at 86 Holdsworth St. in Woollahra.

Ceramics. Some of these are of Aboriginal themes, but not made by Aborigines. Others are just Australian art in their own right. Prices range from $2 for a small pot up to nearly $1,000 for sculptured Australian pottery. We found some of the inexpensive ones to be good, last-minute gifts sold at the airport. (You'll pay more out there, though.) Good ceramics you'll find at the **New Potters Gallery**, 27 Redlub Ave., Wahrooga.

Leather goods. Look for wallets at $7 up or handbags at $45. Jackets zip up to more than $100, now, with coats over $150. The department stores may be your best bets.

Opals and gemstones. Don't just go out and buy an opal. Look in several stores first and talk to the sales people about the product. There are two main types mined in Australia—"white" and the more-valuable "black" opal. Of course neither are really white or black, but the white opals seem to have their vivid blues and greens splashed over and through a sort of milky background. Black opals flash fiery reds and yellows and even dark greens and violets on a natural black background.

You can invest in solid opals, or for much less money you can buy thin slivers made into doublets—a layer of opal attached to a special backing, or triplets—the same as a doublet but with a clear crystal dome fastened above it to protect the opal and slightly magnify the color patterns. Opal products are sold at almost any price from about $5 for a key ring on up to hundreds of dollars for the very best mounted stones. But you may get a very nice triplet ring for $50 or so.

Some reliable stores for buying opals and other jewels include **Percy Marks** (Tel. 233–1355), 79 Castlereagh St., **Flame Opals** (Tel. 27–3444), 119 George St., near Circular Quay, **Staffords** (Tel. 232–3216), at 44 Castlereagh St., **Gemtec Australia** (Tel. 61–4757), 250 Pitt St., the **Sapphire and Opal Centre** (Tel. 233–2346) in the Wentworth Hotel and the Wynyard Travelodge, and **Allison's** (Tel. 223–1677), 15 Park St.

Skin products. Most of these items are made either from sheepskin or kangaroo skin. (Stuffed koala toys use kangaroo skin, generally, because koalas are a protected species.) Sheepskin rugs are a soft, fuzzy bargain from around $30 on up to $50. Sheepskin seat covers for your car are another good idea. They are supposed to keep you warm in the winter and cool in the summer, although we've never tried them. Some drivers like the steering wheel covers, too, and you may get the best bargain on either at a good hardware store—try **Nock and Kirby**, 421 George St.

Coats will run $150 to $300, slippers from $20 to $25, and the stuffed toys (kangaroos, koalas, lambs, rabbits, etc.) from $10 to $40, depending on their sizes. Try **The Sheepskin Shop** (Tel. 27–1599), at 139 George St.

Souvenirs in general. Besides the other categories mentioned here, there are things like small silver souvenir spoons from around $10, pressed wildflower pictures about $6, cork table mats with Australian scenes for perhaps $12.95 for a set of six.

Some general souvenir shops in the center of the city include **The Koala Bear Shop** (Tel. 61–3187), 133 Castlereagh St., and the **Koala Center** at the Wynyard Travelodge. Souvenirs and jewelry are sold at **Prouds** (Tel. 233–4488) at the corner of Pitt and King Street. If you have a car, a nice drive up to Palm Beach will bring you to **Swaggs** at 118 Barrenjoey Road. There are good bargains there for locally made arts and crafts. If a boomerang's your thing, stop in at Duncan Mac-Lennan's **Boomerang School** (Tel. 357–1135), 158 William St. Here you can learn how to pitch the thing before you pitch in to buy it. For some off-beat objects, try **Christies** (Tel. 26–6751) at 248 Pitt St. There are strange T-shirts and obscure military insignia. You'll find some interesting Australian antiques dating back to colonial days at **Aronson Antiques** (Tel. 42–6149) at 154 Castlereagh St.

Wool products. Besides the aforementioned sheepskin rugs, there are many finished wool items that are less expensive and better made in Australia. Cardigans and other sweaters may run $20 and up. You may find some hand-spun pullovers for $40 or $50. Wool blankets could cost about half what you'd expect to pay at home.

Shop hours. Visitors to Australia have an easier time making the rounds of the stores than Australians on the job, due to the generally repressive shopping hours. Throughout the country in general, businesses are open from 9:00 to 5:00, Monday through Friday, and from 9:00 to noon on Saturdays, with one late night per week—on Thursday in Sydney the shops stay open until 9:00 p.m. Last year, some merchants in Sydney began challenging the closing-hours law and staying open until 5:00 p.m. on Saturdays, creating quite a furor. It looks now like the state law will be changed to allow those late closings. On Sundays, forget it! They roll up the footpaths all over the country, and only a very few specialty places are allowed to keep their doors open.

Department stores. The largest in Sydney is **David Jones** (Tel. 2–0664), with entrances on Elizabeth, Market, and Castlereagh Streets and a branch at George and Barrack, followed closely by **Myer** (Tel. 238–0111), with entrances on Pitt, Market, and George Streets. Both are worth a big browse and offer a surprising variety of goods, generally well displayed. (We've seen Aboriginal art at David Jones for lower prices than in Aboriginal country at Alice Springs.)

Other department stores (Aussies say "departmental," by the way) include **Winns** (Tel. 26 – 6342), Oxford and Riley Streets, **Grace Brothers** (Tel. 526 – 0111) out of the central area on Broadway near Victoria Park, **Mark Foy's** (Tel. 2 – 0949) at the corner of Elizabeth and Park Streets, and **Waltons** (Tel. 2 – 0628), 2 Park St. at George.

Shopping arcades. Melbourne might claim the ancestorship of Australian shopping arcades, but Sydney has taken the concept into the twentieth century—tunneling, twisting, and turning through the commercial blocks with modernistic gusto. A good example is the super-slick **MLC Centre** which burrows a new route between King Street and Martin Place. Besides its chrome and mirror-lined shops, it features an unusual circular fountain. (You can walk to its center and never get wet.)

Another is **Centrepoint**, where there are at least 200 shops in the four levels under the pedestal to that dramatic tower. With its bridges and tunnels, it connects the Myer and David Jones Department Stores, too. The **Royal Arcade**, underneath the Hilton, is also popular.

But a beautiful refurbishment of an old Victorian shopping complex is the 1883 **Strand Arcade**, lined with wrought iron and polished mahogany. The narrow, four-floor balconied passageway runs between George and Pitt Streets (No. 193 Pitt is the official address) in the block bounded by Market and King. You *can* miss it, so do search it out. It's a minor masterpiece, from an architectural viewpoint, anyway, but don't lean on the railings! Some of the small stores we found interesting there include **Martinvale** (Tel. 231–3829) for unusual gifts, the **Flamingo Park Frock Salon** (Tel. 231–3027) for some modern, far-out clothes, sweaters, etc., made to order, and **Helen's Bedroom Boutique** (Tel. 231–5810) with some different kinds of blankets and spreads.

Duty Free Shops. We're not very impressed with the special duty free shops, in general. If you know the product you're interested in, how much it costs at home, etc., then have a look in a duty free shop. (You can only order things for planeside delivery if you've a ticket out of the country.)

Another unusual set of shops is the **Argyle Arts Centre** at 18 Argyle St. in the historic Rocks district under the approaches to the Sydney Harbor Bridge. The complex winds around a series of 1829 warehouses, which may have seemed dreary a century and a half ago, but today possess a genuine, old-world charm. In the Centre, have a look at the **Argyle Primitive Art Gallery** (Tel. 241–1853), for the best and most-genuine Aboriginal art. (Manager Peter Brokensha was an oil company executive who chose this peaceful pursuit over the top-management rat race.) Another pleasant stop there is the **Argyle Opal and Gem Centre** (Tel. 27–9125), where A. C. Geary is knowledgeable and helpful on the subject of opals—even if you don't buy. He also sells a few nice souvenir minerals with several kinds of rocks fastened on a souvenir card for $5 or so.

While we're considering the Rocks area, there is an attractive souvenir shop across the courtyard from the Argyle Center. That's the **Voyagers Cottage**, and it's actually at 25 Playfair Street. Not far away is a some-what famous address for malacologists—Lance Moore's **Marine Specimens** (Tel. 27–7357), at 27–A George St. Known also as "the Shell Shop," they nevertheless have more than that, branching out into mounted butterflies, minerals, etc. And at 81½ George St., across from Cadman's Cottage, is **Left-Handed Products** (Tel. 27–3674), a special store for southpaws.

Boutiques at Double Bay. Some call Double Bay "Double Pay," but be that as it may, these are the smart, exclusive shops in a suburb about five miles to the east of Sydney, for—as our friend Alexandra Piechowiak puts it—"all the Guccis and the Puccis." A few samples:

Gianni Boutique (Tel. 36 –6687), 27 Knox St., specializes in imported shoes, some designed for them especially. **Courrèges**, (Tel. 32–0215), Bay Village, Cross St., is the only Courrèges boutique in Australia and **Michal** (Tel. 36 –4016), 12 Cross St., stocks exclusive jewelry designs.

Men's wear. You can be outfitted well at the department stores, of course. Sartorial blokes who want top fashion, though, may head for either **Richard's** at 41 Castlereagh St. or **Richard Hunt** in George Street near Wynyard.

Dime stores. Of course there are no "dimes" in Australia, but the local equivalent to *our* Woolworth's is *their* **Woolworth's**. The main store is in George Street, opposite Town Hall. (There's no connection, incidentally, between the Yank and the Aussie "Woolies.") **Coles** is another chain with similar goods all over the country.

Book stores. Considering that Australians are supposedly always at the beach, in the pubs, or glued to the telly, Sydney has an amazing number of bookstores racking up a large number of sales. At least two should not be missed: **Angus & Robertson Bookshops** (Tel. 231–4066); its national head store at 209 Pitt St., has just about everything in print. And for concentrated Australiana, try **Henry Lawson's Bookshop** (Tel. 61–2365), 127 York St., named in honor of Australia's best-known writer. At some bookstore, incidentally, you should pick up a good map of Sydney for finding your way around the city. Absolutely the best we've seen is Gregory's City of Sydney, Map No. 11 (about 80 cents). For maps of an earlier day, look into **Antiquarian Maps and Prints** (Tel. 326–1919) at 51 Queen St. in Woollahra. And here's a hint for obtaining extremely inexpensive Australian publications produced by the Australian Government Publishing Service: Buy them over the counter at the **AGPS Bookshop** (Tel. 211–4755) at 309 Pitt St. Most of these, of course, are of dull reports and the like. But there are some good maps and a few beautiful pamphlets on Australian nature, history, etc., in full color, and at a fraction of the price you'd expect to pay.

A last thought: The local equivalent of the flea market is **Paddy's Market**, featuring hundreds of stalls and carts selling anything you can imagine, and lots that you can't. It's an ideal Saturday excursion (open from 7:00 to 5:00).

11. Entertainment and Night Life

There is no swinging Las Vegas in Australia, but some segments of the community believe they have one by the tail in Sydney. The after-dark scene there certainly is a shade or two brighter than, say, in Wagga Wagga, Murrumburah, or Dunedoo.

Night clubs. In the traditional sense, there are few. The most ambitious of this genus may be **Le Club** (Tel. 358–1988), 22 Bayswater Road, in King's Cross, and they *do* bring in some acts from Vegas, as a matter of fact. Watch your table choice carefully, here. Several have bad angles on the action. Also it may be difficult to book the show without a dinner. (Monday through Thursday will be less expensive here than Friday and Saturday. Weekdays are also better bets for a good position.)

The **Barrel Theatre** is in our notes as a night club, although we've lost the reason why (!). We haven't been in, but reportedly they don't even wear barrels in there. And the **Town & Country Dance Hall** (Tel. 358–1211) in that burgeoning entertainment complex at the Texas Tavern Hotel, often features some kind of a show.

But much of the action in Sydney actually takes place at the **private social clubs**, sometimes known as "leagues clubs" or "sports clubs." There are dozens upon dozens of these, all supposedly open to members only. Most you can hardly call "exclusive." They may have an active roster of more than 50,000! They are generally joined only by men, incidentally. Women are admitted as wives or girlfriends of members. These clubs are supported not by dues, but by the earnings of their own poker (slot) machines. Under N.S.W. law, they may be installed in such premises. That painless Down Under Way of building an opera house has thus been successfully transferred to keeping the clubs solvent, too!

Several social clubs are more than happy to welcome overseas travelers as "complimentary" members. Just take your passport to the door and you'll get in for a fair admission charge. A good one for that is the **Mandarin** (Tel. 211–3866) downtown at 396 Pitt St., not to be confused with the restaurant by the same name, (although the Mandarin Club also reportedly sells delicious and cheap Chinese meals, we haven't sat down there yet ourselves). There's generally a good cabaret show and dancing—besides that wonderful opportunity to help finance the club treasury while exercising your biceps at the same time. The one-arm bandits, by the way, show poker hands instead of oranges, lemons, bells, and the like.

You may hear a lot about the **N.S.W. Leagues Club**, 165 Philip St., but we call it one of those for the local "rugby, racing, and beer" set, interesting perhaps only sociologically. But the **St. George League's Club** (Tel. 587–1022), on the other hand, welcomes foreigners with open cash drawers. It's at 124 Princess Highway in Kogarah. You might catch a top-flight comedian like Paul Hogan there. But it may feature a full-length musical comedy extravaganza on other occasions.

When name entertainers come to town, it is often the social clubs who can afford to hire them. Otherwise, they must attract a sizable audience to a large hall, something which hardly exists any more. The Opera House's Concert Hall seats only 2,600. This was big enough for John Denver recently, but when Bob Hope came to town, he performed again in the barn-like **Anthony Hordern Pavilion** (Tel. 33–3769), dubbed "Sydney's Garage." (Hope and Australia have a genuine affinity for one another, however, which dates back to World War II.) The Hordern Pavilion also hosts the big indoor rock concerts in Sydney.

Discotheques. The disco scene is alive and well in Sydney, although the choices are smaller—due partly, at least, to the proliferation of the social clubs. By the way, many discos are not true to the definition, often bringing in live bands and singers drawn from Australia's large stable of rock performers or visiting artists.

The city's premier site for Monday-to-Saturday-night fever is **Juliana's**, on the seventh floor of the Sydney Hilton, and associated with the famous Juliana's of London. Open until 3:00 a.m., it has a modest cover of $3 on weeknights and $5 on weekends, at this writing.

The *largest* disco, however, is probably **Ida's**, a mob scene at King's Cross; the *latest* is just opened and called the **Underground**; and the *most attractive* natural setting is at the **Caprice** on Sunderland Avenue overlooking Rose Bay.

Other discos include **Matches** at 87–89 Walker St. in North Sydney (good for high-class singles), **Pips International**, at the corner of Cathedral and Riley in Woolloomooloo (which likes to boast of "name" customers), **Maxy's**, in the old Plaza Cinema on George Street, near Liverpool Street, the **Downunder Disco**, in the shopping arcade underneath the Hyatt Kingsgate Hotel, and **The Loft**, high atop the Boulevard Hotel on William Street.

Pop/rock groups currently on the Australian charts include Sports, Jo Jo Zep and the Falcons, The Angels, Cold Chisel, Split Enz, and the Little River Band. (The Bee Gees, of course, are Aussie alumni who went on to make it big in England, the U.S.A., and the world.)

Three cheers for beer! Before an idealized pub crawl, we should address Australian beer as the Australian does—very seriously. A marvelous, frothy, honey-silk brew, it's a delicious fluid we've had nowhere else surpassed only by the best beers of Germany and Denmark. And Australia is somewhere between the third and the fifth most beer-drinking country in the world.

The nation has two dozen breweries owned by nine different companies which produce more than 70 brands of beer. To avoid argument, you'd better drink a beer of the region you happen to be in at the moment. Most Aussie beers are really lagers, by the way, even though some may be called "ale" or "bitter."

Sydney's many beers are brewed by two corporations with similar names—Toohey's and Tooth's. Among the Toohey entries are Stag Lager (its best), Pilsener, New Special Draught, Hunter Ale (the coal miners' favorite, also called Toohey's Old), a dark beer named Flag Ale, and Miller's Oatmeal Stout. Tooth's has Resch's KB (Sydney's best-seller), Resch's D.A. (Dinner Ale, which we like better), XXX (pronounced "Three-X"), Special New, and a genuinely bitter Tooth's Sheaf Stout.

There are several different sizes of beer glasses, all with individual names. These vary from state to state, but in New South Wales, the "pony" is five ounces, the "glass" is seven, the "middy" is 10 ounces, and the "schooner" sails in at 15. You'll occasionally find a "pint," which is 20 ounces. (Not all pubs will have all sizes.)

The pub crawl. As explained earlier, pubs are more often called "hotels," and they often sell only specific brands of beer. In Sydney, this means that there are Toohey pubs and there are Tooth pubs. Which is which usually will be easily determined by the advertising on the exterior of the establishment.

Until recently, pubs in Australia had a sort of antiseptic look, and you will still find a few which seem to be paved with bathroom tile. It apparently made them easier to hose down after the madding mob had gone home. But this has evidently gone out with the "six o'clock swill," the old practice of declaring drinking illegal when it was time for the men to go to dinner and their long-suffering wives. Now the women, themselves, are coming more to the pubs, and they are insisting on good decoration and carpeted floors.

Some pubs, however, are still for men only. There is no sign to tell you such; it's just a matter of long local custom in certain neighborhoods. In general, women or couples might tell whether or not they'll be welcome by taking a "bo peep" into the bar first. If there are other women in there (other than the occasional hard-bitten local character who may be only technically female), okay. Otherwise, see if the pub has a separate area labeled the "lounge." If so, that's central headquarters for distaff and mixed imbibing.

To confuse things still further, many pubs in the country have several different "bars," often all with their own separate names—perhaps served from the same back bar and perhaps not. Some have dress codes, but the "public" bar may only require that you wear pants.

Fear not. Even Australians become befuddled and often walk into the wrong bar themselves in an innocent attempt to hoist a glass of "the amber." This is especially true today when many of the old customs and standards are being challenged and are in a state of flux.

Here are a brewer's dozen pubs in Sydney, some of which are also open for lunch and dinner: **Australian Heritage**, a century-old watering hole at the corner of King's Cross and Bayswater, has a baby blue exterior and two or three comfortable bars inside. The **Bondi Hotel**, 178 Campbell Parade in Bondi, an ornate building from the 20's, is popular with the young folks. The **Centrepoint Tavern**, on Pitt Street, is a new pub with five bars representing different operatic themes. The building is on the site of Sydney's first opera house. **The Clock**, at the corner of Foveaux and Crown Streets in Surry Hills, is a formerly rough, workingman's pub now converted to a chic "in-spot." **The Grand**, at 30 Hunter St., off Pitt, appeals to members of the stock exchange. The **Grand National Hotel** in "Paddo" is a friendly local pub with an outdoor beer garden and occasional rock entertainment. The famous old **Hero of Waterloo**, at the corner of Windmill and Lower Fort Street in The Rocks, was built in 1817, and is the oldest pub in town. **The Marble Bar** today is technically part of one gigantic "pub" called the Sydney Hilton.

The marble walls and pillars were dismantled from the 75-year-old Adams Hotel and then re-erected in all their glory in the Hilton after it was built on the same site. Don't miss it! The **Royal Hotel**, at Broughton and Heeley Streets in Paddington, also has an outdoor beer garden. Several bars and a restaurant are featured in this 1889 establishment. The **Styne Hotel**, at the corner of The Corso and Manly Beach, is a Manly landmark. There's a soothing ocean view and an inviting open courtyard. The **Surrey Hotel**, at King and Castlereagh, is a good, no-nonsense city pub. The **Tilbury Hotel**, at 22 Forbes St. in Woolloomooloo, is also known as Louis at the Loo. It's open 6:30 to 6:30. That's *a.m. to p.m.* It sometimes features modern jazz on Saturday afternoons. And the **York Hotel**, 48 King St., is another one of those matey drinking establishments in the city. We liked it—as a pub, anyway. (The sleeping accommodations aren't nearly as cozy as the bar.)

Theater-restaurants. These are catching on in Sydney, and they are fun with the right show, the right crowd, and the right meal. One of the most entertaining of the type is the **Music Hall** (Tel. 909–8222), at 156 Military Rd. in Neutral Bay. Here you cheer the hero and hiss the villain at their old-style melodramas. Others featuring floor shows include **Dirty Dick's** (Tel. 929–8888), with a medieval motif, at 313 Pacific Highway, Crows Nest, the **Bull 'N' Bush** (Tel. 31–4627) at 113 William St., near King's Cross. Also, there is the **Speakeasy** (Tel. 663–7442), 107 Anzac Parade, Kensington, and the **Music Loft** (Tel. 977–6585) in Manly.

The **Carousel Cabaret** (Tel. 358–2333), at 2 Roslyn St., King's Cross, featuring all-male reviews, may appeal to Sydney's large population of homosexuals as well as to many others. To some, it's merely a drag.

Other theaters. There are dozens of professional theaters with constantly changing cards featuring Australian, British, and American productions. Check the newspapers, like the Sydney Morning *Herald's* Saturday amusement classified section for the latest on who's playing where, from Shakespeare to "Jesus Christ Superstar."

Some of the well-known Sydney theaters include the **Theatre Royal** at the MLC Centre, **Her Majesty's Theatre** on Quay Street, the **Drama Theatre** in the Sydney Opera House, the **Genesian Theatre** at 420 Kent St., **Seymour Centre** (in the round) at Cleveland Street and City Road, the **Nimrod Theatre**, 500 Elizabeth St., the **Ensemble Theatre**, 78 McDougall St., Milsons Point, and the **Old Tote Theatre**, Anzac Parade, Kensington (opposite the University of N.S.W.).

Australian theatrical standards are indisputably high, and some modern drama by accomplished local playwrights is outstanding. Unfortunately, some of the country's best talent goes to London, New York, or Hollywood—and stays there.

The movies. Sydney has cinemas established all over the metropolitan area, many of them in Pitt Street and more in George Street. One amazing complex called **Hoyts Entertainment Centre**, 505 George St., has no less than seven films showing at once, all timed to break at different moments, keeping a relatively steady demand out at the refreshment stands.

There are four film classifications. R is more or less like the American X—no one under 18 admitted. Then there's M or SOA, suitable for persons 15 and over ("mature"). Then NRC or A—not recommended for children under 12 ("Star Wars" received this classification in parts of Australia!), and finally G, suitable for all ages.

Just as you should try to catch an Australian play while Down Under, you should also see at least one Aussie film production. The number and quality of Australian films is far out of proportion to the country's population with an amazing 75 features produced in the past eight years. Some recent and excellent full-lengthers include "The Last Wave," "Caddie," "The Chant of Jimmy Blacksmith," "Newsfront," "Storm Boy," "The Devil's Playground," and "Picnic at Hanging Rock." (Of course they turn out some bombs, too, and some that are merely a little too pretentious when seen from an international perspective. Try to see some of the above. Otherwise, read the reviews first.)

The Opera. As we mentioned, opera is only performed in one of the four main halls at the Sydney Opera House, the **Opera Theatre**, which seats 1,547 patrons. There are periodic program guides to everything going on in the opera house, by the way. The Australian Opera company, based there, also performs in all other state capitals and in Canberra. The box office is open daily from 9:30 a.m. to 8:30 p.m. for tickets. (Tel. 241–2416.)

Again, Australian opera singers go on to enrich the culture of the rest of the world. Harold Rosenthal, the editor of the British magazine *Opera* wrote, " . . . Not only London, but most of the leading opera houses of the world would, if not actually forced to close their doors, be very hard put to perform certain operas if it were not for the existence of Australian singers."

The ballet. It's also performed at the Opera House, usually in the same Opera Theater. The Australian Ballet handles not only the classics, but it has commissioned dozens of new works from Australian and foreign choreographers. One of the recent Australian ballets is "The Display," which is based on the life of the lyrebird. And "Corroboree," of course, is inspired by Aboriginal ceremonies.

Classical music. Often performing in the Concert Hall, the Music Room, or the Recording Hall of the Opera House are the Sydney Symphony Orchestra, the Elizabethan Sydney Orchestra, and the Australian Broadcasting Commission orchestra, performing works by classical artists as well as those of many contemporary Australian composers like Ahern, Banks, Brumby, Butterley, Conyngham, Dreyfus, and Pemberthy.

The orchestra and choir of the N.S.W. State Conservatorium of Music sometimes perform in the Opera House. The number to call for information on all Opera House events is 2–0588. For some Sunday noon performances, no advance reservations are taken. These programs may be as low as $1.50 for adults and 30 cents for children and students.

Television and Radio Stations. If you're staying home, you can be electronically entertained at least as well as in cities back home. There are four TV channels in Sydney, the government-owned Australian Broadcasting Commission station at Channel 2, and the three commercial channels, 7, 9, and 10. Color transmission is technically superior to the American system. And there are at least nine radio stations, including three run by the government. Their commercial stations are generally devoted to popular music, news, and talk-back programs.

12. The Sydney Address List

(Be aware that there are four different telephone books for Sydney—one for residential numbers only and three others (including the Yellow Pages) for commercial numbers.)

Airlines, International—Air New Zealand, Tel. 233–6888. British Airways, Tel. 233–5566. CP Air, Tel. 233–5711. Continental Airlines, Tel. 232–4108. Pan American, Tel. 233–1111. Qantas, Tel. 436–6111. UTA French Airlines, Tel. 233–3277.

American Consulate, T&G Towers, Park and Elizabeth Sts. (Tel. 235–7044).

Australian Tourist Commission, 5 Elizabeth St. (Tel. 233–7233).

Bank—Bank of New South Wales, 60 Martin Place. (Tel. 233–0500).

Barber—The Stallions Stable, 398 George St. (Tel. 233–2521).

Beauty salon—Adrian Brooks Salon, 868 Anzac Parade, Marouba Junction. (Tel. 349–7128).

British Consulate, 1 Alfred St., Circular Quay (Tel. 27–7521).

Camping equipment rental—Paddy Pallin, 69 Liverpool St. (Tel. 26–2685).

Canadian Consulate, AMP Building, 50 Bridge St. (Tel. 231–6522).

Dental Hospital of Sydney, 2 Chalmers St. (Tel. 211–4322 or 211–2120 after hours).

Dry cleaners—Roylyn Dry Cleaners, 10 Australia Square (Tel. 27–3970).

Emergency (Police, Fire, Ambulance, etc.)—Telephone 000 (no coin is required).

Fishing supplies—The Compleat Angler Pty. Ltd., 127 York St. (Tel. 29–2780).

Florist—Town Hall Florist Shop, Town Hall Station (Tel. 26–5709).

Grocery store—Four Square Stores Ltd., 275 Clarence St. (Tel. 29–1232).

Hospital—Emergency medical attention at Sydney Hospital, Macquarie St. (Tel. 230–0111).

Legal Aid Office, 70 Castlereagh St. (Tel. 233–0233).

Library of New South Wales, Macquarie St. at Hunter St. (Tel. 221–1388).

N.S.W. Government Travel Centre, 16 Spring St. (Tel. 231–4444).

New Zealand Consulate, 60 Park St. (Tel. 233–3722).

Pharmacy (all-night)—Blakes Pharmacy, 28 Darlinghurst Rd. (Tel. 358–6712).

Police station—(General business Tel. 2–0966, but dial 000 for all emergencies, no coin required.)

Post Office—G.P.O., Martin Place, between Pitt and George Streets.

Theater tickets—Mitchell's Box Office, Hunter Arcade, Wynyard (Tel. 29–1932). Also, half-price theater and concert tickets for day of performance—Half a Tic, 23 Castlereagh St. (Tel. 232–2488).

Tourist Information Service—Sydney Visitors Bureau (Tel. 29–5312).
Travelers Aid Society, 358 Elizabeth St. (Tel. 211–2469).
Women's Amenities Centre, Park and Elizabeth Streets (Tel. 26 –2061).
Youth Line—(Tel. 33–4151.)

Australian Capital Territory—Canberra

Map courtesy Australian Tourist Commission

6

Canberra
and the A.C.T.

1. The General Picture

With the intense rivalry between Melbourne and Sydney from the earliest days of the colonies, it was someone's brilliant idea that on federation, Australia should develop an entirely new national capital which would be far enough away from the influences of both ambitious cities.

Canberra was designed about 1910 by an American, Walter Burley Griffin, then a landscape architect in his mid–30's and a former associate of Frank Lloyd Wright. Some of his inspiration may have come from Washington, considering his patterns of circling streets and broad thoroughfares which radiate from various points on the map.

Because of two world wars and a Great Depression in between, plus the inevitable bureaucratic controversy over the grandiose plans, Canberra took its time getting off the drawing board and onto the ground. Nevertheless in the past 30 years the city has come into its own and developed largely into the beautiful swirling patterns envisioned by Griffin. Its population today is fast approaching 250,000, and it's preparing for half a million by the end of the century.

The city is not finished, to be sure. There are empty lots all over the place, but even those help carpet the city with a sort of shaggy green between the spaced-out buildings and the more-manicured lawns. And when autumn comes in April, Canberra with its 4 million imported trees

Canberra

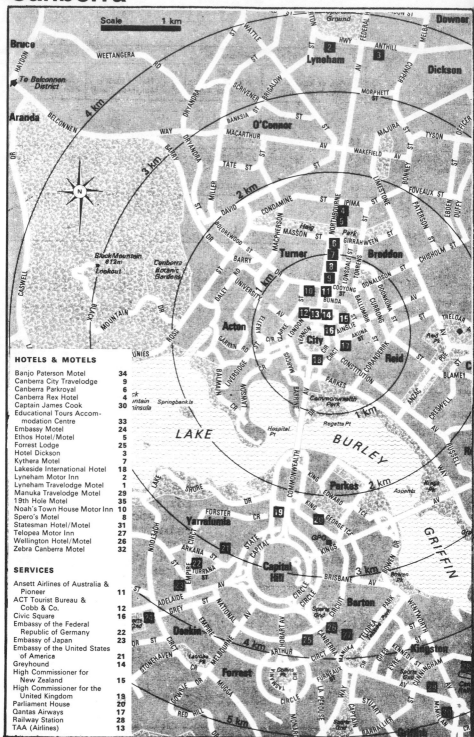

HOTELS & MOTELS

Banjo Paterson Motel	34
Canberra City Travelodge	9
Canberra Parkroyal	6
Canberra Rex Hotel	4
Captain James Cook	30
Educational Tours Accommodation Centre	33
Embassy Motel	24
Ethos Hotel/Motel	5
Forrest Lodge	25
Hotel Dickson	3
Kythera Motel	7
Lakeside International Hotel	18
Lyneham Motor Inn	2
Lyneham Travelodge Motel	1
Manuka Travelodge Motel	29
19th Hole Motel	35
Noah's Town House Motor Inn	10
Spero's Motel	8
Statesman Hotel/Motel	31
Telopea Motor Inn	27
Wellington Hotel/Motel	26
Zebra Canberra Motel	32

SERVICES

Ansett Airlines of Australia & Pioneer	11
ACT Tourist Bureau & Cobb & Co.	12
Civic Square	16
Embassy of the Federal Republic of Germany	22
Embassy of Japan	23
Embassy of the United States of America	21
Greyhound	14
High Commissioner for New Zealand	15
High Commissioner for the United Kingdom	19
Parliament House	20
Qantas Airways	17
Railway Station	28
TAA (Airlines)	13

Map courtesy A.C.T. Government Tourist Bureau

and shrubs changes colors more dramatically than any other metropolis in Australia. In the crisp, cool climes at 1,500 feet, the leaves are reflected in rust and golden symmetry in the artificial lake which bears the name of the young Chicagoan who first drew its banks.

Canberra is more than a political capital. It is also an important intellectual and scientific research center. The Australian National University was established here, as well as the National Library of Australia and the prestigious C.S.I.R.O. (Commonwealth Scientific and Industrial Research Organization).

As Washington has a D.C., Canberra has the A.C.T.—the Australian Capital Territory. It covers an area of nearly 1,000 miles, an elongated patch carved right out of and surrounded on all sides by the state of New South Wales. There are dozens of Canberra suburbs ("new towns") winding between the hills—all built on government leasehold land in order to protect the environment—plus a few other villages that predate the A.C.T. The territory includes an animal reserve in a rural bush setting, and it borders N.S.W.'s Kosciusko National Park, home of the Snowy Mountains.

All together, the Australian Capital Territory turns out to be a lovely bucolic area. If it seems without roots or a distinctive personality, it also appears to be far from the cares of the governmental and political world for which it was created.

2. The Airport and Long-distance Transportation

Canberra's airport, about four miles out Morshead Drive, is a modest construction. Strangely, considering its capital status, it's not even an international facility. (Everyone destined for Canberra must go through customs and immigration somewhere else, like Sydney or Melbourne.) Like most airports in Australia, it is basically divided into areas between **Ansett Airlines** (Tel. 45–0111) and the government-owned airline, **TAA** (Tel. 46–0211). There are several flights daily to and from Sydney (about 30 minutes away) and Melbourne (about 60 minutes).

By train, you take the Canberra-Monaro Express from Sydney (at 7:30 a.m.) all the way to Canberra in about five hours. Tickets are about $10, unless you have the Austrailpass. From Melbourne, it's longer, less convenient, and more expensive. The all-day trip (leaving 8:40 a.m. last we checked) goes first only to Yass. There you change for a bus for the final hour into Canberra, via the **Yass-Canberra Bus Lines** (Tel. 26–1378) arriving at 6:15 p.m. That's around $25, all together. There is also a train from the Canberra station to Cooma, the gateway to the Snowy Mountains recreation area.

Ansett Pioneer (Tel. 48–7555) and **Greyhound** (Tel. 49–8710) offer

Canberra—Kosciusko National Park

Map courtesy Australian Tourist Commission

trips from the major cities to Canberra at prices slightly above train fares. Or it's a pleasant day-long, 200–mile ride in a rented car from Sydney. Take the Hume Highway (No. 31) through Liverpool, Camden, Mittagong, Berrima, and Goulburn, and then the Federal Highway (No. 23) to Canberra. A longer route would be the Princes Highway along the Illawarra Coast (Route 1) to Bateman's Bay and then a local road via Queanbeyan to Canberra.

3. Local Transportation

In spread-out Canberra, you may be better off to rent a car than rely on local transportation. **Avis** (Tel. 49–6088), and **Hertz** (Tel. 49–6211) are at the airport as well as downtown. If you get a car at the airport, you'll begin by saving the $3 taxi—or $1.50 bus—fare into town. A local car rental agency is **Rumbles Rent-A-Car** (Tel. 95–0019) at 5 Bramble St., Red Hill. There's a branch of **Budget Rent-A-Car** (Tel. 48–9788) at 10 Mort St.

Taxis (Tel. 46–0444) are reasonably plentiful. It costs 45 cents to drop the flag, then 40 cents a mile, slightly more on weekends and with extras like 25 cents to telephone them and we've forgotten how much additional for luggage. (For comparison, a rental car may cost you $10 a day plus about 18 cents a mile.)

The orange and blue government bus service run by **ACTION** (Tel. 47–3445), an acronym for Australian Capital Territory Interurban Omnibus Network (!), is allegedly good, but although the service is frequent and convenient for commuters, it's not as well designed for visitors. During "school holidays," however, there is a special Route 901 which travels between tourist attractions. (That would be a couple of weeks in May, maybe two more in August, and a period running from mid-December through the first days of February.) Would that it ran the year around.

In any case, don't try to take ACTION seriously without picking up a copy of their Route Map and Passenger Information folder. Note there is a free bus service (Route 301) over a small circuit in the commercial area generally around London Circuit. And if you see a man in green, he's a bus inspector and available to answer rapid transit questions.

Bicyclists know that Canberra is supposed to be the best two-wheel city in the country. You may be able to rent your bike down by the ferry terminal near the "uni," or out at the youth hostel. Cost is about $3 per day.

4. The Hotel Scene

There are two or three excellent hotels in Canberra among the group that charge about $40 to $60 a night for two. (These are followed by others that are certainly acceptable for the budget range—perhaps $25 to $30 for a pair.)

EXPENSIVE HOTELS

Our top choice is the four-story **Canberra-Rex** (Tel. 48–5311) on Northbourne Avenue and Ipima Street: A large, L-shaped lobby in cool greens and blues with white marble coffee tables; Colonial restaurant to one side; nearby tree-filled patio with pool; coffee shop, the Washington Bar and twin aquaria also downstairs; wide hallways upstairs; the brightest, most-pleasant doubles, in browns and greens, with a view of Mount Ainslie; some with wood paneling; the corner units with balconies; many doubles with an extra single hidden under the window sill; TV, of course, and all luxury amenities. (Reservations from the hotel at Braddon, A.C.T. 2601.) Lyndon Johnson stayed here, and we'd guess he liked it just fine.

Some prefer the **Lakeside International Hotel** (Tel. 47–6244), sometimes called Noah's, a high-rise right on London Circuit at City Hill, and it does win a fifth star from the Royal Automobile Club and that crowd: A proud-looking structure with the flags of eight nations out front; acres of green, in effect, for a front yard; broad, colorful lobby; cozy if a little confusing bar to one side (that fellow bustling about picking up glasses is doing what he does; you place your own order at the bar); respectable restaurant, the Burley Griffin Room at the top; good, rosewood-like furnishings in the bedchambers; subtly striped wallpaper; many nice views over the lake; black-out curtains a thoughtful extra. Some front-desk personnel were not as polished as the furniture on our own stopover, but this may not be all that significant. (We'd avoid using any stock from the fridge next time, though.) (Reservations through the Noah's organization or the hotel at Box 1450, Canberra, A.C.T. 2601.) A good choice for the lake side.

The **Canberra Parkroyal** (Tel. 49–1411) is officially a motel (or "motor inn"), although here, as in most of Australia, we can discern little or no difference between good hotels and good motels. (This one is owned by the university.) Entranceway flanked with flags and fountains at a convenient covered bus stop; over the moat to the purple welcome mat; attractive modern lobby with complimentary coffee; handsome blue and silver Silver Grill and adjoining Swizzle Stick bar; spacious rooms; patterned walls; units with walk-out balconies overlooking the pool. (Reservations at the Parkroyal, 102 Northbourne Ave., Canberra, A.C.T. 2600.) A royal choice.

The **Canberra City TraveLodge** (Tel. 49–6911) at Northbourne and

Cooyong Rd., may be more modest, but it's within walking distance of the city center, and we found friendly, competent young women in charge. There's a small lobby, but the sleeping rooms were sizeable and all due for renovation by now. It's perhaps $5 a night less than its prestigious big sister up the avenue. Recommended for the more modest outlay.

We didn't like the **Town House Motel** for the money. It seemed very hard-used, overpriced, and in danger of harming the reputation of the Homestead chain which maintains some nicer places in other cities.

BUDGET PRICE ACCOMMODATIONS

If you don't have a lot of luggage, the nicest nest in the category is the tiny, friendly **Spero's Motel** (Tel. 49–1388) which sits almost alongside the big boys right on Northbourne Ave. at No. 82. No lobby to speak of, but an attractive French restaurant on the premises; no pool either, and perhaps the reason for the reasonable prices; compact rooms, each as neat and as well-designed as a ship's cabin, with lots of extras like color TV's, free coffee and tea-making materials; a self-service laundromat on the premises. We liked this tidy operation by John Spero Cassidy, and if he can keep his tariffs to $25 or so for two, and $20 for singles, it probably will remain the biggest little bargain in the capital.

Some other budget establishments are all right, too, even if they didn't strike us as solidly as Spero's. The **Kythera** (Tel. 48–7611) just up the street at 98 Northbourne Ave., will do. There's a pool, and it has some good, large family units. The **Ethos** (Tel. 48–6222) also seems older, but you might draw an ethical room here and you might not. TV's are available at extra charge. The **Hotel Dickson** (Tel. 49–6848), in the Dickson Shopping Center (across from McDonald's) has a lot of fancy facilities, but may be a little overrated locally. Choose the room before signing up; we thought some were a little scruffy on our inspection tour.

Youth hostel. Canberra's hostel is the **National Memorial Youth Hostel** (Tel. 48–9759) on Dryandra Street in O'Connor. (Take Bus 29 to Scrivener Street.) Members only may get a bed here for $4.

Accommodations in the snow fields? See Section 8, "Sports" for everything relating to ski fiends.

5. Restaurants and Dining

No restaurant in Canberra stands out as an unforgettable gourmet experience. Reportedly the embassy crowd keeps things cosmopolitan, but we wonder if that isn't just wishful thinking.

One of the most elegant salons, surely, is the **Burley Griffin Room**

(Tel. 47–6244) atop the Lakeside International Hotel. We found it dark enough to enjoy the panorama of lights out the window, but still bright enough to see the menu and the food. Purple and red upholstery and white tablecloths with formal French service by professional waiters. The Chicken Kiev was very nice. The Veal Cordon Bleu had a rather Italianized tomato accent, but we wouldn't complain. Music (organ and drums) began at 8:00 p.m. A well-planned dining choice. In the same hotel, the **London Grill** (same phone number for reservations) has a good local steak-and-chops reputation, but we haven't cut in yet.

But for that kind of fare, we enjoyed the friendly atmosphere at the **Charcoal Restaurant** (Tel. 48–8015) at 61 London Circuit, next door to the tourist bureau. The narrow room is relieved by a wall of mirrors which reflect the open kitchen. Most steaks are in the $5 to $6 range, and you can get a baked potato here—called a jacket potato in local parlance. The house red wine was also good.

Somehow we've not yet made it to the attractive **Paco's Carousel** (Tel. 73–1808). It's a Spanish-style salon perched atop the Red Hill lookout. Paco himself is the proprietor, and he offers imported Spanish wines. You can order a dinner as late as 10:00 p.m., here, but like most non-hotel Canberra restaurants, it's closed on Sunday.

We tried the **Red Door** (Tel. 49–6911) in the Canberra City Trave-Lodge for lunch. It's a pleasant appearing place, but the service and selection were poor. Maybe it's better for dinner.

Chinese food is popular in Canberra, and the most mentioned is the **Mandarin** (Tel. 82–3393). Specializing in Northern Chinese cooking, it's open Tuesday through Sunday at the corner of Townshend Street and Dundas Court in Phillip, up above the Singer Sewing Center. Other Chinese choices include **The Golden Wok** (Tel. 41–2812) in the Yowani Golf Club on the Federal Highway. (Also open Tuesday to Friday.) And **The Emerald Gardens** (Tel. 54–7939) serves seven days a week in the Hawker Shopping Center.

The **Taj Mahal** (Tel. 47–6528), an Indian entry at 39 Northbourne Ave., is pretty good. The **Shalimar** (Tel. 49–6784) is newer but reportedly gaining ground.

The **Private Bin** (Tel. 47–3030), at 50 Northbourne Ave., is informal, cheap, and fun, for the chicken, steaks, beer, and wine from Monday to Friday.

For Italian fare, try **Nero's** (Tel. 88–3146) at Cooleman Court in Weston.

A gregarious Greek motif is apparent at **Zorba's** (Tel. 51–3476) in the

Belconnen Mall shopping center, but it is not limited to Hellenic bill of fare. Not too surprisingly (if you remember that old movie), it's open "Never on Sunday."

For light snacks, pizzas, etc., wander down Garema Place and the little plazas adjoining. Several small cafes are there, some of which will no doubt change their owners and menus again before this perishable research finds its way into print.

Last, and perhaps least, Canberra, too, may be making a bid for recognition as a Dinkum big city at last. It's getting its very own revolving restaurant. This one will begin turning this year in the new telecommunications tower crowning Black Mountain. The view will be wonderful, and who knows? Perhaps the food will be better than that of other spinning dining salons now orbiting the earth?

6. Sightseeing in Canberra (and the A.C.T.)

On wheels, you can make the Canberra itinerary described here in the suggested order. If you're bussing, taxiing, or jogging, consult the map and cut in and out, depending on what seems interesting and practical. You may want to pay a visit first to the **A.C.T. Tourist Bureau** (Tel. 49–7555) in its rather hodge-podge headquarters at the corner of London Circuit and West Row. There's also a **Visitor Information Centre** on Northbourne Avenue near Morphett Street, which is open weekends.

Most itineraries suggest starting at Parliament House, but the best beginning for fellow foreigners, at least, is the **Regatta Point Planning Exhibition** set up by the National Capital Development Commission (NCDC) on the lake shore near the northern end of the Commonwealth Avenue Bridge. See the displays, scale models, etc., explaining the capital's design and development, and don't miss the audio-visual production in the theater. It's open daily from 9 a.m. to 5 p.m.

Just outside, of course, is **Lake Burley Griffin,** the seven-mile-long artificial lake which was finally created in 1963. It was named after the designer of Canberra, Walter Burley Griffin.

Near the Planning Exhibition, and just 550 feet offshore is the 250- to 450-foot high (depending on the winds) jet of water called the **Captain Cook Memorial,** modeled after the taller *Jet d'Eau* of Geneva. Perhaps symbolic of Australia's strict labor laws, even the fountain takes time out for lunch. It shoots generally from 10:00 a.m. 'til noon, and then again from 2:00 to 4:00 p.m. On shore, the Terrestrial Globe indicates the routes of Cook's travels.

Driving across the Commonwealth Bridge and then along Commonwealth Avenue, you pass on the right the commonwealth embassies of Great Britain, New Zealand, and Canada, respectively. (The American Embassy is also nearby, just off State Circle at Perth Avenue.) Many foreign legations are in the area, and all have been inspired by their own native architecture, sometimes to the point of caricature. The American embassy looks like something lifted from Colonial Williamsburg for instance, and it's true that all those red bricks were imported from the U.S.A.

The new parliament building is scheduled to rise in the center of the Capital Circle, but in the meantime the "temporary" **Parliament House,** which was built in 1927, is the long, low building on King George Terrace. If Parliament is in session, you can see much of the old-world froufrou that Australia inherited from Great Britain—the robes, wigs, swallow-tail coats, ruffled shirts, knee britches, buckled shoes, as well as convoluted ceremony like the pointing of the mace, and other rigamarole that will seem more than slightly incongruous to Americans.

You can watch parliamentary proceedings when the Senate or House is in session (normally Tuesday, Wednesday, and Thursday, March–June and August–October), but the free, 25-minute tours are conducted only when sessions are not being held. They're conducted throughout the day from 9:00 a.m. until 4:30 p.m. (except for the inevitable lunch break). King's Hall in Parliament House contains a 1297 issue of the Magna Carta, preserved under a sea of argon gas.

You may notice the Parthenon-like building down by the water. That's the **National Library.** A handsome structure, it's supposed to file everything written on Australia, and we can only hope there's another copy of this modest volume there by now among its 1¼ million works.

Across King's Avenue Bridge, to the left on little Aspen Island, is the three-column tower housing the **Canberra Carillon,** which merrily plays with 53 bells, a 1963 gift from Great Britain. In addition to the automatic "Westminster Chimes" played throughout the day, there are live recitals Wednesday and Sunday afternoons. (By the way, the Australian pronunciation of "carillon" rhymes with "pavilion.")

At the end of King's Avenue, you'll see the **Australian-American War Memorial,** a 258-foot-tall aluminum spire with the American Eagle roosting on top. (It's so tall that the eagle with the upswept wings sometimes looks more like a scared rabbit. Some locals call it "Bugs Bunny.") It commemorates American aid to Australia during World War II.

Drive north a few hundred yards along Russell Drive then Constitution Ave. if you want to look in at the 1858 **Blundell's Farmhouse,** one of the few old buildings around which pre-dated all the rest of the city.

(Open daily, 2:00 p.m. to 4:00 p.m., except Wednesday, 10:00 a.m. to noon.) In any case, it's on the way to **Anzac Parade,** a broad thoroughfare finished in 1965 and honoring the 50th anniversary of Anzac forces landing at Gallipoli. It's lined with Australian blue gum trees and New Zealand veronica shrubs.

At the head of the parade is the fortress-like **Australian War Memorial,** by far the most popular tourist site in Canberra. Filled with relics, pictures, and dioramas of Australia's many foreign campaigns, the copper-domed structure is sometimes criticized for glorifying war more than it laments those who died. There is a wonderful collection of old aircraft and interesting weapons there. The memorial is free and open from 9:00 a.m. to 4:45 p.m. daily. Be sure to get a floor plan to find your way around or take the guided tour.

About a mile east on Fairbairn Avenue a drive leads up to **Mount Ainslie Lookout,** one of three giving an excellent panorama of the city. (The others are Red Hill and Black Mountain.) From here, there are several choices. We recommend returning to the city to have a quick look at the exterior (you can't get inside) of the **Academy of Science.** The copper umbrella at Edinburgh Avenue and McCoy Crescent is at least of architectural interest. The 150-foot diameter igloo shape is sometimes called the "Eskimo Embassy" by Canberrans. In any case, the **Institute of Anatomy,** just across the street, *does* invite visitor exploration. There are two exhibition areas—one on Australian animals, and an excellent anthropological study of the Aborigines. It's open daily until 5:00 (beginning at 1:00 p.m. Sundays, 9:00 a.m. other days).

These latter two buildings are on the fringe of the 358-acre campus of the **Australian National University** (See the Visitor Information Centre on Balmain Crescent, opposite University House). It was founded in 1946 and now has about 7000 students.

Behind A.N.U. on Clunies Ross Street just past the C.S.I.R.O. is the **National Botanic Gardens** (Tel. 47–3822) on the lower slopes of Black Mountain. There are several trails through the 100 acres. They attempt to grow as many species of Australian plants and trees as is possible in the temperate climate.

We might mention two other Canberra sights because so many tour buses make them regular stops on their itineraries. (They may be of more interest to Australians than to international visitors.) One is the little **Serbian Orthodox Church** on National Circuit. There an octogenarian artist is covering the walls with murals of religious significance. And the **Royal Australian Mint** on Denison Street has been set up very well for visitors to see how Australian coins are made.

THE AUSTRALIAN CAPITAL TERRITORY

Out of town, the Cotter Road leads after 10 miles to the **Mt. Stromlo Observatory.** (Like lots of things in Australia, it's the largest "in the Southern Hemisphere," a specious comparison you may find all over the country.) There's a visitor center at this telescopic site, open from 9:30 a.m. to 4:00 p.m. On the same general highway, you can visit the **Tidbinbilla Tracking Station**—one of three satellite stations in the A.C.T., but this is the only one that is partially open to the public with a visitor center, etc.—and then the **Tidbinbilla Nature Reserve,** a highly recommended 13,617–acre piece of protected bush only 25 miles from the national capital. In this forested mountain region are several kinds of native trees among massive boulders. Also living there are possums, swamp wallabies, a colony of koalas, wombats, and spiny anteaters. And you can enter large fenced areas to see the emus and red and grey kangaroos who live there. Some of the roos have room enough to "kanga" along at speeds up to 30 m.p.h. Catching anything out in the open during the cold months of April through October would be pretty chancy, though.

Just south of the A.C.T., the Monaro Highway (No. 23) leads to **Cooma,** gateway to the Snowy Mountains and headquarters for the giant Snowy Mountains Hydro-Electric Scheme, and an interesting town in its own right. Drop in to the Visitors' Centre (Tel. Cooma 2–1108) on Sharp Street to (a) check on road conditions in the mountains and/or (b) see how best to experience some of the massive dams, underground power stations, man-made lakes, etc. The almost incredible water system, completed in 1974 after 25 years abuilding, basically diverts water from the Snowy River, that once flowed to the Pacific, into various other reservoirs and outlets. This allows it to irrigate more than 1,000 square miles of normally dry land to the west and at the same time to run seven power stations producing as much as 4 million kilowatts of electricity.

From Cooma, you can drive through alpine scenery to **Kosciusko National Park,** and its fields of snow or wildflowers. It's ideal ski country (see Section 9).

7. Guided Tours and Cruises

Don't hold us to these, but here was what was available the last time we checked and our estimate of what prices might be:

Ansett-Pioneer (Tel. 48–7555), 62 Northbourne Ave., offers two half-day trips. *Lakeside, Mint, and Library* leaves about 9:15 a.m. daily and may cost around $9. But we would choose the afternoon tour for around the same price called simply *City Tour*. It leaves about 1:50 p.m. Both are a little over three hours. The same company also has its *Canberra in a Day* which combines the points of interest from the other two tours for a seven-hour, 45–mile trip. We'll guess the price at about $16, now. Lunch is extra.

Canberra Cruises and Tours (Tel. 95–0557), Mundaring Drive, Kingston, an excellent local outfit we've had some experience with, offers several good tours every day except Sunday for similar prices. We like their half-day Tour No. 1, leaving at 9:30 a.m., and covering about what Ansett does in the afternoon. (And their afternoon tour is similar to Ansett's morning rounds.) They also have an all-day tour leaving at 9:30 a.m. It costs more—perhaps $21, by now—but it includes the launch and lunch on the lake. This is pretty good if you can take a whole day of regimentation.

Both companies offer tours which include a visit to a nearby country sheep station. We took the approximate equivalent of the *Waltzing Matilda* tour with C.T.&T., and enjoyed meeting the Colverwell brothers (Ray and Rhuben) and watching them at work, herding, shearing, dipping, etc. Equally impressive is their sheep dog who rounds up the "woolies," even running across their backs when necessary.

Get the latest on all these itineraries and any others, either by contacting the tour companies direct or the **A.C.T. Government Tourist Bureau** (Tel. 49–7555) at London Circuit, who can book you on these and a lot more, including fishing trips, tours to Mt. Kosciusko, and the Snow Mountains Scheme.

BOAT CRUISES

Canberra Cruises and Tours lives up to its name by running 1½–hour cruises for around $3 and luncheon cruises of about the same length for $7 or so on Lake Burley Griffin aboard the *Mini Munya* or the *Mimosa*. If the boat isn't too crowded (ours was), it's nice to get out on the water on a hot day, but remember that you can't get very close to anything. The ferry terminal is on the West Basin, near Clark Street, easily walkable from the Lakeside Hotel, or there's ample parking if you drive down.

We haven't tried Canberra's famous **Radio Motorcades** (Tel. 95–7082), where the commentary is given by a tour guide who broadcasts to a convoy of cars. Cost is around $9. Frankly, we'd like a tour guide we could talk back to. If you try it, let us know how you like it.

8. Water Sports

Canberra and the capital territory are the only major land-bound settlements in Australia, so there are no ocean-oriented activities in the immediate area. (It's about 100 miles to the surfing beaches at Batemans Bay.) Swimming in Canberra is confined to the competitions at the Olympic Swimming Pool and different strokes in other calm, rectangular waters.

There are a few river swimming holes (from November to April only in these colder climes) outside the city at Casuarina Sands, Kambah Pool, Cotter Reserve, and Uriarra Crossing—all popular picnic spots, too, incidentally.

You can rent a paddle boat, canoe, or row boat for about $2 per hour for your own private trip on Lake Burley Griffin. Cast off in these down by the ferry landing. (Power boats are generally not allowed on the lake.)

Trout fishing is allowed on the lake from about October 1 to May 31. No license is needed, but the bag limit is 10. The A.C.T. Tourist Bureau can arrange fishing trips to nearby trout streams, too.

9. Other Sports

Spectator sports are often held in the new **Bruce Stadium,** seating 20,000, and put up for the 1977 Pacific Games.

There is an 18–hole public **golf** course at Gloucester Park, Narrabundah, off the Cooma Road. You'll also find four private golf clubs in the territory, the **Royal Canberra** (where you need some sort of good introduction to get on the greens), and the **Federal** (at Red Hill), the **Yowani** (on the Federal Highway at Lyneham), and the **Queanbeyan** (at Queanbeyan, N.S.W., 9 miles away), all of which readily welcome out-of-town players. An outfit now advertising for players is the **Belconnen Golf Centre** (Tel. 54–6740) at the end of Drake Brockman Drive.

There are **tennis** facilities in several areas. Call the A.C.T. Lawn Tennis Association (Tel. 48–5402) for Mr. Willis, the president. If you're into **backpacking and hiking,** you might want to check with the **Canberra Bushwalking Club** (Tel. 81–2132). Skaters, whether on blades or wheels, look in at the **Paradice Ice and Roller Skating Rink,** in the showgrounds off the Federal Highway (at Flemington Road).

Canberra is a good staging area for the **ski country** which is actually headquartered about 100 miles away in the Kosciusko National Park, part of the state of New South Wales. Here in the Snowy Mountains, there are three main alpine villages on the slopes of Mt. Kosciusko—Thredbo, Perisher Valley, and Smiggin Holes.

There are more facilities at Thredbo (three double chair lifts, five T-bars, one poma lift), which hangs from a hillside like a Tyrolean village. The ski season runs from June through September.

We've never skied Thredbo, but friends who have tell us snow conditions are often unstable on the lower half of the mountain, but at the top, actually a plateau about 6,500 feet above sea level, the snowfields stretch for miles and reportedly are bigger than those of Switzerland.

Thredbo, popular with a young singles crowd, has about 15 hotels. Night life centers at "The Keller" (a live band and lots of lively young folks) or at the Schuss Bar, both in the Thredbo Alpine Hotel. At either, the most popular winter beverage is a hot, spicy "gluhwein." Perisher Valley and Smiggen Holes are more family resorts than party communities.

You can get Thredbo snow reports from Canberra by dialing 47–0686, from Sydney at 2–0510, or from Melbourne at 1–1544. Several companies run ski tours to the area.

10. Shopping in the A.C.T.

Shopping is largely decentralized among the several suburbs in Canberra. There is one shopping nexus in the Civic Centre, near the bottom of Northbourne Ave., and some of those Italianesque, arcaded shops are among Canberra's first buildings, built in 1926. A branch of **David Jones** department store is there.

The big shopping centers are Belconnen Mall and Woden Plaza. There are also popular shopping areas at Weston Creek, Manuka, and Kingston. All shopping is carried out during the usual Australian hours, except that late-night shopping in the A.C.T. is permitted on Friday. On Thursday night, capital residents go over to Queanbeyan for the bargains and the bright lights.

Save your serious shopping for Sydney, Melbourne, and other large cities, if you can. But for die-hard shop hounds, here are a few things you might find in the A.C.T.

Souvenir shops. Right downtown, **City Arts & Gifts** (Tel. 49–7102) at 52 Northbourne Ave. has a few oil paintings and prints along with the usual gimcracks. **Lakeside Gifts** (Tel. 48–0956) in the Lakeside Hotel, offers leather goods, sheepskins and suede items. **The Shearing Shed** (Tel. 95–9754), 52 Giles St., Kingston, specializes in leatherwork but also has sheepskin car seat covers and coats and vests made to order. **The Handcraft Center** at Fyshwick Plaza in Fyshwick has souvenirs plus handspun wool for knitting.

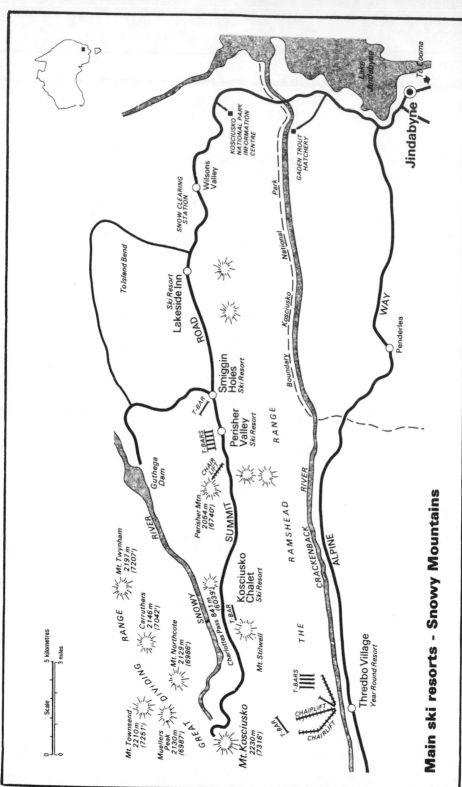

Main ski resorts - Snowy Mountains

Map courtesy Australian Tourist Commission

Galleries. In Woden Plaza, **Aboriginal Arts and Crafts** has a large number of Aboriginal works for sale. **The Fantasia Gallery** at 7 Broadbent St. in Scullin features works by Australian artists, printmakers, and sculptors, and **Narek Galleries,** 23 Grey St., Deakin, offers pottery, weaving, leather goods, jewelry, and paintings.

Books. There are several bookstores. One where we found some Australiana we needed was **Dalton's Bookshop** (Tel. 49–1844) on Garema Place.

11. Night Life and Entertainment

Canberra is not what you would call a swinging town, but there are enough activities to keep things interesting for a city of the size.

The closest thing to a night club is probably the **Queanbeyan Leagues Club,** just over the state line in Queanbeyan, N.S.W. As in Sydney, Leagues clubs usually welcome foreign visitors.

Several discotheques have spun into action in the past couple of years. Three of them are in the city center including **Mahogany**, **The Roxy**, and **Speakeasy**. Also there is the **Gov. Phillip** in Phillip and the nearby **Woden Disco** at the YMCA Centre in Phillip.

You'll find drinking and entertainment, too, at **Kimbo's** at 51 Townshend St. in Phillip, as well as at the **Plaza Tavern** (Tel. 82–3452) at the MLC Tower in Woden.

There's often rock music or something else going on at the Australian National University campus, usually upstairs in the Union bar (on North Road). One of Canberra's own musical groups, by the way, is the Little Jim Band, which seems to be headed for national recognition.

The main theater in town is the **Canberra Theatre Centre** (Tel. 49–7600) in Civic Square. There's a 1400–seat auditorium or a 600–seat playhouse, playing host to traveling theater, ballet or opera companies, or the Canberra Symphony Orchestra.

Theater/restaurant productions have come to Canberra at **Theatre 3** (Tel. 47–4222) at Ellery Crescent in Acton or at **Bard's** (Tel. 82–2983) at Adelaide House in Woden Plaza.

There are movie theaters in several shopping centers including those around Mort and Bunda Streets in the Civic Centre.

12. The Address List

Ambulance—Tel. 49–8133.
American Embassy—Yarralumla (Tel. 73–3711).
Automobile Club—NRMA, 92 Northbourne Ave. (Tel. 49–6666).
British Embassy—Commonwealth Ave. (Tel. 73–0422).

Bus information—Tel. 95–0251.

Canadian Embassy—Commonwealth Ave. (Tel. 73–3844).

Emergency calls—Dial 000; no coin required.

Flower shop—Christine's Flower Boutique, Canberra Arcade. (Tel. 47–0426).

Hospital—Canberra Hospital, Edinburgh Ave., Acton (Tel. 48–9922).

New Zealand Embassy—Commonwealth Ave. (Tel. 73–3611).

Pharmacy (after hours)—City Health Centre Dispensary, Clark Street (Tel. 49–1919).

Police Station—Knowles Place & London Circuit (Tel. 49–7444).

Post office—G.P.O., corner Northbourne Ave. and Alinga Street.

Queanbeyan Information Center—Farrer Place (Tel. 97–4602).

Secretarial service—Western Girl (Tel. 49–7777), 99 London Court.

Tourist information—A.C.T. Tourist Bureau, corner of London Circuit and West Row (Tel. 49–7555).

7

Melbourne,
the Victorian Capital

1. The General Picture

Melbourne suffers from an inferiority complex. She seems to be constantly comparing herself to Sydney, feeling the need to count out one by one the reasons why she is better than—or at least as good as—the N.S.W. capital up north.

Seen from a foreign perspective, she needn't do this at all. But Melbourne, pop. 2¾ million, just doesn't seem to have the confidence in herself as a major, significant, and yet attractive metropolis. And that's too bad.

Melbourne saw flamboyant Sydney get the extravagant opera house—pushing the flashiest kid on the block onto the stage of the world, it seemed—and now she wants an international landmark of her own. Now Melbourne has even appointed a committee to come up with one, and there's an ideal site available if designers can roof over the 74 acres of railway yards that now scar the area between the Cricket Ground and the Yarra River.

The Yarra, which winds to the south of the main part of the city, is often said to be Australia's only river that "flows upside down"—i.e., with all the mud and silt on top. It's an unkind exaggeration. Seen from some of the miles of green parkland skirting the city, the Yarra is a shiny,

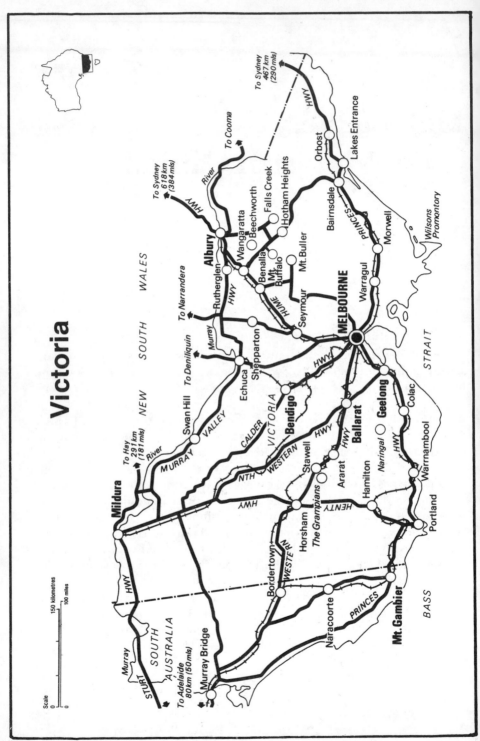

Victoria

Map courtesy Australian Tourist Commission

silvery ribbon reflecting the city's tallest buildings. Yet it's true that you wouldn't want to swim in it.

The Yarra flows to Port Phillip Bay, a body of water too far away to be considered part of the city itself, although the surburban trams and trains eventually roll their way to some handsome beaches at St. Kilda and Brighton.

In the other direction, Melbourne's outskirts now brush up against the Dandenongs, the attractive mountainlets which provide so many viewful weekend drives.

Seen from a distance or from the air, Melbourne seems to be a small forest of skyscrapers, an appropriate configuration for a city known as "everyone's home office." It is a proper business center, but it also has a historical dignity, seen best in a street-level view of the scores of Victorian-era public buildings. These filigreed structures, a legacy from the gold rush days in the latter half of the nineteenth century, give Melbourne its "English" look.

(However, a walk along upper Collins Street, under the speckled patterns created by the leafy trees along the city's proudest thoroughfare, seems more like a stroll along the Rue Madelaine in Paris.)

If Sydney-siders think about Melbourne at all, it is usually as the slightly amusing home of that form of formalized mayhem called Australian Rules Football. Or they know it as the city where it might decide to rain with no prior warning at all. It's true that Melbourne's weather has a "sudden change" quality about it—although statistics prove that more total rain falls in Sydney than in Melbourne.

Whether skies are clement or not, Melbourne shoppers may keep dry and warm by browsing their way through the famous glass-covered arcades, many of which date back 100 years or more. And speaking of shopping, much of Sydney would agree that Melbourne is "fashion central" in Australia. Some of the country's best-dressed women parade along Collins Street or attend civic functions at the quietly wonderful Arts Centre. Though less grandiloquent than Sydney's opera house, its beauty is one of thorough character.

A European living in Australia, and who travels between its two largest cities, might confirm that it is indeed possible to love both Melbourne and Sydney. Sydney, of course, is a perfectly attractive and carefree mistress, full of fun and convivial sensuality. But Melbourne, perhaps, is your wife, the neat, sensible, and loving mother of your children.

A most practical, comfortable, and even lovable life's companion, she is made perhaps even more attractive by her jealousy toward that "other woman" who lives up north.

Map courtesy Victorian Government Tourist Bureau

2. Airports and Long-Distance Transportation

Melbourne's new **Tullamarine Airport** is excellently designed, although unfortunately located a good 12 miles' drive northwest of the city. (When Tullamarine is socked in by fog, flights often land at Essendon, the older aerodrome, somewhat closer to the metropolitan area on the same freeway.)

The airport terminals are designed in a shallow U, with the international section at the middle and the two domestic airlines, **Trans Australia Airlines** (Tel. 345–3344—Be sure to say "double-three, double four!") and **Ansett Airways of Australia** (Tel. 345–1211) taking up space on the north and south arms respectively—a long walk if you're switching between Ansett and TAA.

In the **international terminal,** departures (Gates 1 to 6) are on the second level. There's also a duty-free shop, news stand, etc., and you can visit the observation deck for a five-cent piece in the turnstile. The large Top Air restaurant and cocktail bar are up on the third level, also providing a view over the runways. Arrivals are handled on the bottom floor, and that's where you'll find the bank for currency exchange as well as car rental, buses, and taxis.

The two **domestic terminals** are also arranged for check-in on the upper level and arrivals down below. After checking in, wait for your flight in the departure lounges (Gates 1 to 10, a different set for either Ansett or TAA). Both terminals have cafeterias. On the Ansett side you'll also find a pharmacy, a small bar, a post office, florist, and a "Mother's Room."

Ansett and TAA both have coaches that run to town from their respective terminals at a price of about $3 or so. By taxi, the trip will cost well over $10. Avis, Hertz and Budget cars are now available at the airport, ready to hand you a set of keys seven days a week. (You can even arrange for an Avis car from the air in Australia; ask the cabin crew on the plane.)

By the way, if you're interested in aerial charters, one all-Australia outfit is headquartered in Melbourne. It's Wing-Away Flight Services (Tel. 62–1776), at 51 Queen St. It offers private trips to any place in the country.

All interstate and most country trains arrive at the **Spencer Street Railway Station** (Tel. 62–0771 for reservations) at the foot of Bourke Street. (For information, look for the "Man in Grey.") Daily expresses to Melbourne include the overnight *Southern Aurora* and the *Spirit of Progress* trains from Sydney (about $30 for an economy seat—more for a sleeper), and the *Intercapital Daylight* service from Brisbane, Sydney, and

Canberra. Adelaide runs are made on the daily *Overland* (about $25 economy).

Ships from abroad generally dock at **Station Pier** (Tel. 61–2261) in Port Melbourne, a short suburban train ride out from the city. Nearby is the Tasmanian Ferry Terminal and the **Australian National Lines** (Tel. 62–0681) where you can board the *Empress of Australia* for the Sea-road service across the Bass Strait to the island state of Tasmania. (Fares run from about $25 to $75 each way, depending on arrangements.)

Coach (bus) trips come into Melbourne on either **Ansett Pioneer** (Tel. 345–3144), 465 Swanston St. or **Greyhound Coaches** (Tel. 67–9593), Bourke St., near Spencer St. at prices comparable to train fares.

You can drive to Melbourne on good roads from Sydney and Canberra or from Adelaide. The most scenic route from any of those cities to or from Melbourne is via the coastal Princes Highway—Route 1, which goes nearly around the entire continent. Via this route, it's about 660 miles from Sydney, two or three days' trip. On a circular tour, to or from Sydney, it would be more fun to take Route 1 one way and the other way via the Hume Highway, shorter at 580 miles.

3. Local Transportation in Melbourne

Before you rent a car in Melbourne, consider that the city has perhaps the finest system of public transportation in the country. Trolley cars and suburban trains run nearly everywhere, although a car is ideal for exploring the countryside around the state of Victoria. We tried to tour the Dandenong Ranges in a bus, recently, and were bitterly disappointed. The large vehicle just can't make the tight turns and park in the small areas we wanted to get to.

Although **Avis Rent-A-Car** (Tel. 347–4859) is the biggie at the airport (and downtown at 400 Elizabeth St.), there are several other reliable U-drives to choose from. These include **Astoria Rent-A-Car** (Tel. 347–7766), 630 Swanston St., **Letz Rent-A-Car** (Tel. 329–0222—that's triple-two), corner of Beckett and Queen Streets, and with offices in several states, **Morley Ford Rent-A-Car** (Tel. 62–0321), 29 Yarrabank Road, across the river, **Kay/Hertz Rent-A-Car** (Tel. 663–2901), **Budget Rent-A-Car** (Tel. 663–1872) and **Thrifty Rent-a-Car** (Tel. 347–6322).

Taxis cost about the same as in other Australian cities. Extra charges include 25 cents to telephone them (versus hailing them on the street), 10 cents per suitcase, and a whopping 20 percent surcharge for weekend service. Some phone numbers that will get you taxis in Melbourne: 62–0331, 34–0444, 347–4444, and 347–5511.

Melbourne's streetcars—they call them "trams," though—are legendary. They are run by the Ministry of Transport (Tel. 653–3611 for information). In the city center, at least, there always seems to be a tram approaching that will take you pretty near where you'd like to go, and the chances are that you'll get there for 45 cents or less. (Hold onto your receipt; inspectors often board the cars to have a look at them.) Careful when running for the trolley stops, though; although partly protected by guard rails, they often are out in the street, and Melbourne always has lots of out-of-town drivers who are unsure how to navigate through the tram system.

Try to pick up a Public Transport Map, available for about 20 cents at a bookstore or news agent. It includes color coded descriptions of all tram, bus, and suburban train routes. All those trains, incidentally, leave from that multi-gabled garage with ten clocks on the front called the **Flinders Street Station** (Tel. 653–3533 for information).

Be prepared for walking in Melbourne. Not only is it interesting, but the straightforward street pattern, especially in the central city, makes it easy to find your way around.

4. The Melbourne Hotel Scene

Be sure to see our general comments on Australian hotels under this same section in the Sydney chapter. Also, travelers throughout the country may want to get hold of a copy of the Royal Automobile Club's *Australian Accommodation Guide*. You'll probably have to buy it (for about $2) at RAC headquarters (Tel. 607–2211), 123 Queen Street in Melbourne. Published every six months, it includes the latest room rates on thousands of hotels and motels all over the country, as well as other basic facts and figures in even the smallest settlements throughout the country. (We often disagree with its star system, however.)

EXPENSIVE HOTELS

Rates will change, of course, but generally speaking, we have reserved this category for hotels charging more than $50 daily for two—most will be above $60. Unless otherwise noted, all will have the "international class" amenities like color televisions, air conditioning and central heating, room refrigerator, coffee/tea-making equipment, etc.

It may seem unoriginal, but virtually every Melbournian will agree that the number one house this year has to be the 21-story **Melbourne Hilton** (Tel. 419–3311). Dramatically situated next to Fitzroy Gardens to the west and the Cricket Ground to the south; huge, marble-floored, red-carpeted lobby; overhead glass sculptures glittering by spotlight; a swirling staircase up to the mezzanine; pleasant, tapestry-lined lounge;

opulent Cliveden Restaurant with stained-glass windows (closed Sundays); less-formal Gallery Restaurant (open daily); the MCG Hotel, an old-fashioned Aussie pub attached to the newer building; Juliana's of Melbourne, a disco for Tuesday to Saturday terpsichore; heated swimming pool (pool bar open on the terrace in warm weather).

Outback-sized elevators to 41 suites and 387 spacious, excellently equipped bedchambers, all with standard luxury amenities (color TV, direct-dial phones, etc.); other special touches like the self-service fridge/bar; terrific views from the higher floors; some units available right next to the pool; reportedly excellent service everywhere (or as the locals say, "spot on!"). We looked high and low for anything critical to say about the Hilton. The only thing we could come up with is that some folks may think it's a little far to walk to shopping, theaters, etc.—a very small penalty to pay, especially with the ubiquitous taxis and trams available. (Reservations through the Hilton organization or from the hotel at East Melbourne 3002, Victoria.) We call it "spot on" indeed!

The **Southern Cross Hotel** (Tel. 63–0221), a U.S.-built plant which has had its ups and downs over the past two decades, is on the rise again since its purchase from the InterContinental chain by Melbourne's Fink family. Extremely convenient in the downtown theater and shopping district; modern steel-and-glass structure at the corner of Exhibition and Bourke Streets; direct connection to a modern, two-level shopping arcade; rambling lobby with burbling, cherub-filled fountain and purple-paisley-patterned carpet; several public rooms including the frond-full Palm Court Restaurant, the tartan and brick-lined Club Grill, the Tavern Bar, the Wilawa Piano Bar, etc. No pool; free parking. Nearly all bedrooms recently refurbished with king or queen-size beds; new shag pile rugs in the suites; top-grade accessories in all rooms; excellent decorations with patterned wallpaper or draperies and bedspreads; most rooms with tub and shower together. (Reservations from the hotel at 131 Exhibition St., Melbourne, Vic. 3000). The Southern Cross, like the one on Australia's flag, deserves its five stars.

Somewhat far from the center of things, the **Old Melbourne Inn** (Tel. 329–9344), often called several similar names like the Commodore Old Melbourne Hotel, has excellent facilities if somewhat overdecorated for our personal taste. Designed rather like an old coach house in some parts, a baronial European mansion in other areas; antiques abounding everywhere (ask for the booklet explaining them all). Four-to-six-story building surrounding an interior cobble-stoned courtyard; small lobby with red and pink flocked wallpaper and a bust of Shakespeare (or somebody); Haymarket 1886 Restaurant with blue velvet and more statuary; Norman Lindsay Cocktail Bar (named after the late Australian author and artist); separate piano bar, lit by piano-top candelabrum; Ma's Tea and Coffee Shop with wallpaper on the ceiling, even; Nellie Stewart's Bar; Banjamin's Cellar; ample outdoor swimming pool.

Well over 200 well-maintained bedrooms, 75 percent with walk-out iron-railed balconies; good quality though heavy furnishings. (Reservations from the hotel at 5–17 Flemington Rd., Melbourne North 3051, or through the Commodore chain in Australia.) We think it's strongly saccharin and a mash of mixes, but it's well-run and immensely popular.

With less personality, but more convenience, **Noah's Hotel Melbourne** (Tel. 662–0511), not to be confused with the similarly named above, attracts many to its mid-city location. Large entranceway over some slick bricks; a display of pottery in the reception area; unique ceiling of ball-shaped chandeliers; unusual lighting elsewhere throughout the hotel, too; two restaurants, Bryson Grill and the Cup Room, probably open for late meals; several bars, including the Golden Nugget one flight up; large heated pool on the roof of the 23–level building.

All bedrooms located above the 10th floor, a noise-reducing plus; good luxury equipment in the units; some purple accents; some rooms perhaps still a little under $50, but don't count on it. (Bookings through the Noah's chain or from the hotel at the corner of Exhibition and Little Bourke Streets, Melbourne, Vic. 3000.) Noah's is a dependable, if undramatic ark, in Melbourne.

Still abuilding, and not due to open until late 1980, is the mammoth, twin-towered Qantas-owned **Wentworth Melbourne.** The plans seem magnificent, and we look forward to seeing this place with its massive atrium, elegant restaurants and pillarless ballroom once they get it all together.

MEDIUM PRICE HOTELS

If you're lucky, you'll pay about $35 to $50 for a double in these places. Most of them are far below the quality of those preceding, and penny-squeezers may want to drop directly to our budget entries.

The **Hotel Australia** (Tel. 63–0401), which dates back to 1939, is hoping life does indeed begin at 40. It could hardly be more convenient and central, at 266 Collins St., and with a bottom-level entrance on the Australia Arcade. Lots of stairs to and through a multi-tiered lobby; browns, woods, and oranges predominating in the reception area; Swiss Grill, Terrace Restaurant, and Boomerang Grill for full meals; The Hut, a cafeteria-style eatery; the Woolshed Bar and the Boomerang Bar; some rooms with shower, others with tub; TV's (some in color) and fridges throughout, but no coffee/tea pots; some units at about $48 for two, well in this category, but the fanciest accommodations above $55, not a bargain. Overall, it's a respectable choice, and certainly a winner on location.

The **Sheraton** (Tel. 63–9961) is another of those smallish hotels (like Sydney's) which somehow got hold of the Sheraton name in Australia. Not a bad site at 13 Spring St., across from the Treasury Gardens and a statue of Bobby Burns; small, purple lobby; Terrace Restaurant with park view, slightly above the traffic; 166 neat, clean rooms, some with queen-size beds; some with balcony. (Reservations from the hotel or through the Flag chain.) It's no showplace, but it's okay.

Some rate the old **Windsor** (Tel. 63–0261) as one of Melbourne's top hotels, but it was a bitter disappointment to us. In many ways, it's a mammoth antique, somehow kept breathing through heroic life-support measures far beyond its time. We experienced poor service, shoddy maintenance, only fair housekeeping, and incomplete refurbishments on our own stopover. Without reliving the depressing details which fill our notes, let's say we thought it fun to see, perhaps, but no joy to stay in at the tariffs asked.

Today's travelers deserve efficiency and comfort, too.

BUDGET ACCOMMODATIONS

The **Victoria of Melbourne** (Tel. 63–0441), which has rooms perhaps still running a wide gamut between $15 and $35 for two, has to be number one at this "Bare Bones" price level. Like the Australia and the Windsor, it's also the relic of another age, but one more fairly priced for the fading charms. Very central location at 215 Little Collins St.; popular with out-of-town shoppers of modest means; lobby dominated by a staircase to the mezzanine salon; TV lounge somewhere; creaky corridors; older rooms in the rear with radios about $10 single, $15 double; newer units in the east wing with color TV's about $35 for two by now. We think Vickie's viable for the category.

A very different kind of establishment is the peaceful little **Magnolia Court** (Tel. 41–2782), away from the bright lights at 101 Powlett St. in East Melbourne, not far from Fitzroy Gardens. This is a very clean, family-run bed-and-breakfast place, still offering rooms at approximately $25 for two (maybe $15 for one), including the morning meal in the sun room. Write Mrs. Doyle, the resident manager, at the address above (Zone 3002). The Magnolia is a pleasant blossom.

An old favorite is the **Glensborough** (Tel. 41–5842), not far away at

48 Wellington Parade, and near the Hilton. This is also a "private hotel," which in Australia merely means no alcohol is sold on the premises. (Big deal!) Now it's been sold, but Mrs. Feely, who's still in charge, thinks the new owners will keep things running smoothly. Clean rooms rent for perhaps less than $25 for two, including a light breakfast. (You might get it for a whole week for about $60!) Some are without "private facilities," but all have washbasins at least. Somewhat of a question mark, maybe, but worth a try for sure.

Also very practical, if a little sterile, is the **YWCA Motel** (Tel. 329–5188), 489 Elizabeth St., near the Ansett Terminal. No frills, but it's clean accommodation for women, men, or families for about $22 double, $18 single. There's a TV lounge, a Red Phone at the end of every corridor, etc. We met one American budget-minded family who were staying here, and they thought it was great.

Hosies Hotel (Tel. 62–5521) has some unsurpassed views of the Flinders Street Railway Station. Check out the Mile High Club on the fourth floor. It's filled with leftover furnishings from old airliners, apparently. The rooms, which take off for about $30 double, $25 single, are undramatic, often small, but fairly clean. You'll find it, if you want it, at the corner of Elizabeth and Flinders St. Hosie's not rosie any more, but she's friendly, willing, and probably able.

Youth hostels? There is one, at 500 Abbotsford St., North Melbourne (Tel. 328–2880), which will set you back around $4 a night (but bring your own sheets). You must be a member, of course. If you're not, you can apply to the Youth Hostels Association of Victoria (Tel. 63–5291), Shop 11, Princes Gate Arcade, Flinders St., Melbourne 3000. (At the corner of Swanston Street.)

5. Restaurants and Dining

Melbourne has a deservedly rich reputation for elegant dining, if also one for changeable chefs and peripatetic proprietors who kanga from one kitchen to another, making it difficult to keep up with what's currently "in."

By type of cuisine, we list those dining rooms in the central area—Melbourne, with East, West, and South Melbourne, as well as Carlton (the "uni" neighborhood) thrown in. Following that is a group in greater Melbourne and other out-of-town precincts by the name of their respective areas. Remember that some of Melbourne's best salons are indeed far out from the center—e.g., Baxter Provender in Baxter, the Black Knight in Camberwell, and Glo Glos in Toorak.

AUSTRALIAN AND COSMOPOLITAN

The category may sound a little modest for such an excellent restaurant, but **Petty Sessions** (Tel. 61–3854) is too varied in its ability to be called Continental. A below-street-level site in the law courts and financial district, it offers sensible fare for lunch and then superb evening-out dining later on. We can personally recommend the garlic prawns (Sara had 'em as a full meal!) and the Escalope de Veau Calypso, in which the veal was cooked in a coconut and mango sauce. The Beef Wellington and rack of lamb are also good. Others have praised the crayfish thermidore (that's a lobster, of course) and the supreme of chicken (either "butterfly" or "Rossini").

Most dishes are in the $8 to $10 range. Two with wine and dessert will share a bill of about $35. We had excellent attention from the waiter and the maitre d', and the whole experience was one accented by candlelight and a live orchestra playing by a dance floor somewhere toward the rear. Our only grouse was that like many successful restaurants around the world, they try to crowd too many tables into some narrow spaces. It's officially at 459 Collins St., but look for the striped awning on a side street just a few steps south of the main drag. Petty Sessions was a Grand Session for us. (Closed Sundays.)

Fun for lunch—and we mean especially for long, drawn-out, conversational lunches—is the incomparable **Jimmy Watson's** (Tel. 347–3985) at 333 Lygon St. in Carlton. Cheap drinks, substantial food, and noisy conviviality characterize this place which winds through an old wine shop near the university. It isn't so much what you have here (roast beef and the like) as who you have it with. Say hello to Prop, Alan Watson, jovial son of the founder, and currently a Melbourne city councilman. We enjoyed one of Watson's own wines, a special Tokay, with our own midday munch with Stan Marks, the Melbourne author and *bon vivant* who let us in on it. Fondly recollected and recommended.

The **Windsor Room** (Tel. 63–0261), in the wedding-cake styled Windsor Hotel, 115 Spring St., is supposed to dish out good, English-style food at dinner, and maybe it does. (The Chicken Maryland, a Melbourne institution, is probably dependable.) We only broke our fast in here one morning, and found the greasiest eggs, the weakest coffee, and the most bumbling, amateurish service in six states and two territories. The setting is incomparable, however—a return to an elegant dining room of the last century, complete with ornate skylights, potted palms, and sometimes a string-heavy orchestra in the corner somewhere. Hopefully, there's a different crew guiding things in the evening, and we'll be back for a try.

Eleventy-seven dozen varieties of pancakes are available at **The Pancake Parlor,** off Bourke Street in the theater district at 4 Market Lane. We stayed with something mapley and conservative and enjoyed drawing up to the warm fire on a cold, wet day. (Open daily, but there's that weekend surcharge after 5:00 p.m. Friday.)

In the same neighborhood, American-style sandwiches are supposed to be served at the **Showbiz Deli** (Tel. 662–3711) in the dress circle foyer of Her Majesty's Theatre. (Cnr. Exhibition and Little Bourke Sts.) We haven't yet tried it.

CHINESE RESTAURANTS

Melbourne's foremost Chinese restaurateur is Gilbert Lau, justly famous for **The Flower Drum** (Tel. 663–2531), which beats a fragrant song at 103 Little Bourke St. At last word, Lau has been angling for permission to launch a two-story floating restaurant on the Yarra River. If it's as elegant as the Flower Drum, you won't retreat down the gangplank without spending about $25 for a couple.

Several less-expensive Chinese places are around, including the **Lotus Inn** (Tel. 663–4667) on Market Lane, off Bourke Street (Try the lobster.), **Chopsticks** (Tel. 41–4243) at 10 Wellington St., East Melbourne, or for spicier, Mandarin-style food, the **Shangri-La** (Tel. 347–7922) at Grattan and Drummond Streets in Carlton.

CONTINENTAL AND FRENCH CUISINE

On our own recent ramble over the restaurants of Melbourne, we experienced outstanding cooking at **Balzac** (Tel. 419–6599), at 62 Wellington Parade, a short march from the Hilton. Somehow in our exuberance, we lost our notes, but we remember it as an attractive, streetside cafe, with waiting room in the fountain patio. (The house has been bought and sold a few times, however, so make sure it's still guided by Leon and Vivienne Massoni.) Here is the place for tender veal or roast duckling. We enjoyed the Escalope de Veau a la Savoyarde—served with dry vermouth and cream sauce. There's a long, five-page menu, inspired, perhaps, by Honore de Balzac's history of France. Almost a *tour de force*.

You won't see any advertising for **Fanny's** (Tel. 663–3017), which has consistently held the reputation as the most authentic French restaurant in Melbourne for the past several years. Keeper of the kitchen Edouard Demounoff again won the city's Best Chef Award recently. Try the breast of chicken with hazelnut sauce. Find Fanny's at 243 Lonsdale St., between Russell and Swanston. Expensive and often crowded, but with good reason. (Closed Sundays.)

A smaller and less-pricey place, a little north of the center, near Carlton Gardens, is **Fives** (Tel. 380 –5555), apparently named after its telephone number and address at 555 Nicholson Street. It's open daily except Tuesday, and a woman chef named Marjorie Miller is reputed to be one of the best in town. We haven't been in, but it's on our list for a personal try this year. (Often open late; closed Tuesdays.)

And after our last Melbourne meander, a savor savvy friend named Sally wrote us from there to say she tried **Lazar's** (Tel. 602–1822), a very attractive bluestone restaurant at 250 King St., and loved every minute and morsel. The place has been converted from an old warehouse, she said. Sally advises us to stick to the main restaurant, though, and skip the upstairs bistro. We'll make a booking there our next trip.

ITALIAN FOOD

Melbourne is well-known for the cooking delights of its Italian population, and their delight in opening it all up for everyone to enjoy. One success for us was the **Society** (Tel. 63 –5378) high up at 23 Bourke St., about 25 yards south of Spring. An unspectacular decor with red-flocked wallpaper supporting a few old-masterish oils. We loved the ravioli verdi, filled with a paté and covered with a spicy sauce. Try the osso bucco or the spaghetti marinara, too. The staff is attentive, and the house wine is satisfactory for an average meal. (Closed Sundays.)

For weekdays only, **Florentino** (Tel. 662–1811), at 80 Bourke St., was once Melbourne's premier Italian restaurant. It is still very good and serves some loyal clientele, although some complain of creeping commercialism. Stick with the saltimbocca or the fish specialties.

Sassi's (Tel. 489–5254) is newly opened a little north of the center at 99 Queen's Parade. An old savings bank, it has been converted to an elegant bistro at the end of a tree-lined driveway. Amid brick walls and blue-tiled floors, Tony Sassi and his mother dish out delicious calamari (squid), steak pizzaola, and other recipes emanating from Milano to Palermo. (Open daily except there's no lunch on Saturday or dinner on Sunday.)

A modest affair, but a personal favorite at a reasonable price level is the somewhat hectic **Pellegrini's** (Tel. 662–1885). Officially at 66 Bourke St., it's more like two restaurants—a tiny, narrow corridor at that address and another, larger room behind, best reached via the little alley at the side.

The front section is very much a coffee bar where you can get a decent espresso but at the same time a heaping plate of spaghetti bolonaise, slices of pizza, etc. The rear restaurant is a green-tiled building, at times chaotic. Like a cafeteria, you choose your food by looking and pointing, but then you go sit down and wait for it to be fussed over and then delivered. We had a speedy lasagna in here before attending a nearby theater, and it was cheap, fast, and good. If you can take the noise and rush, then go. It's not "licensed," so BYO wine or take the "fruit cup," a delicious tame drink. (Closed Sundays.)

La Cantina (Tel. 662–1382), a former favorite at 38 Bourke St., is a question mark this year due to the departure of some key personnel. If you go, let us know, please. The **Latin Cafe** (Tel. 662–1985), however, is still a popular gathering spot at 55 Lonsdale Street for Melbourne's communicators. We'd stick with the spaghetti and pasta standards and enjoy rubbing elbows with the city's writers and politicos who show up to gossip and relax. The pasta is much cheaper at the **Spaghetti Theatre,** a BYO spot at 185 Collins St. It's a bit frayed around the edges, but that's undoubtedly the way they like it. Certainly informal and no pressure is applied on anyone to buy anything more than a cup of coffee or a "spider." (That's a sort of Melbourne milkshake.)

OUT OF TOWN RESTAURANTS

We hasten to say that we define "town" a little more narrowly for international travelers than a Melbournian would when it comes to restaurants. Neighborhoods like South Yarra and Collingwood are fruitful gourmet neighborhoods in the metropolitan area if you have a car and know your way around.

Baxter

One of the best and most expensive restaurants in the state, about 30 miles down the southern coastline, is the **Baxter Provender** (Tel. 059 + 77–7337, but you may have to reserve a week or more ahead.) James Beard said in his newspaper column that he loved the Beef Wellington here last year. It's in an 1853 farmhouse on Sages Road. (You'll drop at least 50 bucks for two here, they say. We haven't been.)

Camberwell

About five miles east of the center, the **Black Knight** (Tel. 82–3649) champions the continental cause in Camberwell. It's expensive. Try the Pork Fillet Bohemia.

Collingwood

Much closer, the French-style **Clichy** (Tel. 41–6404) is not far from the Yarra Bend National Park at 9 Peel St. This is good, inexpensive

French fare in quiet surroundings. Bring Your Own Booze. (Closed Mondays, for some reason.)

Prahan

Between St. Kilda and Toorak, an excellent continental restaurant is **Bernardi's** at 34 Punt Road. Although recently damaged by fire, it has been redone with flair. We hear good words, too, about **Percy Pringle's,** also on Punt Road. It's an atmospheric place where large and small model dogs are the stars of the show.

St. Kilda

Check out the inexpensive foreign restaurants along Acland Street, near the Village Bell (a pub). One well-known Bavarian dining room is the **Black Rose** (Tel. 94–6885).

South Yarra

Mention South Yarra in Melbourne, and everyone thinks "food." Indeed there are several good restaurants in this close-in neighborhood. The most famous is **Maxim's** (Tel. 26–5500), at 60 Toorak Road. It's fairly expensive for dinner and very French, of course, although somewhat faded now in its later years.

A smaller and less-expensive continental choice is **Ellie's** (Tel. 269–2030), further along at 278 Toorak Road. Try the Duckling a l'Orange. Two other value-full establishments are **Green's** (Tel. 240–9847), at 425 Chapel St., and **Mr. Bumby's** (Tel. 24–9318) at 505 Chapel St. The much-more-famous **Two Faces** (Tel. 26–1547) is often noisy and food quality may be on the skids.

Toorak

When we were last in Melbourne, **Glo Glo's** (Tel. 24–2615) was *the* chic international dining room. We couldn't see paying the price then, however—maybe $50 per couple. If it holds that reputation, we'll hoe into their tucker before the next edition of this volume. It's open until midnight, and the "in" crowd dines late here. Our reliable informants tell us that although glamorous and glossy, the cuisine is also excellent. (Closed Sundays.)

Also in Toorak are two modest local favorites, **Mostly French** and **Kate's,** both sizzling for good steaks and chops.

A last word on dining. An excellent and most thorough guide to Melbourne restaurants is the paperback *Eating Out In Melbourne*, updated yearly by columnist Peter Smark. We could have saved ourselves a lot of fumbling around if we'd discovered it sooner. It sells for about $4 at bookstores all over the city.

6. Sightseeing in Melbourne (and Victoria)

We certainly don't recommend a hectic round of "musts" in Melbourne. A couple leisurely walks might do the trick.

THE "GOLDEN MILE"

That somewhat expansive term is what Melbournians like to call central Melbourne or "Melbourne City." It's a rectangular cross hatch of about 18 principal streets north of the Yarra River. That network, in turn, is set at an angle to hundreds of other regularly spaced streets and roads.

If you have a map, here's a theoretical walk down Collins Street to about Elizabeth, then back up Bourke to Spring, along Little Lonsdale Street to Swanston, then over to LaTrobe and thence to Russell. We've lopped off quite a bit of the Golden Mile. You may want to add on a few discoveries of your own or to shave some more off this. Feel free to do so.

Collins Street, they say, is nothing like its ambiance in years gone by. Many of its Gold Rush Gothic and Victorian buildings have fallen to make way for the high-rise headquarters of diverse banks and insurance companies. Nevertheless, it has some of that all-mixed-up charm of Fifth Avenue in New York. There are plenty of trees, flagstones, and nineteenth-century structures still standing to provide pleasant backgrounds to a walk down Collins from Spring.

Near Swanston Street, **City Square** has been in the process of renovation amid considerable controversy about the tearing down of nearby buildings. Maybe it will be finished this year; maybe not. Across the street, with its entrance on Swanston Street, the **Town Hall** dates back to 1867. About 3,000 can crowd in for public events, they say, but that mob has never included us.

A sidestep to the left, along Swanston, leads to **St. Paul's Cathedral,** a stylistic mixture that started out with a British architect in 1880. If you're only going to look at one cathedral, however, you might want to save it for St. Patrick's. Across the street, at Number One Swanston, hides Melbourne's truest treasure—at least to hear some speak. There in the bar at **Young & Jackson's** a tiny pub, is the art work that shocked the Melbourne Exhibition of 1880. It's a large, full-length nude oil of "Chloe"—positively Australia's most famous single painting and the subject of countless toasts from Young & Jackson's to North Africa over the past 90 years.

In the next block south on Collins is the ancient **Royal Arcade,** one of several skylit shopping tunnels that burrow through the business blocks. Look for the painted statues of Gog and Magog. When fully operational, they call attention to the time of day every hour. The Arcade, built about 1870, has entrances on Collins and Little Collins Streets and also to the mosaic-tiled Block Arcade. Nearby is the **Victoria Tourist Bureau** (Tel. 63–0202), at 272 Collins St.

At the corner of Collins and Elizabeth Streets, you can shoot up 21 floors for a panoramic view over the city from the **Colonial Mutual Life Building.** Conducted tours to the top are given weekdays at about 2:30 p.m.

At the corner of Elizabeth and Bourke is the **General Post Office,** which owes its rococo design to no fewer than 65 architects. Bourke Street between Elizabeth and Swanston is a walking street, *except for trams,* so watch out! (Motor men are pretty careful, of course, but they can't swerve.) Upper Bourke Street, between Swanston and Spring, is the heart of the cinema and theater district.

At Spring Street, the historic old **Windsor Hotel** still operates to your right. (Peek into the dining room, lounges, etc., if you can, to see how she has weathered the decades since the Gay 90's.) Across Spring Street is the Neo-classic **State Parliament House,** which they began building in 1856 and continued working on for 36 years before giving up. Two sides of the building are still incomplete. In 1901 the National Parliament met here and liked it so much that they continued to do so until 1927 when the lawmakers moved to Canberra.

In the nearby little triangular park called Carpentaria Place is the seated Statue of Adam Lindsay Gordon, the tragic Australian poet (1830–1870).

The corner of Spring and Little Bourke Streets is taken up by the elaborately decorated **Princess Theatre,** built for the Queen's Jubilee in 1887. Large-scale productions are still staged here.

Just up Nicholson Street at Albert Street is the first of Australia's skyscrapers, the **I.C.I. Building** (Tel. 662–0201) put up in 1958. Last information we had was that tours are taken to the top at 2:15 p.m., Monday through Friday, but ring the above phone number to be sure. Not far away, in quite a different world, is **St. Patrick's Cathedral,** the triple-spired gothic structure at Gisborne and Albert Streets, that every architectural enthusiast says we should see. We've yet to go in ourselves, but those in the know say it's got to be one of the best Gothic interiors in the world. Sorry we missed it.

The **National Museum,** at the corner of Little Lonsdale and Russell Streets, presents extensive natural history and ethnographic collections. But its prime exhibit to most Australians, perhaps rivaling the aforementioned "Chloe," is the stuffed Phar Lap, the chestnut gelding who won 37 races, including the Melbourne Cup of 1930. He died in 1932 right after winning the Agua Caliente Handicap at Menlo Park, California. (Australians can't seem to let Phar Lap go. His heart is on display at the Institute of Anatomy in Canberra.) The National Museum is open daily until 5:00 p.m., beginning at 10:00 a.m. weekdays and 2:00 p.m. Sundays.

On the Swanston Street end of that block, in the same building, is the **Institute of Applied Science of Victoria** (Tel. 663–4811). Technological exhibits abound, and there are lots of buttons to push. The **State Library of Victoria** is part of the same complex, with its entrance on LaTrobe Street.

Where Russell Street meets Franklin Street is what's left of the 1841 **Old Melbourne Gaol,** now a penal museum, open daily from 10:00 to 5:00. As every Australian schoolchild knows, this was the site of the hanging of the bushranger Ned Kelly, November 11, 1880. His armor is there, too, along with the cell where his mother admonished him, "Mind you die like a Kelly!"

And still in place, too, is the hangman's scaffold where, at the age of 25, he spoke his last words: "Such is life!"

Many Australians who visit Melbourne wouldn't feel they had done the town at all if they hadn't experienced the whole trinity—(1) the painting of Chloe, (2) the skin of Phar Lap, and (3) the spirit of Ned Kelly in the old jail. We agree.

THE VICTORIAN ART GALLERY

Officially, it's the National Gallery of Victoria Arts Centre (Tel. 62–7411), and that's a much better term than the Victorian Art Gallery, which gives the impression to an out-of-towner that it houses "Victorian" art—that is, art created during the Victorian age. (Unfortunate misunderstandings occur all over the place to foreigners like us because of things named after the *state* of Victoria, not the *era* of Queen Victoria.)

The basalt bluestone structure just across Princes Bridge at 180 St. Kilda Road beckons from a rounded archway across a moat. An inner glass wall supports a sheet of running water. There's also a Great Hall whose roof is made of stained glass panels. Three open courtyards and many halls house sculpture and art that ranges from some of the best Asian and European (contemporary and Old Masters), plus a large collection of paintings by the "Heidelberg School," Australian artists who were strongly influenced by French impressionism. Other periods of the nation's art—Colonial, Edwardian and Contemporary—are also represented, and, in fact, the Australian collection is so large that only about a third of it can be exhibited at once.

The gallery is just the first step in the three-part Arts Center, the rest of which is still a mass of girders, cranes, and concrete that will be formed into a 2,500–seat underground concert hall and a restaurant/theater complex under a 415–foot–high, gold-tipped spire. It was originally due to open in 1973, then later dates were set. Costs have risen astronomically as an almost incredible series of impediments have arisen. Our guess now is that it *might* be unveiled next year.

Don't think of missing the gallery. It was made not only for established patrons but for all us ockers, too. The architect, Sir Roy Grounds, once told John Gunther (*Inside Australia*) that he would fire up enthusiasm among the construction workers on the job about the coming museum: "This is being built for you and your wife and kids," he would say. "I'm trying to get a bloody good job!"

The museum opens at 10:00 daily, except Monday, closing at 5:00 every day except Wednesday when the lights stay on until 9:00 p.m. (Admission 60 cents; 30 cents for children.) Free guided tours are often available.

MELBOURNE PARKS AND GARDENS

Somehow there always seems to be a place to sit down in Melbourne. Or almost always. (If you're a man, better note the occasional benches that are labeled sternly in stone "Ladies Only"—a genteel touch that even the equal rights advocates are not likely to erase.)

Part of the aura of relaxation in this otherwise conservative, businesslike city is due to its extensive parks and gardens system. Nearly a quarter of the city's acreage has been set aside as green areas. It would be impossible to cover them all in this chapter, but here is a J-shaped sequence which, if followed strictly, would keep you generally off the streets and on the grass all day.

Just across St. Kilda Road from the Victorian Arts Centre is **Alexandra Gardens,** a popular lunchtime picnic site by the Yarra River. There stands the statue of Peter Pan. A quick trot across the broad, tree-lined

Alexandra Avenue brings you to the little **Queen Victoria Gardens.** A floral clock there may tell you if it's two carnations past a rhododendron.

Continuing south, crossing another avenue, you'll see the **Sidney Myer Music Bowl**—the tent-like, partially open-air amphitheatre where 100,000 on occasion listen to free concerts. It's in the **King's Domain,** sometimes called the Royal Domain. You have to skirt **Government House** (where the Queen's representative lives, and not open to general peeking) to walk to the **Shrine of Remembrance,** a heavy, classical Greek-style memorial to Australian war dead.

Nearby, though, look for the statue of a donkey with two soldiers. The private leading the animal is John Simpson (Kirkpatrick), an obscure English immigrant who became an Australian hero. He rescued many wounded by carrying them to safety on a stray donkey for 25 days at Gallipoli in 1915 until he himself was killed.

Governor La Trobe's Cottage, the former residence of Charles La Trobe, the first Victoria governor, was prefabricated in England. La Trobe lived in the four-room unit at Jolimont while governing from 1839 to 1854. It was recently restored and moved to the Domain by the National Trust of Australia. Now open about 10:00 a.m. to 4:30 p.m. daily, and worth seeing.

A step across Birdwood Avenue is Melbourne's **Royal Botanical Gardens,** a total of 88 acres of lawns, gardens, and lakes, some of the best classical landscaping in the world. There are ducks and swans and examples of almost everything that will grow in Australia—some 12,000 species, anyway.

Crossing the 1899 Morrell Bridge takes you into the world of sport. The **Olympic Park** with its swimming stadium, sports arena, and velodrome (for cycle racing), which was developed for the 1956 Olympic Games held there. Just north, across Swan Street, is **Yarra Park,** home of three separate cricket fields, of which the most famous is the **Melbourne Cricket Ground** (M.C.G., for short), site not only of that gentlemen's game but of rough-and-rumble Australian Rules Football during the winter season. The M..C.G. has held a crowd as large as 120,000.

Near the Hilton, you can quick march across Wellington Parade into the **Fitzroy Gardens.** On our first foray into Fitzroy, at night, we thought we saw a little wallaby waiting for us. He turned out to be one of a large family of possums who regularly freeload there after dark, and when we had nothing to offer he hopped away. Extend your hand with some food, and you'll receive a warm marsupial welcome.

In the gardens, too, is what's called **Captain Cook's Cottage,** which Cook apparently never lived in. The eighteenth century house belonged to his parents in their later years, however, and it was brought to the park from England in 1934 to celebrate the Melbourne Centennial. (Open 10:00 a.m. to 4:30 p.m.)

Across Lansdowne Street are the **Treasury Gardens.** You have to walk along the traffic of Spring Street for a few minutes, past Parliament House, etc., to get to **Exhibition Gardens,** sometimes called Carlton Gardens. These 60 acres were the site of the Melbourne Exhibition of 1880. On the grounds, look for the **Statue of Burke and Wills,** commemorating the two explorers who left from Melbourne to explore the Outback and establish a land route to the Gulf of Carpentaria in 1861. But after making important discoveries, they died in the desert, needlessly, through an almost incredible combination of unfortunate circumstances.

About four blocks west on Grattan Street is the campus of **Melbourne University,** founded in 1853, and now enrolling about 15,000. There's a famous music exhibit in the **Percy Grainger Museum.** Others could safely skip it, but I was strongly reminded of the time I was a member of an orchestra directed by Maestro Grainger. We halted rehearsal in admiration when he began to conduct a passage of one of his difficult compositions—3/4 time in one hand and 4/4 time with the other, simultaneously!

Royal Park, which begins near the campus, is devoted largely to games and recreation, and includes hockey fields, a golf course, basketball courts, and a baseball diamond. In one corner of the park is the **Melbourne Zoological Gardens,** Australia's first zoo. We'd limit any exploration to the section on Australian fauna, and only that if there was to be no opportunity to see Healesville inthe Dandenongs or Taronga Park in Sydney.

OUT IN THE COUNTRY

Rent a car or hop on a sightseeing bus to take a "Captain Cook" at some of the countryside sights of Victoria, particularly the Dandenongs, Ballarat/Sovereign Hill, and Phillip Island.

The "Beautiful Blue" **Dandenongs,** a range of modest mountains about 30 miles east of Melbourne, features fern gullies and giant eucalyptus trees, some of which reach 300 feet. The highest point in the range is Mount Dandenong itself at 2,077 feet. Unfortunately, the natural feeling there is marred by Melbourne's TV towers and the Sky High Restaurant. It's still a joy on a clear day.

Two or three sights are nestled in the hills. Three miles from Healesville, at the foot of Mount Riddell, you'll find the **Sir Colin MacKenzie**

Wild Life Sanctuary (often called the Healesville Sanctuary). There in the open air are koalas, emus, kangaroos, wombats, possums, and at least one platypus. This research station, where the duck-billed critter was first bred in captivity, was named after the scientist who accomplished it. (Open daily from 9:00 to 5:00.)

Nearer Mount Dandenong, at Olinda, is the **William Rickets Sanctuary.** Rickets, an artist of around 80 years, lives there and carves his Tolkienesque figures in wood, a project partly subsidized by the Victoria Forests Commission. His statues reflect his belief that he must save the Aboriginal spirits, and nature in general, from encroaching modernization.

At Healesville, at the Rickets Sanctuary, or anyplace in the Dandenongs, incidentally, you may hear or even see the lyrebird, that strange twin-tailed creature who can imitate other birds or even chain saws, trucks, and factory whistles.

A favorite diversion for kids of all ages is the little narrow-gauge steam railroad train, **Puffing Billy,** which chugs between Belgrave and Menzies Creek from time to time, especially on weekends. The 1½-hour tour costs about $3 round trip.

About 70 miles to the west of Melbourne is the gold rush town of **Ballarat,** famous as the scene of Australia's almost-revolution, the Eureka Stockade rebellion of 1854. Only a rather sorry monument and a little diorama nearby commemorates this dramatic event in Australia's history.

A pleasant town, today known for its begonias (we enjoyed the flower-filled park along with the busts of past prime ministers), Ballarat is also the location for the commercial theme park called **Sovereign Hill,** a recreation of a gold rush town much like Ballarat in its heyday. Not surprisingly, it seems very similar to Virginia City or some other revived old ghost town in the American West. You can go down in a mine, and even buy a miner's right and pan for gold in the little stream. On weekends, hundreds do. (Open 9:00 to 5:00 daily, admission about $3.) (You can go by train, too; call VicRail at 62–0771.)

If you continue west on the same highway (No. 8), you go through the **Grampians,** a spectacular set of mountains on the way to South Australia. It's one of the few areas where the platypuses still roam free.

Our favorite trip out of Melbourne, however, has to be the 80–mile excursion south to **Phillip Island.** There are fur seals and koalas frolicking about, but the main purpose of the journey is to see the fairy penguins. About 3,000 of these protected birds come home from the sea every day of the year, just at dusk, although they may be viewed only from October through April. After riding in on the waves, they shake themselves a moment, get their bearings, and then begin their "parade" until they find their burrows where their families are waiting for the bacon. (No flash pictures are allowed, but we caught them in the flood-lights on high-speed color film.) It's a charmer. Don't miss it!

7. Guided Tours and Cruises

Probably the easiest way to set yourself up with a guided tour is to arrange it through the Victorian Government Tourist Bureau (Tel. 262–0202), headquartered at 272 Collins St. It's sort of in the tour business itself (Victour). Other agencies include **Ansett Pioneer** (Tel. 345–3144), at 97 Franklin St. (the same as the Ansett Airlines terminal), **Australian Accommodation & Tours** (AAT) (Tel. 347–5555), at 50 Franklin St. (same as the head office for Trans-Australia Airlines), and **Australian Pacific Coaches** Pty. Ltd. (Tel. 92–8555 or 63–5311), 122 Flinders St.

Here are a few coach tours and our estimate of their approximate cost this year. (Be sure to ask where to board the bus, and note that all-day tours will probably stop somewhere for tea as well as for lunch.)

Healesville Wildlife Sanctuary. 4 hours, 2 or 3 afternoons a week. $11. Australian Pacific Coaches and Ansett-Pioneer.

Blue Dandenongs. 3 hours. 2 days a week. $8. AAT, Ansett-Pioneer, and Australian Pacific.

Melbourne Sights and Gardens. 3 hours daily. $10. Ansett-Pioneer and Australian Pacific.

Penguins at Sunset (Phillip Island). 8½ hours, 3 days a week, October through May. $20 (including dinner). Australian-Pacific, Ansett-Pioneer.

Ballarat and Sovereign Hill. 8½ hours. $17. Ansett-Pioneer.

Cruises

The only water tour we know of this year is the jazz cruise on the Yarra River, Saturday and Sunday only. We're unsure of the details, though. Get the latest from the Tourist Bureau (Tel. 263–0202).

8. Water Sports

Melbourne's beaches are nothing to compare with the dramatic surf-ing strands of Sydney, the Gold Coast, or Perth. But they're pleasant for relaxation and gentle swimming. You can take the tram to St. Kilda on Port Phillip Bay in 15 minutes. Further down the eastern coast, avoid the polluted waters between Beaumaris and Frankston, although the beaches between Mornington and Portsea are clear and popular. Cancel at all costs any thought of swimming in the Yarra (yuck!) River.

For serious surfing and swimming in heavy wave action, you'll have to go beyond Port Phillip Bay to the ocean side of Mornington Peninsula, 50 miles from Melbourne. (Portsea and Sorrento almost at the very tip are popular, although Sorrento is unpatrolled and often dangerous.)

You can rent **sailboats** at almost any resort beach, but remember the changeable weather. It's doubly dangerous for boaters with Port Phillip Bay's sudden shifts in wind and waves. Try Black Rock, Frankston, Mardialloc, and Sandringham. If you want to make contact with fellow sailors, call the Royal Melbourne Yacht Squadron (Tel. 94–0227) in St. Kilda.

Water skiers can hire the appropriate equipment at several bay beaches as well as inland lakes. You might make contact with the Victorian Water Ski Association (Tel. 91–1388).

Deep sea **fishing** boats can sometimes be had in towns on Western Port Bay, about 40 miles southeast of Melbourne. Blue fin tuna is the big catch in these waters January to March, followed by Australian salmon. There is trout fishing on several inland lakes and rivers. Get the latest on all this from the Victorian Government Tourist Bureau.

---

9. Other Sports

SPECTATOR SPORTS

From April to September, it seems difficult to get into social conversation in Melbourne that doesn't eventually degenerate into a discussion of Australian Rules Football. Indeed, Melbourne columnist Keith Dunstan once lamented this fact over several weeks and even organized the tongue-in-cheek A.F.L.—"Anti-Football League."

No one took it very seriously, however, including apparently Dunstan himself. But "footy" is taken very seriously in Victoria and other southern and western states. Melbourne's most famous Aussie rules star and later coach Ron Barassi once said flatly, "Getting out of football is just like death."

It may be impossible for Americans, or even Englishmen or New Zealanders, let alone northern Australians, to understand "Rules." Sports fans from Sydney and Brisbane sniff and call it "aerial ping pong," presumably because of the spectacular high jumps in a scramble for the ball, often photographed by the newspapers. For the same reason, others call it "ballet with blood."

As in America, football keeps many glued to the telly on weekend afternoons during the winter. In Melbourne, the Victorian Football League competes in home and away games with about a dozen professional teams. The final series, played in September, may pull in a crowd of 120,000 or so to the VFL's stadium at Waverley, 15 miles from Melbourne, or at the Melbourne Cricket Ground, in Yarra Park near the Hilton.

The football used is ovoid, like an American pigskin or a rugby ball, but scores are made only by kicking it through goal posts. The team receives six points for a goal, but they can also get one point for a "behind," a kick that missed the main posts but got through another set of posts stationed at either side. There's little carrying of the ball allowed. It must be kicked, pushed, or punched down the field, and the long, accurate kicks, sometimes made on the run, account for much of the game's excitement. The whole match is carried out on an oval field, an inheritance from the familiar cricket oval.

It's a rough, fast-paced game, played without padding for about two hours of non-stop action. The true Aussie Rules fan feels the other 99 percent of the world is missing out on the greatest joy in life. Supporters not only carry flags of team colors to the matches, some of them may outfit the whole house—towels, bedspreads, and whatever—in the pattern.

The other kinds of football, rugby and soccer, draw small crowds by comparison in Victoria, but soccer at least is on the rise due to the number of foreign immigrants.

Cricket, of course, is still a popular summer pastime on Melbourne weekends, and you may catch that at the M.C.G. or any of a number of suburban ovals. (One of the prettiest is at Como Park in South Yarra.)

Horse racing, too, is a local passion, and one which peaks in the running of the Melbourne Cup, usually the first Tuesday in November, and the climax of the spring racing carnival. Cup Day, as a matter of fact, is a legal holiday in Victoria. With its high fashion and associated merrymaking, it's comparable to Derby Day in London or Louisville—only much more so.

The Cup is run at Flemington Racecourse, the largest track in the state (320 acres). Located on Epsom Road four miles northwest of the city center, you can travel by tram (No. 404) or by train from the Spencer Street Station. Other tracks include the Caulfield Racecourse, six miles east on Normanby Road in Caulfield, the Moonee Valley Racecourse, on Dean Street at Moonee Ponds, and the Sandown Racecourse on the Dandenong Road in Springvale. Admission to the track is usually about $1.50—maybe twice that for special events.

Racing addicts who haven't had enough with horses can also take in **dog racing.** In Melbourne, the greyhounds run at Olympic Park on Batman Avenue in East Melbourne or at Sandown Park on Dandenong Road in Springvale. Betting is at the track.

PARTICIPATION SPORTS

Australian **tennis** (grass or hard court) is also a top spectator sport, with the Australian championships in January attracting the best players from all over the world, many of whom, of course, are Australians. State championships are held in December and January, and in Melbourne, these would be at the courts run by the Victorian Lawn Tennis Association (Tel. 20 –3333) at Kooyong. The main stadium (also the site of the Australian Open) seats 12,000 spectators, although there are a couple dozen grass courts and a few hard courts there, too.

Phone the association to get some recommendations on sports clubs or public courts that may be available to you near your hotel. There are courts in Royal Park and Albert Park. Commercial tennis courts are also listed in the Pink Pages of the telephone book.

Just as popular in Australia as in the U.S.A., **golf** is also both a spectator sport and a playing sport for everyone. But because of the need for memberships or at least introduction by members, there are few courses where visitors can just show up for a round of 18 holes.

We know of three exceptions, however. The **Victoria Golf Club** (Tel. 93–1254) welcomes strangers. It's on Park Road in Cheltenham, Victoria (post code 3192, if you're writing first). Also check out the beautiful public golf course at **Yarra Bend National Park** (Tel. 48–2171), about four miles northeast of the Golden Mile. And there is the **Albert Park Course** (Tel. 51–5588) in Albert Park. Greens fees may be around $5 or $6—double that if you need clubs.

If you can wangle an introduction, the best course in Australia, and the top of the private club list in Melbourne, is supposed to be the **Royal Melbourne** (Tel. 598–6755) on Cheltenham Road, Cheltenham 3192. It's well-known for sand traps. One of the famous courses where you share the fairways with families of friendly roos is the **Anglesea Golf Course** at Anglesea, along the coastline, about 65 miles southwest of Melbourne (Near Route 1 at Geelong).

And what about **skiing?** Victoria doesn't have the Snowy Mountain resorts we reported on in the Canberra chapter, but the runs in the

Victorian Alps can still be excellent. Mount Buller (Elev. 6,000 feet), 150 miles from the capital, has the most complete facilities. Others swear by Falls Creek and Mount Buffalo National Park. We've yet to try our hickories here.

10. The Melbourne Shopping Scene

In some quarters, Melbourne is known more for shopping than anything else. For the past few years, it's been the trend center for women's fashions, especially, or at least the first in Australia to snap up, re-create, or adapt the latest styles seen in London, New York, and Paris, many of them then sold from exclusive little boutiques in Toorak Road or Chapel Street in the suburbs.

(It's a pity that many Melbournians don't take advantage of the city's fashion leadership, however. As recently as 1973, the British actor Robert Morley—no lover of Melbourne, to be sure—sniffed: "The inhabitants looked as if they had been clothed in some gigantic relief operation, carried out in the dark!")

Much of the serious shopping is accomplished in a 30-block portion of the downtown, bounded by Lonsdale, Spring, Flinders, and Queen Streets. Store hours are 9:00 to 5:00, Monday to Friday and until noon on Saturdays. There is late night shopping on Friday night until 9:00 p.m. Here are some places and purchases to think about:

Aboriginal Arts and Crafts. Although far from the Outback and Aboriginal country, you'll find a considerable amount of native X-ray bark paintings and the like available. Some of the most authentic original pieces (and the most expensive) are found at **Aboriginal Handicrafts** (Tel. 63–4717) on the fourth floor at 167 Collins St. Also, there's the Aboriginal Art Gallery at 42 Hardy Terrace in Ivanhoe.

Melbourne has become known for **antiques** dating back to its affluence during the Gold Rush era. Many shops are in the High Street between Kooyong and Glenferrie Roads in Toorak, southeast of the center. But in Melbourne proper, look for English porcelain and old silver at **Windsor Antiques,** 51 Bourke St., and for antique jewelry, glassware, and silver at **Kosminsky Galleries,** 377 Little Collins St.

Arcades. Melbourne is well-known for its shopping arcades, covered and glassed-in malls which wind through the business area, particularly off Collins Street and Bourke Street. The oldest is the 1870 Royal Arcade which runs under the watchful eyes of the two Beefeater bellringers between Collins and Little Collins. It connects with the **Block Arcade,** which has entrances on Collins, Little Collins, and Elizabeth

Streets. Then there is the Y-shaped **Australia Arcade,** under the Hotel Australia.

That wonderful aroma in the Block Arcade comes from a fast-pie shop called **Dinkum Pies,** in the entranceway called Block Place between the arcade and Little Collins. We saw some nice little things in a tiny notions shop called **Twinkles** at 41 Block Place, too. The **Pru Acton Shop** in the Block Arcade is one of the exclusive shops for original fashion. And in the Royal Arcade, the products are well displayed at the **Australia-New Zealand Sheepskin Centre** (Tel. 63–2687).

Australian Paintings. Some of the commercial galleries include the following (none are in the center): **Tolarno Gallery,** Fitzroy St., St. Kilda. **Realities,** corner of Jackson Street and Grange Road, Toorak. Avant Gallery, 579 Punt Rd., South Yarra. And **Julian's,** 258 Glenferrie Rd., Malvern.

On Saturday and Sunday, don't miss the open air art and crafts markets in St. Kilda, where you might pick up a painting at a fraction of the cost a gallery would charge.

Bookshops. There seem to be several in Bourke Street, for some reason, including the well-known **Collins Book Depot** (Tel. 662–2711) at 86 Bourke St. It offers a good range of Australiana. You might check out **Batman,** both at its 370 Little Book St. and the 224 Swanston St. addresses. It has new and used books and recordings. The well-known **Angus and Robertson** chain is on Elizabeth Street, almost across from the post office. And don't forget the bargains you'll sometimes find at the federally subsidized **Australian Government Publishers Service** (Tel. 663–3010), at 347 Swanston St.

Department stores. One of the world's largest stores is the **Myer Department Store** (Tel. 6–6111) which takes up two blocks on Bourke Street. In addition to the standard items, check here for souvenirs, boomerangs, paintings, books, etc. It also hosts the Miss Myer Boutique, and all the best Australian designers are supposed to be represented. Look for a pretty good shoe department, too.

Other department stores include the elegant **George's** (Tel. 63–0411) at 162 Collins St. (Australian styles), and **Waltons** (Tel. 66–6043), 206 Bourke St., which has a wide variety of goods at less expensive prices.

Opals and Gemstones. As in Sydney, there are lots of Australian jewelry stores featuring black, white, and green opals, as well as other native gemstones. Australia's most famous opal dealers are **Altmann and Cherny,** 227 Collins St. Others include the **Opal Den** (Tel. 63–8385) at 17 Howey St., and **Dunklings,** (Tel. 63–6611), 313 Bourke St. We bought a very nice opal ring from **Nathan Harris** (Tel. 63–1694) up the elevator in the Sportgirl Arcade, 234 Collins St.

Skin products. Sheepskin, kangaroo skin, etc., you might find in several department stores, souvenir shops, etc. Some which specialize, however, include the **Sheepskin Rug Shop,** 237 Little Bourke St., and the shop we mentioned in the Royal Arcade. There's a nice selection of leather and fur of all types at **Andrea's** (Tel. 63–5007), in the London Arcade, 345 Bourke St.

Souvenirs. The traditional leader in souvenirs is **Mond's Australian Souvenirs** (Tel. 63–7542) at 103 Swanston St. The wide range includes toy koalas, kangaroos, and the like as well as the mass-produced boomerangs and barrels of bric-a-brac of one sort or another. A store of a similar persuasion, but smaller, is **Proud's Pty. Ltd.** at 339 Bourke St.

Something unusual? You can buy genuine Australian ANZAC hats at **Mitchell's** (Tel. 63–5785), an Army and Navy store at 134 Russell St.

THE BOUTIQUES OF SOUTH YARRA

For women especially, the exclusive shopping area of Melbourne, comparable to Sydney's Double Bay, is Melbourne's South Yarra, either on Toorak Road or Chapel Street. Here are a few of the addresses which steal the social thunder. None are cheap, of course, and all are currently very "in."

Toorak Road

The **Garb Shop** (Tel. 26 –5369), at 35 Toorak Rd., is a Victorian style boutique with unusual jeans and denim skirts. **Penny Collins Shoe Boutique** (Tel. 26 –3705), 42 Toorak Rd., also features exclusive bags and accessories. **Etre,** 52 Toorak Rd., has international and local styles. **French** (Tel. 267–1052), 65 Toorak Road, is known for conservative European fashions. **Peter Sheppard** (Tel. 26 –4073) has imported leather bags and purses, mostly French and Italian, in his shop at No. 109. **Saba,** 121 Toorak Road, features Italian imports. And **Pru Acton Shop,** 189 Toorak Rd., is a branch of the same designer who has a place in the Block Arcade.

Chapel Street

At 409 Chapel St., **Electrum** (Tel. 240 –9386) offers made-to-order jewelry in gold or silver. Next door is **Blues Point** (Tel. 24–5346) at 409–A. It's an individual fashion boutique, specializing in recycled fabrics with a completely new look. At **Hipparade,** 439 Chapel St., Janine Pimm designs after-dark garments. At No. 441, **Finlandia** (Tel. 24–5999) is one of the best-known made-to-order places for all occasions. It features pure wools and 100 percent cottons. **Scuttle** (Tel. 24–9419), at 467 Chapel St., specializes in unusual clothes. You'll see the Scuttle label all over the country. And **Red Pepper Shoes** (Tel. 240–1942), at 509 Chapel St., has the latest women's imports, local shoes, sports clothing, and bags.

11. Night Life and Entertainment

Melbourne is a conservative town. Get that straight right off the bat. If you're searching for some of the far out fun you can find in Sydney, you'll have to look 10 times harder for it in Melbourne. Still columnist Keith Dunstan said last year that Melbourne has become the massage parlor capital of the world.

Night Clubs. Traditionally, Melbourne's night clubs have led a precarious economic life centered around Fitzroy Street and its side lanes in St. Kilda, the closest thing Melbourne can offer to the King's Cross neighborhood of Sydney. Lately, however, several new clubs have been opening to champagne and fanfare in the city center. One is **Madison's** (Tel. 654–1122), four floors of a former clothing factory at the corner of Flinders Lane and Russell Street. Another is **Elaine's** (Tel. 663–4991), not far away at 170 Russell St., which is billed as a restaurant/supper club.

A long-time club at 141 Bourke St. is the **Lotus Palace**, formerly the Top Hat (Tel. 63–7171).

Discotheques. Discos are turning up more and more in Melbourne, and some even stay spinning past midnight! The most trendy platter palace—where you have to pass inspection or they won't let you in—is the **Underground,** below the surface of 22 King Street. It supposedly cost more than a million Down Under dollars to build, and it will charge you about $5 to experience its nether regions.

There's one of the **Juliana's** chain of discos in the Melbourne Hilton. Other than that, look for **The Love Machine** (Tel. 24–0373) at 14 Claremont St. in South Yarra, and **Silver's** (Tel. 24–8244) at 443 Toorak Rd. in Toorak.

The Beers of Melbourne. Speaking of bars, we're not up enough on Melbourne pubs yet to make a literary pub crawl in this edition, having confined most of our imbibing to our own hotel, in restaurants, or the homes of friends. (We would welcome nominations for the most interesting pubs.) We do have some thoughts on the brews of Melbourne, which rival those of Sydney for their verisimilitude.

If you drank Foster's in the U.S.A., and weren't very impressed, don't let that dissuade you. Foster's is brewed by C.U.B. (Carlton United Breweries) which must make the export stuff bland or the American Feds won't let it in. Foster's in Victoria is fine, although we far prefer one of C.U.B.'s dozen other beers, one called Melbourne Bitter. (Technically it's not a bitter but a strong lager.) There's a milder version, too, called the Victoria Bitter. Similar to Foster's, too, is Carlton Crown Lager and Abbots Lager.

A fizzier C.U.B. brand is Pilsener. We haven't tried their Malt Ale or their alleged low-calorie beer called Dietale. C.U.B. also owns the Ballarat Brewery, now, turning out Ballarat Bitter there.

The other brewery in Melbourne until recently was British, although called Courage Australia. A relative newcomer, Courage has been turning out beers since the 1960's that seem to be named to suggest that they, too, have a long history—1770 Old Colonial Ale, for instance. Their Crest Lager calls itself a pilsener, but hardly seems zippy enough. Courage Draught is nicely dry. Tankard Bitter may have more of a kick to it. In any case, most of Courage's stock has now been sold to Sydney's Tooth's. (It was bad enough being a Pom beer, but now it seems a beer sold in Melbourne is actually owned by Sydney!)

Incidentally, perhaps due to the alleged higher alcoholic content of Melbourne beer, there are some tiny servings offered in some places. The "Pony," or "Small Glass" holds just four ounces. Ask for a "Glass" of beer to get seven ounces or a "Pot" for 10 ounces.

Rock and Jazz. Melbourne is considered a musical town on several different levels. It offers a lot of popular and syncopated beats at several different pubs and wine bars. The scene changes swiftly, and most of it is in the suburbs.

For rock music, check out the **Fun Factory** on Swanston St.; in Richmond, the **Sydenham Hotel** and the **Kingston Hotel;** the **Village Green Hotel,** corner of Springvale and Ferntree Gully Roads, Springvale; the **Martinis Hotel,** 184 Rathdowne St., Carlton; and the **Polaris Inn** (Tel. 347–1871), 551 Nicholson St., North Carlton.

You'll probably find more genuine jazz and folk music at the **Manor House Hotel** at Lonsdale & Swanston Sts. In the university area, look for **La Mama** (Tel. 429–1062), 205 Faraday St. in Carlton. Also the **Lemon Tree,** Rathdowne and Grattan Sts., not far away, jumps Saturday and Sunday.

Theater. Sydney-style theater-restaurants have only begun to come in the Melbourne stage. One gaining an audience is the **Last Laugh Theatre Restaurant and Zoo** (Tel. 419–6226), at 65 Smith St., in the suburb of Collingwood. (About $15 buys dinner and the show.) Also **Foibles**

(Tel. 347–2397), 119 Palmerston St., Carlton, and the **Flying Trapeze Cafe** (Tel. 41–3727), at 201 Brunswick St., Fitzroy.

More than a dozen conventional theaters, for stage plays, opera openings, etc., are firmly established in the Golden Mile, giving credence to Melbourne's reputation as the theatrical capital of the country. Check out what's playing in the newspapers (the morning *Age*—especially the 7-day Leisure Guide in the Friday edition—or the evening *Herald*) or the weekly tourist publication, *This Week in Melbourne.*

The three main stages are the **Princess Theatre** (Tel. 662–2911), 163 Spring St., **Her Majesty's Theatre** (Tel. 663–3716), 219 Exhibition St., where we saw "A Chorus Line" last year, and the **Comedy Theatre** (Tel. 663–3211), 244 Exhibition St. Notice that the **Russell Street Theatre** (Tel. 645–1100), at 19 Russell St., is known for premiering the work of Australian playwrights, along with **Saint Martin's Theatre** in St. Martin's Place in South Yarra and the **Athenaeum Theatre** (Tel. 654–4000), at 118 Collins St. (All three are run by the Melbourne Theatre Company.) And experimental theater is up in the university area. The Australian Performing Group tries out new things at **The Pram Factory** (Tel. 347–7133) at 325 Drummond St., Carlton. Tickets run around $4 or $5.

Movies. The cinemas are also in the theater district in the eastern blocks of the Golden Mile. You'll find many along Bourke Street, between Spring and Swanston. (See our note on film classifications in the Sydney chapter, Section 11.)

Opera. Still without an opera house, Melbourne seldom hosts an operatic production, a situation that will continue until the Arts Center is finished. When the Australian Opera Company comes to call, it chooses one of the large theaters like the Princess. The Victorian Opera Company is headquartered in Abbotsford. It usually performs at the National Theatre in St. Kilda.

The Ballet. The Australian Ballet leaps all over the country from a Melbourne base. At-home productions are usually staged at the three large theaters mentioned above. The ballet, which has made many world tours, too, is known for its penchant for commissioning and performing newly choreographed works on Australian themes as well as the classics.

Classical music. Performances are given generally in the Town Hall (reservations, Tel. 63–0421) by the Melbourne Symphony Orchestra, although sometimes it carries its instruments over to the Sidney Myer Music Bowl in the King's Domain. Pick up concert information from the Australian Broadcasting Commission Concert Department, 10 Queen St.

12. The Melbourne Address List

Airline Bus Terminals—Ansett, 489 Swanston St. (Tel. 345–3144), and
   TAA, 50 Franklin St. (Tel. 345–3344.).
Ambulance—(Tel. 662–2533).
American Consulate (Tel. 699–2244).
Australian Tourist Commission, 414 St. Kilda Road (Tel. 267–1233).
British Consulate (Tel. 602–1877).
Bus, tram, and train information—(Tel. 653–3611).
Canadian Consulate (Tl. 63–8431).
Chamber of Commerce, 60 Market St. (Tel. 62–6681).
Citizens Advice Bureau, 197 Russell St. (Tel. 63–1062).
Dental Emergency Service—(Tel. 347–4222).
Emergencies of all types—(Tel. 000).
Florist—Majorie Milner of Melbourne, 112 Bourke St., (Tel. 663–2008).
Hospital—St. Vincent's, corner Victoria Parade and Nicholson Sts. (Tel.
   419–2611).
New Zealand Consulate (Tel. 67–8111).
Police Station—(Tel. 662–0911).
Post Office—Corner of Bourke and Elizabeth Streets (Tel. 63–0331).
Royal Automobile Club of Victoria, 123 Queen St. (Tel. 607–2211).
Theater tickets—Australia Theatre Bookings, Hotel Australia, 266 Col-
   lins St. (Tel. 63–0401).
Travelers' Aid Society, 182 Collins St. (Tel. 654–2600).
Tourist Bureau—Victorian Government Tourist Bureau, 272 Collins
   St., (Tel. 63–0202).

8

Tasmania,
the Island State

1. The General Picture

For sheer physical beauty, the water-mountain-and-sky setting for Hobart, the capital of Tasmania, actually surpasses that of Sydney.

The city seems small, almost quaint, and a mixture of Georgian, very few Victorian, and some modern buildings are all wrapped together in a comfortable "home town" feeling, apparent even on a short stay. It has a definite appreciation for its roots, too, for the city was founded in 1804, making it the second oldest settlement after Sydney.

Like Sydney, Hobart owes its beginnings to a penitentiary. The infamous Port Arthur was constructed here, and between 1830 and 1877, the name was as feared in England and the rest of Australia as Devil's Island was in Europe. Today the prison city lies in mellow, romantic ruins a short distance from the capital.

Hobart's population now numbers about 162,000, out of the island's total of half a million. Shaped rather like a shield, the state is a rugged, sparsely settled, even partly unexplored area of 26,215 square miles. That's about the size of West Virginia or of Scotland. Were it not so dwarfed physically, culturally, and economically by the continent above it, it would qualify as a big, important island indeed.

Like many scenic lands, Tasmania has a violent history—not only in

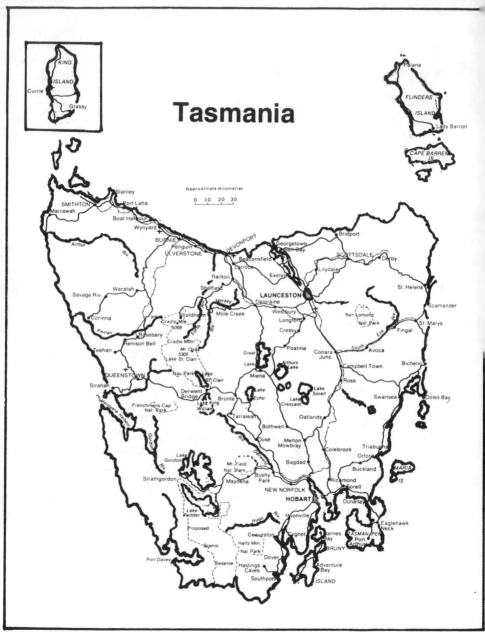

Tasmania

Map courtesy Tasmanian Government Tourist Bureau

the conflicts with convicts but also between the settlers and the indigenous population, a nation of Aborigines of completely different racial stock than the natives of the mainland.

Somehow the early English colonialists managed to slay virtually every one of them. A few older survivors were rounded up, but the last full-blooded Tasmanian Aborigine died about 100 years ago.

It's been a similar story with nature. The Tasmanian tiger hasn't been seen since 1933, although there is some hope that a few may be creeping around the rough country on the west coast. Nevertheless, wildlife conservation is still a controversial issue in Tasmania. People conservation is not. Tasmania has virtually achieved zero population growth, although some of that is because of migration to the mainland.

Among Australians, "Tassy" is still thought of as the "Apple Isle," and some of the world's most delicious apples are grown there. Unfortunately, they've been largely priced out of the export market in recent years. There is considerable industry, now, led by iron mining activities. Much of this has been attracted by the very cheap electricity provided by an ingenious hydroelectric system.

In recent years, Tasmania has come to rely more and more on tourism for income from the rest of Australia, an irony to some who note the typical Tasmanian's traditional hostility toward the mainland Australian. Nevertheless, because of this new commercial interest, things move smoothly in Tasmania, and facilities for visitors today are among Australia's best. If you're going between mid-December and mid-February, however, have all your reservations sewn up tight.

2. Airports and Long Distance Transportation

Major airports are at Hobart, Launceston, Devonport and Wynyard, all receiving frequent flights from Melbourne via **Ansett Airlines** (Hobart Tel. 34–7466; Launceston Tel. 31–7711) and **Trans Australia Airlines** (Hobart Tel. 34–6644; Launceston Tel. 31–4411). There's also a small airline, **Air Tasmania** (book through the Ansett office), which flies between Hobart, Launceston, Queenstown, Wynyard, Devonport, King Island and Flinders Island. Hobart's airport is about a half-hour out the Tasman Highway. Both Ansett and TAA run frequent buses to town from all those cities. Fares range from $1.50 to $2.50 a seat.

By sea, you can take the *Empress of Australia*, which sails from Melbourne overnight to arrive at Devonport. A ship of the **Australian National Line** (Melbourne Tel. 62–0681), you can also reserve passage for it through the tourist bureau (Tel. 34–6911) in Hobart.

This "Searoad" service won't save you any significant money, however,

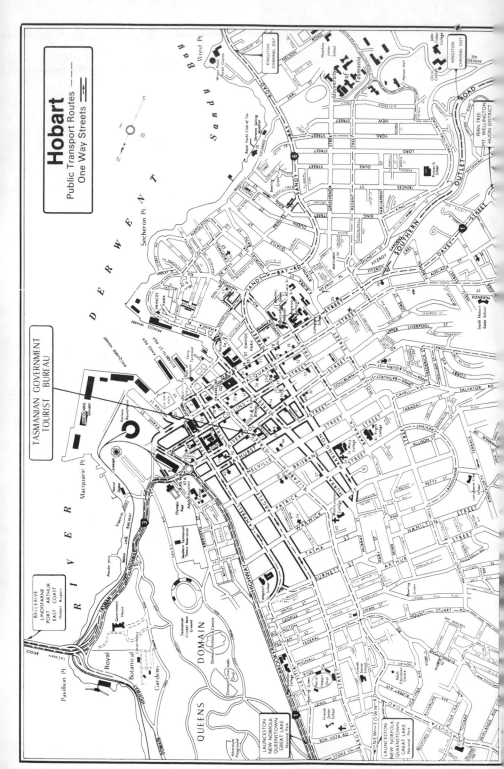

Map courtesy Tasmanian Government Tourist Bureau

unless you're taking your own car to the island. Fares run from about $30 for deck space (pretty cold, and the seas can be equal to the roughest in the world) to about $70 for the best cabin between Melbourne and Devonport—a trip that costs about $60 and takes 45 minutes by air—and you will still have to rent a car or take a bus to the state capital at Hobart.

Unfortunately, the *Tasman Limited*, a passenger train service from Wynyard through Devonport to Launceston and Hobart was suspended indefinitely in 1978.

By bus, you can travel all over the island on the **Tasmanian Coach Lines** (Tel. 34–3477), headquartered at 96 Harrington St. in Hobart. The last we heard, it cost about $16 to bus between Devonport and Hobart.

3. Local Transportation in Hobart

In Hobart and Launceston, there are frequent bus services run by the **Metropolitan Transport Trust** (MTT). In Hobart, these are divided between Western Shore Services—Routes 1–59 (Tel. 34–5670) and Eastern Shore Services—Routes 60–96 (Tel. 44–1599), which run along the opposite side of the Derwent estuary from downtown Hobart. (Notice that all the bus stops are numbered, a handy feature.) Pick up a map from the tourist bureau or the MTT office at 49 Macquarie St.

There's one ferry boat. Leaving from the foot of Murray Street, it plies between Hobart and Bellerive from 6:30 a.m. to 6:40 p.m. The fare is 40 cents, each way.

Taxis seem a little more expensive in Hobart than in other cities. You'll find them waiting at most hotels. Downtown, the biggest stand is near the corner of Elizabeth and Macquarie Streets.

An amazing number of rental car companies compete fiercely all over the island. **Avis Rent-A-Car** (Tel. 34–4222) is the leader. We recently rented a nice little Holden from **Kay/Hertz Rent-A-Car** (Tel. 34–5877), at 223 Liverpool St. or the Wrest Point Casino, for slightly less money. Still cheaper rates are offered by **Auto Rent System** (Tel. 34–5555), the Budget licensee at 119 Harrington St., **Costless Car Rentals** (Tel. 34–3480), **Ajax Rent-A-Car** (Tel. 34–3614), nearby at 156 Harrington St., **Letz Rent-a-Car** (Tel. 72–4555), **Penny's Rent-A-Car** (Tel. 27–8885), and **Southern Cross Rentals** (Tel. 23–2741). There may be several others, however; you can compare rates if you pick up a copy of the Tasmanian Tourism Department's newspaper, *Tasmanian Travelways*.

4. The Hobart Hotel Scene

We have personally stayed in or inspected hotels only in the capital. Following these, however, we'll mention a few other possibilities in the countryside on the basis of current information and personal recommendations.

EXPENSIVE HOTELS

The acknowledged leader, and candidate for the title of Las Vegas in Australia, is the **Wrest Point Hotel-Casino** (Tel. 25–0112), consisting principally of a 21-story cylinder, now dominating Sandy Bay, a couple of miles down the shoreline from the city center. This was the first legal casino in Australia (more are proposed), and the hotel takes its razz-ma-tazz role seriously and slickly. There's a well-regulated casino offering all the standard games plus that Australian institution called "Two Up." Other public areas include a well-designed showroom (often featuring lavish reviews and big name stars) and the revolving restaurant on top, offering peerless panoramas over sea- and mountainscapes. There are several bars and coffee shops, an indoor pool, tennis and squash courts, etc. Rooms in the tower, with all luxury facilities, run from $40 up, and around $80 to $160 for suites, and are as modern as tomorrow. (Suites are decorated in Spanish, classical, or Oriental themes.) There are a few nicely refurbished chambers in the old, original hotel adjoining, these renting in the $25 or $30 range for two. (Reservations from the Federal Pacific Hotel chain or the Wrest Point itself at Hobart 7005.) A thoroughly professional operation.

That out of the way, we can tell you that another hotel we liked every bit as much, but on a very different level, is the historic **Lenna Motor Inn** (Tel. 23–2911), perhaps more officially called the Innkeepers Lenna. The main building is the restored mansion originally built between 1874 and 1880 by a well-known whaling captain. (Locals like to talk of a ghost in the attic!) The wonderful collection of marble, carved wood, patterned wallpaper, gold-framed mirrors, French windows, and the like, exudes the flavor of 100-year-old luxury. The ornate restaurant, with its columns, arches, and piped classical music, is one of the best dining rooms in town.

Rooms in the Italianate original building have more genuine character, but those in the unusually designed open-patio annex are also well-appointed and colorful, with comfortable facilities. (There's no pool, but a self-service laundry is a convenient dip for your duds, anyway.) Doubles rent for about $45 up to $55, or so, in the suites. (Reservations through the Innkeepers or Flag chains or from the hotel at Battery Point, Tasmania 7000). Absolutely charming.

Squatting conveniently in the center of town is **Hadley's Hotel** (Tel. 23–7521), at 34 Murray St., across from the cathedral. Also an old-time hostelry, this one has had many hard years and is in the process of having its face lifted on a three-year plan, perhaps about a third completed by now. The stained-glass, wallpapered, and grandfather-clocked atmosphere is intriguing, as are the plans for expansion of the disco and the theater/night club, open until 3:00 a.m. If the new owners follow through, it could be very nice. But until then, it will depend on the luck of the draw. Rooms of widely varying quality rent for about $20 to $30 for two. We'd check it out before checking in.

Less original, but some say a safer bet, would be one of the four **Four Seasons Hotels** (Tel. 34–6288 for central reservations.) In Hobart, they are the Downtowner (Tel. 34–6333), at 96 Bathurst St., around the corner from the tourist bureau, the Town House (Tel. 34–4422), at 167 Macquarie St., the Westside (Tel. 34–6255), at 156 Bathurst St., all at Hobart 7000, or the Motor Lodge (Tel. 25–2511), at 429 Sandy Bay Road, at postcode 7005.

These all struck us as businessmen's hotels, which rely on such Australian-true color schemes as purple and brown, red brick, etc. We went extensively through the Downtowner and had a brief look at the Town House—or was it the Westside? Our impression was that these four Four Seasons were comfortable for the tabs of around $35 to $45 double, but relatively humdrum spring, summer, fall, or winter.

Last in the price range, the **TraveLodge** (Tel. 34–2911) would do in a pinch, although we thought the heavy travel noise on the freeways below might be a hindrance to peaceful lodging. The rooms we saw were okay, but no more than that. All doubles were around $35.

BUDGET ACCOMMODATIONS

We had a look at two addresses where you might still check in for under $30 for a pair of pillows in Hobart. Right downtown, the **Black Prince** (Tel. 34–3501), at 145 Elizabeth St. (entrance on Melville) may be the champion. It was basic but clean, and you might still get rates of $20 for a couple or $16 for a lone knight, with something to eat in the morning thrown in. And a little further from town, the **Aberfeldy** (Tel. 23–7218), at 124 Davey St., very much like an English bed-and-breakfast hotel, charges about $26 for two in the good rooms. It's not bad, although a little overpriced for its offerings, we thought. It provides electric blankets when needed, a warm touch in the winter time, to be sure.

Other inexpensive hotels in Hobart (which we haven't seen) include the **Brisbane** (Tel. 34–4920) downtown at Brisbane and Campbell Sts., the **Marquis of Hastings** (Tel. 34–3541), at 209 Brisbane St., the **Motel Mayfair** (Tel. 34–1670) at 17 Cavell St., and the **Hobart Tower Motel** (Tel. 28–4520) at 300 Park St. And the youth hostel is across the river at Bellerive (Tel. 44–2552), where members may pay about $2 a bunk.

ELSEWHERE IN TASMANIA

Launceston. There are dozens of places but the most interesting is probably the **Penny Royal Watermill** (Tel. 31–6699), a converted 1825 mill with a waterwheel, etc. Doubles run about $35. **The Coach House** (Tel. 31–5311) is a little less expensive.

Devonport. Try the **Innkeepers Gateway** (Tel. 24–4922).

Burnie. The best bet may be the **Four Seasons** (Tel. 31–4455).

Port Arthur. The **Four Seasons Motor Hotel** (Tel. Hobart 50–2102) and a brand new inn called the **Fox and Hound** (Tel. Hobart 50–2217).

Eaglehawk Neck. Near Port Arthur, the **Penzance Motel** (Tel. Hobart 50–3272), is supposed to be the very first motel in Australia. Rooms are about $25 for two.

5. Restaurants and Dining

Like many vacation spots, Tasmania has many restaurants, most of them somewhat volatile and changeable, depending on the time of year and the ambitions of the chefs and managers. So please take this only as an approximate guide, all of it subject to sudden change. (The local winery, by the way, is Chateau Lorraine, bottling a Rhine Reisling and Cabernet Sauvignon.)

HOBART

One of our personal choices is **Monro's** (Tel. 25–1161) at 664 Sandy Bay Road in Lower Sandy Bay. Warmed by a fireplace and brightened by candlelight and flowers on the tables, it offers a varied Continental menu.

Remembered fondly are the Crayfish Strudel and Oyster Sauce, the Galway Scallops, and the Souvaroff "Gourmet," a beef filet flamed with vodka. We also enjoyed the Piccatina de Vitello "Quadri," veal sauteed in olive oil, tomatoes, white wine sauce, oregano, and *fines herbes,* for around $7. For dessert, the delicious Bulgarian Cream "Gran Sofia" will set you back about $2.50. Professionally run, and a firm favorite. (Closed Sundays.)

The dining room at the historic Lenna Motor Inn called the **Restaurant Lenna** (Tel. 23–2911), at Battery Point, is also fine. In an old-fashioned, Florentine atmosphere, with polished silver and antique china place settings, you dine elegantly in the style of the last century. We loved it and will go again. (Open daily.)

For seafood, try **Mure's Fish House** (Tel. 23–6917), not far away on Knopwood Street. Specialties are flounder and trevally. For dessert, some praise the Creme Courvoisier, although we haven't tried it, yet.

For steak, look into **Dirty Dick's** (Tel. 23–5644) in the same neighborhood at 22 Francis St. For the moment, it's BYO, although they've applied for a liquor license. (Closed Sundays.)

Also in the Battery Point area, the **Ball & Chain** (Tel. 23–2222), in one of those intriguing old warehouses on Salamanca Place (No. 87), recreates the prison theme with grisly exhibits throughout the dungeon-like interior. The food is adequate, but that's not the specialty here. It also serves that great Australian favorite, the sing-along, with the words to the various convict and bush ballads printed on your bib.

Upstairs in the same building, the **Sakura Room** (Tel. 23–1133), which shares the same management, offers authentic Japanese food. (This is a kind of fraternity house for Japanese sailors away from home.) You can get lots of special things with 24 hours' notice. Otherwise, you'll have to take the "set meal," usually Sukiyaki (with soup, appetizers, and dessert) for around $15 per person.

That revolving restaurant at the top of the **Wrest Point** (Tel. 25–0112) isn't bad, considering that no revolving restaurant in the world is ever top notch. (You always pay more for the panorama.) Still, the trevelly, a popular local fish, was certainly okay. Service at our lunchtime meal was not, however. They were pleasant enough, but simply understaffed. Things might go 'round better at night.

We were sent to **Maria's** (Tel. 25–2511) in the Four Seasons Town House, which is enjoying some current popularity. (That's pronounced like "Mariah's," by the way.) We found red bricked walls, high-backed booths, and a too-loud sound system unsuccessfully trying to drown out the noisy conviviality of Maria's regular patrons. It served a decent steak at $5 or $6, but so do lots of places in Australia. Maybe fun for a crowd. The house red wine was good and cheap, anyway.

Some other possibilities in the capital: For Italian fare, try **Don Camillo** (Tel. 34–1006), a tiny place at 6 Magnet Court, Sandy Bay, or **Mondo Piccolo** (Tel. 23–2362), at 196 Macquarie St. in Downtown Hobart. A locally popular Indian restaurant is the **Kasmir,** 109 Elizabeth St., also right downtown. (Open daily.) For seafood, drop into **Vader's**

Cellar (Tel. 23–6063) at 13 Cromwell St., Battery Point. The Dutch family who runs it gives excellent service.

KITCHENS IN THE COUNTRY

Here are a few reliable choices elsewhere around the island:

Launceston. **The Owl's Nest** (Tel. 31–6699) in the Penny Royal Watermill serves good roast beef and other things. But go to **Dicky White's** (Tel. 22–206) in the Launceston Hotel for shish kebab. Another favorite—for light meals and a heavy view—is the new **Gorge Restaurant** (Tel. 31–333), at the foot of the dramatic Cataract Cliffs. Drive there via Gorge Road, or take Basin Road to the end and board the chairlift to the restaurant. (We haven't done this yet, ourselves, but plan to this year.)

Port Arthur. We weren't terribly impressed with our buffet lunch in the **Four Season Motel** (Tel. 50–2102) at Port Arthur. Next time, we're going to take someone's advice and eat down the road at the **Penzance Motel** (Tel. 50–3272) at Eaglehawk Neck (Pirate's Bay).

Richmond. We lunched once in the **Richmond Arms Hotel** (Tel. 62–2109) in that historic community a few miles from Hobart. This is a no-nonsense, typical Aussie pub operation—cheap and substantial. (Place your order at the bar. They'll deliver it to your table.) It was a Monday, because we had been heading for the well-known 1830 **Prospect House** (Tel. 62–2207), outside of Richmond, which is closed Mondays. We still haven't hit it, but the old mansion is famous for excellent and gracious home cooking. Still on our list—but never on Monday!

Evandale: The leader is **Casey's** (Tel. 91–8484). *Perth*: At the **Leather Bottell Inn** (Tel. 98–2248), a country tavern on the Main Road, they may still make their own beer. *Ross*: The same is true, we think, at the **Scotch Thistle Inn** (Tel. 81–5213), on Church Street, another colonial building in a historic town. (Closed Sunday.) *Devonport*: Home cooking is touted at **The Country Kitchen** (Tel. 24–4341), at 93 Oldaker St. *Burnie*: Try the **Martini** (Tel. 31–3408), 63 Wilson St.

6. Sightseeing in Hobart and Tasmania

Your first stop should be the **Tasmanian Government Tourist Bureau** (Tel. 34–6911), 80 Elizabeth St., to see what there is to see.

In Hobart, **Battery Point,** with its early nineteenth century buildings and traditions, is the local equivalent to Sydney's Rocks area. If you have the pamphlet *Let's Talk About Battery Point* (one of a series of "Let's Talk About . . . " folders), you can follow a well-designed walking tour of this historic area.

At **Salamanca Place,** a terrace of 150-year-old storehouses provides a colorful backdrop to a Saturday open-air market in good weather. And look for "Narryna" which houses the **Van Diemen's Land Folk Museum,** Hampden Road, in that area, whose displays reflect colonial life in Tasmania. (Monday to Friday until 5:00 p.m.; admission 80 cents.)

Other museums include the **Post Office Museum** on the Castray Esplanade, the **Tasmanian Museum,** 5 Argyle St., with its sad exhibits on the fate of Tasmanian Aborigines, a race which no longer exists, the **Allport Library,** 91 Murray St. (corner of Bathurst) with its books, maps, and antiques (open weekdays, 9:00 to 5:00), and the **Maritime Museum of Tasmania,** at Cromwell Street, Battery Point, which has many models of ships from windjammers to modern liners. (Open daily from 2:00 to 4:30 p.m.)

Elsewhere, you'll of course notice **Mount Wellington,** southwest of the city. You can drive for about 10 miles right to the top of the 4,166-foot peak, where it often snows in winter. (Wear something warm and water resistant, and skip it if the weather is not clear.)

On the opposite side of town, the large green area is the 640-acre **Queen's Domain** and the adjoining **Royal Botanical Gardens.** Nearby the attractive $14.7 million **Tasman Bridge,** built in 1965, spans 3,364 feet over the River Derwent. In 1975, it was closed after a ship crashed into its pilings, causing part of the roadway to collapse. Counting the victims whose cars fell into the river, a total of 12 persons died. The bridge was repaired and reopened over two years later.

Also in Hobart, but a sight we've never made it to, is the **Model Tudor Village** (Tel. 25–1194), a miniature marvel, they say, at 827 Sandy Bay Road (Bus Stop 30). How about your telling us about that one?

PORT ARTHUR

An absolute must is an excursion out of Hobart, by coach or car, to Port Arthur, about 60 miles by road from the capital. The old penal institution, which held as many as 12,000 convicts at one time, is largely in ruins but is maintained as a historical exhibit. Knowledgeable National Park Rangers and a small museum there explain the background of the famous—or notorious—prison. It's $1.50 for a guided tour of the grounds, one of the best bargains in Australia. (Take Route 3 to Sorrell, then Route 7 to Port Arthur.)

THROUGHOUT TASMANIA

Elsewhere in the state are many scenic towns, historic villages, and dramatic natural features. By all means see **Cataract Gorge,** if you're going to Launceston. On the northwest coast, the old town of **Stanley** features an unusual rock formation called "The Nut" at the end of its peninsular site. And there is some spectacular scenery on the narrow Lyell Highway into **Queenstown.**

For a detailed description of virtually every site on the giant island, pick up the *Official Visitors' Guide* produced by the Tasmanian Tourist Council, and available for $1.50. (The most recent edition we saw was the tenth, produced in November, 1978, but beware that newsagents may still be selling an edition as old as the seventh—undated, but presumably printed back in 1976, or before.)

A last word: Tasmania has lots of distinctive wildlife, but you'll have a dickens of a time seeing it. Since our last visit to the island, we've heard of a fellow named John Hamilton who has opened up the **Tasmanian Devil Wildlife Park** in Tarrana, near Port Arthur. If you go before we get there, let us know about it. And by the way, stay away from any snake in the wild. Every species in the state is deadly poisonous. (They say, however, that the snakes are shy and prefer not to bite humans!)

7. Guided Tours and Cruises from Hobart

Book all tours through the Tasmanian Government Tourist Bureau (TGTB) (Tel. 34–6911), 80 Elizabeth St. (Some of these may not run from June through November.)

Historic Port Arthur: Eight hours. About $10. *D'Entrecasteaux Channel, Huon Valley, and Mount Wellington*: Seven hours. About $10. *Hastings Caves*: (Via Huon Highway.) Seven hours. About $10. *Gordon River Road via Russell Falls and Mt. Field National Park*: (We've never taken this but have heard the falls are spectacular.) Nine hours. About $15.

Some boat cruises up the River Derwent may cast off this year. See the T.G.T.B. for details.

Air tours? Try **Tasmanian Aviation Services** (Tel. Hobart 48–5172) which reportedly offers some scenic air routes.

8. Water Sports

Good beaches line much of Tasmania, including some sands on the Derwent Estuary near Hobart, like Kingston and Long Beach. There are more choices on the Eastern Shore, however.

Scuba diving is consistently popular. Rent equipment from the **Aqua Scuba Diving Services** (Tel. 34–5658) at 54 Collins St. For boating, check first with the secretary of the **Royal Yacht Club of Tasmania** (Tel. 23–7394) at the Marieville Esplanade, Sandy Bay 7005. (Hobart, of course, is the terminus for the annual Sydney to Hobart and Melbourne to Hobart Ocean Yacht Races. The first boats usually arrive New Year's Day.)

Big game fishing is a big sport in Tasmania during the summer, and some of the best tuna is caught at Eaglehawk Neck, near Port Arthur. Charter boats cost about $100 to $225 a day. In Hobart, try **S. P. Dwyer** (Tel. 23–2122), 163 Macquarie St., Hobart 7000. The tourist bureau will have the names of other skippers and boats. There's plenty of trout fishing on lakes, streams, and rivers, particularly in northern Tasmania. Rainbows regularly tip the scales at more than 30 pounds up at Lake Crescent, they say.

9. Other Sports

Hobart's most famous sport is indoors. The gambling casino at the Wrest Point Hotel offers roulette, blackjack, craps, baccarat, poker, keno, and "two up," the traditional Aussie coin toss.

The casino operates from 1:00 p.m. to 3:00 a.m., or to 4:00 a.m. on weekends. If you're going to gamble, ask the Wrest Point for its little booklet *Introduction to Gaming*, and read it first. (Note that there are no slot machines allowed in Tasmania.) Ostensibly for tourists, gambling actually attracts more Tasmanians to the tables as players. Many tourists just come to watch. (Gambling may also begin somewhere in Launceston during 1980.)

Horse races are run every Saturday, alternately at **Elwick Racecourse,** on Elwick Road, Glenorchy, about three miles up Route 1, and at **Mowbray Racecourse** in Launceston.

Tennis addicts, if there are no nets at your hotel, look for facilities at the **Domain Tennis Centre** in that big park overlooking the bridge. You can call the Tasmanian Lawn Tennis Association there (Tel. 34–2365), who will help put you on a hard court.

For golfing, by far the most outstanding course is the private **Tasmanian Golf Club** (Tel. 48–5098), which spreads over a spectacular promontory surrounded on three sides by the waters of Barilla Bay, near the Cambridge Aerodrome. Then there is the **Royal Hobart** (Tel. 48–6161) at Seven Mile Beach, near the Hobart Airport, which is also good. A little closer to town, and open to all comers is the **Rosny Park** (Tel. 44–1297), a public course in Bellerive (Bus Stop 7).

Tasmania is not the antarctic refrigerator most Australians think it is. Nevertheless, skiing is a popular sport June to September at the higher elevations in Mount Field and Ben Lomond National Parks and sometimes at Mt. Mawson. Snow conditions are not as reliable as those in Victoria and New South Wales, however.

10. Shopping in Hobart

As the second oldest settlement in Australia, Hobart not surprisingly comes up with several antique shops, many of them at Battery Point. Also there, or more specifically on Salamanca Place, be sure to wander through the colorful and musical open market held under the umbrellas and plane trees on Saturdays, when the regular Hobart shops are closed.

The main department stores downtown are **Fitzgerald's** on Collins Street and a branch of the Melbourne-based chain, **Myer's** on Liverpool Street.

Also downtown, some general souvenir and antique shops worth looking into include **Ward's Gift Shop,** 93 Liverpool St., **Barclay's Souvenir Centre,** 24 Elizabeth St., and **Excelsior Antiques,** 111 Elizabeth St., plus the charitable handicrafts and jams and jellies sold at the **Country Women's Association Gift Shop,** at 165 Elizabeth St.

Don't miss a walk through Centrepoint Hobart, The Place, or Elizabeth Mall, three new complexes with small, interesting specialty shops, or the little **Cat and Fiddle Arcade** which tunnels between Elizabeth and Murray Streets in the block also bounded by Liverpool and Collins. The name honors a pub once there and is symbolized by some mechanical nursery rhyme figures which animate on the hour at an interior courtyard. A shop we liked near the fountain is **Ornamo's** (Tel. 34–3744) which offers a lot of unusual kitchen things. And the **Sanitorium** features lots of Tassy goodies, including honey, apple juice, etc.

Out of town, if you get up to Hamilton, about 47 miles northwest, you'll find a good selection of local crafts at the **Old School House.**

In Launceston, check out the souvenirs and crafts at **Emma's Arts,** 78 George St.

You may see some of the island's apples sold in roadside stands. Look for Red Delicious, Golden Delicious, Jonathan, and, of course, Granny Smiths.

11. Night Life and Entertainment

The average Tasmanian doesn't much believe in a lot of fuss after dark, but the state's new reputation as "Tasmania, the Treasure Island" is forcing some changes in that attitude.

Not the least, of course, is the influence of the casino at the Wrest Point Hotel, and the new one which may open this year in Launceston. We covered those activities under Section 9.

To complete the Nevada image at the Wrest Point is the large **Cabaret Room** (Tel. 25–0112) which generally features a lavish, full-scale revue. The tables are well arranged in three tiers, so everybody gets a good look at the action.

You'll find a Friday matinee, perhaps still serving lunch and show together for around $9. Dinner shows will run about twice that Monday to Friday and perhaps $20 on Saturdays and holidays. We thought the best bargain was to take the show only (without dinner) Monday to Friday at about $9, or the late Saturday night show only at 12:30 for $10. (Remember, these are sample prices only; they could be up this year in general or even more for specific shows.)

We like the show we saw there, except we thought it strange that the small live band was sometimes supplemented or replaced by recordings of a big orchestra—a practice which cast somewhat of a provincial tone to an otherwise professional production.

You'll find some other action scattered here and there. One theater/restaurant, the **Cedar Court** (Tel. 23–7521) has opened up in the refurbished Hadley's Hotel at 34 Murray St.

The **Hobart Repertory Theatre** group as well as traveling productions often appear in Hobart. The capital is the headquarters of the **Tasmanian Symphony Orchestra** as well as a choir from the Tasmanian Conservatorium of Music. Visiting live rock bands might appear at the Hobart City Hall or at the theaters.

Hobart theaters include the **TVT Entertainment Centre** (Tel. 34–5998), 174 Liverpool St., the **Theatre Royal** (Tel. 34–6266), 82 Campbell St., the **Playhouse** (Tel. 34–1536), 106 Bathurst St., and **ABC Odeon** (Tel. 30–9903), 163 Liverpool St. There are also several motion picture theaters.

A few pubs feature live jazz on the weekends. Try **Tattersalls Bar & Bistro** at 112 Murray St. Last we knew, there were a few discos spinning around the island—**Goldie's** at the Casino, and at the **Pancake Parlor,** corner of York and Kingsway, in Launceston.

And beer? Of course! The popular Hobart brew is Cascade (Est. 1824), which now also owns its former Launceston competitor, Boag's. Both the Cascade Red Label and Cascade Blue Label are fairly mild beers. Green Label is stronger and more bitter, and there's a Cascade Stout with quite a stout kick to it. Boag's also has a Red and Blue Label, both a little stronger than the direct Cascade equivalent. And both breweries also produce an ale, which we haven't tried.

In the pubs, beer comes in four, six, eight, and ten-ounce glasses.

12. The Tasmanian Address List

Bank—The Bank of New South Wales, 74 Elizabeth St., Hobart (Tel. 23–2961); 109 Brisbane St., Launceston (Tel. 31–4533).

Books and magazines—O.B.M. Newsagents & Booksellers, Collins Street, near Elizabeth (Tel. 34–4288).

Bus information—Western Shore buses, Tel. 34–5670; Eastern Shore buses, Tel. 44–1599.

Camping equipment—Outdoor Equipment, 212 Liverpool St., Hobart (Tel. 34–6213).

Emergencies of all types—Telephone 000.

Hiking and backpacking information—Federation of Tasmanian Bush Walking Clubs, P. O. Box 106, Bellerive 7018.

Post Office—Corner of Elizabeth and Macquarie Streets (Tel. 20–7207).

Royal Automobile Club of Tasmania, Murray and Patrick Streets, Hobart.

Tourist information—Tasmanian Government Tourist Bureau, 80 Elizabeth St., Hobart (Tel. 34–6911), or St. John & Paterson Streets, Launceston (Tel. 31–5833).

Youth Hostel Association, 105 Macquarie St., Hobart, Tel. 23–6497.

9

Adelaide
and South Australia

1. The General Picture

Adelaide seems just about the most alive city in Australia.

They used to call her the "City of Churches." Now she seeks—and deserves—the title of the "Festival City," since the 1970 construction of a $21 million arts complex on the banks of the Torrens River. There she hosts a biennial extravaganza that brings every kind of performer and artist from the rest of Australia and from other cultural centers of the world.

But throughout non-Festival years, too, there is a feeling of activity in Adelaide—of something going on somewhere that should not be missed.

The capital is also one of the most well-designed cities in the world. It was laid out midway between the coastline and the Mount Lofty Range by its 1838 founder and surveyor, Colonel William Light. The main portion of the city today is almost completely surrounded by extensive park lands.

The town seems divided into two parts—the southern square mile grid of 75 blocks contains nearly all the business, government, and cultural centers. To the north, across the Torrens and the wide green belt, is a city of homes, gardens, and parks.

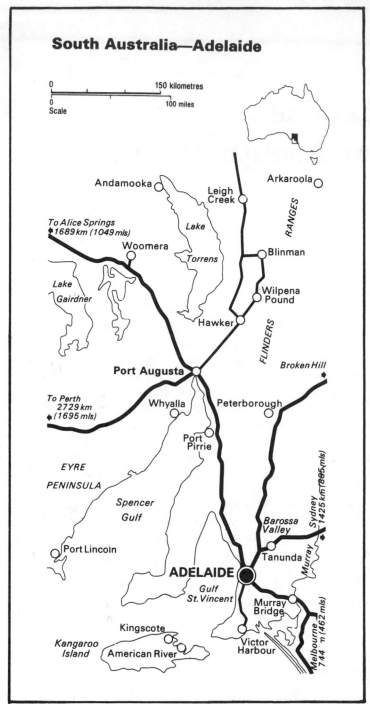

South Australia—Adelaide

Map courtesy Australian Tourist Commission

The entire state of South Australia likewise divides itself in two different regions. Adelaide sits in the southern third of the state—fertile coastland with a Mediterranean climate and hills and valleys that provide excellent soil for olives, almonds, and especially the European grapes which have made the region famous for wine production. The 1,600 mile long Murray River also passes its final 400 miles through southern South Australia before emptying into the Great Australian Bight.

Adelaide, though green, is also dry. It averages only about 20 inches of rain a year. But the northern two-thirds of South Australia, the second region, receives only half as much rain, and seemingly twice as much heat. These are the beginnings of the great deserts for which Australia as a whole is known world wide.

There are first the Flinders Ranges, colorful and rugged mountains, and popular with "bushwalkers" and lovers of spring wildflowers. Beyond those, the country is flatter and less inviting, although spectacular in a different way. Here is Lake Eyre, which most years has no water at all—just 3,000 square miles of glaring white salt. Here, too, is the opal country, where man lives underground, not just to dig out the precious stones, but to protect himself from the oppressive heat. And in this section is the shadeless Nullarbor Plain, where the Trans-Australian Railway sets out on a stretch westward that includes 300 miles of perfectly straight track.

South Australia, gateway to the Outback, has the distinction of being the most lively and the most deadly state at the same time.

2. The Airport and Long-Distance Transportation

The interior of the Adelaide airport terminal is in a "T" shape, with the check-in counter for **Ansett Airlines** (Tel. 212–1111) resting inside the left arm of the T and its departure lounges and gates lined along the left side of the stem. The check-in for **Trans Australian Airlines** (Tel. 51–8233) occupies the mirror image on the right arm with the right side of the T-stem devoted to TAA gates and lounges.

Although compact, the airport squeezes in several facilities. Across from Ansett is the Walkabout Restaurant, Coffee Shop, and Grill, and there's a "canteen" (takeout stand) nearby, too. As befits this vineyard vicinity, there's a wine store there. Across the walkway, the newsagent displays a good collection of books and pamphlets about S.A.

If you're flying out to Kangaroo Island—about $25, each way—you may look for the little **Emu Airways** (Tel. 352–3128), whose counter almost hides under the stairway. (We don't know why an airline to an

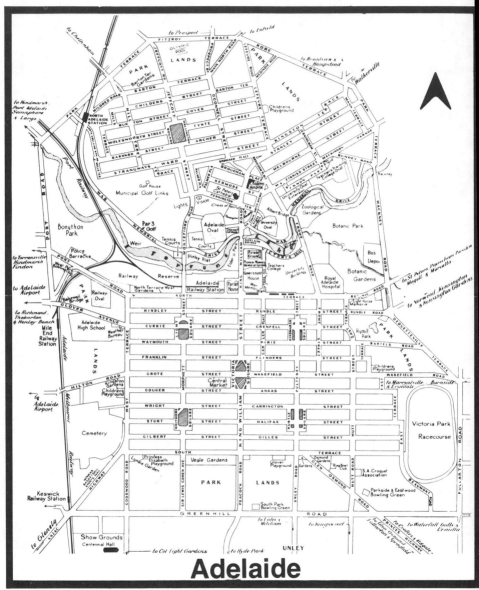

Adelaide

Map courtesy South Australian Division of Tourism

island called Kangaroo is named Emu—an emu is a flightless bird, after all—although maybe it's got something to do with a short hop!) Sara took one of their little low-altitude Cessnas out there recently and had a wonderful time. (More conservative folks may prefer Ansett Airlines of S.A.)

Baggage areas for Ansett and TAA are opposite their respective check-ins, and both offer coaches at about $1.50 per seat for the five miles into town.

There's a newer small airline around called **Opal Air** (Tel. 212–1111), which is inaugurating flights and aerial tours to the gemstone areas of Andamooka and Coober Pedy, and even up to Ayers Rock in the Northern Territory. We know little about them, however.

Daily railroad services from the rest of Australia connect with Adelaide. To or from Melbourne on the *Overland* (about $25 Economy Class—extra for sleepers) you can ride for 12 hours all the way on the same train. To and from other major capitals requires a change at Port Pirie. This is the way to connect with the famous transcontinental *Indian Pacific* (west to Perth or east to Sydney) or—if you want to chance it—the historic Central Australian Railway called the *Ghan* which moseys on Mondays up to Alice Springs and wanders back again on Wednesdays. (1980 is to be its 103rd and final year. Remember that there are sometimes washouts on the line, with resulting delays, jammed hotels, changed plans, and the like.)

Train reservations are handled by the **Australian National Railways** (Tel. 212–6699), on North Terrace, or through the **S.A. Government Tourist Bureau** (Tel. 51–3281) at 18 King William St. Trains come in to the Adelaide Station, conveniently located on North Terrace, next to the Festival Centre and several hotels.

Bus services to Adelaide are launched from Alice Springs, Darwin, Brisbane, Canberra, Melbourne, Perth, and Sydney via **Ansett Pioneer** (Tel. 51–2075), 140 North Terrace, and **Greyhound Coaches** (Tel. 212–1777). The Central Bus Station is at 111 Franklin St., and several small feeder lines head for destinations within South Australia.

There is an automobile ferry boat service from Port Adelaide to Kangaroo Island. For information and reservations, contact **R. W. Miller & Co.** (Tel. 47–5577), 14 Leadenhall St. in Port Adelaide. Allow about seven hours for the crossing, and remember it's only about 30 or 40 minutes by plane.

Driving into Adelaide, you'll most likely wheel in on Highway 1, either the Princes Highway from Melbourne (about 600 miles) or the Eyre Highway from Perth (about 1700 miles). Both roads are generally excellent, but plan the Adelaide-Perth excursion carefully. The section across the Nullarbor is not to be taken lightly.

People we've talked to now say this recently improved desert section is more easily done. Nevertheless, in the past this section of road has fallen victim to an Outback bacteria that actually eats asphalt for breakfast. In any case, your car should be in excellent condition, you should carry extra water, and your nightly reservations should be pre-booked all along the way. We advise a membership in—and the latest information from—the **Royal Automobile Association of S.A.** (Tel. 223–4555), 41 Hindmarsh Square, Adelaide 5000, before making the trip.

Driving to Alice Springs? Forget it! Take the train, or better yet, the plane. (The roads are real axlebusters.)

One caveat when traveling to or from South Australia by any means. Remember that it's on a bastard time zone. Under normal circumstances, it's *one-half hour* earlier in South Australia and the Northern Territory than it is in the eastern states. And it's *one and one-half hours later* than the state of Western Australia.

This, of course, is when all parties are observing standard time. Western Australia, the Northern Territory, and Queensland do not observe Daylight Saving Time, but South Australia and much of the rest of the country do. So this will obviously confuse the time picture still further for those reading airline, train, and bus schedules between South Australia and other states.

Forewarned is forearmed. Good luck!

3. Local Transportation in Adelaide

With the city's wide, easily understood streets, driving is relatively simple, and there are several rental car agencies clamoring for your business. At the moment, and subject to a sudden shift of gears, the best rates seem to be with two or three companies, **Ajax Rent-A-Car** (Tel. 223–1786), 106 Frome St., **Letz Rent-A-Car** (Tel. 51–7088), 18 Magill Road, and maybe **Thrifty Rent-A-Car** (Tel. 212–3366), 194 Currie St.

Most rates will be well over $20 a day, however, including those at **Budget Rent-A-Car** (Tel. 223–1400), 274 North Terrace, **Hertz Rentals** (Tel. 51–2856), 30 Morphett St., and **Avis Rent-A-Car** (Tel. 51–8000), 298 Hindley St.—the only one of this group charging a combination of daily rates plus so much a kilometer. (All the others offer flat daily and weekly rates.)

If you're a pedal bicycle fan, Adelaide with its parks and gardens is one city where it might be practical. You can rent these ("push bikes," they call them in Australia) from **Super Elliotts** (Tel. 223–3946), at 200 Rundle St., and in several other addresses throughout the suburbs.

Metropolitan Bus Services (Tel. 223–4791 for information) are well described in the color-coded *Public Transport Map*, issued by the Ministry of Transport from time to time. (Ask for one at the tourist office or the railroad station.) Maximum fare on the silver vehicles is 40 cents, but note the free "Bee Line" service (99-B) shooting between the railroad station and the Victoria Square tram terminal. Adelaide is gradually air conditioning its entire fleet of buses in an attempt to lure riders back on board.

There is now only one trolley left. That's the little chocolate car called the **Bay Tram.** You get it at Victoria Square and it takes about a half-hour to get to the seaside suburb of Glenelg on the Gulf St. Vincent. (Other Adelaide streetcars were retired years ago, but the Glenelg line had its own right-of-way so it never had to war with motor vehicles. Now Adelaide is considering inaugurating a new tram service to other outlying districts.)

4. Hotels in Adelaide

There are three obvious leaders in the city center—the Gateway, the Town House, and the Grosvenor. The viewful Oberoi Adelaide (Tel. 267–3444) in North Adelaide is reportedly much improved since it was last known as the Hotel Australia, but we haven't seen it since the transformation.

EXPENSIVE HOTELS

You'll pay $40 to $55 for two in most rooms of these five or six choices. All have the standard luxury features—color telleys, fridges, air conditioners, tea makers, newspapers, etc. Following those, we'll list a few possibilities at a lower tariff.

An absolutely perfect location goes a long way to recommend the 21-story **Gateway Inn** (Tel. 217-7552) at 147 North Terrace, across from the railroad station, Parliament, the Festival Centre, the river, and a grand view of North Adelaide—and also around the corner from the business section. Down on the bottom level, too, is the Ansett airport bus terminal, which means that the coach carries you and your goods and chattels right from the plane to your hotel. Lots of central facilities, including laundry, dry cleaners, swimming pool, the Chelsea Restaurant, Portico Grill, cocktail bar, travel agency, etc.; colorful, well-lighted, nicely designed bedrooms (notice the little breakfast tray hatch accessible from the hallway); convenient bathrooms with good showers and tubs. We experienced friendly, efficient service. Our only small criticism of the Gateway is that if you travel a lot between Adelaide, Perth, and Brisbane, you may have to look out the window in the morning to be reminded which of these cities you're in, because the three links in the chain look like identical triplets inside. (Reservations through Ansett, of course, or write to the hotel.) There's nothing in Adelaide today that matches it.

The venerable old **Grosvenor** (Tel. 51–2961), a few doors down the street, has been brought fairly smoothly into the 1970's, and the refurbishment is still continuing. The hotel was first built in 1918 by a farmers' cooperative organization who wanted a decent place to take their families when they came to town, and it still fulfills that role nicely. Modernized, wood-paneled lobby with blue and gold monogrammed carpet; Coolibah Room for breakfast, lunch, or dinner; cozy Pioneer Bar; no pool; no views to speak of; free parking; 280 widely varying bedchambers, but most with air conditioning, stocked refrigerator, color TV's, tea makers, subdued colors; good staff *esprit de corps* exemplified by Paul Andrews, the head porter. Rates run a little less here, and it's a good bargain. (Reservations from the hotel at 125 North Terrace, Adelaide 5000.) An admirable job of preserving a 61-year-old model.

Still, some will prefer the **Town House** (Tel. 51–8255), a modern candidate around the corner at the conjunction of Morphett St. and "swinging" Hindley Street: Red brick facade; covered porte-cochere; reception area with some unusual lamps and a certain amount of clutter; Lipizzaner Dining Room reflecting the manager's love for horses; bar and coffee lounge open to guests only; large, heated pool on the roof, with wind-protected sundeck; several conveniences catering to businessmen. Amply proportioned bedrooms and many suites; some with walk-out balconies; good, full bathrooms; color TV's and many luxuries in all units; some with views over the rooftops. Prices, beginning at about $50 doubles, are a little steeper than we think they should be. (Reservations through the M.F.A. chain in Australia, or from the hotel at Adelaide 5000.) Certainly comfortable, although without the sparkle of the Gateway or the cheerful informality of the Grosvenor.

If you can't get into any of the above, you might try the **Parkroyal** (Tel. 223–4355), somewhat inconveniently situated at 226 South Terrace. (It's fine with a car.) Imposing façade with fountains playing; large, outdoor pool in the back garden; pleasant Copper Grill restaurant; well-arranged rooms, many with balcony.

The Parkroyal is one of a trio of TraveLodge-owned hotels, all next door to one another, for some reason, including the **Adelaide Trave-**

Lodge (Tel. 223–6177) and the **South Terrace TraveLodge** (Tel. 223–2744). The Parkroyal is okay, if you like the location. The other two we judged clean, neat, and dull.

BUDGET PRICED ACCOMMODATIONS

"Absolutely charming" is the comment we keep hearing about one of our favorite bargains in the entire country for the price level. That happens to be the **"Teasers" Newmarket** (Tel. 51–3836), at the corner of West and North Terraces, the end of the Port Road, and a hotel with genuine creaky character since it dates back about 130 years.

The centerpiece of this house is its wonderful, free-standing cedar spiral staircase swirling from the lobby to the upper floor, an architectural feature now protected by the Australian National Trust. It's worth stopping in to see even if you don't stay there.

An active place throughout the day and night, the Newmarket includes the popular Stockyard restaurant, a cocktail lounge, and a weekend discotheque. The entire establishment is filled with old oil paintings, Tiffany skylights, crystal chandeliers, marble-mantle fireplaces and other Victoriana. The bedchambers, though no longer young, tend to be large, trim, and cheap. For $30 or so for a double, you'll draw a B&W TV, a phone, a fridge, and an electric jug to boot. Some singles may still be under $20. (Write the hotel for reservations at 1 North Terrace, Adelaide 5000.) You may have to lug your luggage up those historic steps, but at those non-spiraling tariffs, it could be worth it.

Even at slightly higher rates, a few may prefer the more central site of the **Ambassadors Hotel** (Tel. 51–4331) at 107 King William St., another supposed oldie-but-goodie. There's a lift, here, and you'll get color television and all that. But the rooms are cramped by comparison. Most have showers, but few have tubs.

We also had a look at the **Astor** (Tel. 51–6408), at 95 Gawler Place, and the **Plaza** (Tel. 51–6371) at 85 Hindley St. Either will do for traveling Spartans. (Singles might get a cell for a ten-spot.)

Youth hostel? For members, only, remember, it's at 290 Giles St. (Tel. 223–6007), and has lots of rules. You may check in for about $3.50—a little less if you provide your own bed sheet. Headquarters of the Youth Hostels Association of S.A. (Tel. 51–5583) is at 72 South Terrace.

5. Restaurants and Dining

Adelaide folks like to eat out, and it's a truism oft-repeated that the city has more restaurants per gullet than any other metropolis in Australia.

Observers of Adelaide's restaurant scene say, in fact, that the city has too many, and this results in a serious lack of consistency at the top addresses—this, in a city which would otherwise rival Melbourne for elegant dining rooms.

SEAFOOD

Adelaide is famous for ocean specialties, particularly (1) crayfish, (2) prawns, and (3) whiting, whether in restaurants calling themselves seafood houses or in more wide-ranging kitchens. It's not surprising when you consider there are two large bays, or rather gulfs—Spencer Gulf and Gulf St. Vincent—to harvest.

Look out for dishes labeled "fried or grilled whiting" or "crumbed prawns." More than likely, they will be frozen—not fresh. And skip whiting dishes which are smothered with French sauces, as these mask the delicate, distinct flavor of whiting.

Other favorites, if you can find them are fresh gemfish (something like barramundi, which is a Northern Territory specialty), tuna, and rock lobster.

And don't forget that some of Australia's best wines—particularly whites—are produced in the nearby Barossa Valley and are just about perfect complements to the seafood specialties.

There are two outstanding seafood restaurants. The most beautiful setting, and certainly the most convenient, is **Benjamin's** (Tel. 51–6280), a city council-sponsored (but privately run) two-story glass house right on the riverside in the park beside War Memorial Drive. (Ask for a window table—easier for a group of four than for two, incidentally.) We liked the fillet of flounder with prawns. All main dishes in the $7 or $8 range. The whiting and lobster is certainly recommended, too. Some steak dishes are offered (and dependable).

The other seafood star is **Swain's** (Tel. 79–6449), which now packs 'em in at 207 Glen Osmond Road in Frewville, a little southeast on Route 1. Here's a good place to try whiting or crayfish, but you'd better count on paying a bill of $30 for two, with wine. (Closed Sundays.)

For fish fanciers with a thinner wallet under their gills, try one of the little ocean-oriented cafes in Gouger Street, an even greater saving when you can bring your own wine. Don't expect the Ritz, but we liked **Gouger's Cafe** (Tel. 51–2320) at No. 98. If you don't mind formica and bright lights, you may come up with an excellent garfish or whiting for about $3.50. It's very popular; reservations are not mandatory, but you may have to wait. Similar favorites include **Paul's,** at No. 79, and **George's,** at No. 108, the only one of the three which is air conditioned and also open Sunday.

OTHER RESTAURANTS

Many of Adelaide's best restaurants will also do very nicely with seafood, of course. This is certainly true at **Henry Ayers** (Tel. 223–2852), in the historic, state-owned Ayers House at 288 North Terrace. Be warned right away that (a) this is supposed to be the most expensive restaurant in Australia and (b) we haven't yet eaten there, even though we have actually touched a few people who have! According to Sol Simeon's excellent guide, *Eating Out in Adelaide,* it is Adelaide's most spectacular restaurant, decorated in "Edwardian decadence." We cadged a copy of their 1979 menu, however, and in our dinner of the mind, we are finding it difficult to choose between the Langouste Chantecler (lobster sauteed in butter with curry powder—served on a bed of rice, coated with curry sauce and nantua sauce and garnished with mushrooms) at $17.50 and the Tournedos Esterhazy (two small fillets, pan fried in butter with julienne of celery, carrot, green peppers, onions seasoned with paprika and capers, and finished with cream) at $12.95. (Remember, that was a 1979 menu!) In the near future, they say, you and your dining partner won't leave without settling a total tab of $75 or $100. (There's no smoking in the dining room, by the way, which might save you a few pennies.)

Other top-drawer choices include the **Chelsea** (Tel. 217–7552), in the Gateway Inn. You might try the Porc a la Scandinave, with red cabbage, for something different. They're proud of one crayfish dish, too, the Chausson de Langouste Haleakala, named for a Hawaiian volcano. It's baked in pastry with celery, chestnuts, and mushrooms.

Besides that, you'll find good international fare in the **King's Court** (Tel. 223–4355) in the Parkroyal Hotel, the **Festival Centre Restaurant** (Tel. 51–6430) right next to the main auditorium (Adelaide *Advertiser* food writer Stan James said he had his best barramundi there, pan fried in butter and topped with Hollandaise sauce), and at **Little Amsterdam** (Tel. 223–2573) in Gay's Arcade, just off the Rundle Mall, specializing in Dutch Indonesian, but offering a wider selection than that. **Dillinger's,** 58 North Terrace, we think is overpriced. But **Decca's Place** (Tel. 267–2745), 93 Melbourne St., near the boutiques, in North Adelaide, is as well-loved for its garden atmosphere as its Wiernel Schnitzel.

There are bargains to be had in little Hindley Street, particularly in the little Greek or Serbian-run barbecue cafes there. One is **Lubo's** (Tel. 51–2848) at No. 108, and not bad except for the glaring fluorescent light in part of it. My shashlik was fine. Sara didn't go for the schnitzel which came with cold vegies. Some say the **Barbecue Inn** (Tel. 51–3033) at No. 196 is much better, especially for Serbian sausages. And the **Hin-**

dley Bar-B-Q (Tel. 51–2090) at No. 179 is also very popular. All are inexpensive.

For Italian food, the best bet is **Sorrento** (Tel. 51–6740) at 135 Hindley St., although the **Billy Bunter Cellar,** at 168 Gouger St. is where owner Libero De Luca serves good calamari—whole baby squid flown fresh daily from Kangaroo Island. It's an excellent lunch for around $3.

Adelaide now teems with pizza joints, but the best is **Don Giovanni's** (Tel. 223–2125), at 201 Rundle St., just off the mall. Lots of other standard Italian dishes like canneloni and scallopini marinara are also good; servings are large, and prices are reasonably cheap. **The Adelaide Pizza House,** 169 Hindley, is also popular.

And Chinese fare? Adelaide has several, including **Chinatown** (Tel. 212–2501), at 33 Hindley St., usually a good bet, **Dynasty** (Tel. 51–7036), at 26 Gouger St., specializing in dim sum (chinese snacks), and the **Lantern Inn** (Tel. 297–1629), at 295-B Anzac Highway in Plympton (halfway to Glenelg) where the Peking Duck is excellent (but 24 hours' notice is required for that), and the **Manchurian** (*all* the way to Glenelg).

In Kent Town, a little east of the city, is an English find called **Maggie's Tavern** (Tel. 42–2686). At 107 Rundle St. (not to be confused with the Rundle Street downtown), a fan named John Anderson wrote us that "it has a warm atmosphere, with fireplaces in several of its small rooms, a large wine cellar, and the service is friendly." Thanks, John. The corned beef and cabbage is good, too, and it's well known for reasonable prices.

Open 24 hours a day, seven days a week, is the **Pancake Kitchen** (Tel. 51–9469) in that tiny L-shaped lane called Gilbert Place. We enjoyed a capuccino cup at **The Coffee Pot** (Tel. 212–1613) upstairs in the Rundle Mall. It's a little expensive, but good. The second cup is free, and there are newspapers and magazines to read. (No substantial food, though.)

BAROSSA VALLEY

In the famed wine-growing region, one of your best bets for wein and wurst Germanic atmosphere might be **Gramps Weinkeller Restaurant** (Tel. 085 + 63 – 8266), at Jacobs Creek (near Rowland Flat). We were very disappointed in **Die Galerie** in Tanunda. The weingarten *gemütlichkeit* was delightful, but we felt as if the owner was trying to trick us into ordering more than we really wanted. We did not experience that anywhere else in Australia.

6. Sightseeing in Adelaide and South Australia

Get all the latest information, maps, folders, tour information, etc., from the South Australian Government Tourist Bureau (Tel. 51–3281), at 18 King William St. It's just about the most on-the-ball state tourist office in Australia.

Ask the Tourist Bureau for the pamphlet and map entitled *Walks in Central Adelaide*. The three routes described and mapped are easy strolls covering the most important sites and sights in the city center. The points noted on the walking tour which are also in the following alphabetical list receive an asterisk (*). (There are several points on the walk, of course, which are not on the following list.)

Adelaide Festival Centre (*). In Elder Park, alongside the banks of the Torrens, the complex includes a 2000-seat multipurpose auditorium, a two-level drama theater, an experimental theater, and an amphitheater. The Adelaide Festival of the Arts takes place in the fall of even-numbered years. The next is March 1982. (Public tours of the Centre are offered from 10:00 to 3:00 on the hour.)

Art Gallery of South Australia (*) (Tel. 223–8911), sometimes called the National Gallery. An international collection particularly rich in Australian paintings, ceramics, and sculpture. (Open Monday–Saturday, 10:00 to 5:00.) Nearby the Frome Road is very attractive in summer with its copious overhanging trees.

Ayers House (Tel. 223–1196), 288 North Terrace. Now the headquarters of the South Australian National Trust, this elegant bluestone home of the middle nineteenth century is also maintained as a museum. (Two restaurants are on the property—Henry Ayers, very expensive, and Paxton's, less formal , but still not cheap.) Try to catch a guided tour of the house, Tuesday through Friday at 12:00, 1:00, 2:00, 3:00, and 4:00. (Open also weekends and holidays from 2:00 to 4:30 p.m. Closed Mondays. Admission $1.)

Botanic Gardens. In the parklands to the northeast of the center, its collection of water lilies is noted worldwide. (A small zoo is there, too.) The gardens are open daily until sunset. By the way, there's a small river boat called *Popeye* that sails on the Torrens every 10 minutes between the zoo and the Festival Theatre. The fare is 70 cents.

Civic Buildings (*). These include the structures just north of Victoria Square—the twin clock towers of the General Post Office and the Town Hall, the Treasury Building, and the gothic-styled Stow Memorial Church. Of more interest to many is the little pie cart alongside the GPO. The specialty is the floater, an upside down pie floating in a sea of green pea soup. Adelaideans lap it up with a dollop of tomato sauce. (Another good pie cart is usually outside the Adelaide Railway Station.)

Central Market. Running between Grote and Gouger, the stalls sell vegies, fruit, cheeses, meats, flowers, nuts, caviar, smoked salmon, and you name it. It's open Tuesday until 6:00, Friday until 10:00 and Saturday until 2:00 p.m.

Light's Vision. In North Adelaide, overlooking the city from Montefiore Hill, this memorial and statue of Colonel Light is considered a good place to begin a tour of his city.

South Australian Museum (*) (Tel. 223–8911), sometimes called the Museum of Natural History. It has an outstanding mob of stuffed birds and animals. Be sure to stop inside long enough to have a good look at the ground-floor skeleton of the giant Diprotodon, an ancestor of the wombat. (Photograph its portrait head-on, and we'll guarantee you'll have a startling slide to shake up your audience!) Like many sites, the museum is on the elegant North Terrace. (Open 10:00 to 5:00, Monday to Saturday, Sunday, 2:00 to 5:00.)

State Library (*), next door. You'll find an excellent collection of current newspapers in its reading room.

University of Adelaide (*), also a neighbor to the above, provides a scholarly looking campus and a route to the little footbridge over the Torrens to the Angas Gardens.

KANGAROO ISLAND

A good, one-day aerial tour is a trip to the island they call "K.I." It features lots of unpenned wildlife—yes, including kangaroos, plus penguins, goannas, koalas, "flying foxes" (a type of bat), and an occasional platypus. At Seal Bay, you can walk among and photograph closeup the laziest colony of seals you ever saw. Have a look, too, for squadrons of pelicans and the rare Cape Barren goose, as well as a group of remarkable rocks, called the Remarkable Rocks. "Camel Safaris" are also available.

Kangaroo Island, discovered in 1802 by Mathew Flinders, has a colorful history all its own, and we could easily do an entire chapter on the place—and a book on S.A.—but neither is practical. If you go to K.I., however, say hello for us to Joan and Jim Sanderson, owners of the American River Motel, who carted Sara on one of her most efficient tours in Australia.

MOUNT LOFTY TO THE MURRAY

A day's driving tour from an Adelaide base is to head for the **Adelaide Hills** along Route 1 (Princes Highway or Mt. Barker Road) and thence to **Mount Lofty,** via the Summit Road. The outlook is great, but the real purpose of the journey is to enter the well-designed Native Fauna Zone of the **Cleland Conservation Park.** (If you didn't go to Healesville in Victoria, Cleland is a must.) There you may walk among and even pet some of the several different types of Australian animals in residence. The park is still being developed, but it already has begun to rank with the best in the country. (Open 9:30 a.m. to 5:00 p.m. daily. Feeding time for koalas, dingos and birds, from 2:00 p.m. to 4:00 p.m. Be sure to get a map.)

On the same trip, you might drive through, or even stop for lunch at the little German-styled town of **Hahndorf,** 18 miles east of Adelaide. Many Germans immigrated to South Australia because of religious and economic problems around 1840. The Old Mill Restaurant there is well known. Tours around the village are available from the blacksmith's shop.

About 30 miles further along the Princes Highway, you eventually come to Murray Bridge, boarding point for cruises along Australia's famous **River Murray.** Totaling around 50 miles from Adelaide, it should perhaps be a separate excursion, at least if riding the old steamboats is your goal. (Fares are about $205 for an all-inclusive, 5½-day cruise.)

In addition to the cruises from Murray Bridge (See Section 7), you can hire houseboats from the town of Berri, 130 road miles from Adelaide (upstream, near the Victoria border) and sail around anywhere you like. They cost about $275 for seven days, sleep five or six people, and are supposed to be "unsinkable." Similar vessels are available at Mannum, Loxton, and Renmark.

BAROSSA VALLEY

This is wine country, and if that doesn't interest you, so be it. But for those who appreciate the fermented grape, a visit to the best vineyards of Australia is virtually essential.

Since you will want to stop at one or two established wineries, perhaps the best way is to take one of the guided tours from the Tourist Bureau. But if you want the freedom of driving, pick up the thorough brochure, *Sightseeing Guide to the Barossa Valley* from them and head for **Tanunda,** about 45 miles away. This is the center of the valley and headquarters for many of the German families who brought their skill to South Australia a century and a quarter ago.

On odd numbered years—the opposite to the schedule for the Adelaide Festival—the Barossa Wine Festival is held in April.

Some of the wineries that offer tours, tastings, and "cellar door" sales are **Yalumba** (site of our own recent taste test), **Kaiser Stuhl** (which now sends wine to the U.S.), and **Seppeltsfield.** There are dozens more. (Tours and tastings are generally free; sales are usually about 10 or 15 percent less than retail prices in bottle shops in Adelaide.)

Visitors who want to get thoroughly into the wine scene should call the Wine Information Bureau (Tel. 71–0191) in Adelaide.

NORTHERN SOUTH AUSTRALIA

About 125 miles north of Adelaide begins the rugged mountains called the **Flinders Ranges,** actually an extension of the Adelaide Hills. The Flinders' bright colors, majestic trees, and granite peaks make them a favorite of landscape painters. From September to October, the hills are covered with wildflowers. As a base for Flinders explorations, head for the town (and mountain) of Wilpena Pound.

Further out is the salt lake, that is usually *all* salt, called **Lake Eyre.** It may be difficult to get much of a feeling for the salt flats without taking a plane over it. For the past couple of years, the 44 mile by 81 mile lake has been largely filled with water again, for the first time in a generation or more.

Near the center of the state are the desolate opal mining areas of **Andamooka** and **Coober Pedy,** the latter of which is a somewhat more practical destination for a casual visitor. About $3 million worth of opals is mined per year, much of it by intrepid individuals, many of whom are recent immigrants. The residents live mostly underground in former opal digs where the temperatures are tolerable. Outside, it can easily reach 130 degrees Fahrenheit.

They say Coober Pedy in the local Aboriginal tongue means "white man in a hole." (The town is lucky to have a simple name. A nearby salt lake is called Lake Cadibarrawirracanna.) Sightseeing tours of both communities are available, and they even have a couple of motels. At Coober Pedy you can stay underground inside the Umoona Opal Mine, but you'll pay 50 cents for a shower! We'd advise flying in—not driving—because of the hazardous roads in the area.

If you want to "gouge" for some opals yourself, you must buy a Precious Stones Prospecting Permit for $10. Otherwise you can "noodle" through a "mullock heap" gratis. If you want to *buy* opals, we'd advise staying with established dealers. You *might* get a bargain from a miner, but if you're not an expert, you're taking a big chance.

7. Guided Tours and Cruises

There are a potentially confusing number of tours offered by several different agencies throughout South Australia, and the picture changes frequently. Better get the latest from the South Australian Government Tourist Bureau at 18 King William Street.

Half-day tours. *City Sights*, 3 mornings a week, about $8. *Mount Lofty Ranges and Wildlife Sanctuary*, 2 afternoons a week, about $8. *City Lights*, 2 evenings a week, about $6.

Full-day tours. *Barossa Valley*, 3 days a week, about $16, including lunch. *Goolwa and Murray Mouth* (including a short launch cruise), Saturdays, about $11. *Hahndorf and Mt. Lofty Ranges* (including the Cleland Sanctuary), 2 days a week, about $16, including lunch.

Murray River Cruises. At the moment, long passenger cruises are available on the *Murray River Queen* (5½ days, Goolwa to Swan Reach and back for around $260) and the *Coonawarra* (5 days from Murray Bridge to Morgan and back for around $160). Both paddlewheelers will soon be supplemented by the new $1.8 million *Murray Explorer*, which will carry 120 passengers on 5½-day cruises between Renmark and Morgan for $275.

Kangaroo Island. There are a few combination plane/bus one-day tours, including a picnic lunch and sometimes a dinner at Kingscote. About $60.

Longer tours. The S.A.G.T.B. can book any number of combinations of trips (including hotels) to popular and obscure sites throughout South Australia. Some of the most interesting appear to be the "safari tours" by Landrover and camel to places like the Simpson Desert. We hope to have the time and energy to try one of these one day. Some of the best itineraries we've seen are offered by an outfit called **Desert Trek Australia Pty. Ltd.** (Tel. 085 + 261–0055). We have had no personal contact with them, however.

8. Water Sports

Adelaide's principal seaside resort is the town of **Glenelg.** Together with other shoreline sites on the Gulf St. Vincent, like **West Beach** and **Grange,** it offers about 20 miles of good, safe swimming beaches, with no surf. The beaches are virtually shark-free, even though white pointer sharks, measuring 25 and 30 feet, are caught off South Australia. **Maslin's Beach,** about 45 minutes' drive south of Adelaide, was the nation's first official nude beach.

Surfers head for **Victor Harbor, Pondalowie Bay** and **Cactus Beach** on more exposed waters of the Bight. Skin divers like both gulfs (St. Vincent and Spencer) to view the reefs and wrecks there. You can rent skindiving equipment from **Adelaide Skindiving Centre** (Tel. 51–6144), 7 Compton St., Adelaide.

There is water skiing on the **Murray River,** as well as on **Lake Bonney.** Deep sea fishing boats cast off from **Port Lincoln** and **Kangaroo Island.**

9. Other Sports

For spectator sports—and in S.A., that means cricket and Aussie rules football—the main sports ground is the Adelaide Oval, just across the river from the Festival Centre. Horseracing, however, is in the parklands southeast of the main grid at **Victoria Park Racecourse.** You can watch free, if you walk up to the side of the track, but you have to pay to get a grandstand view. Other courses include **Morphettville,** four miles southwest, where the Adelaide Cup is usually run the third Monday in May, **Cheltenham,** 5 miles northwest, and **Globe Derby Park** in Bolivar for trotting races.

Tennis courts are everywhere, notably the **Memorial Drive Tennis Courts** next to the aforementioned Adelaide Oval. You can book them for about $20 a day or $4 per hour, the last we heard. Recheck that with the S.A. Lawn Tennis Association (Tel. 51–4371) on War Memorial Drive.

For golfers, the **North Adelaide Municipal Golf Links** (Tel. 267–2171) are also right in town, in the parklands. Some enjoy the unique character of the **Royal Adelaide** in Seaton (Tel. 356–5511), which has a railway line through the course. But the best and most impeccably groomed course is the **Kooyonga Golf Club** (Tel. 43–6163), at May Terrace, Lockleys, S.A. 5032.

10. Shopping in Adelaide

Shopping activities center around two very compact areas—the Rundle Mall, a block south of North Terrace, with the several arcades that open onto the mall, and the smart boutiques along Melbourne Street in North Adelaide. Most shops are open weekdays from 9:00 to 5:30. Thursday night is late night shopping in the suburbs. Friday, shops in the city operate until 9:00. Saturday morning, everything goes dead at 11:30 a.m. sharp.

On the Rundle Mall, you'll find the three main department stores. First, there are the two branches of the Melbourne and Sydney headquartered outfits, the **Myer Emporium** and David Jones. But there is also one sharp local firm, too, **John Martin's of South Australia.**

For opals, a well-recognized house is **Precious Gems of Australia** (Tel. 212–3493) at 4 Peel St., which divides its selections between opals mined at Coober Pedy, at Andamooka, and at Lightning Ridge. Other dependable opal shops include **The Opal Mine** (Tel. 223–4023), 30 Gawler Place, the **Opal Shop,** 30 Adelaide Arcade, and **The Opal Scene** (Tel. 51–5759), 25 Bank St.

General gifts and souvenirs are pretty good at **The Australian Scene** (Tel. 43–6916) at 235 Henley Beach Road in Torrensville, the **Aboriginal Artists Centre** (Tel. 51–4756) at 140 Rundle Mall, and the **Mungara Arts Gift Shop** (Tel. 223–3140) in the Da Costa Arcade at 68 Grenfell St.

For antiques, poke around the numerous shoppes along Unley Road (try **Antique Galleries**), King William Road (near Hyde Park), or, of course, in Melbourne Street. You'll probably pay less here for items also sold in Melbourne and Sydney.

Artworks are for sale at **David Sumner Galleries,** 170 Goodwood Road. In Goodwood, some handcrafted jewelry and pottery are at **Andis Lidlums Gallery,** 88 Jeringham St. in North Adelaide, and you'll find more jewelry and pottery as well as sculpture at **Greenhill Galleries** (Tel. 267–2887), 140 Barton Terrace in North Adelaide.

An unusual arts and crafts operation is at **The Jam Factory** (Tel. 42–5661), 169 Payneham Road, in St. Peters. No longer turning out jam, of course, it's a project by the South Australian government to boost local crafts, most of them made on the premises. (It's open daily from 10:00 to 5:00 and on weekends from 2:00 to 5:00.)

Books? There are three or four well-stocked bookstores in Adelaide, and lots more featuring special interests. Browse through **Liberty Bookshop** (Tel. 223–2386), 32 Hindmarsh Square, **City Books** (Tel. 212–1563) at 103 Gawler Place, and then there's the well-known **Third World Bookshop** at 103 Hindley St., which never closes!

11. Night Life and Entertainment

The closest thing Adelaide has to Sydney's Kings Cross area is Hindley Street, a three-block long stretch of after-dark activity that, by and large, is pretty tame.

All the standard drinks are available, bolstered by perhaps more kinds of wine than you might find elsewhere in Australia. Neighborhood pubs, of course, are still loyal bastions of beer, and despite the state's reputation for wine, it also brews some fair samples of the amber.

Cooper and Sons, the only family brewery in the country, produces a wonderful sparkling ale (although it doesn't really sparkle). It packs quite a punch, though. They also turn out a light dinner ale, and a somewhat sweet and very stout extra stout (5½ percent alcohol).

A second brewery, the South Australian Brewing Company, produces

West End and Southwark, which we haven't tried. We liked its special Stuart Draught, honoring the 1862 explorer John Stuart, although we bought that in Alice Springs in the Northern Territory, and were told it wasn't available in Adelaide.

Most beer glasses come in "butcher" sizes—that's six ounces. Don't be frightened by the "schooner." Unlike N.S.W., where it is 15 ounces, the S.A. schooner has only nine.

Out of the pubs, now, and back on Hindley Street, a couple of night clubs we haven't seen are the **La Belle,** which we understand is more a strip show now, and the **To Kendro,** which probably has a better show.

Discotheques and rock music are featured at the **Old Lion Hotel** on Melbourne Street in North Adelaide. Also **Jules,** 94 Hindley St. and **The Wellington** at Wellington Square, North Adelaide, feature some heavy beats. Further out (that is, further away), there's the **Arkaba Disco** (Tel. 79–3614), also a restaurant at 150 Glen Osmond Rd. in Fullarton, and the **Buckingham Arms Hotel,** 1 Walkerville Terrace in Gilberton, which caters somewhat to the gay community.

Something a little cooler, more conservative? The **Creole Room** (Tel. 267–3335), corner of George and O'Connell Streets in North Adelaide, likes to call itself the 'Home of Modern Jazz.' You'll also find live jazz on Thursdays at the **Flagstaff Hotel** (Tel. 296–6677), South Road, Darlington, but you'd better recheck the days and hours by phone.

In theatre-restaurants, that double medium taking Australia almost like football and pavlova, the choices include the **Bull 'N' Bush** (Tel. 262–3944) at the Hotel Enfield, 184 Hampstead Rd., Enfield, which features Elizabethan trappings, and **Dirty Dick's** (Tel. 223–4166), at 289 Pirie St., near Hindmarsh Square, for perhaps a little more raw approach. Another dinner/floor-show combination is at the **After Dark Club** (Tel. 212–4580), 63 Light Square. And in the little German town of Hahndorf, 18 miles from Adelaide, the **Old Mill** (Tel. 388–7255) provides a spectacular feast and show.

Live theater is a frequent occasion in Adelaide, with performances often at the **Festival Centre** (Tel. 51–2291). The 600-seat Playhouse there is the home stage for the South Australian Theatre Company.

Other commercial theaters include the **Sheridan Theatre** (Tel. 223–2050), at 50 MacKinnon Parade, North Adelaide, and the **Q Theatre** (Tel. 223–5651) at 89 Halifax St.

For classical music, the South Australian Symphony presents concerts usually in the 2000-seat concert theater at the Festival Centre but sometimes in the **Adelaide Town Hall.** Get the latest from the S.A.G.T.B. or the Australian Broadcasting Commission Concert Department, Gawler Place, in Adelaide.

12. The Adelaide Address List

Ambulance—Tel. 272–8822.

American Consulate—Tel. 212–3879.

American Express, 32 Gawler Place (Tel. 223–5680).

Bank—Bank of Adelaide, 81 King William Street (Tel. 51–0291).

Beauty Salon—Mary-Ann, 156 Hutt St. (Tel. 223–6248).

Bus and Tram Information—Tel. 212–6311.

Citizens Advice Bureau, 51 Grenfell St. (Tel. 212–4070).

Dental Emergency Service—Tel. 79–7878.

Doctor service after hours—Tel. 332–3433.

Emergencies in general—Dial 000.

Fire Department—223–3000.

Hospital—Royal Adelaide Hospital (Tel. 223–0230).

Jaycees—Tel. 293–1162.

Kiwanis—Tel. 295–6945.

Pharmacy—(24-hours chemist) Burden Chemists, 13 Hindley St. (Tel. 51–4701).

Poisons Information Centre—Tel. 267–4999.

Police—Tel. 217–0333.

Rotary Club—Tel. 267–3625.

Royal Automobile Association, 41 Hindmarsh Sq. (Tel. 223–4555).

S.A. Government Department of Public and Consumer Affairs, Grenfell Centre, Grenfell St.

Tourist office—S.A. Government Tourist Bureau, 18 King William St. (Tel. 51–3281).

Train information—Tel. 51–0231.

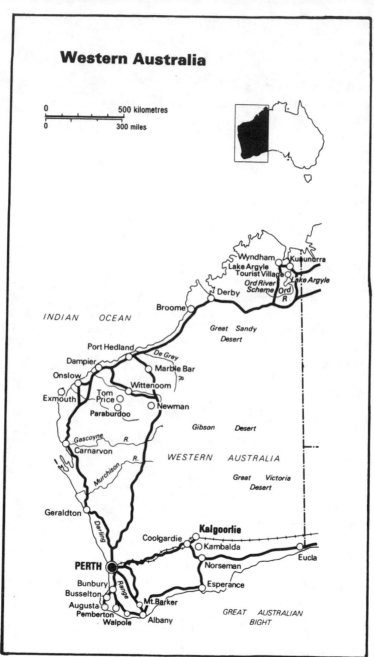

Western Australia

0   500 kilometres

0   300 miles

INDIAN OCEAN

Wyndham   Kununurra
Lake Argyle
Tourist Village   Lake Argyle
Ord River
Scheme   Ord R

Derby

Broome

Great Sandy
Desert

Port Hedland
De Grey
Dampier
Marble Bar
Onslow   R
Wittenoom
Tom
Exmouth   Price
Paraburdoo   Newman

Gibson   Desert

Gascoyne   R
Carnarvon
R
WESTERN   AUSTRALIA
Murchison
Great   Victoria
Desert

Geraldton
Darling
Kalgoorlie
Coolgardie
Kambalda
PERTH
Norseman   Eucla
Bunbury
Busselton   Esperance
Range
Augusta   Mt.Barker
Pemberton
Walpole   Albany   GREAT   AUSTRALIAN
BIGHT

Map courtesy Australian Tourist Commission

10

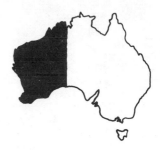

Perth,
The Star of W. A.

1. The General Picture

Everyone likes Perth.

You can hold debates at the drop of a beer can about every other city in Australia, but somehow when you come to Perth, the argument stops.

Nitpickers say there are things to criticize about the Westralians— their provincialism, perhaps, their overestimation of their importance in the scheme of things. But isn't that a complaint that could be registered in greater or lesser degree toward any other area in the world?

The storied "Tyranny of Distance" should be visited on the people of "W.A." (as they like to say) more than anywhere else in Australia. For the westerners are cut off by thousands of miles of desert, not just from the world but from the cultural centers of their own land. And people from Perth who travel at all, will probably not choose Brisbane, Sydney, or Melbourne for a holiday. More likely they'll fly to Jakarta or Singapore.

Still, there is something special about Perth. It is the sunniest capital in the country, receiving a yearly average of eight hours of sunshine per day, and reminding many visitors of the Italian Riviera or Southern California. It is also unpolluted, with the many heavy mining and manufacturing industries of W.A. installed hundreds of miles away.

Central Perth

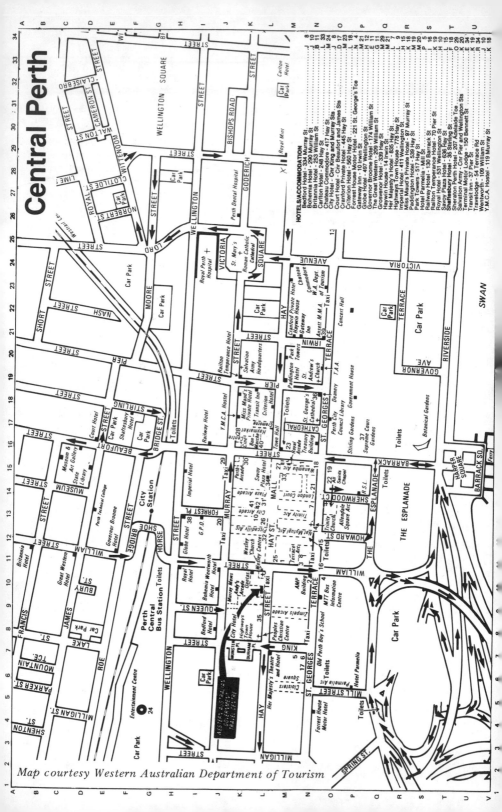

Map courtesy Western Australian Department of Tourism

There is an attractive river estuary, the Swan, which widens almost into a lake through the city limits. (It was named in 1696 when Dutch explorers first saw black swans on its waters.) And overlooking the river is King's Park, a large portion of flowered bushland atop a hill directly within the city. Below it is an architectural pattern of filigreed nineteenth-century buildings set against a few modern skyscrapers. Somehow, it's all spread out enough so that visually, it works. Esthetically, they live together.

Perth also likes to call itself the "City of Light," a tradition which dates back to 1962 when the citizens turned on every lamp as a greeting to pioneer astronaut John Glenn when his orbital path carried him directly over the city. It was also the light of inspiration, bringing the city of Perth to the attention of the world. Soon, investors in New York, London, and Tokyo came to town, and the city and state grew during the 1960's and 1970's to a degree that could not have been previously imagined.

It was development on sound principles, too. Western Australia is without a doubt the most prosperous state in the country. Iron ore is mined in the Hamersley Ranges. Elsewhere there is oil, natural gas, bauxite, and uranium. Nickel is mined from the rough and tumble towns where Australia's second gold rush occurred in the 1890's. And yes, some gold is still brought up there today.

It seems that the people of every Australian state like to talk about seceding from the rest of the country, a generally acknowledged impractical action. They talk about independence, too, in W.A., and if they ever did it there, Perth could conceivably become the richest nation per capita on the globe. Population is still only a little over a million in W.A., and more than three-fourths of that number live in Perth.

They like Perth not only because of its material goods and money-making opportunities. The people, too, are said to be somehow "more Australian" than the rest of the country—less jaded, more open, and a repository of friendly optimism that seems to some countrymen to exist today in the history books.

Give a Westralian some sympathy for some sort of personal setback, and he's likely to exclaim, "No worries!"

And he means it. He'll be back on his feet in no time.

2. Airports and Long Distance Transportation

Perth's attractive airport, 11 miles from town center, has a terminal that seems to be one long room. At one end are the main domestic airlines, including **Ansett Airways** (Tel. 25–0251), **MacRobertson Miller**

Airline Services (MMA) (Tel. 25–0451)—now an Ansett subsidiary, and **Trans Australian Airlines (TAA)** (Tel. 323–8413).

At the opposite end of the structure are an amazing number of international carrier counters, including Qantas, British Airways, South African Airways, Singapore Airlines, Air India, Cathay Pacific, and more. The terminal offers all the usual facilities, including a Wines of Australia shop, your last chance to pick up a·favorite vintage on the way out, for it's difficult to get W.A. wines anywhere else.

The coach to town will run about $1.50, taxi fare about $1.50 more, so two or more together may prefer to split a cab.

Ships all dock at Fremantle, the port for Perth, 12 miles west along the Swan River. You'll tie up at Victoria Quay on the Inner Harbour. You can take a bus into the big city if you want. By taxi, the Fremantle-Perth connection will cost around $5.

To go to Perth by train, you can take the famous *Indian Pacific*, the transcontinental express that originates in Sydney. It's three days of travel time from there or two days from Adelaide. (Interstate trains come in somewhat inconveniently at the East Perth Terminal on Summers Street—information, Tel. 29–2370. Suburban trains have all just been cancelled, and they're considering tearing up the tracks to build freeways.

There are air conditioned buses to Perth over the Eyre Highway from Adelaide, Brisbane, Melbourne, and Sydney via **Ansett Pioneer** (Tel. 25–8855), 26 St. George's Terrace, and via **Greyhound Coaches Pty Ltd** (Tel. 321–9188), Barrack Street between Hay and Murray. It will cost you approximately $80 to make the trip by bus from Adelaide, about $20 less than the train.

Driving to Perth? Don't try it from Darwin without four-wheel drive and years of Outback expertise. From Adelaide, you can do it, but see our remarks in the previous chapter.

3. Local Transportation in Perth

As compared with Sydney and Melbourne, anyway, finding your way around by car is fairly simple. Rentals are also a highly competitive business, so you may be able to get some good rates. The three national firms, as usual, are **Avis** (Tel. 325–7677), 46 Hill St., but also at the airport, of course; **Hertz** (Tel. 321–7103), at 39 Milligan St.; and **Budget** (Tel. 321–9721), 33 Milligan St.

But you might get some good bargains for local travel from **Houghton** (Tel. 362–2329), 960 Hay St.; **Econo-Car** (Tel. 325–6700), 23 Bennett St.; **Sydney Anderson's** (Tel. 328–1477), 216 Stirling St.; and

Ryan's (Tel. 325–2042), 299 Wellington St. On all, note there are many variations between kilometer and unlimited distance plans, etc. Some have 150 free kilometers and charge after that.

Local bus, train, and ferries are run by the city-owned **Metropolitan Transport Trust (MTT)** (Tel. 321–8624), 125 St. George's Terrace, the most efficient public transportation system in the country. By all means, pick up their route map and other free folders there. They'll even show you exactly where to wait for a bus in the center of the city.

There are two free buses, the "Red Clipper" and the "Yellow Clipper" following short circular routes downtown. Ferry boats span the Swan every half hour between the Barrack Street Jetty and Mends Street, South Perth. Price: 20 cents.

Check with the MTT about their special ticket bargains that allow unlimited travel within certain time periods on buses, ferries, and trains.

4. The Perth Hotel Scene

Perth's acknowledged leader among hotels, and absolutely one of the very finest in Australia, is the 270-room **Parmelia Hilton International** (Tel. 322–3622), taking up the entire block on one-block-long Mill Street. Elegant, marble-floored lobby combining modern sculpture with brass pillars and a grandfather clock; an arcade of smart shops to one side; three well-decorated bars; two excellent restaurants including the green-toned Garden Restaurant and the relatively reasonable Adelphi Steak House; heated, windless, outdoor swimming pool; lavish convention facilities.

In the sleeping areas, the most desirable rooms are on the river side with balconies, although the city views are also good. Widely varying types of accommodations, including 85 singles, 62 twins, 40 doubles, 28 double suites, 36 twin suites, and 17 VIP suites (those on the 10th—the VIP—floor, running from $100 to $300 a day); all luxury amenities in every room, even down to the ample businessman's singles; colorful wallpapering and good lighting; suites with antiques, famous art, and other extra touches; reportedly highest service standards throughout the premises. The Parmelia, built in 1968 to be the best international hotel in the country, perhaps still succeeds. Hilton International has just taken over its operation, and standards seem to have remained as high as ever. Remember, doubles run $55 to $65 a day here, but to those who can afford it, it's worth every gilt-edged biccie.

Occupying a firm second in our book is the sometimes uneven but generally pleasant **Sheraton-Perth** (Tel. 325–0501) which overlooks the scene from 207 Adelaide Terrace: W-i-d-e lobby with patterned carpet and multiple chandeliers; three restaurants—the well-regarded River Room, the Clinker Grill, and the Wandarrah Coffee Shop; Downunder bar and disco; three comfortable drinking bars; good pool and pool deck; sauna; a set of liberated elevators which seem to change their minds; 427 generally comfortable rooms, with good furnishings in excellent floor plans; unsurpassed views over the city and river; rates a little less than the Parmelia, thank heavens—about $50 to $55 for two in regular units, $70 to $200 in the suites. (Reservations from any hotel in the Sheraton family.) Unlike the chain's weaker links in Sydney and Melbourne, this house seems like a genuine Sheraton—not "spot on," but still a top spot.

Ansett here has one of its dependable trio, each called the **Gateway Inn** (Tel. 325–0481). Somehow it seems a little more formal in Perth than it does in Adelaide or Brisbane: tiny lobby off busy little Irwin Street; a preponderance of browns and greens; attractive Silver Swan restaurant (with a genuine silver swan sailing over the salad bar); cozy Opal Cocktail Bar; sunny pool and pool deck; long, well-designed bedrooms all with ample space for two or even three; all luxury fittings; direct dial phones with message light; 24-hour room service; Ansett coaches pulling up on the premises downstairs, of course. Rates begin at about $41 for two. (Reservations through Ansett Airways or the hotel at 10 Irwin St.) As usual, a convenient, comfortable landing place.

Many Australians prefer the **Chateau Commodore** (Tel. 325–0461) over the Sheraton, and that's a reasonable assessment if the service is good. (We couldn't tell on a short inspection.) Somehow it seems overdecorated and hokey with all its medieval frou-frou. There are relatively few views, too, but try for a chamber with a balcony. Soothing rates in the $36 to $46 range for two will make up for a lot. (Reservations from the hotel at Hay Street and Victoria Avenue.) A little odds bodkins, but a comfortable castle nonetheless.

The **Transit Inn** (Tel. 325–7655), a Flag entry, waves from 37–45 Pier St. Combination foyer/terrace/swimming pool; Boodles Coffee House to one side; Ruby's Restaurant to the other; 120 well-maintained bedrooms; views from the very highest floors; some extras like in-house movies available on the TV, toaster to augment the usual tea-maker, nice long bathtowels, etc.; No. 702 a favorite double about $42; also one single room on each floor about $30. (Reservations from the Hotel, 37–45 Pier St.) Not too fancy, but likeable.

Another possibility is the **Highways Town House** (Tel. 321–9141) at 778–788 Hay St. There's a dining room and an indoor pool. Everything was clean and neat, but the rooms seemed relatively colorless to us, and some were quite small. Rates around $35 for twins.

BUDGET ACCOMMODATIONS

At rates of about $25 for two (including breakfast) the cheerful little **Railton** (Tel. 325–2133), at the corner of Pier and Murray Streets, has to be the leader. Some keep it at arm's length when they find out it's run by the Salvation Army, but this is no lumpy-bed "People's Palace." Instead, it's a family oriented, colorful establishment with comfortable furniture. (Some rooms have color TV's; other patrons can use the lounge; viewful nests are on the sixth and seventh floors.) And there are things the big boys don't have like an automatic laundry and ironing room for wash-it-yourselfers. There's a pleasant roofgarden and a snack bar, too. Single rooms go for around $18 and triples for around $30. Efficient management by Marge Bevan. (Reservations from Perth, WA 6000.) It's not the Ritz, to be sure, but for a rent of the few brass razoos it asks, we'll rave about the Railton.

The **Paddington** (Tel. 325–6877), at around the same price for doubles (a little cheaper for singles), seemingly dates back to the Gold Rush. Some rooms are without private bathrooms here, so choose carefully. Some have air conditioning. But watch TV in the lounge. Overall, it'll do—I guess.

A bare bones establishment is the **Imperial** (Tel. 325–8877), at 411 Wellington St., across from the suburban railroad station. This place looked on its last legs to us. Sleeping space was renting for $14.20 for two, $6.45 for one, when we peeked in, but the whole place had just been sold and plans were indefinite. Meanwhile, we'd skip it.

Australia's busiest youth hostel is the **Perth City Hostel** (Tel. 328–1135) in an 80-year-old former guest house at 60–62 Newcastle St., Perth 6000. Members with regulation sheets will pay about $3.50 for a night's bunk.

5. Restaurants and Dining

There are a large number of ethnic cafes in Perth. Many good dining rooms are in the hotels, of course, but the more exotic establishments you'll find "North of the Line"—that is, on the other side of the railroad tracks from downtown Perth. These are generally along William Street. Many will change owners, managers, prices, and menus more rapidly than some of the long-established central salons.

FRENCH AND INTERNATIONAL

One of the best combinations for views and viands is the **Kings Park Garden Restaurant** (Tel. 321–7655), overlooking Perth from the park. Lunch from 12:00 to 2:30; dinner 6:00 until 11:00. We enjoyed our Dhufish (jewfish), a local specialty, at around $5.

The Garden Restaurant (Tel. 322–3622), in the Parmelia Hilton, is formal, expensive, elegant, and delicious. A good place to try W.A. Rock Lobster, perhaps (about $10). Another specialty is the Tournedos Cordon Rouge, topped with a paté, ham, and mushroom sauce, about $8.50.

European fare with a Yugoslavian accent is a specialty at **Bohemia** (Tel. 328–7163) at 309 William St. A favorite of owner Mie Andrijcich is Govedina u Vinu—Beef in Red Wine, plus the usual selections of shishkebabs, goulashes, etc. Some like the seafood, too. Most main courses are in the $5 to $6 range. (Closed Sundays and Mondays.)

We enjoyed our meal so much at **Le Coq D'Or** (Tel. 325–2208) that we apparently left our notes stuffed in a wine glass or something. This is an upstairs BYO address (walk or take the tiny elevator) above some kind of a shop at 645 Hay St. Choose from the blackboard menu—perhaps the Escalope Viennoise at around $5, then while Paul or Mike prepares it, run across the street to the pub for a bottle of wine. (Perhaps a Sandalford or Houghton Cabernet Sauvignon or a Valencia burgundy.) There are no views nor, indeed, we don't even recall a window. But the meals were excellent for the type.

Other French choices locally respected include **Le Chef** (Tel. 381–9858), Hay Street, and **Luis** (Tel. 325–2476), 2 Sherwood Court. The **River Room** (Tel. 325–0501) at the Sheraton is moving up. Figure $12 to $15 for main courses.

SPECIALIZING IN SEAFOOD

The championship oceanarium is still **Mischa's** (Tel. 328–6741) at 137 James St., also a BYO operation. (Some good local white wines to bring include a Swanville Riesling or Chablis or Sandalford's Swan Valley White Burgundy.) Here you might get some of Perth's blue marlin, or the mangrove crabs, which are similar to the mud crabs of Queensland.

The Oyster Bar (Tel. 328–7449), down the road, is less expensive, cafeteria style, and closes early. **Gardi's**, at the corner of James and Lake Streets, doesn't mask the flavor of good seafood with heavy sauces or batter.

ITALIAN RESTAURANTS

The kitchens of Perth are blessed with several seasoned sons of Italy. Across the river in South Perth, the leader is **Pontevecchio** (Tel. 367–7886), which, as its name indicates, features Florentine and Northern Italian dishes, with main courses about $6 to $8. (Closed Sundays.) Lower priced, but also popular, is the recently redecorated **La Tavernetta** (Tel. 328–3763), next door to Mischa's on James Street (large veal cutlets a specialty), and the **Romany** (Tel. 328–8042), also north of the line at 188 Williams St.

INDONESIAN CUISINE

If you like that sort of thing—and we do—we can personally recommend **Opa's** (Tel. 325–2120), a Dutch Indonesian Restaurant at 326 Hay St. (corner of Hill), just a block's walk up from the Sheraton. The split-level interior, decorated by more plates and bottles on the wall than on the tables, is dark but not too dark. We ordered a Nasi Pedang for two (the closest thing we could get to a Rijstafel, which required 24 hours' notice). Service is hectic but willing. It can't hold a candle to Amsterdam's famous Bali, but it's the only one of its kind in Perth, and it's good.

CHINESE FARE

We haven't picked up chopsticks in Perth, but reports indicate that **Cheong On** (Tel. 325–5187) is now the leader. The new **Emperor's Court** (Tel. 328–8860), 66 Lake St., has won a rave review from TV personality Alison Fan. Some still swear by the **Golden Eagle** (Tel. 328–5420) in James Street.

MEXICAN RESTAURANTS

Verdad! There are some, and *delicioso*. The best of the best lately has been **El Gringo's** (Tel. 381–9513), a BYO place at 13 Rokeby Road. We know a displaced *gringo* named Duncan MacLaurin in Perth, and join him in his heartfelt *oles*. If the lines are too long there, try instead the place entitled **The Mexican Restaurant** (Tel. 328–4728) at 276 William St., run by a couple of expatriate Yankees themselves. Also good and cheapo.

SPANISH AND PARTLY SPANISH

We must draw a difference between Spanish and the Mexican entries above, even if the Westralians might be forgiven for mixing them together. **Franco's** (Tel. 325–4843) is cater-corner from Opa's at 323 Hay

St., if we remember right. The paella is only available Tuesdays. Other nights, the cuisine is more international. Also popular is the **Casa Latina** (Tel. 328–1769), at 245 William St., and the unusual **Casa Pepe** (Tel. 321–8184) on Wellington Place near the Metropolitan Markets. The latter combines *Spanish and Greek* specialties—honest!

INEXPENSIVE DINING

In addition to some of the Mexican, Italian, and Spanish candidates above, look for other bargains near the shopping areas. One possibility is **Miss Maud's Swedish Restaurant** (Tel. 325–3900) at the corner of Pier and Murray. Last we saw it, the all-you-can-eat smörgasbord was selling at $5.95, $8.25, and $9.45, depending on the time of the day and the day of the week. (Probably up "something-ti-five" by now.) Next door is **Glutton's Paradise**, run by the same Swedish miss, with lunches or dinners in the $4 range. The **New York Cafe**, 125 Barrack St., looked interesting for its $3 special, and the **Petite Steak House** at 137 Barrack had a luncheon special for under $4.

The most fun of all, at least for lunch, is to eat your way from one door to another in the barn-like **Haymarket**—not really a restaurant but a way of enjoying yourself a la Singapore. On Murray Street, it opens deceptively into an arcade of individual stalls, selling more exotic comestibles than you can shake a satay stick at. I once had a Burmese Beef-and-Bean dish which was terrific, even if the hot sauce *did* take the roof from my mouth. I then cooled down at the hip salad and vegetable bar next door. The city keeps threatening to close the Haymarket (sometimes it doesn't look very sanitary), but we enjoyed it nevertheless.

6. Sightseeing in Perth and W.A.

Just as in South Australia, your sightseeing headquarters in Perth ought to be the official T.O. That's the **Western Australia Government Travel Center** (Tel. 321–2471), at 772 Hay St. In addition to their free folders, maps, and advice, they will also book you on any sightseeing tours. The state is currently celebrating its 150th birthday, and there are still many special events to get in on, especially in Perth.

Here are some town targets to consider:

The **Art Gallery and Museum**. This complex at Francis and Beaufort Streets exhibits contemporary and traditional Australian paintings in the brand-new gallery (enter from James Street). In the museum are some dramatic blue whale skeletons, and an Aboriginal history and culture section. Also on the grounds, check out the old jail dating back to

1856. (Open 9:30 to 5:00, most days; 10:30 to 5:00 on Saturdays and 2:00 to 5:00 Sundays.)

Out of all the green spaces, the big one to see is **King's Park** and its bordering **Botanic Gardens**. The 1000-acre park is largely natural bushland which is carpeted with unusual wildflowers August through November. (There are 7,000 varieties of wildflowers in W.A., two-thirds of the number found in the entire world. Try to find the weird green and red fingers of the "kangaroo paw.") Buses 25, 27, and 28 drive right through the park.

London Court. This unusual Elizabethan-style shopping arcade, a study in "Pseudor Tudor," looks like the 16th century but was actually built in 1937. It runs between the Hay Street Mall and St. George's Terrace.

The Old Mill in South Perth, which dates back to pioneer days, has been restored as a folk museum.

Stirling Gardens hosts several government buildings including the interesting Old Court House (1836). The Georgian building is the oldest one remaining in Perth.

The **Town Hall**, at the corner of Hay and Barrack Streets, was built by convicts from 1867 to 1870 in the style of an English Jacobean market hall. The nearby Colonial-style **Treasury Building**, around the corner on St. George's Terrace, was put up between 1874 and 1897.

OUT OF TOWN

Fremantle, the port for Perth, was settled 12 miles downstream, at the mouth of the Swan River. At Memorial Park, we enjoyed a wide panorama of the city and harbor. Another stop is the excellent Maritime Museum, originally built as an asylum, at the corner of Finnerty and Ord Streets.

Offshore by about 12 miles is the popular resort at **Rottnest Island**. It was named by a Dutch sea captain who mistook the little quokkas of the island for rats (*rott*, in Dutch). Thousands of these "midget kangaroos" still live there, and almost nowhere else. The diminutive marsupials have proven useful in research which has recently made medical history in the muscular dystrophy field. Dr. Byron Kakulas, a Perth pathologist, has used quokkas for experiments which show that paralyzed muscles can sometimes be regenerated.

(We might stay away from Rottnest on busy public holidays, however, when drunken larikens and other unsavory elements sometimes visit the place, occasionally throwing the helpless quokkas through windows, etc.)

The Rottnest Passenger Service (Tel. 325–7373) offers a good hydroplane service between Perth (Barrack Street Jetty) and Rottnest Island via Fremantle for a round-trip fare of around $10. A slower service is the regular passenger ferry. It takes about two hours each way, about twice the hydroplane time, and costs about half as much.

Two other sites promoted in the Perth area include **Yanchep National Park** (with its caves) and the Andalusian stud farm at **El Caballo Blanco** near Wooroloo. We've seen them both, and they're pleasant, but perhaps of more interest to Australians for the time spent than to international travelers. Some may disagree, of course.

THE REST OF W. A.

If you can easily visit **Kalgoorlie and Coolgardie** and the surrounding gold rush country 375 miles east of Perth, then do so. Due to an inconvenient air schedule—an early morning arrival from Perth, a late night departure to Perth—we were at the hands of one of the local tour drivers all day, and had every bloody grade school in a 50-mile radius pointed out to us—when he wasn't cursing the "Abos." We would have enjoyed driving around on our own, going down into the **Hainault Tourist Mine**, seeing the ghost town buildings at Coolgardie, etc., and then choosing when to leave.

It might be fun to take the train called "The Prospector" one way (8 hours for about $25), stay overnight—perhaps at the Tower Motel— rent a car for sightseeing and then return to Perth with a taste of Outback driving under your belt. (In Coolgardie, drop in to see Harry Boucher on the main street, a most amazing rock merchant.)

The south is the spring **wildflower country**, blooming generally around the towns of Bunbury, Busselton, Augusta, Pemberton, and so forth. Other times of the year, the 250-foot-tall karri forests are still impressive. We've yet to make our way down there, but we will.

North of Perth on Route 1 about 315 miles is **Geraldton**, the center of the crayfish industry and the gateway to the spectacular gorges of Kalbarri National Park. Then, 350 miles north of Perth is the strange **Hutt River Province**, where Leonard Casley has declared himself "prince" of an 18,000-acre desert domain that no one else wants for the moment and "seceded" from Australia.

Locals disagree as to exactly how serious Prince Leonard is, and the Federal government at Canberra ignores him, perhaps realizing with some sensitivity that some important elements in Western Australia would like to cut off the entire rich state from the rest of the country. Meanwhile, the prince is doing a terrific souvenir business, selling stamps, visas, etc.

The **Hammersley Ranges**, 800 miles north of Perth and including the towns of Tom Price, Newman, Marble Bar (hottest town in Australia), is the center of massive iron mining operations, but reported to be ruggedly scenic by survivors of those roads. (Recent discoveries of microfossils by scientists in this neighborhood have shown life to be 3½ billion years old, about 200 million years older than previously imagined.)

Broome, on the northwest coast, is a romantic area once the center of a massive pearl diving industry, which is still partly carried on there. Further north, the town of **Derby**, gateway to the iron-rich Kimberley Ranges, is famous for its baobab or boab trees, whose bottle-shaped trunks actually store water. One particularly fat tree in Derby is hollow and was supposed to have once been used as a jail. Further, **Kununurra** is the site of the Ord River Dam and becoming a recreational center on Lake Argyle. So far, we've only seen it from the air.

7. Guided Tours and Cruises

Some tour operators include **Ansett Pioneer** (Tel. 345–3144), **Feature Tours** (Tel. 371–1131), **Motive Travel** (Tel. 322–5709), and **Parlorcars Tours** (Tel. 325–5488). We'd book all tours from the Western Australian Government Travel Centre (Tel. 321–2471) at 772 Hay St., Perth, W.A. 6000.

Half Day Tours. *City Sights, Beaches, and Landmarks*, about $7. *City Lights*, about $6. *Swan Scenic Drive* (to Fremantle and back by separate routes), about $7.

Full Day Tours. *Perth in a Day*, about $13. *Wildflower Tour* (August through October), about $10.

There are also longer wildflower and other types of "fully accommodated" tours over several days throughout Western Australia. See the tourist office for details.

Cruises. The city-owned MTT (Tel. 325–0491), the same hot-shot outfit that runs the buses, offers afternoon cruises on the river, too. The MV *Vlaming* goes upstream from the Barrack Street Jetty about three afternoons a week for about $3, and the SS *Perth* makes a downstream cruise perhaps on Sunday only for around the same price.

The **Rottnest Passenger Service** (Tel. 325–7373), headquartered at the same jetty, also has several cruises on several vessels, some to Fremantle and back, others to Rottnest Island. Its hydrofoil service via the

Hydroflite H26 is fastest, making Rottnest Island in an hour each way for around $10 round trip.

And the **Swan River Queen** goes upstream to the Houghton Winery once a day for a ticket of around $15, including lunch. Reserve through the tourist office.

8. Water Sports

There are several popular Indian Ocean beaches along the shoreline north of Fremantle. You can get to **Cottesloe** on the train. Both it and **City Beach** (Buses 80 and 81) are good surfing beaches October to March. The most famous surf beach, however, is **Yallingup** much further north. **Leighton Beach** (train to Leighton Station) and **North Beach** (Bus No. 250 then transfer to 255) are gentler strands. And **Swanbourne** is the local site for swimming and sunning in your birthday suit. (Look out. No lifeguard on duty there.)

You can also swim in the Swan. It's clean, believe it or not. Two river beaches are **Crawley** (Bus 201), near the university, and **Como** (Bus 32), south of South Perth.

Skin diving is supposed to be good on the shallow coastal shelf where you find the occasional wreck of seventeenth- and eighteenth-century Dutch ships. Skin-diving conditions around Rottnest Island, an undersea sanctuary, are also said to be excellent. Contact the W.A. Skin Diving Association (Tel. 321–4979) at 486 Murray St.

Boats and water skiing equipment may be rented from the Indiana Ski Academy for skimming over the surface near the Narrows Bridge. You might also like to rent the little "surf cat" boats there for about $5 an hour. Check with the tourist office.

Deep sea fishing is available the year around from ports all along the coast, and it's recently becoming more popular. Blue marlin is the big catch. Some charter boats are based at Fremantle. You can also fish on the Swan River. We heard of a chap who got a 76 pound mulloway right on the doorstep of the city!

9. Other Sports

The big spectator sport, of course, is the same as in Melbourne, Tasmania, and Adelaide—Australian Rules Football. Most matches are at the Perth Oval, Lord and Bulner Streets. Cricket is played at the W.A. Cricket Association Oval at the end of Hay Street in East Perth.

Westralians are nuts about racing—horses, dogs, cars, and motorcycles. Flat races are held at the two racecourses, **Ascot** in the summer and **Belmont** in the winter. Night trotting races, particularly popular in

Perth, are held October through July at the super modern facilities at **Gloucester Park** on Nelson Avenue, in East Perth. Greyhounds run in the new stadium at Cannington. Cars and motorcycles tear up the turf at Claremont.

In golf courses, Terry Smith, the knowledgeable golfing writer for the Sydney *Sun* and other publications says that **Lake Karrinyup** (Tel. 47–5777), on North Beach Road, is the pride of Perth, although he complains about the need to wear a collar and tie in the clubhouse and the summertime swarms of bushflies out on the links. John Glendon, another golf writer, praises the public courses at Perth suggesting visitors try **Hamersley** (Tel. 347–1922), on Marmion Avenue at North Beach (18 holes for around $3). There are about two dozen more in the neighborhood, and serious duffers should talk to the W.A. Golf Association (Tel. 349–2166).

Tennis courts are available in the public parks for about 50 cents an hour, but check first with the tourist office or with the W.A. Lawn Tennis Association (Tel. 321–9977), P.O. Box 138, Perth, W.A. 6005.

10. Shopping in Perth

The principal shopping street is the Hay Street Mall running from Barrack Street to William Street, and the little arcades shooting off from it, including the Wanamba Arcade, London Court, Plaza Arcade, Trinity Arcade, City Arcade, National Mutual Arcade, and the Piccadilly Arcade. (Shopping hours are 9:30–5:00, Monday to Friday, except on Thursdays until 9:00 and Saturdays until noon.)

The most unique product of Western Australia in the shops is iron ore jewelry, a product which we never knew could be turned into a stone before! It certainly does seem appropriate in a state known for iron ore, but you'll have to decide for yourself whether or not you like the sparkling form of the product. You can buy it as a pendant for as little as about $11.50. Try the **Gem Center and Opal Cave** (Tel. 325–5528), at 534 Hay St., for iron ore and other stones.

For a wider selection of Australian souvenirs, look into the **Australian Gift Shop** (Tel. 321–3074) in the National Mutual Arcade off Hay St. Kangaroo skin poofs are around $30, pillows for about $11.50, change purses at $6, even a kangaroo bag for about $12, as well as a good selection of opals, iron ore stones, etc.

For stones in a rougher state, peek into the **Perth Lapidary Centre** (Tel. 325–2954) at 58 Pier St. It's a rock hound's delight with everything for chip-it-yourselfers.

Perth has a well-recognized cadre of ladies' boutiques, specializing in designer fashions, foreign imports, etc. Some of these include **Bigi** (Tel. 325–4953), International Arcade, **Celeste** 126 Murray St., **Ulla** (Tel. 325–4010), 645 Central Hay St., **B2 Boutique** (Tel. 325–5276), 40 Pier St., **Poi Boutique** (Tel. 322–2363), Mutual Arcade, Hay Street, **Garbo's** (Tel. 321–5420), 792 Hay St., and the **Village Gate** (Tel. 325–3573), Wanamba Arcade, Hay Street.

There are five department stores on Hay Street, including Ahern's, David Jones, Walsh's, Big-W, and Cole's. Myers is on Murray Street, and **Boans** Department Store is always having a sale. On its Wellington Street side there's a permanent-looking flashing sign which proclaims "SALE!"

11. Night Life and Entertainment

Popular night clubs include **Romano's** (Tel. 328–4776) at 187 Stirling St., a restaurant, too. Also there is often a show at the **Old Melbourne** (Tel. 321–2865), 942 Hay St., and at **La Tenda**, whose address has slipped away from us.

On William Street, "North of the Line," occasionally a lavish illegal casino will begin spinning until it gets shut down by the law, so you'd better not count on that.

The top discotheque in Perth today is **Hannibal's** (Tel. 328–1065), carved out of an old church at 69 Lake St. The DJ is suspended in a glass box above dancers who jump on a lighted glass floor. Membership requirements waived for holders of foreign passports. Other hot spots include **Eagle One**, with its chrome and black "spaced-out" decor, **Gobbles,** at 613 Wellington St., and **Beethoven** (Tel. 321–6887) at 418 Murray St. The largest disco is the **Downunder** in the Sheraton Perth, and some singles consider it the best for pickups. Then there's **Pinocchio's** (Tel 321–2521), which may be a bit teeny-boppish. And the gay crowd is said to like the **Connexion**—along with some other young "trendies."

All the beer you'll find in W.A. pubs is made by the Swan Brewery, that building that lights up like a ship on the edge of the river. Besides Swan Draught and Swan Lager, it also produces a brand called Emu in Perth, and over in Kalgoorlie, a stout and a lager under the name Hannan's. By the way, a "glass" of beer has five ounces and the "middy" is seven. A "pot" can be either 10 or 15 ounces.

For more genteel entertainment, there is usually good live theater in Perth at the **Playhouse** (Tel. 325–3500), at 3 Pier St., the headquarters of the National Theatre, Inc. At the University of Western Australia, at Crawley, downstream a bit, is the **Dolphin Theatre**.

Special events are usually staged at the modern **Perth Concert**

Hall (Tel. 325–3399), 5 St. George's Terrace, also the home of the West Australian Symphony Orchestra, or at the **Perth Entertainment Center** on Wellington Street.

12. The Perth Address List

Airport bus terminals—Ansett, 26 St. George's Terrace (Tel. 325–0251), TAA, 32 St. George's Terrace (Tel. 323–8413).

Bank—Commercial Bank of Australia, 40 St. George's Terrace (Tel. 325–9877).

Bus information—Bus Information Centre, 125 St. George's Terrace (Tel. 322–3022).

Citizens Advice Bureau, 19 Irwin St. (Tel. 325–9999).

Dental Emergency—Perth Dental Hospital, 196 Goderich St. (Tel. 325–3452).

Emergencies Fire, police, ambulance, etc. Dial 000.

Ferry information—Tel. 325–0491.

Hospital—Royal Perth Hospital, Wellington & Lord Sts. (Tel. 325–0101).

Immigration Department, 862 Hay St. (Tel. 325–0521).

Laundromat—20 Bennett St. (Between Adelaide Terr. and Hay St.)

Library—State Library, 40 James St. (Tel.328–7466).

Pharmacy—Craven's Pharmacy, Barrack and Hay Sts. (Tel. 325–4375).

Police Station—Hay St. East. (Dial 000 for all emergencies.)

Post Office—Forrest Place near Wellington St. (Tel. 326–5211).

Royal Automobile Club, 228 Adelaide Terrace (Tel. 325–0551).

Tourist Office—W.A. Government Tourist Bureau, 772 Hay St. (Tel. 321–2471).

Trains (interstate) information—Tel. 326–2811.

Travelers' Aid Society, Westrail Centre, West Parade, East Perth (Tel. 326–2811).

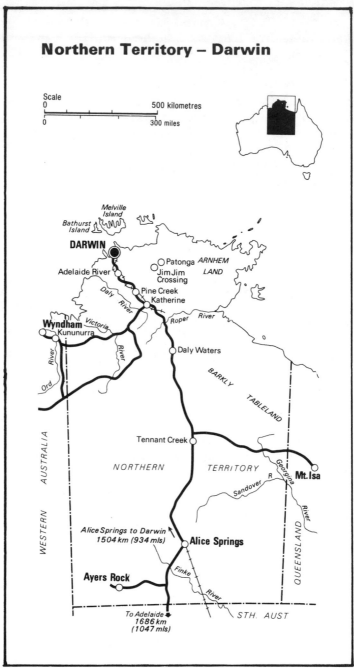

Northern Territory – Darwin

Scale
0   500 kilometres
0   300 miles

Melville Island

Bathurst Island

DARWIN

Patonga
Jim Jim Crossing

ARNHEM LAND

Adelaide River

Daly River

Pine Creek
Katherine

Roper River

Wyndham
Kununurra

Victoria River

Daly Waters

BARKLY TABLELAND

Ord River

WESTERN AUSTRALIA

Tennant Creek

NORTHERN TERRITORY

Mt. Isa

Georgina River

Sandover R

NORTHERN

QUEENSLAND

Alice Springs to Darwin
1504 km (934 mls)
Alice Springs

Finke River

Ayers Rock

To Adelaide
1686 km
(1047 mls)

STH. AUST

Map courtesy Australian Tourist Commission

11

The Northern Territory—
Darwin and Alice Springs

1. The General Picture

The Northern Territory is what most of the world imagines when it thinks of Australia.

Here is the Red Centre—the baked desert and stone that has served as the setting for nearly a century and a half of Outback adventures. It's studded by that massive red granite monolith which almost marks the geographic hub of the entire continent, Ayers Rock—what the ancient Aborigines called the sacred Uluru.

The staging area for visiting The Rock and other sights in Australia's Dead Heart is the strange, often lonely little town of Alice Springs, which was sparked by a telegraph relay station and grew up along the banks of a usually dry river. It was made world famous by Nevil Shute's wartime novel, *A Town Like Alice*.

"The Alice" may be the informal capital of the Outback, but the official center of government for the Northern Territory (N.T.) is in the small coastal city of Darwin, bordering the Timor Sea in the tropical climate near the tip of Australia's "Top End." Some 50,000 people now live there, half the population of the entire territory.

Many of the city's residents are foreign born or are descended from a variety of nationalities and races, including the black Aborigines. (More

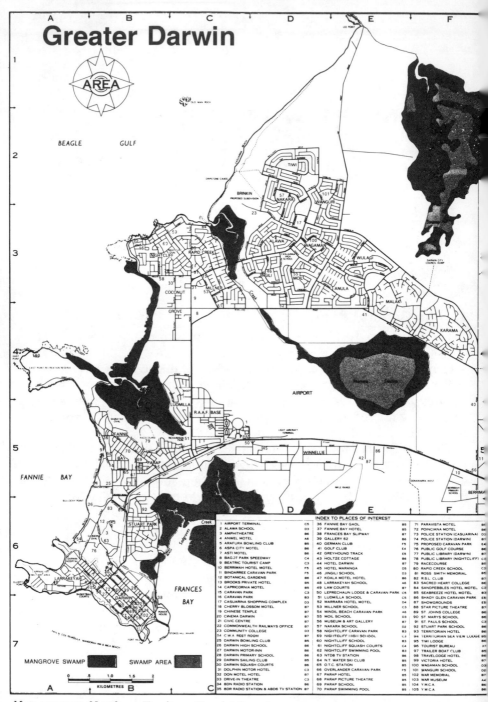

Greater Darwin

AREA

BEAGLE GULF

FANNIE BAY

FRANCES BAY

	INDEX TO PLACES OF INTEREST	
1 AIRPORT TERMINAL	C5	37 FANNIE BAY GAOL	B5	71 PARAVISTA MOTEL	B6
2 ALAWA SCHOOL	D3	38 FANNIE BAY HOTEL	B5	72 POINCIANA MOTEL	B5
3 AMPHITHEATRE	B6	39 FRANCES BAY SLIPWAY	B7	73 POLICE STATION (CASUARINA)	D3
4 ANIWEL MOTEL	A6	40 GALLERY 62	B6	74 POLICE STATION (DARWIN)	B7
5 ARAFURA BOWLING CLUB	B5	41 GERMAN CLUB	F5	75 PROPOSED CARAVAN PARK	E4
6 ASPA CITY MOTEL	B6	42 GOLF CLUB	E5	76 PUBLIC GOLF COURSE	B7
7 ASTI MOTEL	B6	43 GREYHOUND TRACK	E5	77 PUBLIC LIBRARY (DARWIN)	B7
8 BAGOT PARK SPEEDWAY	C4	44 HOLTZE COTTAGE	B6	78 PUBLIC LIBRARY (NIGHTCLIFF)	C3
9 BEATRIC TOURIST CAMP	C4	45 HOTEL DARWIN	B7	79 RACECOURSE	C4
10 BERRIMAH HOTEL MOTEL	F5	46 HOTEL MARANGA	D5	80 RAPID CREEK SCHOOL	C3
11 BINDARREE CARAVAN PARK	F5	47 JINGILI SCHOOL	D3	81 ROSS SMITH MEMORIAL	B5
12 BOTANICAL GARDENS	B6	48 KOALA MOTEL HOTEL	B7	82 R.S.L. CLUB	B6
13 BROOKS PRIVATE HOTEL	B5	49 LARRAKEYAH SCHOOL	A6	83 SACRED HEART COLLEGE	B6
14 CAPRICORNIA MOTEL	B5	49 LAW COURTS	B7	84 SANDPEBBLES HOTEL MOTEL	C3
15 CARAVAN PARK	C3	50 LEPRECHAUN LODGE & CARAVAN PARK	C5	85 SEABREEZE HOTEL MOTEL	B3
16 CARAVAN PARK	B3	51 LUDMILLA SCHOOL	B5	86 SHADY GLEN CARAVAN PARK	E5
17 CASUARINA SHOPPING COMPLEX	D3	52 MARRARA HOTEL MOTEL	D4	87 SHOWGROUNDS	B5
18 CHERRY BLOSSOM MOTEL	B7	53 MILLNER SCHOOL	C3	88 STAR PICTURE THEATRE	B7
19 CHINESE TEMPLE	B7	54 MINDIL BEACH CARAVAN PARK	A6	89 ST. JOHNS COLLEGE	B5
20 CINEMA DARWIN	B7	55 MOIL SCHOOL	D3	90 ST. MARYS SCHOOL	B7
21 CIVIC CENTRE	B7	56 MUSEUM & ART GALLERY	B7	91 ST. PAULS SCHOOL	C3
22 COMMONWEALTH RAILWAYS OFFICE	B7	57 NAKARA SCHOOL	D2	92 STUART PARK SCHOOL	B6
23 COMMUNITY COLLEGE	D3	58 NIGHTCLIFF CARAVAN PARK	B3	93 TERRITORIAN HOTEL	B7
24 C.W.A. REST ROOM	B7	59 NIGHTCLIFF HIGH SCHOOL	C3	94 TERRITORIAN SEA VIEW LODGE	B5
25 DARWIN BOWLING CLUB	B6	60 NIGHTCLIFF SCHOOL	C3	95 TIWI LODGE	D2
26 DARWIN HIGH SCHOOL	B6	61 NIGHTCLIFF SQUASH COURTS	C4	96 TOURIST BUREAU	B7
27 DARWIN MOTOR-INN	B6	62 NIGHTCLIFF SWIMMING POOL	B3	97 TRAILER BOAT CLUB	B5
28 DARWIN PRIMARY SCHOOL	B6	63 NTDB TV STATION	B3	98 TRAVELODGE HOTEL	B6
29 DARWIN SAILING CLUB	B5	64 N.T. WATER SKI CLUB	B5	99 VICTORIA HOTEL	B7
30 DARWIN SQUASH COURTS	B6	65 O.T.C. STATION	B5	100 WAGAMAN SCHOOL	D3
31 DOLPHIN MOTOR HOTEL	C3	66 OVERLANDER CARAVAN PARK	F5	101 WANGURI SCHOOL	D2
32 DON MOTEL HOTEL	B5	67 PARAP HOTEL	B5	102 WAR MEMORIAL	B7
33 DRIVE-IN THEATRE	C3	68 PARAP PICTURE THEATRE	B5	103 WAR MUSEUM	A6
34 BDN RADIO STATION	C5	69 PARAP HOTEL	B5	104 Y.M.C.A.	B5
35 BDR RADIO STATION & ABD6 TV STATION	B7	70 PARAP SWIMMING POOL	B5	105 Y.W.C.A.	B5

MANGROVE SWAMP   SWAMP AREA

0   0.5   1.0   1.5   2
KILOMETRES

Map courtesy Northern Territory Tourist Board

than half of Australia's Aborigines live in the N.T., as a matter of fact, most of them on special reserves.)

Darwin deserves a book of its own. This multiracial society has survived despite repeated ravages of war and weather over the past 110 years. Thousands of Americans were stationed in Darwin during World War II, one reason the settlement suffered no less than 64 air raids by the Japanese. The town is smack in the middle of the Indian Ocean cyclone (hurricane) belt, and it has been directly hit by three of these storms. The first was in 1897, another was in 1937, and the last was the devasting Cyclone Tracy which stripped Darwin to the bone during a 5½-hour siege on Christmas Day, 1974. Five years after the disaster, Tracy's scars are still visible.

Darwin and Alice Springs are connected by the thousand-mile Stuart Highway, locally called simply "The Track." This road, paved by the American Army during the War, passes through such history-steeped settlements as Adelaide River, Katherine, and Tennant Creek. It serves as the arterial route from which other tracks lead to poverty-stricken Aboriginal reserves, to huge, battling cattle stations, to teeming wildlife sanctuaries, to current iron mines, and to future uranium mines.

The Northern Territory is full of anomalies, but one which concerns visitors directly is that it has only two seasons. In Alice Springs, this is interpreted as summer (hot days and warm nights) and winter (warm days and cool nights). In Darwin, they talk about "The Wet," a monsoon summer season, raining nearly non-stop from about December through March, and "The Dry," the cloudless warm days and balmy, pleasant nights occurring from about April to October—the ideal season to experience some of the most varied bird and animal life you'll see in Australia.

This makes the N.T. a practical vacation for Americans and Europeans during their Northern Hemisphere summer—i.e., Australia's winter—when the Alice and Darwin are just right. During the Australian summer, we'd skip them both, unless we could arrange to at least overnight at Ayers Rock. No photograph, no word description does justice to this natural wonder. It's hard to explain, but we firmly believe that a lifetime is hardly complete without having experienced Uluru at first hand.

2. Airports and Long Distance Transportation

Airports at both Darwin and Alice Springs are simple affairs, often crowded with waiting friends and relatives when big flights are due in or out. Also when planes are due, both **Ansett Airlines** and **TAA** run

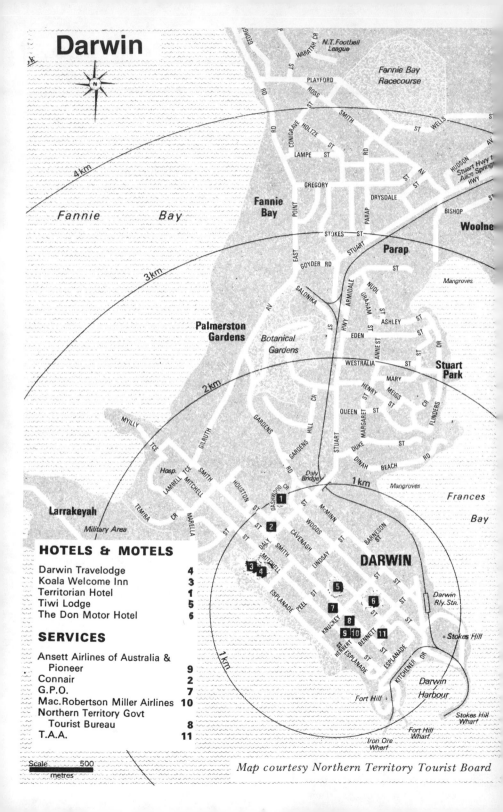

buses to and from town. Near the baggage claim area at Darwin, look for the free telephones to the two or three taxi companies. Pick up one receiver and give them your name, and the driver will "sing out" for you when he arrives.

Darwin and Alice Springs are connected over "The Track" by **Greyhound** and by **Ansett Pioneer** coaches. The trip, which takes more than 20 hours straight through, costs approximatly $70, about half the plane fare. It's approximately the same fares again to continue on the often-rough trip between Alice Springs, N.T., and Adelaide, S.A.

You can also take the historic old train called **The Ghan** until November, 1980, when it is to be replaced. The 1,000-mile trip to Alice Springs from Adelaide (Port Augusta) has its roots in 1877 when the "Afghan Express" was built along an old camel caravan route across what was then believed to be a drought area. But it turned out to be one of the most flood-prone regions of the country.

Adventurous it is still, because the line washes out often, leaving its passengers stranded for days or weeks in the Never Never. (Bus lines are no better, of course, and if you're on a tight schedule, the airplane is your best chance of keeping on it.) The old narrow-guage line is to be superseded by a new set of tracks about 100 miles to the west, reducing the 60-hour trip to only 22. **The Ghan** costs $139 First Class or $107 Economy one way, including berth and meals.

We certainly don't recommend rental cars for long-distance transportation in this neck of the desert. Therefore you'll find them straight ahead in this chapter filed under local transportation.

One more word: Try not to arrive in either of these or any small Aussie towns on a Sunday. They're closed all day.

3. Local Transportation

There are no public buses in Alice Springs. Darwin has a few which run to the suburbs from the terminal on Harry Chan Avenue (Tel. 81–2151). Thank heavens, the taxi service in both Darwin and Alice Springs is pretty good, although you'll have to pay extra for telephoning and, of course, the weekend supplements when appropriate.

Although you can walk around the central districts of both towns pretty easily, it's probably a good idea to rent a car for some medium-distance exploring, particularly in Alice Springs where the interesting sights are just out of town.

Several firms compete in both settlements. For the best bargain, you might consider picking up a popular, jeep-like "Moke," a mobile tin can which will negotiate some rough roads with ease, although admittedly

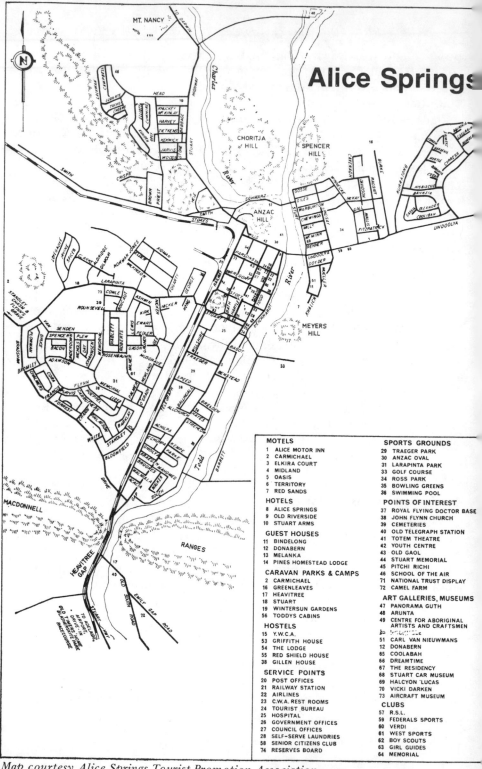

Alice Springs

MOTELS
1 ALICE MOTOR INN
2 CARMICHAEL
3 ELKIRA COURT
4 MIDLAND
5 OASIS
6 TERRITORY
7 RED SANDS

HOTELS
8 ALICE SPRINGS
9 OLD RIVERSIDE
10 STUART ARMS

GUEST HOUSES
11 BINDELONG
12 DONABERN
13 MELANKA
14 PINES HOMESTEAD LODGE

CARAVAN PARKS & CAMPS
2 CARMICHAEL
16 GREENLEAVES
17 HEAVITREE
18 STUART
19 WINTERSUN GARDENS
56 TODDYS CABINS

HOSTELS
15 Y.W.C.A.
53 GRIFFITH HOUSE
54 THE LODGE
55 RED SHIELD HOUSE
38 GILLEN HOUSE

SERVICE POINTS
20 POST OFFICES
21 RAILWAY STATION
22 AIRLINES
23 C.W.A. REST ROOMS
24 TOURIST BUREAU
25 HOSPITAL
26 GOVERNMENT OFFICES
27 COUNCIL OFFICES
28 SELF-SERVE LAUNDRIES
58 SENIOR CITIZENS CLUB
74 RESERVES BOARD

SPORTS GROUNDS
29 TRAEGER PARK
30 ANZAC OVAL
31 LARAPINTA PARK
33 GOLF COURSE
34 ROSS PARK
35 BOWLING GREENS
36 SWIMMING POOL

POINTS OF INTEREST
37 ROYAL FLYING DOCTOR BASE
38 JOHN FLYNN CHURCH
39 CEMETERIES
40 OLD TELEGRAPH STATION
41 TOTEM THEATRE
42 YOUTH CENTRE
43 OLD GAOL
44 STUART MEMORIAL
45 PITCHI RICHI
46 SCHOOL OF THE AIR
71 NATIONAL TRUST DISPLAY
72 CAMEL FARM

ART GALLERIES, MUSEUMS
47 PANORAMA GUTH
48 ARUNTA
49 CENTRE FOR ABORIGINAL
   ARTISTS AND CRAFTSMEN
50 MULGARE
51 CARL VAN NIEUWMANS
12 DONABERN
65 COOLABAH
66 DREAMTIME
67 THE RESIDENCY
68 STUART CAR MUSEUM
69 HALCYON 'LUCAS
70 VICKI DARKEN
73 AIRCRAFT MUSEUM

CLUBS
57 R.S.L.
59 FEDERALS SPORTS
60 VERDI
61 WEST SPORTS
62 BOY SCOUTS
63 GIRL GUIDES
64 MEMORIAL

Map courtesy Alice Springs Tourist Promotion Association

leaving you vulnerable to dust in the open-sided vehicle. (It is not, however, a four-wheel drive.) You might manage a Moke for $10, plus 10 cents a kilometer (but no promises) from the **Intertourist Centre** at the Hotel Darwin (Tel. 81–8896), or in Alice Springs at a related company, the **Dreamtime Moke Rentals** (Tel. 52–1405) opposite Ansett on Parsons St.

The ubiquitous **Avis** (Alice Tel. 52–1375), (Darwin Tel. 81–9745) also has Mokes (for more), along with conventional sedans. Other companies represented in Alice Springs are **Budget** (Tel. 52–4133) and **Hertz** (Tel. 52–2644).

In Darwin, look into **Cheapa Rent-A-Car** (Tel. 81–8400) or **Hunters** (Tel. 81–6686), either of which might have a four-wheel drive if you need it. **Hertz** (Tel. 81–6686) is also in Darwin with Datsuns and Holdens on tap.

4. The Hotel Scene

There are no luxury hotels in either Darwin or Alice Springs, although comfortable rooms are available in either, if you reserve ahead. If you haven't booked, you might still get a place, but don't expect the Ritz. In the summer, air conditioning is a must. In the winter, it's still highly desirable in the daytime.

HOTELS IN DARWIN

The best hotel in Darwin, and a proud, 11-story survivor of Cyclone Tracy, is the 186-room **TraveLodge** (Tel. 81–5388) on the Esplanade, somewhat of a hoof from the center of town. (We walked it in ten minutes or so.) Reserve the inland side for the more interesting views (the ocean side is just that—lots of blank water). There's a good, beef-accented restaurant, swimming pool, and all luxury facilities (including a fridge and bar) in the ample rooms. Since we stayed here the price has been jacked up considerably— to about $60 for two— and we can't help wondering if it's improved all that much. (Reservations from the hotel or through the TraveLodge chain.) Certainly, it's a solid choice.

Another good house, for around $25 less per couple, is the low-rise **Koala Welcome Inn** (Tel. 81–6511), just around the corner from the above, efficiently managed by Mr. and Mrs. Bräutigam. This one has a large number of bars and restaurants and is one place to take in the local action.

With more tropical character, and almost right downtown, is the 1939-model **Hotel Darwin** (Tel. 81–9211) which was partly rebuilt after the storm. Here you'll find the overhead fans (besides air conditioning, of course), and other tropical accouterments, along with a few rough edges. At double rates of from $40 to $45, however, it could be a little overpriced. This would depend on your individual accommodation.

Right smack in the center of town is the **Don Hotel** (Tel. 81–5311), with 40 not-too-fancy but adequately furnished rooms (even with color tellies)renting for around $35 for two.

Other possibilities include the 8-story **Telford International** (Tel. 81–5333), about $35 twins, and the **Leprechaun Lodge** (Tel. 84–3400), somewhat far out directly across from the airport for about $30 for a double. The cheapest hotel in Darwin, which we haven't seen, we think is now the **Aspa City** (Tel. 81–6695), selling doubles on Dashwood Crescent for around $20.

The youth hostel is at Tracy Village (Tel. 27–1860) where beds for members go for around $4 per mattress.

HOTELS IN ALICE SPRINGS

Keeping in mind that Alice Springs is synonomous with "roughing it" in most Australians' lexicon, there is one amazingly comfortable and attractive spread called the **Oasis Motel** (Tel. 52–1444), which we wish we could have stayed in recently: Tiny, 24-hour reception room where one or two friendly faces try to do everything at once (register guests, answer the switchboard, sell newspapers, etc.); an excellent restaurant (but always reserve hours ahead); pleasant Afghan Camel Drivers Bar; motel-type courtyards lined with colorful orange and lemon trees, hibiscus bushes and various tropical and desert flowers; pool in the middle of the campus; private aviary maintained by manager Mullins and a tiny zoo with family of kangaroo; many different types of well-kept, cool accommodations, most (but not all) with wall-to-wall carpeting, excellent furniture and luxury extras. The only trouble with the Oasis, as a matter of fact, is that you might get the erroneous impression that The Alice is no longer a difficult, frontier community; but that and its rates of $35 to $40 for two, seem a small price to pay for comfort. To sum up, I'm not sure we'll ever go to Alice Springs again unless we can get in at the Oasis.

We've stayed in two other hotels in The Alice, though, and of those we rather liked the management and facilities at the **Alice Motor Inn** (Tel. 52–2322), which unless you have a car is somewhat inconveniently located at 27 Undoolya Road. Rates are about $30 for two. There's a pool, but you'll have to look elsewhere for a restaurant, etc.

More central than either of the above, and a neat choice is the **Melanka Lodge** (Tel. 52–2233) at the corner of Todd Street and Stuart

Terrace. We thought it a little sterile, but certainly it's a good deal for $25 to $30 for two.

Our experience at the **Territory Motel** (Tel. 52–2066) was much less than fun. Without going into the depressing details, let's say that if you insist on the *refurbished* rooms only, you might be okay. (And let us repeat our warning against arriving in any small Australian town on a Sunday evening, or you may not get anything to eat or have anyone to carry your luggage upstairs). Rates are around $35 to $40 for two, here, which we thought more than the hotel is worth. Some may disagree.

We inspected the **Stuart Arms** (Tel. 52–1811) right on Todd Street, and we definitely wouldn't pay $35 for two, which is about what it charges (admittedly with breakfast).

The old **Hotel Alice Springs** (Tel. 52–1055, but better recheck that number) has been bought by the Telford organization since we were there. Reportedly the ancient three-story structure on Parsons Street has been completely de-gutted and re- gutted during 1979 and now may be worth the prices of $33 to $64 double that it charges. (Actually, it's supposed to be the center of an entirely new tourist complex. A built-in library there is to contain "U.S. and German newspapers"—don't ask us why!) We'll be back to check the quality of its repairs—and at least read its Yankee gazettes—as soon as we can.

Alice Springs' youth hostel is Griffiths House (Tel. 52–1880) at 34 Hartley St. Members pay about $4 per set of Alice springs.

5. Restaurants and Dining

There are no gourmet palaces in the Northern Territory. Darwin, at least, is fortunate to have such an ethnically diverse population that you can find some variety in its restaurants. Alice Springs is big on beef, although "buffalo steaks" are sometimes available in both areas. That's cut from water buffalo, of course. We've tried it, and it's very good, too.

DARWIN DINING

We enjoyed the modest, outdoorsy **Cri Restaurant** (Tel. 81–2756), on aback street called Austin Lane. (Not to be confused with the Capri, below.) In a rectangle of red-clothed tables and hanging plants, it features Italian and Australian food and some seafood. Most main courses run in the $6 or $8 range. If you're not going to Queensland, you might try a Morton Bay Bug for $6 or so. On the same street, the **Olympic** (Tel. 81–3298) is also popular.

The **Capri** (Tel. 81–2931), 37 Knuckey St., also features Italian specialties and bakes the town's best pizza. **The French Restaurant** (Tel.

81–6511) in the Koala Hotel on Daly St., has some night-time glamour in its green-and-yellow interior, and true to Darwin's beer-drinking image, it serves up a Soupe a la Biere for $1.50. Seriously, a good local fish offering is Barramundi Grenoboloise for $7 or so.

Steak leads the blackboard menu at the **Safari Room** (Tel. 81–5388) in the TraveLodge. Sit in the cool inside or outdoors by the pool.

A well-respected Chinese establishment is the **Hong Kong** (Tel. 81–3498) at 29 Cavenagh St., open evenings only near the waterfront. It hasn't changed a bit over the past 10 years, catering to all comers, including Darwin's population of about 1,200 Chinese, of course. (The mayor of Darwin was for many years Chinese, an amazing fact in Australia. The current mayor is a woman.) We want to try an Indonesian restaurant named **Ramath**, when we come back, but first we'll have to find the address which we lost.

Perhaps an attractive dining spot by now is the restaurant reopened in the historic **Vic Hotel**, which wasn't quite refurbished our last trip. (We think they saved the bullet holes from a Japanese air raid, so have a look.) There's a well-respected health food cafe simply called **Simply Foods** in the Central Mall off Smith Street.

Several hotels in Darwin will, of course, offer a "counter lunch," generally involving a slab of steak or a piece of local fish or something inexpensive and uncomplicated.

ALICE'S RESTAURANTS

We had a pleasant meal at the **Oasis Restaurant** (Tel. 52–1730) at the motel by the same name on Gap Road. It was not fancy, but the service and the steaks were "spot on," (orchestrated by Walter the *maitre*). The **Territory Restaurant** (Tel. 52–2066), in that motel on Leichardt Terrace, was more decorative with its green and raffia accents, but less tasty. We had a look at—but didn't eat at—a popular western-style room called the **Overlanders Steakhouse** (Tel. 52–2159) at 72 Hartley St. It's attractive, with rough wooden tables, buffalo horns on the wall, etc. A filet mignon runs around $8, and there's an orchestra on Fridays and Saturdays.

An inexpensive Italian address is **Papa Luigi's Bistro** (Tel. 52–2000). We dropped in for a lasagna lunch at two or three dollars. Simple, but good and efficient.

A new place for smörgasbord (about $7) is the **Old Riverside Hotel** at the corner of Todd and Wills Sts. We also enjoyed lunch at **Lasseter's Restaurant** (Tel. 52–1065), at 52 Todd St., where the theme is "Lasseter's Reef," a mountain of gold supposedly in the nearby Peterman

Ranges, found and lost in 1897—similar to Arizona's "Lost Dutchman" legend. (Note the gold-painted reef outside.) We just had a couple of gilt-edged sandwiches, and they were fine. And the local champion Chinese place is supposed to be **Chopsticks** (Tel. 52–3873) in the Ermond Arcade on Hartley St. (untried by us).

6. Sightseeing in the Northern Territory

You'll get all the latest on what there is to see and do from the Northern Territory Government Tourist Bureau (Tel. 81–6611) at 33 Smith St. in Darwin and (Tel. 52–1299) at 9 Parsons St. in Alice Springs.

One thing you should look for—but certainly not count on—in the N.T. is an Aboriginal *corroboree*. This singing and dancing extravaganza is unfortunately not often available to visitors, and not well explained on the rare occasions when you can see one.

The rich Aboriginal culture, in general, has almost been erased from the country, due to repressive religious missions and other unenlightened policies of the past, many of which are still in effect in the present. Hopefully, some of their ethnic dignity and colorful ceremonies will be restored in years to come, for the benefit of the Aborigines themselves as well as for the appreciation of international visitors and Australian tourists, too.

Be sure to dress practically for excursions "out bush." Jeans are worn out of town by both men and women, as well as tough, comfortable shoes. Use sandshoes or sneakers for rock climbing, but for other serious hiking, you should have a stronger sole. Also a sun hat is advisable any time of year. And long sleeves and long trousers help combat sun, brush, and insects.

DARWIN

The 34-acre **Botanic Gardens**, badly damaged by Cyclone Tracy, are still worth seeing for the tropical flora. Then, about four miles out at **East Point**, wander through the fortifications left from World War II and the **Artillery Museum** (Tel. 81–9702)—admission 50 cents.

An almost incredible collection of undersea life is on living display at **Indo Pacific Marine** (Tel. 81–5906), in a private home at 36 Phillip St., Fannie Bay. We hope Helene Pretty will show you through the reef life aquaria herself and explain some of the dangerous and beautiful creatures so well exhibited. (Admission $2, and well worth it!)

In another suburb, try to catch sight of (you can't go in) the silo-like, five-story, 12-room residence of architect Peter Dermoudy. It's made principally from two 40-foot-high metal drums which were once used to mix uranium ore and sulphuric acid. It's naturally cooled and built to withstand any future cyclone. The house is also termite proof, resisting that voracious pest which causes most other Darwin homes to be built on metal posts several feet above the ground.

A pleasant water trip is the half-hour cruise across the harbor from Darwin to Mandorah Beach. Then, 13 miles down "The Track," you can view **Yarrawonga Park**, a garden of tropical wildlife including crocodiles, buffaloes, brolgas, emus, dingos, and snakes. And if you visit **Fogg Dam**, near Humpty Doo, 36 miles southeast of Darwin, you may see thousands of water birds, parrots, and other winged creatures on the floodplains of the Adelaide River (See Section 7.) On the nearby **Marrakai Plains** are the wild wallabies, water buffalo, and the vertical ant hills built by different varieties of termites.

ALICE SPRINGS

Alice Springs perhaps qualifies more as a staging area for outback sightseeing rather than hosting many points of interest within its city limits. Nevertheless, don't miss the restored **Old Telegraph Station**, now a national park, about three miles north of town on the billabong that was the real, original Alice Springs. (It was named for the wife of the S.A. superintendent of telegraphs, Sir Charles Todd. His own name stuck on the dry river.) Signs posted around the buildings will explain it all pretty well, and it's a great place for a picnic lunch.

The **Royal Flying Doctor Service** is headquartered on Stuart Terrace, between Todd and Simpson Streets. Contrary to most opinion, the doctors seldom fly to the distant cattle and sheep stations any more, but mostly diagnose patients and dispense medical advice by radio. You can watch and listen weekdays 9:00 to 11:00 and 1:00 to 4:00, and Saturdays 9:00 to 10:00 (admission 50 cents). Nearby is the **School of the Air** where you can sometimes listen to children in Outback homesteads taking part in their radio lessons. Classes begin at 1:30 each weekday. Check at the tourist office to make arrangements to sit in.

The **Pitchi Richi Bird Sanctuary**, just three miles south of town, features sculptures by William Ricketts. Open daily 9:00 to 5:00; admission 60 cents.

We haven't been there yet, but **Noel Fullerton's Emily Gap Camel Ranch** is out on the airport road, and there you can ride a camel for around a dollar. There may be 20,000 wild camels roaming the Red Centre. They were introduced in the 1840's for transportation. (The Camel Cup races, organized by the Lions Club, are run on a Saturday in late August or early September in Alice Springs.)

Be sure to stop by that strangely shaped building at 51 Hartley St. to see the **Panorama Guth**, (Tel. 52–2103), the unusual 360-degree, 200-foot painting by Henk Guth, who might well be the gent selling you the ticket. Entrance is about $3, as we recall. It's worth it, in any case, and don't miss the mini-museum he has outside the principal panorama.

AYERS ROCK

Nothing seems more of a shame than for a northern hemisphere visitor to fly all the way to Australia and *not* go to Ayers Rock (see cover). To any but the most jaded or the most superficial traveler, it is not "just a big pebble." Ayers Rock, 210 air miles southwest of Alice Springs is, of course, the largest monolith in the world. It is two miles long, 1½-miles wide, and 1,143 feet high.

But beyond that, the rock, a type of feldspar-rich sandstone called arkose, was the sacred Uluru to the Aborigines, and their paintings and the remains of ancient rites and ceremonies are in evidence in the rock's folds and caverns. If you're in good physical condition, and wearing appropriate shoes, you can climb the rock, something many Aussies feel they must be able to boast they have done. (You can then buy yourself a T-shirt or other certificate to declare you have accomplished this.)

The rock is interesting from dawn until dusk, while it changes colors throughout the day, ending usually with a brilliant orange blast exactly at sunset. No photograph we've seen does it justice, and yes, it's worth a special trip from Sydney if you can swing it. (You'll have to change airlines in Alice Springs.) It's also worth all the annoying flies you'll find in hot-weather months. (Take some kind of repellent.)

Ayers Rock is only one of the big lumps in the area. Also in the same national park is **Mount Olga**, or as it is better known, "The Olgas." It consists of about 30 dome-shaped protuberances down an orange dusty road 20 miles from Ayers Rock. Some think they're more dramatic than Ayers, and if you can put out of your mind some of the other famous rock formations in the world, perhaps they are. The Olgas are not related to Ayers Rock, incidentally. Look closely and you'll see the stone is a conglomerate of many other rocks—a sort of pre-Cambrian concrete, if you will.

(There are four motels at Ayers Rock. We've only stayed at the Uluru, which was passable, but no gem. The Ayers Rock Chalet could be better. Unless you're driving in yourself, you'll probably be limited to whichever motel your airline or tour bus has made advance arrangements with anyway.)

Alice Springs—The Great Outback

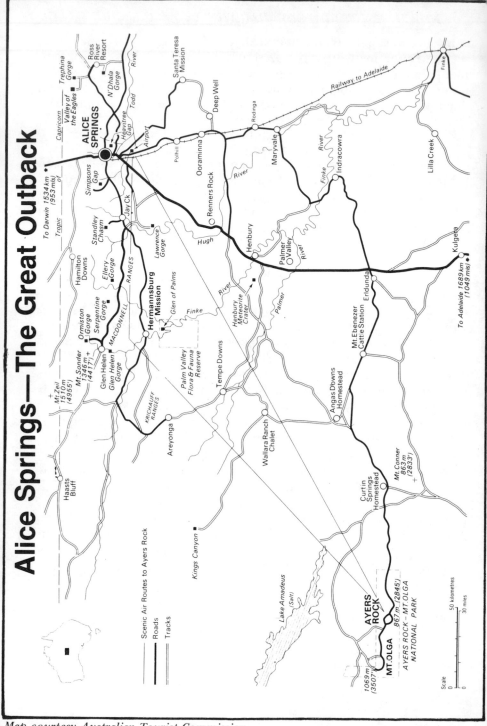

Map courtesy *Australian Tourist Commission*

MACDONNELL RANGES

The mountain ranges to the west and east of Alice Springs contain several worthwhile tourist targets: **Simpson's Gap**, 14 miles west, is a colorful park. Further on, 30 miles from Alice, is the well-known **Standley Chasm**, which you're supposed to see at exactly noon to appreciate the 200-foot cliffs which are just 12 feet apart. **Ormiston Gorge** (80 miles west of town), features red and purple rock walls rising above the creek, and five miles south of that, **Glen Helen Gorge** displays remarkable vertical rock formations known as the Organ Pipes. **Hermannsburg Mission** (83 miles west) contains the school where the late Aboriginal artist Albert Namatjira learned to paint.

East of Alice Springs about 50 miles, **Trephina Gorge** displays the magnificent "ghost gum" trees. The nearby **Corroboree Rock** and the **Valley of the Eagles** have considerable ancient Aboriginal significance. (The roads are dangerous, and are even frightening on a guided tour. Sara said she could hardly open her eyes as the bus skittered over the loose gravel!) And 50 miles east of town is the **Ross River Resort** (Radio Tel. 135), Australia's equivalent to the dude ranch.

KATHERINE

The small town of Katherine, about 200 miles down "The Track" from Darwin, is famous mainly for **Katherine Gorge**, 20 miles east of town. You can arrange cruises on the river and safaris through the park through the Katherine Gorge Tourist Agency (Tel. 72–1810) on Katherine Terrace.The gorge, incidentally, is the home of the Johnstone River crocodile, apparently the most benign crocodile in the world, taking no interest in man whatsoever. (But we'd take no chances whatsoever, either!)

TENNANT CREEK

Further down the same Stuart Highway, Tennant Creek is closer to Alice Springs, but still more than 300 miles from it. The town is the commercial center of a few mineral mines. South of the settlement about 30 miles are the **Devil's Marbles**, a group of granite gibbers, some about 20 feet in diameter.

7. Guided Tours and Cruises

Up here, there's a chance to enjoy the genuine wilderness of Australia—not only strange land forms, but flocks of bright-colored parrots and other strange birds, plus beasties like wallabies, buffalo, dingos, goannas, crocodiles, etc., without the formality of a zoo or fenced-in sanctuary.

The Outback is ideal guided tour country. Many of the trips are called "safaris," and with good reason. These sights and sites take expert drivers and lecturers, usually a combination of the two. On your own, you not only might get stuck in a bog, you won't know what you're looking at either.

(Some of the safaris are multiple days or week arrangements up from Sydney or Melbourne. We hope to be able to report on these in a future edition of this book. Meanwhile, here are a few of the locally conducted tours.)

DARWIN

In Darwin, our experience has been solely with one outfit that we liked so much that we haven't brought ourselves to take any others. That's **Anne's Courtesy Tours** (Tel. 81–8403), Box 4467, Darwin, N.T. 5794, run by Anne and Colin Ross.

Col led us on the $20 five-hour *Sunrise Wildlife Tour*, picking us up in the dark at 6:00 a.m. so we wouldn't miss the awakening birds and beasts at Fogg Dam. Then we saw the ant hills at Marrikai Plain on the way home. We went with Anne's group in the evening for the three-hour *Sunset Town Tour* (about $10), and learned more about Darwin that way than we could have done otherwise.

Other well-respected Darwin tour outfits include **Matilda Tours** (Tel. 81–8055), 44 Mitchell St., featuring two- and three-day tours to the Arnhem Land Aboriginal Reserve, the new Kakadu National Park, and Jim Jim Falls, as well as some city and wildlife tours, along with a harbor cruise; **Stefan's River Safaris** (Tel. 85–2703), which plies the crocodile-inhabited Adelaide River; and **Keetley's Tours** (Tel. 81–4422), which has a three-day trip to Katherine Gorge. We no longer recommend **Boothy's Safariland Tours.**

ALICE SPRINGS

A bewildering number of tours leave from Alice Springs, the traditional jumping-off place for nearly everything of interest in the Outback. Here are just a few of the operations:

Legion Trailway Tours (Tel. 52–4588), P.O. Box 321, Alice Springs (64 Hartley St.) has short tours around two for about $15, as well as overnighters as far afield as Ayers Rock (about $125 with meals and hotel room).

CATA (Central Australian Tours Association) (Tel. 52–1700), Box 1020, Alice Springs 5750, operates bus/air packages with TAA and offers about two dozen tours ranging from an *Alice Town Tour* to air tours of several days. Its 6-hour *Standley Chasm* tour costs around $20, including lunch.

Ansett-Pioneer (Tel. 52–2422), corner of Todd and Parsons Sts. This local branch of the national outfit has at least a half dozen offerings. Sara took the 10-hour *Valley of the Eagles* tour (about $28), which was enjoyable, if sometimes frightening because of road conditions.

Connair (Tel. 52–1755), 51 Todd St., is not only the airline to Alice Springs, they handle an entire tour there, too. We took their $137 overnighter recently, and had a terrific time despite the rain that washed out the runway at Ayers Rock (yes, it can and does happen occasionally!), and the somewhat dumpy hotel room we drew at the Uluru. (The dinner and breakfast were okay.) (At this writing Connair is due to be sold. Some of its operation could change in an unforeseen way.)

And since our first edition of this guide, R. Fraback of Portland, Oregon, has written us to highly recommend **John Dare's Visitours** (Tel. 52–2350), an Ayres Rock fly/drive combination which can also be booked through the above Connair folks at P.O. Box 1 in Alice Springs: "John Dare is very experienced in the Outback and takes only small groups on a three-day trip—fly one way and drive the other. It was the highlight of my trip." (Currently Dare's all-inclusive price is about $180, and like many independent tours, it is operated winter only—early April to mid-October.)

8. Water Sports

Do not swim in the ocean near Darwin in the summer time! That's a warning we'll get in right off the bat because of an often-deadly jellyfish that lives there December to May called the sea wasp. Other times of the year, swimming is pleasant and safe. Popular beaches include **Mandorah Beach**—take the ten-minute *Darwin Duchess* (Tel. 81–3894) across the harbor from Stokes Hill Wharf, **Mindle Beach**, on East Point Road, site of the world-famous Beer Can Regatta in June (all kinds of boats made from empty beer cans compete in various classes), and **Casuarina Beach**, at the end of Trower Road. For freshwater swimming, drive 20 miles down "The Track" to **Howard Springs**, a cool and green swimming hole near a popular picnic area. (Notice the bower birds and the ibis, too.) And boaters can rent a catamaran or a windsurfer at Mindle Beach during the dry season.

Deep sea fishing is catching on in Darwin, with most anglers casting about for queenfish, Spanish mackerel and, from January to May, barramundi and barracuda. Check at the tourist office for a charter boat.

9. Other Sports

You'll find the Territorians interested in football—rugby, "rules," and soccer—cricket, and horse racing, of course. In Alice Springs there's quite brisk competition in basketball, baseball, and softball, partly brought on by the number of American military men and dependants living in or near the community. (A super-secret American communication base is at Pine Gap, outside of Alice Springs).

The big spectator sport of the year, however, is the Henley-on-Todd Regatta, held in late August or early September. It's run on the dry Todd River bed, and contestants fashion boatlike contraptions with sails but no bottoms so that the eight-man "crew" can pick it up and run with it.

Most times, however, the Todd is the venue for a sad surfeit of Aboriginal drinking.

Golfers visiting Darwin should make contact with the **Darwin Golf Club** (Tel. 27–1365) at McMillan's Road. In Alice Springs, visitors are welcome at the 18-hole **Alice Springs Golf Club**.

Tennis courts are installed at some hotels. Otherwise, in Darwin, call the **N.T. Tennis Association** (Tel. 81–2181) on Gilruth Avenue. And in Alice Springs, you can rent public courts at **Traeger Park** (arrange it at the Council Offices in Hartley Street, though).

10. Shopping

In either Darwin or Alice Springs, some of the widest choices are in Aboriginal products, and you'll find some local shopkeepers able to discuss the differences in patterns and styles made by various Aboriginal tribes. Be aware that much Aboriginal material is turned out almost in mass production by artisans under central direction at various mission stations.

In Darwin, the best of the type is the **Arnhemland Aboriginal Art Gallery** (Tel. 81–5457), corner of Knuckey and Cavenagh Streets. Be sure to see the fabric designs as well as the better-known wood carving and paintings. (By the way, a more representative boomerang is not the common returning type, but the hook-style hunting boomerang.)

In Alice Springs, have a look at products at two addresses. For N.T. Aboriginal work only, try the **Center for Aboriginal Artists and Craftsmen** (Tel. 52–3408), at 86–88 Todd St., also open Sunday afternoons, 2:00 to 5:00. But a wider selection from all over the country is at the little store run by Judy Vaughan and Heather Shortus called the **Donabern All-Aboriginal Art Gallery** (Tel. 52–3662), at 58 Bath St., near the corner of Scott Terrace (also open Sunday afternoons).

Rock hounds in Alice Springs will dig **The Gem Cave** (Tel. 52–1079), 99 Todd St., which sparkles with an excellent collection of semi-precious stones—opalite, mica, amethyst, even rock salt destined to whet the appetite of a minerals gourmet. Also, **The Rockhole** (Tel. 52–1480), at 50 Hartley St., has similar specimens presented more informally. We wished later we'd picked up the souvenir card of 20 gemstones we saw there for $5.50.

For books, magazines, postcards and the like, see the **Darwin Newsagency** (Tel. 81–8222), at 28 Smith St., Darwin, or in Alice Springs, **Marron's Newsagency** (Tel. 52–1024), on Todd Street, opposite the Flynn Church, and the **Connoisseur Book Shop** (Tel. 52–4057) in the Fan Arcade.

11. Night Life and Entertainment

As elsewhere in Australia—and *more* than anywhere else in Australia—the principal nighttime entertainment throughout the N.T. is drinking, mainly beer. There's a brewery in Darwin, jointly owned by C.U.B. and Swan, turning out local beers, notably the brand called N.T.

In a vain attempt to beat the heat, draft beer is often sold too cold in these climes—as low as 35 degrees F., whereas the most flavor is released at temperatures closer to 42 degrees. Before buying a *bottle*, be sure you want what you'll get. The famous "Darwin Stubbie" contains 75 ounces of beer! (The bottles are becoming a collector's item, by the way—even empty.)

In Alice Springs, we enjoyed a canned beer called Stuart Draught, actually brewed in Adelaide, but not sold there. We took home the empty can—with its Outback scene—as a souvenir.

Some of the pubs in Darwin can be a little rough. We looked at each of a group of better-run bars in the Koala Welcome Inn: **The Beachcomber**, serving tropical drinks, probably will have live entertainment. **The Board Room** is the "gentlemen's club bar." Then there's **The Verandah**, a "saloon" bar, for eating in, too, and **The Sportsman**, a "public bar," which means minimum dress standards (footwear and a shirt) and not for the ladies.

You'll notice some interesting patterns of apparel in the N.T. Normally, men wear shorts, long socks, and short-sleeve, open-neck shirts during the day. In Darwin, "Darwin Rig" is worn for formal occasions—dark trousers, white, long-sleeved shirt and tie. At Alice Springs, a similar evening uniform is adopted, except that jackets are worn in the winter (it's cool in the desert then). Women wear light dresses during the day and cocktail dresses in the evening. During the day, comfortable walking shoes and a sun hat are also recommended.

You'll find night club and disco entertainment in Darwin at the **Aspa Cabaret Room**, Dashwood Crescent, the **Bougainvillea Room**, (Tel. 81–2163), on Gregory Street, Parap, and the **Don Hotel** (Tel. 81–5311), 12 Cavenagh St. The new casino is open in the Don, the first legal gambling in Australia, outside of Hobart, Tasmania.

At Alice Springs, there's usually some kind of a show at the **Stuart Arms Hotel** (Tel. 52–1811) on Todd Street. There's a disco nearly every night in the **Old Riverside Hotel** (Tel. 52–1255), on Wills Terrace— sometimes even an act plays there someplace, too. Alice likes to drink all right, but generally speaking, she turns in early.

12-A. The Darwin Address Book

Airlines—Ansett/MMA, 32 Mitchell St. (Tel. 80 –3211), TAA, 8 Bennett St. (Tel. 80 –1222), Connair, 30 Daly St. (Tel. 81–9899), Qantas, 50 Mitchell St. (Tel. 80 –1212).

Ambulance—Tel. 81–2244.

Beauty salon—Shirley Ann, Cavenagh Street (Tel. 81–9711).

Bridge players—Darwin Bridge Club (Tel. 85–4568).

Dental Clinic, 48 Mitchell St. (Tel. 81–9688).

Fire brigade—81–2222.

Florist—Gardener's World, 63 Smith St. (Tel. 81–4607).

Hospital—Darwin Hospital, Mitchell St. West (Tel. 81–2171).

Laundry—City Laundromat, Smith St. West (Tel. 81–3561).

Lions Club—Bill Binns, 913 Chrisp St., Rapid Creek (Tel. 85–3267).

Pharmacy—Jim Berry, 7 Westralia St. (Tel. 81–8075).

Police Station—Mitchell Street (Tel. 81–5555, 85–2444).

Post Office—Knuckey Street.

Supermarket—Alawa Supermarket, 53 Alawa Crescent, Casuarina.

Swimming pool—Casuarina Pool, opposite the shopping center.

Taxis—Darwin Co-op (Tel. 81–8777), Keetley's (Tel. 81–2933).

Tourist office—Northern Territory Government Tourist Bureau, 13 Smith St. (Tel. 81–6611).

12-B. The Alice Springs Address List

Ambulance—Tel. 52–2200.

Camping equipment rental—Outdoor Territorian, Milner Road and Elder Street (Tel. 52–2848).

Fire Brigade—Tel. 52–1000.

Hospital—Alice Springs Hospital (Tel. 50 –2211).

Laundry—Whistlestop Laundromat, Todd St., opposite Melanka Lodge (Tel. 52–4461).

Library—Hartley Street, behind the Court House.
Pharmacy—Alice Springs Pharmacy, Todd Street (Tel. 52–4274).
Police—Tel. 52–2777.
Post office—Hartley Street, between Parsons and Gregory.
Supermarket—Egars, Todd Street. (Tel. 52–4000).
Tourist Office—Northern Territory Government Tourist Bureau, 9 Parsons St. (Tel. 52–4711).

Queensland

Cape York

GULF OF
CARPENTARIA

Cooktown

Lakeland
Downs

SOUTH

Normanton

Cairns

PACIFIC

To Tennant Creek

Agate Creek

377 km
(234 mls)

GREAT

GREAT

BARRIER REEF

OCEAN

Townsville

Cloncurry

414 km
(257 mls)

Mt Isa

DIVIDING

396 km (246 mls)

Mackay

Colston
Sheep Station

Longreach

Anakie

Rockhampton

QUEENSLAND

Jundah

Carnarvon
National Park

Fraser
Island

Hervey Bay

Charleville

720 km
(447 mls)

RANGE

Maryborough

SOUTH

Rosevale
Sheep
Station

Maroochydore

Sunshine
Coast

Caloundra

AUST

Glass House Mtns.

Toowoomba

BRISBANE

Cunnamulla

Warwick

N.S.W

To Sydney
1043 km (648 mls)

To Sydney
1021 km
(634 mls)

Scale
0   300 kilometres

0   200 miles

Map courtesy Australian Tourist Commission

12

Brisbane
and Queensland

1. The General Picture

Queensland might hit you in three stages.

At first, the state seems to be Hawaii—coastlines of yellow sand, solid blue waters, bright green islands, then fertile plains of sugar, pineapple, rustling palms, and hills of flowering trees and plants—all backgrounded by the mountains of the Great Dividing Range.

But just beyond the first impression, the state begins to feel more like Florida. Its capital, Brisbane, bears the remnants of a traditional "wowserism" that is not unlike the "cracker" influence still at work in America's southern resort state.

Still later, Brisbane and Queensland take on their own personalities, as complex and as interesting as any other location in Australia.

Queensland's conservative tradition is an outgrowth of a long agrarian history. In the past, the great labor-intensive industries were operated by those who shanghaied and shipped in thousands of "kanakas"—Pacific islanders—to provide the brawn needed to harvest the sugar, pineapple, and banana plantations. There was little but scorn for the Aborigines who understandably enough did not see the percentage in this kind of backbreaking work.

And the racist attitudes of the past have still not entirely disappeared in Queensland. This, together with its otherwise hospitable personality,

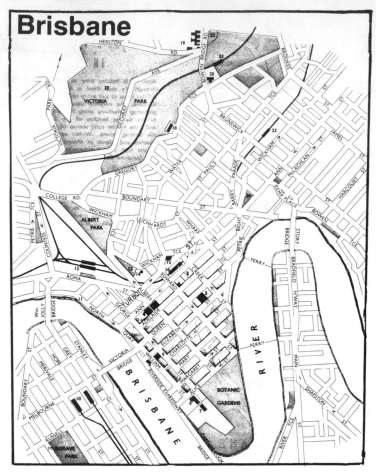

Brisbane

Map courtesy Queensland Government Tourist Bureau

1   Queensland Government Tourist Bureau
2   Anzac Memorial Park
3   G.P.O.
4   City Hall
5   King George Square
6   Parliament House
7   Brisbane Technical College
8   Public Library
9   Queen's Gardens
10 Interstate Railway Station
11 John Oxley Memorial
12 Roma St. Railway Station
13 Wickham Park
14 Observatory
15 City Council Car Park
16 Central Railway Station
17 Municipal Golf Links
18 Centenary Swimming Pool
19 Brisbane General Hospital
20 Museum
21 Exhibition Grounds
22 Bowen Park
23 Brunswick St. Railway Station
24 Centenary Place

makes it a paradox comparable to the anomalies still found in the American south.

Physically, Queensland varies from the treeless, fly-ridden mining country and desert Outback in the west, through jungle-like Aboriginal reserves and other little-explored and hardly civilized territory to the north, especially in the York Peninsula. One feature of its sun-bathed north west coast is world famous—the 1,250-mile-long Great Barrier Reef, a massive ridge of coral, once hazardous to navigation and today a repository of some of the world's most varied and beautiful marine life.

And to the southern Australian, Queensland is a winter playground— the tropical home of the Sunshine Coast, a string of beaches and resorts from Brisbane north to Noosa, and most especially, the Gold Coast, a long, narrow equivalent to Miami Beach extending along the southern shore for the last 20 miles before reaching the border of New South Wales.

Queensland's premier for the past several years is an authoritarian figure who some say sets an anti-intellectual, ultra-conservative tone for the state, Joh Bjelke-Petersen. He has the power, which he exercises, to ban public demonstrations and to arrest those who challenge this authority, which they do.

When rich bauxite was found on ancestral land at a Queensland Aboriginal reserve recently, the premier's decision was merely to move the tribe off the property and start mining. When church missions came to the aid of the Aborigines, Bjelke-Petersen closed down the churches, too! (With the help of the Federal government in Canberra, there has since been some compromise, although the controversy is continuing on the issue.)

Outside of the undeveloped areas, the countryside is still very agricultural, and in addition to the giant sugar plantations, there are vast acres of vegetables and fruits plus huge cattle stations raising some of Australia's best beef. An occasional impediment to this activity are numbers of wild animals who compete for the forage of the plains. Most of these are shot on sight—animals like kangaroos, dingos, and "brumbies"—wild horses which cannot be captured.

Brisbane (they pronounce it "Briz-b'n") grew from a crude convict settlement in 1824 to a very large country town. There it remained until recently. Thousands of American GI's who were stationed in Brisbane during World War II would hardly recognize it today. It has also grown now to a population of nearly a million.

With a few exceptions, Brisbane is not known for holding onto evidence of its past. Many of the city's landmarks, including the famous hotel where General Douglas MacArthur issued orders during the darkest days of the war, have been razed to make way for other, more-modern, more-lucrative structures.

Happily, its tropical gardens and parks remain, as well as some of its sandstone, Victorian-style public buildings. These, in fact, are being gradually cleaned and sandblasted in preparation for the capital's hosting of the 1982 Commonwealth Games.

With her face becoming freshly scrubbed again, Brisbane is becoming a very bright-looking place to visit.

2. Airports and Long Distance Transportation

The Brisbane Sunday *Sun* recently dubbed the city's aging international airport terminal at Eagle Farm, the "Jet Shed," and it's certainly true that the hodge-podge left over from WW II seems to have outlived its usefulness. At the moment, it seems certain that the new terminal will not be built in time for the Commonwealth games, in 1982.

Meanwhile, you stand a very good chance of getting rained on between the plane and the shelter, and fighting with hundreds of others for *lebensraum* in the building. You may have to wait forever for a cab, so if it's a toss-up anyway, better take the airport bus for the four-mile trip into town.

Unless you come in on one of the international flights from New Zealand or a few other foreign gateways, you'll most likely arrive either on **Ansett Airlines** (Tel. 224–0222) or **Trans Australia Airlines** (Tel. 33–2011). Some flights from Sydney are also shuttled by **East West Airlines** (Tel. 31–0311, same as for TAA).

Arriving by train from Sydney, you'll step out at the Interstate Station in South Brisbane after a 15-hour trip on the air-conditioned *Brisbane Limited*. Fares run about $30 Economy and about $54 First Class (which includes a sleeping berth). Another well-known train is the *Sunlander* between Brisbane and Cairns, a two-day trip for about $50 Economy and $80 First Class (with berth).

Three long-distance bus (coach) lines link Brisbane with other capitals, **Ansett Pioneer** (Tel. 229–4455), 16 Ann St., the **Greyhound Express** (Tel. 44–7144), 79 Melbourne St., or **Cobb & Co.** (Tel. 44–4015), 167 Stanley St. If you don't have the special passes, the fare between Sydney and Brisbane runs $40 each way for a 17-hour overnight trip.

Travel by rental car throughout most of Queensland—at least along the East Coast—can be delightful, and you'll find several competing companies in Brisbane. **Avis** (Tel. 268–5322), of course, is at the airport as well as in the city at Ann Street and North Quay (Tel. 52–7111), and its rates start at about $15 a day and 15 cents a kilometer. A well-known local outfit, **Manx Rent-A-Car** (Tel. 52–7288), at 325 Wickham St. (Fortitude Valley) is considerably cheaper, with some rates beginning at around $5 or $6 daily plus 10 to 15 cents per kilometer. Also you might check out **Ajax Rent-A-Car** (Tel. 52–5535), 341 Wickam St., **Scotty Rent-A-Car** (Tel. 52–7540), 108 Breakfast Creek Rd., and **Letz Rent-A-Car** (Tel. 262–3222), 9 Amy St.

United may also have some campervans for rent. Others are rented by **Annand and Thompson** (Tel. 52–0161) and by **Sun Seeker** (Tel. 397–0695).

3. Local Transportation

The urban bus service (Tel. 225–4444) run by the City Council isn't bad. You can buy a Day Rover ticket and go anywhere all day for a dollar, if you want. There's a good suburban train service to several suburbs, most of which depart from the Central Station.

Despite the ubiquitous bridges across the meandering Brisbane River, there are still a few ferry boats bouncing back and forth, notably the **Edward Street Ferry** which crosses between the Botanic Gardens and Kangaroo Point and the **Customs House Ferry**, a few hundred yards downstream.

We recently found one place right downtown where you can rent a bicycle for $1.50 an hour: **Brisbane Bicycle Hire** (Tel. 229–2592) is at the corner of Alice and Albert, right next to the Parkroyal Hotel.

Taxi services include **Ascot** (Tel. 221–1422), **Black & White** (Tel. 229–1000), and **Yellow** (Tel. 391–0191).

4. The Brisbane Hotel Scene

Our prediction is that if Brisbane does not get busy, it's going to find itself short of hotels, the more international air fares go down and the closer it gets to the date of the 1982 Commonwealth Games. Meanwhile, nail your bookings down well, or you may find yourself camping at the airport during busy periods.

EXPENSIVE HOTELS

It's almost a horse race between the top two or three, the Lennons Plaza, the Parkroyal and the Gateway. Nevertheless, we prefer them in that order.

The seven-year-old **Lennons Plaza** (Tel. 32–0131), is at 66–76 Queens St., over three blocks from the site of the original historic Lennons, where General MacArthur publicly vowed to return to the Philippines (now occupied by the COMALCO tower): Very convenient site in the center; large, plush, high-ceiling lobby in modern "grand hotel" style; several thick-carpeted, very decorated bars; three different dining areas, including the elegant Colosseum Restaurant, the tropical-toned Hibiscus Room on the top floor, and a coffee shop down below; several function rooms; 128 well-designed accommodations, all with luxury fittings; higher floors featuring the views. Doubles in pleasant colors like yellow, dark green, and maroon, begin at nearly $45 up to about $55. Spacious suites are about $70 to $100. (Reserve from the hotel direct or through the Zebra chain.) This was our own recent address, and we found it a top-class, solidly professional operation.

Perhaps with a little more distinguishable personality, though, is the **Brisbane Parkroyal** (Tel. 221–3411), which is labeled a "motor inn." (For some reason, Australians insist on drawing such a difference between "hotels" and "motels," although the latter term is going out of favor.) Lovely green and growing site next to the Botanic Gardens and within walking distance of the river ferry; long, purple-carpeted lobby (with courtesy coffee) leading eventually to a refreshing outdoor pool; wood-lined sauna available; recently expanded cocktail bar; dark-paneled Walnut Room Restaurant; ample, warm-toned rooms, all with small balconies; front units overlooking the gardens and the river beyond; all top-class amenities installed; $1 extra for some units with a water bed. Doubles begin about $45, but the best views are higher at about $65; 9th and 10th floors equipped with king-size mattresses; some swellegant VIP suites at around $100. (Reservations through the TraveLodge organizations or the hotel, corner of Alice and Albert Streets.) We're going to try for this one next time.

We've also had a brief stay at the **Gateway Inn** (Tel. 221–0211), a successful and well-concocted formula by the Ansett organization above their bus terminal at 85 North Quay, off Ann Street. Its efficiently designed rooms are virtually—if not exactly—duplicates of the Gateways in Adelaide and in Perth, except that if you draw a front room here, you get a nice view of the developing Cultural Center, Victoria Bridge, and the mid-channel Elizabeth II Jubilee Fountain that springs to life from time to time in the Brisbane River. There's a pool, restaurant and bar, too, of course. Even though we might prefer the balconies and the more open feeling of the Parkroyal, we have no complaints about the Gateway, which may be more convenient for some folks, anyway. About $45 up. (Book through Ansett or at the hotel at Brisbane 4000.) Recommended.

The **Zebra Hotel** (Tel. 221–6044)—and remember to pronounce that "*zeh*-bra"—is also near the center of things at 103 George St. Modern entrance decorated by stickers proudly displaying the scores of credit cards and travelers checks it accepts; outdoor advertising pushing for more restaurant business ("gourmet grills" from 12 to 2 for $4.95); dining and dancing in the Raindrop Room; swimming pool; bedchambers all neat and clean; mostly showers (not tubs); some TV's in color; furniture running toward raffia; some with kitchenettes; not as much view when compared to the previous two; rates about $10 less than for the Lennons, its partner in the profession. (Reservations through the Zebra chain or the hotel direct.) A businessmen's favorite, and a very fair deal for the price.

Somehow we missed an inspection of the **Crest International** (Tel. 221–7788), an oversight we will correct on our next trip. The well-regarded establishment is directly on King George Square.

BRISBANE BEDS ON A BUDGET

You might draw a very nice double for $25 at the **Parkview Motel** (Tel. 31–2695), at 128 Alice St., near the more prestigious Parkroyal. A member of the Flag chain, it runs up an outdoor pool but no restaurant. Almost next door, at 132 Alice St., is the **Motel Regal** (Tel. 31–1541), which does have a restaurant, as well as a pool. It's also a Flag, waving rooms at around the same price. You'll find TV's, complimentary newspapers, and several touches associated with the big boys.

The well-advertised **Canberra Hotel** (Tel. 32–0231) up the hill at Ann and Edward Streets, has a plaque outside declaring it to be a temperance hotel since opening day July 20, 1929. We've nothing against their not selling liquor, but we wonder what they've got against pictures. The rooms in the new wing would look nice if it weren't for those acres of blank space above the furniture. Doubles were running a fair $20 to $32 when we looked in, most with TV, tea/coffee makers, etc. Not a bad choice—especially if you want some place to project your slides.

At the **Embassy Hotel** (Tel. 221–7616), the "XXXX" outside the old red brick building do not a 4-star hotel make. That's just the brand of beer it features in the pub. A convenient location (No. 37 bus stops right outside), it's been recently renovated, taking the edge off some of that 1924 mustiness. Believe it or not, it has just 20 sleeping nests and seven bars. Try for a corner double at $27. It's a pretty good bargain—*if* you can squeeze in.

The **York Hotel** (Tel. 221–0605), at 69 Queen St., will take you back into the past via its open-cage, gold-grilled lift. A modest twin with "private facilities" still goes—we hope—for $10 per person, double or single, *with* breakfast. It's not the Ritz, but Mr. and Mrs. Meiklejohn seemed efficient and receptive. The rooms are small, and we didn't see any telly (maybe there's one in the lounge?). Better have a look at your headquarters before signing in, perhaps.

If you don't mind getting a little outside the center, you could get a little more for a little less. In Fortitude Valley you may pay $8 per person single or double in the **Mornington Private Hotel** (Tel. 52–4204), at 527 Gregory Terrace. We haven't seen this one yet, but we understand there's a TV lounge, a pool, laundry facilities, and all around convenience. Sounds good, at least!

Last, Brisbane's youth hostel is about five miles out at 15 Mitchell St. in Kedron. (Book through the YHA in town, Tel. 57–1245.) Beds run about $3 for members here.

5. Restaurants and Dining

An unsubtle delicacy, the Queensland Mud Crab is famous, gigantic, and delicious. Also the Moreton Bay Bug, a lobster, is brought in from the bay outside Brisbane.

The restaurant for seafood is **Gambaro's** (Tel. 269–1928) at 34 Caxton St. in Petrie Terrace. Dominic Gambaro is famous for his Cold Seafood Platter, which includes the bug and the crab, along with oyster and other seasoned goodies. This is not a fancy-looking place. In fact, it started out as a fish and chips shop, although it's now been built up into one of the best of its type in the country.

Another fish house getting along swimmingly is **Finigan's** (Tel. 229–2355) in the Pavilion Shopping Centre in Queen Street. This one is also open for lunch. (Try the Quelltaller Rhine Riesling with your fish.) Service is a little iffy, so it's not universally popular, though.

Just across the street from Gambaro's, **Rag's** (Tel. 36–6794) at No. 25 Caxton, has a name which belies its serious French intent. Try the Boeuf Grand Veneur (beef marinated in red wine).

On the Italian front, we liked our own excursion into Scallopine Picante at **Milano's** (Tel. 229–3917), 78 Queen St., a short lob from Lennons. Hmm. Or was that "Veal Stuffato di Manzo al Barolo?" Our notes are not clear on the subject, but our memory is of a vividly excellent meal, well prepared and served faultlessly. The elegant upstairs setting featured white tablecloths, a rosebud in a stainless steel vase, pivoting, hip-hugging chairs, and someone playing Gershwin on the goanna somewhere in the background. There are many French specialties on the menu, and we understand they're good, too. We paid about $35 for two, with an obscure (but quite acceptable) house wine.

A full-fledged French establishment is **Scaramouche** (Tel. 221–0431), set in a century-old church beautifully renovated with antiques, stained glass, and Renaissance prints at the corner of Turbot Street and North Quay. The menu frequently changes, and some things must be pre-ordered. (Closed Sundays.)

Crowning culinary achievements are the rule at the **Coronation** (Tel. 36–0055) in Milton. It's expensive though—about $45 for two, with wine. **The Courtyard** (Tel. 52–5431), 67 O'Connell Terrace, near the Brisbane Hospital, has indoor tables as well as seating *al fresco*. The atmosphere amongst the greenery is delightful, and the specialty is dependable Queensland beef. And **Arts & Battledress** (Tel. 36–2406), at 216 Petrie Terrace, displays gourmet skills in a tiny, midtown setting. The Steak Bermuda combines beef, bacon, banana, and brandy!

For lunch, you might look for the outdoor beer gardens that are gradually coming to Brisbane. One very modest one is the **Port Office** (opposite the old post office) which offers 60-cent hamburgers and other sandwiches. They go down well with a glass of Brisbane Bitter or Castlemaine XXXX. Also the garden of the **Breakfast Creek Hotel** (Tel. 262–5988), at 2 Kingsford Smith Drive, is good. It has a good reputation as a no-nonsense steak house, day or night. (Open Sundays, too, but only from 5:00 to 8:30 p.m.)

Back downtown again, there are reasonably priced meals in the **Wool Press Restaurant** (Tel. 229–5064) in the SGIO Building on Albert Street, and in **The Bistro**, in the new Civic Centre (fried Barramundi, about $3.50). Another inexpensive choice for day or night dining is **Mamma Luigi's** (Tel. 52–2320), a pasta palace at 240 St. Paul's Terrace that's 43 years old this year. Bring your own wine and enjoy the simple spaghetti and chicken served on rough-hewn wooden furniture. *Molte bene*, and you may get away around five biccies!

6. Sightseeing in Queensland

Long a vacationland for Australians, Queensland lays out an incredible number of attractions, only a relative few of which we can touch on in a guidebook for international visitors to Australia. We've divided this section up into four areas—Brisbane, the Gold Coast, the Great Barrier Reef, and the Cape York Peninsula (Cairns, etc.).

BRISBANE

Pay a visit before anything to the **Queensland Government Tourist Bureau** (Tel. 31–2211), at the corner of Adelaide and Edward Streets.

This is the place to ask for maps and folders, not only of Brisbane but the attractions throughout the state. They'll book you on tours, too, if you want, or for trips north, south, or west of the city.

If you see nothing else in Brisbane, don't miss a visit to the privately owned **Lone Pine Koala Sanctuary** (Tel. 378–1054), about seven miles up the river. (In fact, a delightful way to arrive is by launch; see Section 7.) The sanctuary was established in 1927 specifically to protect the koala (the Australian "Teddy Bear") then being slaughtered in huge numbers. At Lone Pine, the Queensland koalas prove their penchant for gentleness, and the curators will even photograph you with a Polaroid holding a koala in your arms—just about the only place in Australia where you can get away with that.

Other animals at Lone Pine include kangaroos and emus (you can walk among them, scratch their ears and feed them all you want—but *they'll* want only a little, being so well fed), plus a platypus, wombats, echidnas (spiny anteaters), Tasmanian devils, dingos, and various kinds of weird reptiles and native birds, including kookaburras, cockatoos, galahs, etc. We thought the whole experience was wonderful. (Open 9:30 a.m. to 5:00 p.m. daily.)

On the way to or from Lone Pine, many newcomers drive up to **Mount Coot-tha Forest Park**, a piece of natural bush which also provides a view over Brisbane, the meandering river, Moreton Bay and the surrounding area sometimes as far as the rock pillars called the Glasshouse Mountains, 50 miles away. (The people who live there are said to be easygoing, and not inclined to throw stones.) The park features many kinds of aromatic gum (eucalyptus) trees, and lots of tropical flowers like fragrant frangipani (plumeria), poinciana, etc. (We've never found anyone who could tell us why Coot-tha is hyphenated.)

Other gardens worth looking into include **New Farm Park**, a "must" during early summer: Some 12,000 rose bushes bloom from September to November, but even more dramatic and unusual, millions of lavender jacaranda blossoms come out during October and November and the brilliant red poinciana trees bloom in November and December. Also, right in town, the **Brisbane Botanic Gardens** surrounding Parliament House and other public buildings provide Queenslanders with some serendipitous Sunday walks.

In the center of the city, a stop at the symbol of Brizzie, the 1930 Queensland stone **City Hall** is considered a must by some. They say it's still worth the 10 cents or so they charge to take the elevator up into the tall clock tower, but we've never gotten around to that ourselves. **King George Square**, in front of the building, gives a pleasant open look to this area of town. A couple blocks up either Ann Street or Adelaide Street is **Anzac Square**, with a memorial made from that same handsome sandstone. The park also sports one water-swollen boab (baobab) tree, and stairs to walk up the steep hill from Adelaide to Ann Street in front of the Central Station.

Further up the hill, next to Wickham Park, is the **Tower Mill**, also called the Old Observatory. It was built by convicts to be a windmill, but somehow it didn't work. The sails were then removed, and it was converted to a treadmill, run by convict footpower, used to grind corn. (We wonder if the same convicts turned it after failing to build it correctly.) The tower was also used for experimental television transmission in 1935.

Two museums are in the city, ready for rainy-day visitors. The **Queensland Art Gallery** (Tel. 229–2138), temporarily housed in the M.I.M. Building, 160 Ann St., exhibiting about 200 modern and classical works, and the **Queensland Museum** (Tel. 52–2716), temporarily housed at the corner of Gregory Terrace and Bowen Bridge Road. Both are now open 10 to 5:00 Monday to Saturday and 2:00 to 5:00 Sunday. Note that both these institutions are to be installed eventually in the new **Cultural Center** which will continue under construction for some time on the riverbank south of Victoria Bridge.

Also in Downtown Brisbane, don't miss the intricate facade of the 1888 **Treasury** Building. The collection of columns and archways carved from local sandstone is now dubbed "one of the finest Italianate buildings in (you guessed it) the Southern Hemisphere." Like many of the city's public buildings, it has recently been sandblasted back into the elegance it possessed a century ago. It is perhaps at its most dramatic on a floodlit evening.

We shouldn't leave Brisbane without mentioning two islands in Moreton Bay, **Moreton Island** and **North Stradbroke Island** ("Straddie"), both of which are potentially excellent resorts. They're worth a visit if you have time on your hands. Both have some fine, uncrowded beaches.

THE GOLD COAST

Many Australian tourists are surprised to learn that the Gold Coast is one long city, stretched out for 20 miles by about a half-mile wide. It begins at a place called **Southport**, on the coast, about 50 miles down the Pacific Highway from Brisbane. It continues through a dozen and a half other communities along the shoreline, notably **Surfers Paradise**, Burleigh Heads, and **Coolangatta**, the latter of which is next to the border of New South Wales.

There are lots of ockerous things to see and do on the Gold Coast—fake medieval castles, wax museums, zillions of lion parks, miniature golf courses, and the like. Without going into detail, however, three locations we rather liked were **Sea World** (Tel. 32–1055) in Surfers, whose dolphin and seal performances are terrific for the nippers ($4.50 grownups, $1.50 nippers), and the nearby **Bird Life Park** (Tel. 32–5999), like Sea World, also owned by Keith Williams, a fun-loving entrepreneur.

I've never been big on old cars (Sara likes them), but the demonstrations make the difference at **Gilltraps Yesteryear World** (Tel. 36 –1500), down near Coolangatta. Admission $2. We missed the **Currumbin Sanctuary** at Currumbin Beach nearby, but Phillip and Marie Stoneham tell us you can't beat it for birds and kangas.

Before we went to the Gold Coast ourselves for the first time last year, we received a succinct description by letter from an observant reporter, John Anderson—a friend gifted with a talent for summing up a place accurately and compactly:

" . . . And yes, Bob, there really is a place called Surfers Paradise. It's one of several resort towns strung along a strip of highway from the N.S.W. border north. The area is a miniature Waikiki, with skyscraper hotels crowding the shoreline, lots of boutiques and discotheques, and a few typical Aussie pubs, which are actually more like filling stations, hidden away here and there.

"But there is a beautiful new shopping mall at Surfers, featuring a MacDonald's hamburger stand. And bathers are alerted at regular intervals by the local radio station, which is broadcast across the beach through loudspeakers:

> *'Time to change your pose,*
> *Or you'll burn your nose.*
> *And even more so,*
> *You'll burn your torso!'* "

The English novelist and playwright, J. B. Priestley, dismissed Surfers Paradise as "a cardboard Miami," but that's perhaps a little unfair today. Although it has suffered from years of unplanned growth, and commercialism is rampant, it serves as an attractive playground for a young segment of Australia's population, and its higgledy-pigglediness at least gives an interesting insight into the directions taken by an unbridled antipodean pop culture.

It's also worth noting that because of the fierce competition between facilities here, prices for such attractions as hotels and restaurants are some of Australia's lowest for quality among the highest. (In Surfers, for example, you can stay at the Chevron Paradise—Tel. 39-0444—a top address, for about $35 double. And some say the queen of Queensland's restaurants is the River Inn—Tel. 31-6177—at 32 Ferny Avenue, just across the street.)

We can't say goodbye to the Gold Coast without mentioning its most well-known assets—the meter maids. As the brief bathing suit is the unofficial uniform of the place, these maids are bobby-dazzlers dressed in gold lamé bikinis. Their job is not to ticket overparked cars but to put coins *into* the meters for forgetful motorists as a public-related service of the Merchants Progress Association. Good-on yer, Gold Coast. Yer cahn't be all bad, at that!

THE GREAT BARRIER REEF

The massive coral growth which extends along 1,250 miles of the east coast from Gladstone to Cape York is, of course, one of the genuine wonders of the world. Who hasn't seen the magnificent, colorful creatures spread across the pages of *National Geographic* and other magazines. It's the site of some of the best underwater photographs ever taken. As the travel posters say, you *can* see at the reef more kinds of fish in the sea than anywhere else on earth.

But here's the rub. To fully appreciate the Great Barrier Reef, one should be a qualified scuba diver. At least, you must find a good, shallow location to put on a face mask and snorkle and paddle around on the surface to see things as clearly and as close-up as they should be. If you can't do that, you could still be lucky, of course. If conditions are perfect for the day you go out, you *might* be able to get some idea about coral patterns and a few small fish that float by under a glass bottom boat. And again, when conditions are just right, you can put on a pair of boots or old tennis shoes to protect your feet and walk on the reef at low tide, getting one on one with the sea in that manner.

Most Australians who go to the reef do very little of this. The G.B.R. to many of them is a holiday on a tropic isle, with plastic leis and old-fashioned, syrupy Hawaiian guitar music, community sings, and 1940's dance steps. And if you want to learn how to do the "sugar shake," try Brampton Island, for one. There are surely others, too.

A couple more general observations. There are two types of islands in the G.B.R. One is an island like any other, the tip of an undersea range of hills. The other is a genuine reef island, having been built up on an even level by sand, dirt, and life caught up on the coral itself and building above the surface. In general, we believe the latter is more likely to

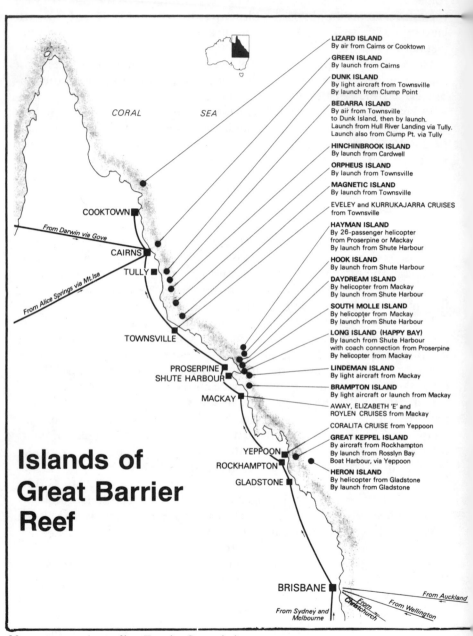

Islands of Great Barrier Reef

CORAL   SEA

LIZARD ISLAND
By air from Cairns or Cooktown

GREEN ISLAND
By launch from Cairns

DUNK ISLAND
By light aircraft from Townsville
By launch from Clump Point

BEDARRA ISLAND
By air from Townsville
to Dunk Island, then by launch.
Launch from Hull River Landing via Tully.
Launch also from Clump Pt. via Tully.

HINCHINBROOK ISLAND
By launch from Cardwell

ORPHEUS ISLAND
By launch from Townsville

MAGNETIC ISLAND
By launch from Townsville

EVELEY and KURRUKAJARRA CRUISES
from Townsville

HAYMAN ISLAND
By 26-passenger helicopter
from Proserpine or Mackay
By launch from Shute Harbour

HOOK ISLAND
By launch from Shute Harbour

DAYDREAM ISLAND
By helicopter from Mackay
By launch from Shute Harbour

SOUTH MOLLE ISLAND
By helicopter from Mackay
By launch from Shute Harbour

LONG ISLAND (HAPPY BAY)
By launch from Shute Harbour
with coach connection from Proserpine
By helicopter from Mackay

LINDEMAN ISLAND
By light aircraft from Mackay

BRAMPTON ISLAND
By light aircraft or launch from Mackay

AWAY, ELIZABETH 'E' and
ROYLEN CRUISES from Mackay

CORALITA CRUISE from Yeppoon

GREAT KEPPEL ISLAND
By aircraft from Rockhampton
By launch from Rosslyn Bay
Boat Harbour, via Yeppoon

HERON ISLAND
By helicopter from Gladstone
By launch from Gladstone

COOKTOWN

From Darwin via Gove

CAIRNS

TULLY

From Alice Springs via Mt. Isa

TOWNSVILLE

PROSERPINE
SHUTE HARBOUR

MACKAY

YEPPOON
ROCKHAMPTON
GLADSTONE

BRISBANE

From Auckland
From Wellington
From Christchurch
From Sydney and
Melbourne

Map courtesy Australian Tourist Commission

be able to provide the true flavor of the reef, despite what some would consider the monotonous flatness of the territory.

Here is our island-by-island description of the ones easily reached, beginning in the south and continuing north. Nearly all are accessible by boat and/or plane from ports on the nearby mainland. Unless indicated, all offer accommodations for overnight or longer. (If you're going to stay, we would choose either Heron, Hayman, Dunk, Green, or Lizard islands as the best bets.)

Heron Island: A small coral cay catering to scuba divers and snorkelers and perhaps outfitted for that better than anyone else. Some wonderful big "bommeys"—coral heads—where you can hand feed the fish who live there. A nesting site of the sea turtle and hundreds of sea birds. Perhaps the best choice also because the coral in this area has not yet fallen prey to the crown-of-thorns starfish, which has been ravaging the reef in many places further north.

Great Keppel Island: It has been "upgraded" into a big, go-go entertainment center recently—something going on every minute from water skiing to rock bands. Also has a glass-bottom boat.

Brampton Island: The top of an undersea mountain, it's not a true coral island. We enjoyed walking entirely around it one afternoon, accompanied at times by a tame, high-stepping emu named George. We also liked a hostess named Hazel who did her best with a bad job. Without going into depressing detail, the resort itself struck us as the pits.

Lindeman Island: Owned by P&O Lines, it's very much a family resort on a hilly island. Lots of organized entertainment. It wouldn't be our first choice, but some reef activities are also featured. **Long Island** (Happy Bay): Another one bigger on community sings and Bingo, apparently, than on reef experiences. **South Molle Island**: a mountain island once considered a fairly good compromise between isolation and sociability. But the resort appears to be slipping in recent years.

Daydream Island: This one is very tiny and has chosen a Hawaiian/Mexican motif for its resort. There's an unusually large swimming pool—nay, a sort of swimming lagoon. This one may depend a lot on the crowd. **Hook Island**: You don't have to scuba dive or snorkel here, because you can go down under the water in a special observatory. (The fish float by thinking that you are the one in the aquarium!) No hotel rooms on the island; a daily launch comes over from Shute Harbour.

Hayman Island: Perhaps the most sophisticated resort in the G.B.R. islands, it's an Ansett operation that has a wider choice of everything, both in day and night life. Generally appeals to a young crowd equally at home with rock music as they are with oxygen tanks and flippers.

We're looking forward to seeing this one personally, but haven't made it yet. **Magnetic Island:** It attracts hundreds of day trippers every weekend due to its closeness to Townsville, and it's big enough to be a national park and host several resorts. You might pick this one for bush walking and animal appreciation, but hardly for coral and fish viewing. **Orpheus Island:** A seven-mile-long island in the Palm group, it's fringed with reef. Some consider it the ultimate away-from-it-all location. **Hinchinbrook Island:** A national park with dense rainforest, waterfalls, and wildlife. **Bedearra Island:** Small, tropical and isolated, its resort sleeps only 10 souls.

Dunk Island: Finally finished with its $3 million development program, Dunk is beginning to appeal to the sophisticated over 30's vacationer. Capped by 800-foot-high Mount Koo-tal-oo, it's a tropical rain forest and a biologist's paradise, with an amazing variety of birds, bats, lizards, and the fierce-looking (but harmless) rhinoceros beetle. It's always been an enjoyable place, but prices have gone up to $30 to $50 per person a day, full board.

Green Island: A genuine coral cay, it's 16 miles offshore from Cairns and officially a Marine National Park. Snorkeling and coral viewing are near perfect here, and the underwater observatory now installed is effective. It's about $30 per person full board, and lots of Green graduates report a good time here. **Lizard Island:** Closer to Cooktown, with a magnificent coral reef, it now has a tiny hotel sleeping only 10 people. Perhaps a good choice for isolationists.

CAPE YORK PENINSULA

Much of the Peninsula is uninhabited, and this is some of the most wild-and-woolly, tropical jungle you'll find anywhere, virtually impossible to see except on safari.

Cairns (Pop. 35,000) is the principal town on the shores of the Coral Sea. It comes alive from September to December, acting as the base for big game fishermen from around the world, all in search of record marlin. It's also the launching point for Green Island (see above). The historic Hides Hotel in Cairns has just been refurbished.

In this town, you can board the dramatic narrow-gauge railroad for a 21-mile scenic ride through the rainforest. It climbs through canefields and dense jungle, skimming past the Great Barron Falls and Barron River Gorge to the village of **Kuranda** on the edge of the Atherton Tableland.

About 200 miles north of Cairns, **Cooktown** stands on the Endeavour River, where Captain James Cook beached and repaired his ship *Endeavour* during his historic 1770 voyage. Early relics are preserved in the Cook Museum.

7. Guided Tours and Cruises

In Brisbane, **Boomerang Tours** (Tel. 221–9922) operates morning and afternoon tours of different parts of the city, either one for around $5 per ticket. Several full-day tours are also offered. Boomerang runs one to the *Gold Coast* and another to the *Sunshine Coast* (a less-developed resort shoreline north of Brisbane), either one for around $10. **Scenic Tours** (Tel. 48–0060) has a full-day excursion called the *Jungle Day Tour* to Lamington National Park for around $10.

Cruises in Brisbane include the trip up the Brisbane River past the University of Queensland to *Lone Pine Sanctuary*. It's run by **Hayles Brisbane Cruises** (Tel. 221–0020) from the quay off Queens Wharf Road under the expressway near Victoria Bridge. The 3½-hour trip costs around $5. Hayles also operates a full-day guided cruise to *North Stradbroke Island* and another to *Bishop Island and Saint Helena Island* in Moreton Bay for around $10. (The easiest way to arrange all these cruises and tours, incidentally, is through the aforementioned tourist office at Adelaide and Edward Streets.)

A plethora of tours are cranked up on the Gold Coast itself. Check at the tourist office above in Brisbane or at the branch office in Surfers Paradise at 3177 Gold Coast Highway.

Several cruises wend through the islands along the Great Barrier Reef, and this could be one of the best ways to see the area, depending on a number of variables—like the condition of the vessel, the food offered, and the make-up of your fellow passengers. From Mackay, the 112-foot cruiser *Elizabeth E* carries 24 passengers on a four-day cruise in the Whitsunday group for about $250. Also, **Roylen Cruises** operates several vessels, of which the *Petaj* is the best. It makes a five-day cruise for around $300.

Several day cruises, ranging from around $12 to $25, are run by different companies from Shute Harbor near Mackay. Look over their itineraries carefully. The latest information is on tap at the tourist office on River Street in Mackay.

From Townsville, five-day cruises are operated on the 85-foot *Evely Beaver* by **Evely Cruises**, perhaps still for under $200.

8. Water Sports

As already indicated, surfing and swimming on the Gold Coast are some of the best in the world. Go in the water only at designated beaches, however. These are protected with effective shark nets. Virtually the entire coastline is lined offshore by these Nylon meshes at least as far up as Noosa at the top of the Sunshine Coast. Jim Matheson of the Queensland Department of Tourism told us that in the 15 years the nets have been in place, there have been no shark attacks along these shores.

You can go water skiing at Sea World, Southport, at Lake Terranora, and on the Tweed River. You can rent boats from most resorts, too.

Skin diving is best, of course, on the islands of the Great Barrier Reef, mostly done with masks and snorkles. However scuba equipment can be rented at Heron Island, Daydream Island, Hayman Island, and Dunk Island. That's the best way to appreciate the reef.

Big game fishing at Cairns is world famous, with many anglers trying for the elusive 2,000-pound black marlin. There's a $100,000 prize waiting for the first to get one. (You might catch Marlon Brando, Lee Marvin, Ernest Borgnine, and other famous fisher-folk at Cairns during the October-December marlin season.) Some other kinds of fish regularly brought in include barracuda, sailfish, wahoo, several kinds of tuna, and Spanish mackerel. Dozens of boats are available for charter at Cairns at around $150 to $300 for a day's outing, depending on the size of the boat and the season. One of the most well-known is Peter Bristow's *Avalon*, which has landed more than 20 marlins in excess of 1,000 pounds.

Book all boats through the Great Barrier Reef Travel Agency (Tel. 51–3877), on Shields Street in Cairns 4870. Or the Queensland Government Tourist Bureau, at 81 Abbott St., Cairns 4870, is also ready to hand out good oil on the fishing scene.

9. Other Sports

New athletic facilities are being developed in South Brisbane for the Commonwealth Games. Meanwhile, being a northern state, Queensland is nuts about **Rugby**, of course, both the professional League and the amateur Union, with New South Wales the principal rivals. The big matches are played at Lang Park. **Cricket** is also big, again with the custody of the Sheffield Shield at stake, usually in competition with N.S.W. Cricketmatches are played at Woolloongabba, more commonly called just "Gabba."

Racing, both with dogs and horses, is popular. The principal tracks are at Eagle Farm, a fast grass track and the home of the Queensland

Turf Club, and at Albion Park, a sand track. Also you can "go to the trots"—trotting races—at Albion Park. Greyhound racing takes place at "Gabba," and it's considered most fun while eating dinner at the picture window restaurant, just a nostril or two away from the dogs.

You can play **tennis** by hiring a court at Milton (Tel. 36–4983), Milton Road, the home of the Queensland Lawn Tennis Association as well as the Davis Cup. Courts cost $5 or $6 for a half day.

If you like **golf**, the Royal Queensland (Tel. 268–1127) in Hamilton and the Brisbane Golf Club (Tel. 48–1008) in Yeerongpilly, are private clubs known to be hospitable to visitors, although they apparantly hate each other with an intense rivalry that goes back to 1921. (Either club may give you their version of the story.) Public golf courses, more convenient for visitors, include the one in **Victoria Park** (Tel. 52–4244), off Gilchrist Avenue.

10. Shopping in Brisbane

As in most of Australia, stores are open until 5:00 p.m. weekdays and until 11:30 a.m. Saturdays. Brisbane has two main shopping areas— downtown in the center of the city, and out in "The Valley"—Fortitude Valley, to be specific. Both are open until 9:00 p.m. on Fridays.

Art galleries, Aboriginal craft, and souvenirs: Of this group, the best may be **Barry's Art Gallery**, 205 Adelaide St., which offers an extensive range of Australian art. There's a branch, too, in Surfers Paradise. The **C.A.Q. Galleries**, 37 Leichardt St., Spring Hill, is the place members of the Craft Association of Queensland display their skills.

The official Aboriginal outlet is **Queensland Aboriginal Creations**, 135–147 George St. (If you buy a boomerang, see if they still have the little pamphlet explaining how to throw it.) **Arunga** (Tel. 221–0892), at 197 Adelaide St., corner of Edward, has a fairly wide selection—some good, some junk. At the **Artifacts and Souvenir Center** (Tel. 229–6242), 183 Edward St., Mr. and Mrs. Beard also feature a lot of things from New Guinea and the Pacific islands. **Currans Corner** (Tel. 229–3690), 174 Adelaide St., across from the tourist office, also displays a bewildering variety of things, plus a book, magazine, and foreign newspaper section. **The Rock Shop** (Tel. 229–6009) at 193 Adelaide St., has souvenirs but especially Australian rocks and gemstones.

11. Night Life and Entertainment

It may be a while yet before conservative Brisbane develops much of a reputation for after-dark shenanigans. A commuting city, the central area says goodnight to most of its citizens while the sun is still high in the sky.

A few pubs—they call them hotels, but they are more known for their libations than accommodations—stand out. The **Crest Hotel** (Tel. 221–7788), on King George Square, houses several good bars, at least one of which sometimes has live music. The **George Hotel** (Tel. 221–2211), 85 George St., is also converted to a discotheque when the spirit moves them. Another good drinking spot is the **Waterloo Hotel**, at Anne Street and Commercial Road, in Fortitude Valley. Popular pubs also include **Wilson's 1870**, underneath 103 Queen St., with a nice friendly piano bar, and the **Treasury Hotel** whose address we left locked up in a vault somewhere. You'll usually hear some good jazz at the **Melbourne Hotel** on Browning Street in South Brisbane, or at the **Twelfth Night Club**, Cintra Road in Bowen Hills. (Brizzie's most popular beer, by the way, is Castelmaine XXXX—pronounced "Fourex"—Bitter Ale, a strong beer by any standards.)

Some nascent night life now is in Fortitude Valley. Two clubs are **Romeo's** at 693 Ann St. and **Mamie's** (Tel. 52–4070), 195 Brunswick St. (Sometimes the crowd is a little rough at both.) The premier disco is the **Brisbane Underground** (Tel. 36–2633) at Caxton St. and Petrie Terrace.

You'll find six or seven legitimate theaters—quite a few for a town supposedly lacking in culture. The 600-seat **S.G.I.O. Theatre**, in the S.G.I.O. Building on Turbot St., is the home of the Queensland Theatre Company. **Her Majesty's Theatre** on Queen Street, dating from 1888, is Brisbane's oldest (used for both stage productions and films). **LaBoite**, 57 Hale St. in Milton, is the headquarters for the Brisbane Repertory Company, and it often stages contemporary and experimental productions. The **Schonell Theatre** is part of Queensland University in St. Lucia but is open to the public, too.

If you're heavily into films, you might want to skip them in wowserist Queensland where they are subject to itchy-scissored censors. And we'd avoid any opera, concert, or ballet at the **Festival Hall** on Charlotte Street. The acoustics are awful, the air conditioning is often faulty, and the seats are rock-hard.

If you're in Brisbane in late September, don't miss **Warana**, the annual Mardi Gras type "Blue Skies" festival. Starting on the last Saturday in the month, it's a week-long wing ding with an assortment of activities like art shows, concerts, beer festivals, an air race, a rodeo, you name it. A dinkum shivoo!

12. The Brisbane Address List

American Chamber of Commerce in Australia, 139 Leichardt St. (Tel. 221–8542).

American Consulate, 359 Queen St. (Tel. 229–4677).

American Express, 165 Elizabeth St. (Tel. 221–7815).

American Families Association (Tel. 266 –4976).

Beauty shop—Coiffure Francaise, 444 George St. (Tel. 221–0839).

Bridge players—Brisbane Bridge Club, 17 Manning St., South Brisbane (Tel. 44–2672).

Brisbane Chamber of Commerce, 288 Queen St. (Tel. 211–1766).

British Consulate, 193 North Quay (Tel. 221–4933).

Bus Information—Tel. 225–4444.

Citizens Advice Bureau, 168 Ann St. (Tel. 221–4343).

Emergencies (Fire, Police, Ambulance)—Dial 000.

English U.K. Club—Tel. 229–4158.

Hospital—Royal Brisbane Hospital, Herston (Tel. 253–8111).

New Zealand Consulate, 288 Edward St. (Tel. 221–0005).

Royal Automobile Club of Cleveland, Ann and Boundary Streets (Tel. 221–1511).

Square Dancing Society, 9 Belgrave Rd., Hawthorn (Tel. 399–7606).

Tourist office—Queensland Government Tourist Bureau, Adelaide and Edward Streets (Tel. 31–2211).

Index

309

Please tell us about your trip to Australia below.

(You may use this page as an envelope. See over.)

TO ORDER ADDITIONAL COPIES OF:

The Maverick Guide to Australia $8.95   _____
The Maverick Guide to Hawaii $8.95   _____

Enclose check. Add $1.00 postage and handling for each copy ordered.

Fold along dotted lines to make an envelope.

Place
first class
postage
here

Bob and Sara Bone
The Maverick Guides
Pelican Publishing Company
1101 Monroe Street
Gretna, LA 70053